The European Social Charter

Volume 17, Procedural Aspects of International Law

The Procedural Aspects of International Law Series
RICHARD B. LILLICH, editor (1964–1977)
ROBERT KOGOD GOLDMAN, editor (1977–)

The European Social Charter

David Harris

University Press of Virginia

Charlottesville

THE UNIVERSITY PRESS OF VIRGINIA

Copyright © 1984 by the Procedural Aspects of
International Law Institute, Inc.
200 Park Avenue, New York, New York 10017

First published 1984

Library of Congress Cataloging in Publication Data

Harris, D. J. (David John)
  The European Social Charter.

  (Procedural aspects of international law series ;
v. 17)
  Rev. version of thesis (Ph.D.)—University of London.
  Bibliography: p.
  Includes index.
  1. Labor laws and legislation—Europe.   2. Social
legislation—Europe.   3. Council of Europe.   European
Social Charter.   I. Title.   II. Series.
LAW   344.4   83-23318
ISBN 0-8139-1004-8   344.04

Printed in the United States of America

Foreword

This volume, the seventeenth book in the Procedural Aspects of International Law Series sponsored by the Procedural Aspects of International Law Institute, presents a much-needed and thoroughly detailed study of the implementation of the European Social Charter.

While most existing books on this instrument were written shortly after its creation in 1961 and generally focus narrowly on its text and legislative history, Professor Harris's book analyzes instead the actual implementation of the Charter and the evolution of its system of supervising states. In addition, Professor Harris offers thoughtful insights into the relevance and importance of social and economic rights to contemporary European efforts to promote and to protect fundamental human rights. The successful implementation of supervising states' policies to guarantee the Charter's social and economic rights complements, in large measure, the system created under the European Convention of Human Rights to protect civil and political rights.

The European Social Charter is the most authoritative publication in the English language on the Charter. As such, it is a welcome contribution to this Series and to the dissemination of knowledge of human rights law.

I want to acknowledge with thanks the considerable time that Richard Gittleman and Lindsey B. Lang, my previous Dean's Fellows and Beatrice Maugeri, my current Dean's Fellow, devoted to the editing of this book. Thanks are similarly due to Richard B. Lillich, Howard W. Smith Professor at the University of Virginia Law School, for arranging for the publication of this volume.

Robert Kogod Goldman

Washington, D.C.

Contents

Preface

This book is a revised version of a thesis submitted to the University of London for a Ph.D. I wish to thank Richard Lillich for his help and encouragement during its preparation. I also wish to acknowledge my indebtedness to the Council of Europe and to the British and Irish Governments. The Council of Europe employed me as a *stagiaire* at Strasbourg where I was able to observe the system of supervision of the Charter at first hand. The British and Irish Governments were extremely cooperative, answering all of my questions fully and providing me with materials. I am particularly grateful to the British Government for allowing me access to the official government records of the drafting of the Charter. I am happy also to have the opportunity to record my gratitude to the late Sir Otto Kahn-Freund, former General Rapporteur of the Committee of Independent Experts; Mr. A. M. Morgan and Mr. W. Adams, successively members of the Committee of Independent Experts; Mr. J. A. Hargreaves, Head of the International Department of the British Trades Union Congress; and the several civil servants in the U.K. Department of Employment who gave freely of their time. Finally, I wish to thank Mr. F. Millich, Head of the Social Charter Section of the Council of Europe, who read the manuscript and made many valuable comments, and Miss Fiona Boyd, who prepared the index. Any errors or omissions remain my responsibility. Every effort has been made to record the law and practice of the Charter as far as the seventh cycle, which was completed in March 1983. No account is given, however, of the First Icelandic Report, which was submitted very late.

D. J. Harris

Nottingham

Abbreviations

C I to C VII	Conclusions I to VII of the Committee of Independent Experts
CA	Consultative Assembly of the Council of Europe (renamed the Parliamentary Assembly in 1974)
CE	Council of Europe
CIE	Committee of Independent Experts
CM	Committee of Ministers
CMSC	Committee of Ministers' Social Committee
ECHR	European Convention on Human Rights
GC	Governmental Committee of the European Social Charter
GC I to VII	1st to 7th *Reports* of the Governmental Committee of the European Social Charter
ICCPR	International Covenant of Civil and Political Rights
ICESCR	International Covenant on Economic, Social and Cultural Rights
ICEFRD	International Convention on the Elimination of All Forms of Racial Discrimination
ILC RP	International Labor Conference, Record of Proceedings
ILO	International Labor Organization
PA	Parliamentary Assembly of the Council of Europe (the new name of the Consultative Assembly from 1974 onwards)
Rec Proc TC	Record of Proceedings of the Strasbourg Tripartite Conference of December 1958 convened by the ILO at the request of the CE, ILO publication, 1959 (roneoed)
TC	Tripartite Conference
UNCHR	UN Commission on Human Rights
UDHR	Universal Declaration of Human Rights

Introduction

The story of the movement toward the protection of human rights in international law after the Second World War is a familiar one. Action upon a universal scale has resulted mainly in the United Nations Charter, the Universal Declaration of Human Rights 1948, and, after much delay, the two 1966 International Covenants on Civil and Political Rights and Economic, Social and Cultural Rights. During the long gap between the Declaration and the Covenants, the focus of attention turned to Western Europe with the adoption of the European Convention on Human Rights in 1950. The Convention was drafted under the auspices of the Council of Europe. The Council is the modest outcome of the initial attempt at European unification in the postwar period. It has a Parliamentary (formerly Consultative) Assembly, composed of members of parliament of the member states, and a Committee of Ministers, on which member states are represented by Foreign Ministers or (usually) their deputies. The no more than peripheral role of the Council in the political and economic affairs of Europe is a matter of record. A happier side to its work has been its achievements in the field of human rights, particularly its sponsorship of the European Convention on Human Rights and, a decade later, the European Social Charter in 1961. The European Convention, which protects civil and political rights, is by far the most successful and well-publicized international human rights guarantee that there has been. The right that the Convention gives to individuals to petition an independent adjudicative authority is a considerable breakthrough, and its development of human rights law in Europe is gathering pace and commanding increasing attention.

The Convention's achievements have been such as to overshadow the Social Charter, its more recent counterpart in the field of economic and social rights. In one sense, the Charter cannot complain at this; it should rather be thankful that it is alive at all. By 1961 interest on the part of the member states in the projects of the Council of Europe generally was much less than it was in 1950, and enthusiasm for a treaty guarantee of economic and social rights as a companion to the European Convention on Human Rights (which was beginning to cause difficulties for states) was particularly limited. Even so, after a long and difficult period of gestation, the Charter was born, and, despite gloomy pronouncements by early witnesses that it was not a strong infant, it has survived. Its success in establishing itself during its first years of life has been the result not of loving nurture by the states that conceived it, who have instead tended to neglect their offspring, but of the care and attention of the foster mother charged with the Charter's implementation, the Committee of Independent Experts. Led by a forceful Chairman, the Committee approached its task with remarkable zeal during early cycles of implementation and has since continued to show its full commitment to the realization of the Charter's objectives. It has examined every corner of the national reports submitted to it and commented frankly and fully upon the shortcomings of the contracting parties disclosed by them. In the course of doing so it has found many breaches of the Charter and itemized them in a series of *Conclusions,* or reports, which now constitute a wealth of material interpreting and applying the Charter. What is apparent from even a cursory examination of this jurisprudence is the breadth and potential depth of coverage of the Charter and the demanding nature of the test to which it subjects the economic and social policy of the states that accept it. In the hands of the Committee of Independent Experts, the Charter has become far more than a "paper" guarantee.

One consequence of the Committee of International Experts' enthusiasm for its role has been to lead it into conflict with the other main supervisory organ of the system of supervision, the Governmental Committee of the Social Charter, which is composed of civil servants representing the governments of the contracting parties. Not surprisingly, the Governmental Committee has seen matters in a different perspective from that of the Committee of Independent Experts and has disagreed with the latter on many questions of interpretation and approach. This has posed something of a dilemma for the Committee of Ministers, which is charged with the task of making recommendations to recalcitrant states and of supervising the operations of the Charter generally. If the experience of the Charter to date demonstrates the need for a system of implementation to give meaning to a treaty guarantee, it also has a lot to say about the need for that system to be an independent one.

It is an interesting fact that whereas there are many books (and a continuing stream of articles) on the European Convention on Human Rights, the Charter has been largely neglected. There were quite a few articles when the Charter appeared which analyzed its text and commented upon its drafting, but with one exception there has only been a modest trickle of comment since then, very little of which has used the mass of materials now available. The primary reason for this is almost certainly the low rating that states and academic writers in the Western World (in contrast with those in Eastern Europe and in the developing states) give to economic and social rights when compared with that which they give to civil and political rights. Some writers balk even at calling the former "human rights" at all. While it is true that economic and social rights are essentially different in kind from civil and political ones in the response that is needed from a government to secure them, there seems no good reason to deny them the status of human rights if they are in conscience felt to be fundamental to the condition of man. A person who thinks of the right to equal pay for work of equal value as fundamental is as much entitled to call it a human right as the person who thinks of freedom of religion in the same way. Although the potential for abuse and disagreement in such an approach is clear, the test of conscience would seem to be as defensible as others.

A second ancillary reason for the lack of publications on the Charter is the absence of a system of petitions—particularly individual petitions—leading to rulings on the facts of particular cases by a court or comparable body. Such rulings catch the eye and are much more the stuff of legal articles or news stories than the abstract, impersonal conclusions to be drawn from a general report. Further to this is the absence of a satisfactory arrangement for the publication of the documentation concerning the Charter and of many other activities that could draw attention to it.

It is to be hoped that enough has been said in the preceding paragraphs to justify the claims that it is time for a comprehensive study of the Charter of the sort the present book contains. The book's primary purpose is the simple one of recording and analyzing the guarantee in the Charter as it has been interpreted in the key formative years of its existence and of explaining and examining the working of the system of supervision. In the course of realizing this purpose, it is believed that some light may be thrown not only on the meaning and working of the Charter itself but also on matters of more general concern such as the level at which an international guarantee of economic and social rights can realistically be pitched, the difficulties that states genuinely have in satisfying such guarantees, and the potential and limitations of a report system of supervision. Consideration of such matters is particularly opportune now that the International Covenants on Human Rights are at last in force. It may also be of service in the current debate within the Council of Europe on the twin questions whether the European Convention on Human Rights should be extended to protect certain economic and social rights and whether the Social Charter should be revised to strengthen its substantive guarantee and to change its system of supervision by introducing a right of petition for individuals and a European Court of Social Rights.

The European Social Charter

CHAPTER I

The Background to the Charter

THE DRAFTING OF THE CHARTER[1]

The European Social Charter[2] was signed by thirteen of the member states of the Council of Europe in Turin on October 18, 1961.[3] It entered into force on February 26, 1965.[4] There are now thirteen contracting parties. They are, in order of ratification or approval, the United Kingdom, Norway, Sweden, Ireland, the Federal Republic of Germany, Denmark, Italy, Cyprus, Austria, France, Iceland, the Netherlands, and Spain.[5]

The Charter is a creature of the Council of Europe. When the Council was established in 1949 it directed its attention at once to the protection of human rights. The incentive to do this came generally from a wish to prevent a recurrence of the conditions that Europe had recently witnessed and to secure Western Europe against the threat of communism. More particularly, it came from the terms of the Statute of the Council of Europe.[6] In realization of the Aim of the Council[7] and in

---

[1]*See* Janssen-Pevtschin, *Les Engagements des Parties Contractantes et la Mise in Oeuvre de la Charte Social Européenne,* 1966 REVUE DE L'INSTITUT DE SOCIOLOGIE 9; A. ROBERTSON, HUMAN RIGHTS IN EUROPE 140–44 (1963); Tennfjord, *The European Social Charter—An Instrument of Social Collaboration in Europe,* 1962 EUR. Y.B. 71 (Council of Europe); Wiebringhaus, *La Charte Social Européenne* 9 ANNUAIRE FRANÇAIS DE DROIT INTERNATIONAL 710 (1963).

[2]European Social Charter, *signed* Oct. 18, 1961, 1965 Gr. Brit. T.S. No. 38 (Cmnd. 2643), 529 U.N.T.S. 89.

[3]The Charter is open to members of the Council of Europe for signature. Art. 35(1). Six more states have become signatories since 1961. For a full list of the signatory states, see Appendix I. The Charter was signed in Turin to commemorate the centenary of the unification of Italy.

[4]According to Art. 35(2), the Charter was to enter into force 30 days after the fifth state had ratified or approved it. It remains in force so long as five contracting parties are bound by it. Art. 37(1).

[5]For further details, see Appendix I.

[6]Statute of the CE, *signed* May 5, 1949, 1949 Gr. Brit. T.S. No. 51 (Cmd. 7778), 87 U.N.T.S. 103.

[7]Art. 1 reads:

(a) The aim of the Council of Europe is to achieve a greater unity between its
    Members for the purpose of safeguarding and realising the ideals and principles

order to define further the "human rights" obligations of membership,[8] the European Convention on Human Rights[9] was adopted in 1950. The Convention protects only civil and political rights. This was a matter of priorities and tactics.[10] While it was not disputed that economic and social rights required protection too, the immediate need was for a short, noncontroversial text which governments could accept at once, while the tide for human rights was strong. Given the values dominant within the Council, this meant limiting the Convention to the civil and political rights that were "essential for a democratic way of life";[11] economic and social rights would have been "too controversial and difficult of enforcement even in the changing state of social and international development of Europe"[12] to have been included at that stage.[13]

For once, this was a "shelving" that proved only temporary. A year after the signature of the Convention, the Consultative Assembly recommended to the Committee of Ministers "that a

which are their common heritage and facilitating their economic and social progress.

(b) This aim shall be pursued through the organs of the Council by discussion of questions of common concern and by agreements and common action in economic, social, cultural, scientific, legal and administrative matters and in the maintenance and further realisation of human rights and fundamental freedom.

[8]Art. 3 reads:

Every members of the Council of Europe must accept the principles of the rule of law and the enjoyment by all persons within its jurisdiction of human rights and fundamental freedoms, and collaborate sincerely and effectively in the realisation of the aim of the Council as specified in Chapter 1.

[9]European Convention on Human Rights and Fundamental Freedoms, *signed* Nov. 4, 1950, 1950 Gr. Brit. T.S. No. 70 (Cmd. 8969), 213 U.N.T.S. 221. The Convention came into force on Sept. 3, 1953. All of the 21 members of the CE are parties now.

[10]*See* the Report of the Consultative Assembly Committee on Legal and Administrative Questions, Eur. Consult. Ass., 1st Sess., Doc. No. 77, paras. 4 & 5 (1949).

[11]Mr. Teitgen, EUR. CONSULT. ASS. DEB. 1ST SESS. 408 (Aug. 19, 1949).

[12]Sir David Maxwell-Fyffe, *id.* at 448.

[13]The above approach was generally maintained, however, where there was some overlap between the ECHR and the Charter. *See* note 52 *infra*. On the concepts of economic and social rights, see M. CRANSTON, WHAT ARE HUMAN RIGHTS 65–71 (1973); C. JENKS, SOCIAL JUSTICE AND THE LAW OF NATIONS 69–88 (1970); H. LAUTERPACHT, INTERNATIONAL LAW AND HUMAN RIGHTS 284–86, 354–55 (1950); Luard, *Promotion of Human Rights by UN Political Bodies*, in THE INTERNATIONAL PROTECTION OF HUMAN RIGHTS 315–16 (E. Luard ed. 1967); Bossuyt, *La Distinction Juridique Entre les Droits Civils et Politiques et les Droits Economiques, Sociaux et Culturels*, 8 HUMAN RIGHTS J. 783 (1975); and Papadatos, *The European Social Charter*, 7 J. INT'L COMM'N JURISTS 214, 214–18 (1966).

common policy in the social field should be adopted by Member States of the Council of Europe."[14] Although the Assembly made no specific mention of a Social Charter in its recommendation, the memorandum[15] prepared for the Committee of Ministers by the Council of Europe Secretariat as a result of the Assembly's initiative did. In a key passage, it read:

> The social progress which the Members of the Council of Europe have set forth as an objective[16] should therefore be based on common principles. It thus appears that the first task of the Council in the social field should be to define and develop these principles. The importance of so doing is such as to warrant their enunciation in the form of a European Social Charter. This Social Charter would, together with the Convention on Human Rights and Fundamental Freedom, constitute a solemn declaration by the European states of the spiritual values underlying western civilization. The principles enshrined in the Social Charter would serve as a guide for the future action of the Council of Europe in the realization of social progress and in the achievement of greater unity between its Members.

The idea of a Social Charter was approved unanimously by the Consultative Assembly[17] but had a mixed reception within the Committee of Ministers. Doubt was expressed about the value of such a document. It was suggested that the proposed Charter would duplicate the work of the International Labor Organization and of the United Nations and would be unlikely to do more than define economic and social rights in other than vague and consequently unhelpful terms. To this was opposed the view that the Charter could spell out principles specifically applicable to Western Europe and that, in so doing, it could, as the Secretariat had suggested, provide the necessary guidelines for the social policy of the Council of Europe and thereby contribute to European unification. Nonetheless, the Committee was able, on May 20, 1954, to agree unanimously upon a text instructing its new established Social Committee to "endeavor to elaborate a European Social Charter."[18] The Charter "would define the social objectives

---

[14]Recommendation 14, TEXTS ADOPTED, December 1951.

[15]CE Doc. SG (53) 1 (Apr. 16, 1953).

[16]See Art. 1, quoted in note 7 supra.

[17]Opinion 5, TEXTS ADOPTED, September 1953.

[18]Special Message of the Committee of Ministers transmitting to the CA the Programme of Work of the CE, para. 38, Eur. Consult. Ass., 6th Sess., Doc. No. 238

aimed at by Members and would guide the policy of the Council in the social field, in which it would be complementary to the European Convention on Human Rights and Fundamental Freedoms."[19] It was left to the Social Committee to decide whether the Charter should contain obligations binding upon states in law.[20]

The Consultative Assembly at once approved the Committee of Ministers' action and expressed the hope that preparation of the Charter by the Committee's Social Committee might "begin without delay."[21] Not satisfied with this, it set about drafting a Charter of its own. Although this proved difficult,[22] in 1956 the Assembly drafted a text which it submitted to the Committee of Ministers for consideration.[23]

Meanwhile, the Social Committee of the Committee of Ministers had also been at work. The differences of opinion that had been voiced by member states in the Committee of Ministers were echoed by their representatives in the Social Committee, and it seemed for a time as if the opponents of a Charter would win to the extent that the Committee would recommend only a declaration of principles and objectives that would not be binding in law. But the proponents of a treaty text pressed their case, and a compromise was reached which is reflected in the final text of the Charter.[24] In February 1958 the Committee agreed upon a draft Charter[25] which, as far as its substantive undertakings were concerned, con-

---

(1954). Unanimity, which was necessary for the adoption of the Special Message, was achieved by changing the original wording of para. 38 ("Our Committee has accepted the principle of a European Social Charter") to "Our Committee will *endeavour to* elaborate a European Charter" in order to satisfy the less enthusiastic states. (Emphasis added.)

[19]*Id.*

[20]*Id.* at 39.

[21]Opinion 9, TEXTS ADOPTED, May 1954.

[22]*See* note 1 *supra.*

[23]Recommendation 104, TEXTS ADOPTED, October 1956. The draft submitted to the CM (Eur. Consult. Ass., 8th Sess., Doc. No. 536 [1956]) was a compromise text which was not voted upon by the CA for fear of its being rejected. Two earlier drafts submitted to the Assembly by its Committee on Social Questions (Eur. Consult. Ass., 7th Sess., Doc. No. 403 [1955]) and Committee on Economic Questions (Eur. Consult. Ass., 8th Sess., Doc. No. 488 [1956]) had been rejected. The main problem had been a split within the Assembly over the system of implementation.

[24]The decision to draft a text that was a least partly binding upon states was in line with CM Resolution (56) 25 in which the CM, probably because of the pressure that was building up in the CA and among trade union organizations, indicated its preference for a binding text.

[25]Eur. Consult. Ass., 11th Sess., Doc. No. 927 (1959).

tained two parts. Part I, which all contracting parties would accept in its entirety, indicated policy objectives across the whole field of economic and social rights and would be hortatory only. Part II contained obligations that would be binding in law. These were not nearly so ambitious as the text submitted by the Consultative Assembly had proposed and were drafted on the supposition that they would allow ratification on the basis of existing law. A state would not have to accept all of the obligations in Part II in order to become a party to the Charter; it would be sufficient for it to accept a prescribed number of them which it could freely choose from among the whole. The draft also proposed a report form of supervision which was adopted in its essentials in the final text.

The Social Committee's draft was examined by a Tripartite Conference at Strasbourg in December 1958 at which members states of the Council of Europe were represented by delegations composed, in International Labor Organization fashion, of government, employers', and workers' delegates.[26] The Conference, which had a purely consultative role, proposed a number of amendments to the Social Committee's text. Most significantly, it proposed that there should be a common core of obligations accepted by all of the contracting parties and recommended (mainly on the initiative of the workers' delegates) changes in almost half of the paragraphs of Part II. Above all, it asked for express recognition of the right to strike and a commitment to full employment.

Following the Conference, the Consultative Assembly submitted a revised draft Charter[27] to the Committee of Ministers. This was based upon the Social Committee's 1958 draft Charter but incorporated all of the suggestions that had been agreed upon unanimously by the Conference and certain other suggestions put forward by the Assembly itself. The Social Committee accepted some, but by no means all, of these alterations to its 1958 text. Most significantly, it was unable to accept the Assembly's proposal on the extent of a contracting

---

[26]The Conference was convened by the ILO at the request of the CM under Article III(2), General Agreement between the CE and the ILO, *approved* Nov. 23, 1951, 126 U.N.T.S. 331. The debates and reports of the Conference are documented in ILO, REC PROC TC. On the considerable importance of the technical assistance given by the ILO in the drafting of the Charter during the Conference and at other stages, *see* A. ROBERTSON, *supra* note 1, at 150, and Papadatos, *supra* note 13, at 218.

[27]The draft was appended to Opinion 32, TEXTS ADOPTED, January 1960. *See also* Eur. Consult. Ass., 11th Sess., Doc. No. 1035 (1959).

party's undertaking. Whereas the Assembly had identified a core of six articles which all states should accept, the Committee preferred the more flexible approach of the final text by which a state might become a contracting party if it accepted any five out of seven specified Articles. Even so, this was an improvement upon its 1958 text, which had contained no core of Articles at all. The Social Committee also rejected the Assembly's proposal that a contracting party should be required to accept the remaining obligations in Part II within five years of ratifying the Charter. A joint meeting between representatives of the Social Committee and the Assembly in October 1960 did not lead to any change in these respects. Thereafter, the Social Committee continued work on the Charter by itself until a final text was adopted by the Committee of Ministers in September 1961 and signed in Turin the following month, some eight long years after work had begun.

It will be evident from this account that the Charter is mainly the work of the Social Committee of the Committee of Ministers. This was inevitable for the reason that the member states of the Council of Europe eventually had to sign and ratify it and the Social Committee was the forum within which they could express their views about what they were prepared to accept. It is important, however, to record the contributions of the Consultative Assembly and the Tripartite Conference. Although the substantive guarantee and the system of supervision in the final text were not greatly influenced by the Assembly's 1956 draft, there is no doubt that the continual badgering of the Social Committee by the Assembly's parliamentarians (representing in some cases international trade union organizations)[28] and their later initiatives on particular matters contributed to the drafting of a stronger document than would have emerged had the Social Committee been left to its own devices.[29] Without them there might have been no treaty at all. Similarly, the open discussion between government representatives and others at the Tripartite Conference, when the former had to answer for the Social Committee's text to the latter, helped to give it

---

[28]See E. HAAS, CONSENSUS FORMATION IN THE COUNCIL OF EUROPE 40 (1960).

[29]Cf. Delperée & Gilon, La Charte Sociale Européenne, 1958 REVUE DU TRAVAIL 1217. On the importance of the role of the CA in the initiation and drafting of CE conventions generally, see A. ROBERTSON, THE COUNCIL OF EUROPE 248–49 (2d ed. 1961), and E. HAAS, supra note 28, at 69.

more substance than that Committee had previously proposed. The *travaux préparatoires* of the Charter thus bear witness to the curious ambivalence that is constantly present in the attitude of state and that makes such "irresponsible" pressure worthwhile. States may agree to international guarantees of human rights for commendable, idealistic reasons,[30] but, even as they do so, the domestic legal and political consequences of their acts are seldom far from their minds. As negotiations progress, the temptation to minimize their obligations gathers force, and such pressure as may be brought to bear from outside becomes increasingly important in pricking a state's conscience and reminding it of the reason for the whole exercise. Striking examples of its value can be found in the case of the Charter in the improvements that were made following the Tripartite Conference and the further work of the Assembly.

Equally informative is the background to the rule concerning the scope of the Charter *ratione personae*. This question was only fully discussed at the very end of the drafting process, after the Tripartite Conference and the Assembly had had their say. At that late stage, despite doubts expressed by some members, a view prevailed within a closeted Social Committee which severely restricts the Charter's application.[31]

The scope of the Charter *ratione personae* was just one of several features that made the initial reaction to it in 1961 markedly unenthusiastic. Although a number of European newspapers dutifully noted its adoption,[32] none commented editorially upon its significance. Most academic commentators were critical,[33] and the mood of the Consultative Assembly was one of disappointment at an opportunity lost.[34] Generally, the

---

[30]In some cases, it may be for more devious reasons or a matter of not losing face.

[31]*See* note 35 of Chapter IV.

[32]*See, e.g., Le Monde*, Sept. 16, 1961, at 14, col. 4, and *The Times* (London), Sept. 18, 1961, at 14, col. 4.

[33]*See, e.g.,* Janssen-Pevtschin, *supra* note 1, at 17–28, for a particularly caustic attack upon the Charter. For a spirited early defense, see Pugsley, *The European Social Charter*, 39 Y.B.A.A.A. 97 (1969).

[34]*See* the discussion in EUR. CONSULT. ASS. DEB. 13TH SESS. 679 *passim* (Jan. 16, 1962). The following remarks by Mr. Montini (Italy) were typical:

... this Charter makes no great changes in our European world. The fact is ... that the burst of enthusiasm which at the outset united us in our determination to create a European Social Charter has gradually dwindled. I will not say "*parturiunt montes, nascetur ridiculus mus*"; but it is certain that what we now have before us is appreciably different from the Social Charter we envisaged.

impression that the Charter gave was of a document recording
past standards rather than setting new ones. This was true of
the rights included and the level at which they were protected.
There was also the feeling that it was a workers' Charter which
paid inadequate attention to other social rights.[35] The modest
demand made of states in terms of the number of obligations
that they had to accept to become parties was also stressed.[36]
At the same time, there was a reluctant acceptance by critics
that it was no mean achievement, in 1961, to obtain a Charter
at all. Although it was not a perfect document, at least the
Charter provided a coherent, if conservative, blueprint from
which the Council of Europe could work in building a social
policy for Western Europe and contained some commitment
in law to the protection of the existing economic and social
rights of West Europeans.[37] It was, as one commentator
noted,[38] far too early to write the Charter off as a pointless
exercise; the test would be how many states ratified it and
how it came to be interpreted and applied by its supervisory
organs.

AN OUTLINE OF THE CHARTER

The provisions of the Charter are considered in detail in the
following chapters. It may be helpful, however, to provide a
short synopsis of them now. The Charter consists of a Preamble, five Parts, and an Appendix. The Preamble, which is
very brief, confirms that the object and purpose of the
Charter is to provide a counterpart, or "pendant,"[39] to the

_Id._ at 682. The general tone of the debate was remarkably similar to that which had
greeted the CM draft of the ECHR when that had fallen short of the Assembly's
expectations: _See_ EUR. CONSULT. ASS. DEB. 2D SESS. 322 _passim_ (Aug 14, 1950).

[35]_See, e.g.,_ Mr. Montini (Italy), note 34 _supra._

[36]_See, e.g.,_ Mr. Molter (Belgium), _supra_ note 34, at 681.

[37]See, in defense of the Charter, the following comment made by one of the
British negotiators, Mr. Spain, after its signature:

. . . what the Charter does is make it very difficult for any Government in future to
deny certain rights. Do not expect too much of the Charter. It's not revolutionary,
but rather it codifies principles. Twenty or thirty years ago you would not have got
these European Governments to agree by charter to such a thing.

The Manchester Evening Chronicle, Oct. 26, 1961.

[38]Valticos, _La Charte Sociale Européenne: sa Structure, son Contenu, le contrôle de son
application,_ 26 DROIT SOCIAL 466, 474 (1963).

[39]The Charter is frequently referred to, sometimes somewhat skeptically (_see, e.g.,_
Cohen-Jonathan, _Droits de l'Homme et Pluralité des Systèmes Européens de Protection Internationale,_ 5 HUMAN RIGHTS J. 613, 638 [1972]), as the "pendant" to the Convention.

European Convention on Human Rights in the realization of the Aim of the Council of Europe[40] by securing economic and social rights.[41] The Charter protects nineteen such rights. They are first listed in brief and general terms in Part I of the Charter, in which the contracting parties "accept as the aim of their policy . . . the attainment of conditions" in which the rights may be "effectively realized." Each right is then taken separately in one of the nineteen Articles of Part II and made the subject of one or more legal obligations. The two basic undertakings that a state must accept in order to become a contracting party are set down in the one Article that constitutes Part III. In the first place, it must undertake "to consider Part I of this Charter as a declaration of the aims which it will pursue . . . ." Second, it must undertake to consider itself bound by at least ten of the nineteen Articles that make up Part II in their entirety or forty-five of the seventy-two numbered paragraphs of which these Articles consist. In addition, on whichever of the above bases a contracting party accepts the Charter, the obligations that it chooses must include all of those in five of seven specified Articles. The machinery by which the Charter is enforced is set out in Part IV. This supposes the submission of biennial reports by the contracting parties on the obligations in Part II that they have accepted and of occasional reports on the others. The reports are examined by the Committee of Independent Experts, which adopts *Conclusions* based upon them. They are reexamined (with the *Conclusions*) by the Governmental Social Committee, which adopts a *Report*. This goes to the Committee of Ministers, together with the *Conclusions* and an *Opinion* of the Parliamentary Assembly which is based upon the *Conclusions* and the *Report*. The Committee of Ministers is competent to "make to each contracting party any necessary recommendations."[42] Part V contains ancillary provisions on such matters as derogations in time of war or public emergency, restrictions that may be imposed upon the rights protected, relations between the

The term was first used in this way in the French text ("pendant") of the CM's Special Message to the CA in 1954, *supra* note 10, at 18, and was then used by the CA in both the English and French texts of its Opinion 5, *supra* note 17, at 11.

[40]*See* Art. 1, note 7 *supra.*

[41]*Cf.* Lannung, *Human rights and the Multiplicity of European Systems for International Protection,* 5 HUMAN RIGHTS J. 651 (1972)

[42]This is the procedure for biennial reports; that for occasional reports is similar.

Charter and domestic law or other international agreements, implementation of the Charter by collective agreements, and its territorial application. It also has provisions concerning the signature, ratification or approval,[43] and entry into force of the Charter and concerning amendments to and denunciation of it. Finally, the Appendix to the Charter, which forms "an integral part of it,"[44] contains a series of unnumbered clauses which interpret or add to other provisions of the Charter.

THE INTERNATIONAL CONTEXT

It may also be helpful, by way of introduction, to place the Charter in the context of other international human rights treaties and declarations. As far as the United Nations is concerned, it coexists primarily with the Universal Declaration of Human Rights 1948,[45] the International Covenant on Economic, Social and Cultural Rights 1966,[46] and the International Convention on the Elimination of All Forms of Racial Discrimination 1966.[47] Also on the world level, there are the large and increasing number of International Labor Organization conventions and recommendations protecting individuals in employment and hence, directly or indirectly, economic and social rights.[48] This last parallel is particularly relevant since much of the Charter is modeled upon the precedents set by the International Labor Organization.[49] What is new in the Charter is partly the formulation in terms of human rights of

[43]Provision was made for approval, as opposed to ratification, because of French constitutional practice. CM/Del./Concl.(61) 98, 14.

[44]Art. 38.

[45]Universal Declaration of Human Rights, G.A. Res. 217A (III), U.N. Doc. A/810, at 71 (1948).

[46]International Covenant on Economic, Social and Cultural Rights, *adopted* Dec. 19, 1966, G.A. Res. 2200, 21 U.N. GAOR, Supp. (No. 16) at 49, U.N. Doc. A/6316 (1966), 1977 Gr. Brit. T.S. No. 6 (Cmnd. 6702). The Covenant entered into force in 1976.

[47]International Convention on the Elimination of All Forms of Racial Discrimination, *opened for signature* Mar. 7, 1966, 1969 Gr. Brit. T.S. No. 77 (Cmnd. 4108), 660 U.N.T.S. 195. The Convention entered into force in 1969.

[48]*See ILO*, CONVENTIONS AND RECOMMENDATIONS: 1919–1966, and loose-leaf supplement (1967 onwards) for the text of ILO conventions and recommendations. *See also* C. JENKS, HUMAN RIGHTS AND INTERNATIONAL LABOUR STANDARDS (1960).

[49]*See The European Social Charter and International Labour Standards*, 84 INT'L LAB. REV 354 (1961). There is little evidence of any influence of the early drafts of the ICESCR in the final text of the Charter.

many undertakings found in International Labor Organization conventions and recommendations and partly their assembly, usually in more general terms, in a single document.
The ILO system is one that allows for continual updating and
supplementation of the International Labor Code; the con-
trasting rigidity of the Charter is to some extent made good by
the interpretative role of its supervisory organs and the possibility of adding to it by protocols (none so far) and by other
Council of Europe conventions. In addition, the undertakings
in the Charter extend beyond the individual's interests as a
worker. At a regional level, there are the American Declaration of the Rights and Duties of Man[50] and the American
Convention on Human Rights.[51] More significantly, there are
several companion European guarantees. The European Convention on Human Rights 1950 overlaps to a small extent in
the rights it protects,[52] and its system of implementation provides an instructive contrast with that of the Charter. There
are also the laws concerning migrant workers and on other
matters of social policy of the European Communities,[53] with
its more direct impact upon the laws of member states, that
also overlap with the commitments of the Charter. Finally, the
Council of Europe has adopted other conventions in the field
of social policy that predate or supplement the Charter.[54]

[50]American Declaration of the Rights and Duties of Man, O.A.S. Res. xxx, *adopted
by* the Ninth International Conference of American States, Bogotá, 1948, *reprinted in*
HANDBOOK OF EXISTING RULES PERTAINING TO HUMAN RIGHTS 15, OEA/Ser. L/V/II.
23, doc. 21, rev. 6 (1979).
    [51]American Convention on Human Rights, *signed* Nov. 22, 1969, O.A.S.T.S. No.
36 at 1, *reprinted in* HANDBOOK OF EXISTING RULES PERTAINING TO HUMAN RIGHTS 27,
Off. Rec. OEA/Ser. L/V/II. 50, doc. 6, (1980). The Convention entered into force in
1978. Its guarantee of economic and social rights is very limited. *See* Art. 26.
    [52]*Cf.* Art. 1(2), Charter, and Art. 4(2), ECHR; Arts. 5 & 6, Charter, and Art. 11,
ECHR; and Article 16, Charter, and Article 8, ECHR. The ECHR, unlike the
Charter, also protects the rights to property and to education. *See* Arts. 1 & 2, First
Protocol to the ECHR, *signed* Mar. 26, 1952, 1954 Gr. Brit. T.S. No. 46 (Cmd. 9221),
213 U.N.T.S. 262.
    [53]*See, e.g.*, K. LIPSTEIN, THE LAW OF THE EUROPEAN ECONOMIC COMMUNITY 304–10
(1974).
    [54]*See* the two 1953 European Interim Agreements on Social Security, *signed* Dec.
11, 1953, 1955 Gr. Brit. T.S. No. 41 (Cmd. 9511), 218 U.N.T.S. 153, and 1955 Gr.
Brit. T.S. No. 40 (Cmd. 9510), 218 U.N.T.S. 211; European Convention on Social
and Medical Assistance and Protocol, *signed* Dec. 11, 1953, 1955 Gr. Brit. T.S. No. 42
(Cmd. 9512), 218 U.N.T.S. 255; European Convention on Establishment and Protocol, *done* Dec. 13, 1955, 1971 Gr. Brit. T.S. No. 1 (Cmnd. 4573), 529 U.N.T.S. 141;
European Code of Social Security and Protocol, *opened for signature* Apr. 16, 1968,
1968 Gr. Brit. T.S. No. 10 (Cmnd. 3871), 648 U.N.T.S. 235; European Convention of

INTERPRETATION OF THE CHARTER

Since much of the rest of this work consists of a consideration of the meaning of the Charter, it will be appropriate to end this introduction by indicating the rules of interpretation that apply. The Charter is a treaty and "must be interpreted according to customary rules for interpreting international treaties"[55] as codified in the Vienna Convention on the Law of Treaties 1969.[56] The European Court of Human Rights has emphasized a teleological approach in the interpretation of the European Convention on Human Rights. In the *Wemhoff* case it stated: "Given that it is a law-making treaty, it is also necessary to seek the interpretation that is most appropriate in order to realize the aim and achieve the object of the treaty, not that which would restrict to the greatest possible degree the obligations undertaken by the Parties."[57] It is submitted that, within the limits allowed by the clear meaning of the text,[58] the same emphasis should be placed in the interpreta-

the Adoption of Children, *done* Apr. 24, 1967, 1968 Gr. Brit. T.S. No. 51 (Cmnd. 367), 634 U.N.T.S. 155; European Agreement on Au Pair Placement, *done* Nov. 24, 1969, Europ. T.S. No. 68; European Convention on Social Security and Supplementary Agreement, *done* Dec. 14, 1972, Europ. T.S. No. 78; European Convention on the Social Protection of Farmers, *done* May 6, 1974, Europ. T.S. No. 83; European Convention on the Legal Status of Children Born out of Wedlock, *done* Oct. 15, 1975, 1976 Gr. Brit. Misc. No. 2 (Cmnd. 6358), Europ. T.S. No. 85; and European Convention on the Legal Status of Migrant Workers, *done* Nov. 24, 1977, Europ. T.S. No. 93. All of these instruments are in force.

[55]C III xiii. This statement by the Charter's Committee of Independent Experts is, it is submitted, true of Part I of the Charter as well as of the remainder of it. Although Part I contains a political and not a legal undertaking (*see* note 10 of Chapter II), it resulted from the same drafting process as led to the adoption of the rest of the Charter and is an integral part of it.

[56]Vienna Convention on the Law of Treaties, *adopted* May 22, 1969, 1969 Gr. Brit. Misc. No. 31 (Cmnd. 4140). The Convention entered into force in 1980. The rules of interpretation in the Convention (Arts. 31–33) can be taken to reflect customary international law. *Cf.* Golder Case, 57 I.L.R. 200, 213–14 (Eur. Court of Human Rights 1975). U.K. practice is to the same effect. *See* Cmnd. 4589, at 15.

[57]Wemhoff Case, 41 I.L.R. 281, 302–03 (Eur. Court of Human Rights 1968). *See*, more recently, the Golder Case, *supra* note 56, at 218. *Contra* the separate opinion of Judge Sir Gerald Fitzmaurice in the Golder Case, *supra* note 56, at 251. The European Commission has also adopted a teleological approach and rejected the principle of restrictive interpretation. *See* Morrison, *Restrictive Interpretation of Sovereignty-Limiting Treaties: the Practice of the European Human Rights Convention System*, 19 INT'L & COMP. L.Q. 361 (1970). *See also*, F. JACOBS, THE EUROPEAN CONVENTION ON HUMAN RIGHTS 17 (1975).

[58]For this necessary limit to the teleological approach, see the Interpretation of Peace Treaties with Bulgaria, Hungary and Romania Case, 1950 I.C.J. 65, 221.

tion of the Charter upon its object and purpose. The principle of restrictive interpretation of treaty obligations limiting national sovereignty,[59] which was rejected in the *Wemhoff* case, is a doubtful one in any context;[60] it is particularly so in the field of human rights at a time when international law is becoming increasingly concerned to protect the individual against the state.[61] It has been rejected in the interpretation of the European Convention on Human Rights and should have no place in the interpretation of the Charter either.

One final comment is that the Charter is drafted in a strikingly slipshod way. There are the ambiguities and gaps in the text that one associates with any treaty, particularly one accommodating the views and proposals of a large number of states and other bodies and with two language texts. The complaint being registered here is that there are also an unusual number of inadequacies of translation and other inconsistencies and mistakes that should have been avoided on a careful final reading. The result is that there are sometimes differences in wording which do not seem to have any significance,[62] and occasionally it can be shown from the *travaux préparatoires* that the meaning a word or phrase would clearly seem to have from the text is not the intended one.[63] The approach adopted in such situations in the following chapters has been to discount differences in wording that appear to result only from poor drafting and to make free use of the *travaux préparatoires* to clarify or confirm the intention of the drafters.

[59]*See* Wimbledon Case, 1923 P.C.I.J., ser. A., No. 1, at 24–25.

[60]*See* A MCNAIR, THE LAW OF TREATIES, App. A at 765 (2d ed. 1961).

[61]*See, e.g.,* Barcelona Traction, Light & Power Co., Ltd. Case, 1970 I.C.J. 3, 32, and the many steps taken by the U.N. in recent years to extend the protection afforded to human rights. *See* J. CAREY, UN PROTECTION OF CIVIL AND POLITICAL RIGHTS (1970); R. LILLICH & F. NEWMAN, INTERNATIONAL PROTECTION OF HUMAN RIGHTS: PROBLEMS OF LAW AND POLICY 1–544 (1979); and L. SOHN & T. BUERGENTHAL, INTERNATIONAL PROTECTION OF HUMAN RIGHTS 505–997 (1973).

[62]*See, e.g.,* the introductory wording in Art. 5, discussed at note 279 of Chapter II.

[63]*See, e.g.,* the French text of Art. 15 (2), discussed at note 713 of Chapter II.

The Undertakings in the Charter

Article 20 (1) of the Charter reads:

Each of the Contracting Parties undertakes:

(a) to consider Part I of this Charter as a declaration of the aims which it will pursue by all appropriate means, as stated in the introductory paragraph of that Part;

(b) to consider itself bound by at least five of the following Articles of Part II of this Charter: Articles 1, 5, 6, 12, 13, 16 and 19;

(c) in addition to the Articles selected by it in accordance with the preceding sub-paragraph, to consider itself bound by such a number of Articles or numbered paragraphs of Part II of the Charter as it may select, provided that the total number of Articles or numbered paragraphs by which it is bound is not less than 10 Articles or 45 numbered paragraphs.

In the present chapter it is intended to consider these three undertakings in turn, looking briefly at that in respect to Part I of the Charter first and then examining in detail those in respect to Part II. The chapter ends with an appraisal of the record of compliance with the undertakings in Part II of the Charter and the standards set by them.

OBJECTIVES OF ECONOMIC AND SOCIAL POLICY

In the "introductory paragraph" to Part I to which Article 20(1)(a) refers, the contracting parties "accept as the aim of their policy . . . the attainment of conditions" in which the nineteen "rights and principles" listed in Part I "may be effectively realized." As a result, the Charter is not only a source of obligations of immediate effect (through Part II) but also of general guidelines for future economic and social development. This second, "missionary" side to the Charter distinguishes it from its counterpart, the European Convention on Human Rights. Whereas it was reasonable to ask the members of the Council of Europe to protect at once all of the key civil and political rights to which that Convention is addressed,[1] a similar request in respect of economic and social rights was too ambitious.

The "rights and principles" in Part I correspond to those that are later the subject of the nineteen Articles of Part II and are listed in Part I in the same order as they are in those Articles.[2] The "conditions" that the contracting parties undertake to seek to attain for their realization are, for the most part, those which will be attained by compliance with the obligations in Part II. The equation, however, is not an exact one. Several of the "rights and principles" in Part I are so narrowly worded that the "conditions" for their realization must be taken to be less than those which will result from compliance with all of the obligations in the relevant Article of Part II. Paragraph 1 of Part I, for example, clearly covers the ground of Article 1(2) of Part II only.[3] In other cases, the question arises whether the required "conditions" are necessrily attained by compliance with all of the equivalent obligations in Part II. Although it might be inferred from the texts of Parts I and II that this is all that is required,[4] this is not expressly stated, and the object and purpose of the Charter suggest otherwise (so far as the wording of Part I allows) where economic or social circumstances have changed so that the "conditions" attained by realization of the undertakings in Part II can be seen as ones upon which improvement may be expected.

[1]This obligation is subject to any reservations that a state might make. *See* European Convention on Human Rights and Fundamental Freedoms, Art. 64, *signed* Nov. 4, 1950, 1950 Gr. Brit. T.S. No. 70 (Cmd. 8969), 213 U.N.T.S. 221.

[2]It is a curious feature of the drafting of the Charter that Part I precedes Art. 1. It consists of 19 numbered paragraphs immediately after the Preamble but before Art. 1.

[3]Para. 1 reads: "Everyone shall have the opportunity to earn his living in an occupation freely entered upon." *See also* para. 7, which corresponds to Art. 7(10) only, and para. 18, which is more limited than Art. 18. There is no evidence that these discrepancies were intended; they lead to a curious and unsatisfactory position which would seem to result from poor drafting. In some cases (*see, e.g.*, Arts. 16 and 17) the text of the article in Part II is no more precise than its counterpart in Part I. In such cases, the meaning of the article, and hence the "conditions" that need to be attained for the purposes of Part I, is a matter of interpretation for the supervisory organs to a larger extent than usual.

[4]*Compare* the wording "may be effectively realised" in Part I *with* the introductory wording "With a view to ensuring the effective exercise of" in nearly all of the articles in Part II. *See also* the wording of Art. 31, which applies equally to Part I and Part II.

It is not clear whether Part I establishes a legal or a political obligation for the contracting parties. Since the Charter is undoubtedly a treaty, placing Part I after the Preamble and in the body of the Charter leads to the prima facie conclusion that it establishes a legal obligation. The use of the same term—"undertaking"—in Article 20 in respect to Parts I and II when the "undertaking" in respect to the latter is undoubtedly legal suggests the same.[5] The general nature of the undertaking in Part I is not against such an interpretation; there are other human rights treaty obligations of a legal character which are no more specific.[6] But there is also evidence to the contrary. Part I precedes the first Article in the Charter, which comes at the beginning of Part II. This is unusual and may indicate that the obligation in Part I has a different character from those in Part II, which obviously are legal. The wording of Article 20 supports this view insofar as the obligation in respect to Part I is to accept it as a "declaration of . . . aims" whereas that in respect to Part II is for a contracting party to "consider itself bound." Although a "declaration" may be legally binding in international law, the precedent of the Universal Declaration of Human Rights[7] in the human rights context may suggest otherwise in this particular case.

If the textual evidence is inconclusive, the *travaux préparatoires* support the conclusion that no legal obligation exists. The Committee of Ministers proposed to have two parts in the Charter delineating the different rights protected when it decided that the Charter should not be a purely hortatory document but should contain some obligations that were binding in law. Consequently, the United Kingdom suggested that the Charter could consist of a first part of a declaratory character applicable to all of the states and of a second part containing

[5]The same lack of terminological distinction between the two undertakings is found elsewhere in the Charter. *See* Art. 31 and the Appendix. *See also* the declarations made by states accepting the Charter, printed in COUNCIL OF EUROPE, 1 EUROPEAN CONVENTIONS AND AGREEMENTS 360 (1971). All of the declarations that refer specifically to Part I as well as Part II was the legal-sounding term "stipulation" to refer to each.

[6]*See* U.N. CHARTER Arts. 55 & 56. On the legal character of the obligations in these articles, see the discussion in H. LAUTERPACHT, IINTERNATIONAL LAW AND HUMAN RIGHTS 148–49 (1950). Lauterpacht refers to and rejects (persuasively) the view that they are not legal obligations.

[7]Universal Declaration of Human Rights, G.A. Res. 217A (III), U.N. Doc. A/810, at 71 (1948).

obligatory provisions from among which each state could choose those which it wished to be binding upon it.[8] In accepting this suggestion, the Committee clearly understood that what ultimately became Part I (the "declaratory" part in the U.K. scheme) did not, in contrast to what became Part II, contain any binding obligation. Unusual though it may be for a treaty to contain an obligation which is not binding in law,[9] the evidence of the *travaux préparatoires* suggests that this was what was intended.[10]

Looked at realistically (or cynically), the question whether Part I imposes a legal obligation is purely an academic one for the reason that no machinery is provided to enforce it.[11] In this situation, a political undertaking as to social policy is likely to be as successful and significant as a legal one, both nationally and within the Council of Europe. In practice, its legal or nonlegal character has not affected the use to which the supervisory organs have put Part I in the interpretation of the obligations in Part II.[12]

---

[8]The suggestion was made during the Fourth Session of the Committee of Ministers' Social Council, January/February 1957.

[9]For another example, see Art. 19(1), Geneva Convention on the Territorial Sea and the Contiguous Zone, *done* Apr. 29, 1958, 516 U.N.T.S. 205.

[10]The majority of commentators take the view that Part I is not legally binding. *See* A. ROBERTSON, HUMAN RIGHTS IN EUROPE 145 (1963); Benvenuti, *Les Buts Sociaux et Politiques de la Charte Sociale Européenne*, 4 REVUE BELGE DE SÉCURITÉ SOCIALE 657, 664 (1962); Delperée, *Les Droits Sociaux et la Charte Sociale Européenne* 1 HUMAN RIGHTS J. 549 (1968); Janssen-Pevtschin, *Les Engagements des Parties Contractantes et la Mise en Oeuvre de la Charte Sociale Européenne*, 1966 REVUE DE L'INSTITUT DE SOCIOLOGIE 9; Tennfjord, *The European Social Charter—An Instrument of Social Collaboration in Europe*, 1962 EUR. Y.B. 76 (Council of Europe); Van Asbeck, *La Charte Sociale Européenne: sa Portée Juridique, sa Mise en Oeuvre*, in MÉLANGES OFFERT À HENRI ROLIN: PROBLÈMES DE DROIT DES GENS 427, 438 (1964); and Wiebringhaus, *La Charte Sociale Européenne*, 9 ANNUAIRE FRANÇAIS DE DROIT INTERNATIONAL 713 (1963). Commentators who take the opposite view are Bleckmann, *Interprétation et Application en Droit Interne de la Charte Sociale Européenne, Notamment du Droit de Grève*, 1967 CAHIERS DE DROIT EUROPÉEN 388, 390; Papadatos, *The European Social Charter*, 7 J. IINT'L COMM'N JURISTS 222 (1966); and Troclet, *Dynamisme et Contrôle de l'Application de la Charte* 2, paper presented to the Brussels Colloquium on the European Social Charter, Institut d'Etudes Européennes (1976). The present author took the view that there was a legal obligation before having the opportunity of reading the *travaux préparatoires*. Harris, *The European Social Charter*, 13 INT'L & COMP. L.Q. 1076, 1080 (1964).

[11]This may, as Van Asbeck, *supra* note 10, at 432, suggests, be another pointer indicating that Part I is different in character from that in Part II (which has an enforcement system). Indirectly, the Part II system of supervision helps in achieving compliance with Part I.

[12]*See, e.g.,* the use of para. 18 in the interpretation of Art. 18, note 787 *infra*.

INTRODUCTORY ASPECTS

The General Undertaking

In order to become a contracting party, a state must accept at least ten of the nineteen Articles that make up Part II or forty-five of the seventy-two "numbered paragraphs" of which these Articles consist.[13] Although urged upon them, the possibility that a state might be required to accept all of the obligations in Part II was never seriously countenanced by the drafting states.[14] This was partly because economic and social progress within the membership of the Council of Europe was too diverse; if compliance with the mainly negative and abstentional requirements of the European Convention on Human Rights was within the power of all members, the fulfillment of many economic and social rights required positive government intervention that was dependent upon the availability of economic resources. It was also because Western Europe has emphasized the classical civil and political rights of man and only in fairly recent times paid attention to his economic and social aspirations and come to recognize them as rights.[15] For this reason too the Charter could not be as exacting as its counterpart. A system of variable and progressive acceptance was in-

---

[13]Art. 20(1)(c). An odd consequence of providing for the alternative of ratification on the basis of "numbered paragraphs" is that, even allowing for the "core" requirement, it is possible for a state to become a contracting party by accepting only eight articles in toto instead of ten if the "numbered paragraphs" in those articles are counted and not the articles themselves. For example, Articles 1, 2, 4, 6, 7, 12, 13, and 19 contain more than forty-five "numbered paragraphs."

[14]Had it been just a matter of certain states having doubts about one or two provisions, the case for a reservations clause, which was not included in the Charter, would have been a strong one. An attempt by the CA to tighten the arrangement for progressive acceptance of the Charter (see Art. 20[3]) by requiring contracting parties to accept all of the undertakings in Part II within five years of ratification failed. Opinion 32, TEXTS ADOPTED, January 1960. *See also* Eur. Consult. Ass., 11th Sess., Doc. No. 1035 (1959).

[15]*See* M. CRANSTON, WHAT ARE HUMAN RIGHTS 65–71 (1963); C. JENKS, SOCIAL JUSTICE AND THE LAW OF NATIONS 69–88 (1970); H. LAUTERPACHT, INTERNATIONAL LAW AND HUMAN RIGHTS 284–86, 354–55 (1950); Bossuyt, *La Distinction Juridique Entre les Droits Civils et Politiques et les Droits Economiques, Sociaux et Culturels*, 8 HUMAN RIGHTS J. 783 (1975); Luard, *Promotion of Human Rights by U.N. Political Bodies*, in THE INTERNATIONAL PROTECTION OF HUMAN RIGHTS 315–16 (E. Luard ed. 1967); and Papadatos, *supra* note 10, at 214, 214–18.

evitable if the Charter was to be widely ratified and if the standards it set were to be worthwhile.[16]

A result of the complicated and unusual scheme that was devised is that a state need accept only between a half and two-thirds of the substantive undertakings in Part II in order to become a party. In fact, the thirteen contracting parties so far have almost all accepted far more than this; although one (Cyprus) has accepted the bare minimum of provisions, two (Italy and Spain) have accepted every one of them, and the contracting parties as a whole have accepted over 80% of the provisions that could be selected.[17] If only two states have added after ratification[18] to the list of provisions accepted by them, no state has yet withdrawn its acceptance of any provision.[19]

To accomplish one of the Charter's avowed purposes of furthering European unity in the social field by imposing a core of obligations common to all contracting parties,[20] it is provided that a contracting party must, whether it ratifies on

---

[16]There were precedents in certain ILO Conventions, particularly the ILO Social Security (Minimum Standards) Convention (ILO Convention No. 102), *adopted* June 28, 1952, 210 U.N.T.S. 131, and the ILO Plantations Convention (ILO Convention No. 110), *adopted* June 24, 1958, 348 U.N.T.S. 275, which both contain schemes for partial acceptance and a "core" of obligations.

[17]Expressed in terms of "numbered paragraphs" accepted, the contracting parties have accepted the following number of paragraphs:

Italy: 72 paragraphs
Spain: 72 paragraphs
France: 70 paragraphs
Netherlands: 70 paragraphs (less a part of Art. 6(4))
F.R.G.: 68 paragraphs
Ireland: 63 paragraphs
Austria: 62 paragraphs
U.K.: 62 paragraphs
Norway: 60 paragraphs
Sweden: 62 paragraphs
Denmark: 45 paragraphs
Iceland: 41 paragraphs
Cyprus: 34 paragraphs (consisting of ten whole articles)

For further details, see Appendix II. As Valticos has pointed out, such facts and figures may, although relevant, be somewhat misleading in assessing the significance of the undertakings given since much must depend upon what provisions contracting parties have accepted; some provisions (*e.g.*, Art. 4[3]) are more important and exacting than others (*e.g.*, Art. 2[2]). *See* Valticos, *La Charte Sociale Européenne: sa Structure, son Contenu, le Contrôle de son Application*, 26 DROIT SOCIAL 468 (1963).

[18]*See* Art. 20(3). Sweden and Denmark have accepted three and one more provision(s) respectively.

[19]*See* Art. 37(2).

[20]For other reasons for the core provision, see Papadatos, *supra* note 10, at 223–24.

the basis of Articles or of "numbered paragraphs," accept in their entirety at least five of seven specified Articles.[21] These seven Articles and the rights they concern are:

Article 1: the right to work
Article 5: the right to organize
Article 6: the right to bargain collectively
Article 12: the right to social security
Article 13: the right to social and medical assistance
Article 16: the right of the family to social, legal, and economic protection
Article 19: the right of migrant workers and their families to protection and assistance

The Articles were chosen not because they necessarily protect the seven most important rights but in order to achieve a balance between the different groups of rights in the Charter. The arrangement imposes some degree of uniformity, but the choice of five Articles out of seven that is given[22] has limited its effectiveness.[23]

Dynamic Provisions

The political undertaking in Part I as to the aim of a contracting party's economic and social policy gives the Charter a dynamic, or progressive, character.[24] It is dynamic also insofar as certain of the provisions in Part II that require a set level of achievement upon ratification are sufficiently generally phrased as to allow them to grow as expectations and economic conditions improve. The undertaking "to recognise the right of workers to a remuneration such as will give them . . . a decent standard of living" (Article 4[1]), is an example of this kind of provision.[25] In its practice, the Committee of Independent Experts has characterized a small number of provisions in Part II of the Charter as "dynamic" in yet a third sense, viz., that they "impose an obligation to adopt over the years a course of con-

[21]Art. 20(1) (b).

[22]On the attempts to strengthen the arrangement at the drafting stage, see Eur. Consult. Ass., 11th Sess., Doc. No. 1035 (1959).

[23]It was theoretically possible for all of the member states of the CE to ratify the Charter without any of them accepting the same set of five articles. This has not happened in fact. The level of acceptance of the "core" articles has been well above the minimum that was possible. *See* Appendix II.

[24]*See generally* Troclet, *supra* note 10, at 3–4.

[25]*Cf.* Pugsley, *The European Social Charter*, 39 Y.B.A.A.A. 97 (1969)

duct so as to achieve a development in a stated direction."[26] In the case of these provisions, compliance turns upon effort and improvement rather than attainment. It is not necessary to show improvement in every cycle; it may be sufficient in a particular cycle to show that a program of action is being planned or is under way that will bear fruit later. The economic situation may also prevent or limit progress in a particular cycle. There is also an ultimate limit to the progress that must be made in the implementation of most "dynamic" provisions in this third sense. For example, once the formalities surrounding the taking of employment by migrant workers have been simplified to a certain point (Article 18[2]), there is no more to be done.[27] At this stage, as in the case of other provisions, a contracting party need in future cycles only maintain the level of achievement that it has reached. Other dynamic provisions, such as that concerning the level and nature of social security benefits,[28] remain unceasingly dynamic, subject only to economic limitations.

ANALYSIS OF ARTICLES

Article 1: The Right to Work[29]

It is appropriate that the first right protected by the Charter is the right to work. This indicates the importance of economic

[26]C I 9. The following provisions have been so characterized: Arts. 1(1), 2(1), 12(3), and 18(1), (2), (3). *Id.* Art. 14 would appear to have been so characterized also (C I 69), although it is difficult to distinguish it from comparable undertakings, such as that in Art. 10 to "promote or provide" vocational training and to "encourage" its use, which the Committee has not identified as "dynamic." For these provisions it is "incumbent on every Government concerned to inform" the CIE of such changes as have occurred during the cycle to allow it to assess the progress that has been made. A "purely static description of a state of affairs at a given moment does not suffice." C I 9.

[27]C II 59.

[28]Art. 12(3).

[29]*Compare* Art. 23(1) of the UDHR, note 7 *supra, with* Art. 6 of the International Covenant on Economic, Social and Cultural Rights, *adopted* Dec. 19, 1966, G.A. Res. 2200, 21 U.N. GAOR Supp. (No. 16) at 49, U.N. Doc. A/6316 (1966), 1977 Gr. Brit. T.S. No. 6 (Cmnd. 6708). The Covenant entered into force in 1976. *Cf.* in respect to Art. 1(1), ILO Employment Policy Convention (ILO Convention No. 122) *adopted* July 9, 1964, 569 U.N.T.S. 65; in respect to Art. 1(2), ILO Forced Labour Convention (ILO Convention No. 29), *adopted* June 28, 1930, 39 U.N.T.S. 55, ILO Right to Organise and Collective Bargaining Convention (ILO Convention No. 98), *adopted* July 1, 1969, 96 U.N.T.S. 257, ILO Abolition of Forced Labour Convention (ILO Convention No. 105), *adopted* June 25, 1957, 320 U.N.T.S. 291, and ILO Discrimination (Employment and Occupation) Convention (ILO Convention No. 111), *adopted* June 25, 1958, 362 U.N.T.S. 31; and in respect to Art. 1(3), ILO Unemployment Convention (ILO Con-

rights in the Charter and is consistent with the fact that a guarantee of the right to work is, according to the Committee of Independent Experts,[30] a condition for the realization of certain other economic rights in the Charter, such as the right to just conditions of work (Article 2) and the right to a fair remuneration (Article 4). The nature of the right to work was well expressed by Mr. Even (F.R.G.) in debate in the Consultative Assembly: "One of the first social requirements is necessarily the provision and guarantee of a livelihood for our working people. . . . It is a very hard fate for men with the will and the ability to work to be unable to earn a living, to be overcome by fears for their life and existence and hence to acquire an inferiority complex."[31] The "right to work" is an emotive concept which has often been used for propaganda purposes. Upon examination, however, it cannot mean what it appears to mean: that a state must guarantee a job for every person who wants one.[32] This guarantee is impossible to fulfill for the availability of work is too dependent upon the economic climate and the skills and capacity of each individual. Accordingly, Article 1 does not aim to provide work for everyone in search of it; it consists instead of four specific undertakings that will improve opportunities for work.[33]

Article 1(1): Full Employment.

By Article 1(1), the contracting parties undertake "to accept as one of their primary aims and responsibilities the achievement and maintenance of as high and stable a level of employment as possible, with a view to the attainment of full employment."[34] The Committee of Independent Experts has re-

vention No. 2), *adopted* Nov. 28, 1919, 39 U.N.T.S. 41, and ILO Employment Service Convention (ILO Convention No. 88), *adopted* July 9, 1948, 70 U.N.T.S. 85.

[30]C I 13.

[31]Eur. Consult. Ass. Deb. 8th Sess. (Oct. 24, 1956).

[32]*Cf.* Mr. Corish, Eur. Consult. Ass. Deb. 7th Sess. 435 (Oct. 18, 1955).

[33]On the control of employment by international law generally, see C. Jenks, The Common Law of Mankind Chap. 6 (1958).

[34]The words "with a view to the attainment of full employment" were added as a result of a suggestion made by the workers' delegates to the TC. REC PROC TC 194. "Full employment" is not defined in the Charter. A common definition is a situation in which unemployment does not exceed the minimum due to seasonable and frictional factors. "Full employment" is also one of the objectives of EFTA, which had just been established. *See* Stockholm European Free Trade Convention, Art. 2(a), *signed* Jan. 4, 1960, 370 U.N.T.S. 3. On full employment, *see generally*, Rehn, *Attainment and Maintenance of Full Employment*, Working Paper for the Strasbourg Symposium on the European Social Charter 1977, CE Doc. AS/Coll/Charte 2-E.

quired parties that accept this undertaking first to demonstrate that they have a coherent economic policy specifically addressed to the achievement of as high and stable a level of employment as possible, with full employment as the ultimate goal.[35] The Committee has indicated the features that this policy should contain. It should be concerned with the short-term, the medium-term, and the long-term employment situation;[36] it should aim at avoiding or reducing regional imbalance;[37] it should seek to improve or maintain the position of all groups of workers within society, including women, the young, the middle-aged, and the elderly;[38] and it should be concerned with all sectors of the economy, including agriculture.[39] The Committee has also confirmed what is evident on even the most undemanding reading of Article 1(1), viz., that "if a state at any time abandoned the objective of full employment in favour of an economic system providing for a permanent pool of unemployed, it would be infringing the Social Charter."[40] The Committee of Independent Experts has been persistent and vigorous in its requests for information that will allow it to judge whether a coherent economic policy of the required kind exists. It has demonstrated dissatisfaction with a short, general affirmation of compliance.[41]

Second, the Committee of Independent Experts has expected that measures be taken to implement the required policy[42] and, here too, has insisted that information sufficient to evaluate implementation be submitted.[43] The Committee has, for the most part, refrained from suggesting to a contracting party what particular measures it should adopt.[44] There is

[35]C II 3 (Denmark, U.K.).

[36]C II 3 (U.K.), C IV 5 (Italy), C IV 3 (Austria).

[37]C I 14 (Italy, Norway, U.K.), C IV 3–5 (Italy, Denmark, U.K.).

[38]See, e.g., C IV 5 (Italy) and C IV 4 (Denmark).

[39]C II 179 (Cyprus).

[40]C I 14.

[41]Thus it was not until the fifth cycle that the U.K. was found to have provided sufficient information. C V 5 (U.K.).

[42]C I 14 (U.K., Denmark), C II 65 (F.R.G.).

[43]C III 4 (Ireland) and C V 4 (France).

[44]In the first cycle, the CIE did specifically ask for information in Ireland's Second Report on the success of efforts made to attract foreign capital investment into the country, implying that this was a means of improving employment which Ireland ought to adopt. C I 165 (Ireland). Art. 1(2) of the Charter, with its ban on forced labor, prohibits for those states that accept it the most obvious example of a means of increasing employment levels that would be unacceptable in the light of the "ideals and principles" which are the "common heritage" of the member states of the CE

evidence to support such an approach in the *travaux preépa-ratoires* of the Charter. Attempts were made to include in Article 1(1) guidelines indicating the kind of steps that should be taken to improve employment. However, these attempts failed, probably because it was felt that this was a matter of some political delicacy which states should determine for themselves.[45] Moreover, the supervisory organs are so composed that they are not competent to give expert guidance on the complex and controversial matter of tackling unemployment.

The key to the assessment by the Committee of Independent Experts of the adequacy of the measures taken to satisy Article 1(1) is its characterization of that provision as "dynamic."[46] To comply with Article 1(1) in a given cycle a contracting party must take measures to improve upon the employment situation that existed at the beginning of the cycle. Actual improvement is not necessary; the essence of compliance with a dynamic provision is the adoption of measures to achieve its objective.[47] Accordingly, the fact that unemployment has increased or decreased in a particular cycle of supervision is, although important,[48] by no means conclusive evidence of noncompliance or compliance with the Charter.[49] Thus, in the third cycle, the Committee of Independent Experts found that Sweden had complied with Article 1(1) even though there was a "fairly considerable increase in unemployment in Sweden" during the period concerned because the Swedish authorities had made "a substantial effort to improve

referred to in the Preamble to the Charter. Art. 1(3) of the ILO Employment Policy Convention 1965, note 29, *supra* states that full employment "shall be pursued by methods that are appropriate to national conditions and practices."

[45] Art. 1(b) of the CA 1956 draft Charter, Eur. Consult. Ass., 8th Sess., Doc. No. 536 (1956), proposed that states should realize high employment "through the pursuance of policies which will ensure adequate opportunities for work, such as, for example, the fixing of national employment targets, the preparation of national manpower budgets, and the establishment of long-term development programmes, including the planning of public works, which may be adapted to the changing employment situation." This wording was omitted in the 1959 CMSC draft, Eur. Consult. Ass., 11th Sess., Doc. No. 927 (1959). The reason for its omission was not indicated. An attempt by the workers' delegates to the TC to reintroduce it was sucessfully opposed by the employers' delegates and some government delegates. REC PROC TC 193.

[46] C I 13. *Cf.* GC VI 6.

[47] On dynamic provisions, *see* note 27 *supra*.

[48] C I 14 (U.K.).

[49] C III 3.

the labour market situation."[50] In contrast, the reduction in unemployment in Italy during the third cycle was not by itself "a sufficient indication of an effort to achieve full employment," at least "when the level of unemployment was still about 5 per cent of the working population."[51]

One problem which the Committee of Independent Experts had to consider in the fourth cycle was the consistency with Article 1(1) of measures that a contracting party takes to deal with inflation or with an economic recession which increase unemployment in the short term but are expected to reduce it later on. This had become a problem for all of the contracting parties by the end of that cycle (1972–73) as a result of the oil crisis and the worldwide recession that had developed. Although recognizing the exigencies of the situation and the permissibility of such action, the Committee of Independent Experts stressed that "measures to sustain employment should be taken, in pursuance of Article 1, paragraph 1, to offset the side effects of action, such as anti-inflation measures, made necessary by the current crisis, in order to avoid an excessive rise in unemployment."[52] In particular, "special measures should be taken to help those people who are at a disadvantage in seeking work either because of regional imbalance or disparities based on sex or because of age, since older workers, like the young, run a greater risk of unemployment."[53] Simi-

---

[50]C III 4 (Sweden). *Cf.* C V 3 (Cyprus). Contrast the ruling on Denmark's Report in the sixth cycle. Although measures had been taken to combat unemployment, these were not sufficient. This is the only case yet in which a breach of Art. 1(1) has been found. Ruling reversed in C VII 3 (Denmark). The GC impliedly disagreed with the sixth cycle ruling. GC VI 6.

[51]C III 4 (Italy).

[52]C IV xiv. The GC has criticized the CIE for tending "to underestimate medium and long-term employment measures, whose intended results only become apparent at a later stage, but which also deserved to be taken into account when assessing the overall efforts undertaken by governments." GC VI 6.

[53]C IV xiv. The problem was foreseen so far as inflation is concerned by Mr. Federspiel (Denmark), Chairman of the CA Economic Committee, in a letter to the President of the CA of October 17, 1955, Eur. Consult. Ass., 7th Sess., Doc. No. 407 (1955):

The principle of full employment and that of the stability of the purchasing power of money . . . each constitute very complex problems upon which there is heated argument, not to mention that the two have been most difficult to reconcile in the recent past. The problems that will arise whenever a priority must be established between them—and that need will often be felt—will obviously depend on the conditions at hand in a given country at a given time.

larly, in the sixth cycle the Committee indicated that when the economic climate was such that the prospects for employment were poor, Article 1(1) required contracting parties to "intensify their efforts, as a priority objective, with a view to reducing unemployment especially among the groups most affected by it. . . ."[54]

Article 1(2): The Right of the Worker to Earn His Living in an Occupation Freely Entered Upon

By Article 1(2), the contracting parties undertake "to protect effectively the right of the worker to earn his living in an occupation freely entered upon." It is clear that this undertaking does not, any more than that in Article 1(1), require a state to ensure that each person has a job. What it does require is that a state provide protection against (i) forced labor and (ii) discrimination in employment practices.[55]

Forced Labor. The guarantee against forced labor stems from the wording "freely entered upon" in Article 1(2). By this wording the Committee of Independent Experts has understood "that the coercion of any worker to carry out work against his wishes, and without his freely expressed consent, is contrary to the Charter."[56] The Committee has also interpreted this provision as prohibiting "the coercion of any worker to carry out work he had previously freely agreed to do, but which he subsequently no longer wanted to carry out."[57] It therefore prohibits not only a requirement that a person do work to which he has never consented but also the imposition of criminal sanctions for failure to comply with the terms of a contract of employment which has been freely made.

The Committee of Independent Experts did not find any instances of forced labor in the first sense during the first seven cycles. Presumably provisions such as the Swedish law authorizing the government to call upon citizens to help fight fires[58]

---

[54]C VI xii.

[55]C II 5, C III 5, GC IV 4.

[56]C II 5.

[57]*Id.* For other definitions of "forced labor," see ILO Forced Labor Convention 1930, Art. 2(1), note 29 *supra*, and ECHR, Art. 4(1), note 1 *supra*, as interpreted by the Eur. Comm'n of Human Rights in the Iversen Case, 1963 Y.B. Eur. Conv. on Human Rights 278 (Eur. Comm'n of Human Rights). For a discussion of these definitions and their application, *see* J. Fawcett, The Application of the European Convention on Human Rights 43–57 (1969).

[58]Fire Law of Mar. 30, 1962.

and the Norwegian law concerning compulsory service by dentists,[59] which were both reported to the Committee of Independent Experts and not commented upon by it, were thought justifiable under Article 31 of the Charter.[60]

In contrast, it did find instances of forced labor in the second sense in respect to merchant seamen, air personnel, and public servants. At the beginning of the operation of the system of supervision almost all of the contracting parties of the Charter provided criminal penalties for merchant seamen who failed to return to ship; some parties imposed criminal penalties for disobedience to other lawful orders in certain circumstances. In the opinion of the Committee of Independent Experts, "penal measures could, in appropriate circumstances, be justified when they are applied in cases where the act giving rise to the charge endangered, or was capable of endangering, the safety of the ship or the life or health of those aboard.[61] In such cases, it implied, Article 31 of the Charter would apply. Otherwise, in the opinion of the Committee of Independent Experts, it is contrary to Article 1(2) to use the criminal law to enforce a contract of employment.[62] By the end of the seventh cycle, five contracting parties had changed their law on the matter so that it met the Committee of Independent Experts' test; four states—France, Ireland, Italy, and the U.K.—had not and remained in default.[63] The position of the U.K. is

[59]Act of June 21, 1956. This law was found not to be in violation of Art. 4 by the Eur. Comm'n of Human Rights in the "Iversen" Case, note 57 *supra. See also* Gussenbauer case, [1972] Y.B. EUR. CONV. ON HUMAN RIGHTS 448, 558 (Eur. Comm'n of Human Rights), in which the arrangement in Austrian law for compulsory legal aid work by lawyers was questioned under Art. 4 of the ECHR, note 1 *supra.* The case was settled without any ruling on the point. Report of the Eur. Comm'n on Human Rights, Oct. 8, 1974.

[60]As to which, *see* note 11 of Chapter IV. See also the lists of permitted forced labor in the ILO Forced Labour Convention 1930, Art. 2(2), note 29, *supra* and ECHR, Art. 4(3), note 1 *supra.*

[61]C III 5. *Compare* the approach of the ILO CE in the application of the ILO Forced Labour Convention 1930, note 29 *supra, with* the Report of the Committee of Experts, Int'l Lab. Conf., 53d Sess., Report III (Part 4A), 71 (1966).

[62]Enforcement of a contract of employment by means of civil law remedies would seem to be acceptable. Such remedies have been limited in English law to damages and have not included specific performance. *See* Kahn-Freund, *On Uses and Misuses of Comparative Law, 36* MOD. L. REV. 1, 24 (1974). *Quaere* whether "coercion" in the form of an order of specific performance would be "forced labor."

[63]C VI 608. The states that had changed their law were Cyprus, Denmark, the F.R.G., Norway, and Sweden.

particularly interesting since that state has thrice relaxed its law during the life of the Charter, by the Merchant Shipping Acts of 1970, 1974 and 1979. Although the Committee of Independent Experts never ruled upon it in respect to the U.K., the law under the Merchant Shipping Act 1894, which preceded the 1970 Act, clearly ran counter to the Committee of Independent Experts' interpretation of "forced labor."[64] Reviewing the changes made by the Merchant Shipping Act 1970, the Committee of Independent Experts found in the third cycle that there were still cases in which a seaman could be convicted of a criminal offense for conduct in breach of contract that did not endanger the safety of his ship or of persons on board.[65] Two of the offenses criticized by the Committee of Independent Experts were those of a seaman (i) being absent without leave when his ship sailed[66] or (ii) "wilfully [disobeying] a lawful command relating to or likely to affect the operation of the ship or its equipment."[67] Both of these offenses were repealed by the Merchant Shipping Act 1974.[68] The offense of being on duty as a seaman under the influence of drink or drugs so as to impair one's capacity to carry out one's duties has also been repealed other than in respect of seamen on fishing vessels.[69] But it remains an offense in U.K. law for a seaman (i) "persistently and wilfully" to neglect his duty or to disobey lawful commands or (ii) to combine with other seamen employed in his ship to disobey lawful commands or to neglect any lawful duty required to be obeyed or discharged while the ship is at sea or to impede at sea the progress of a voyage or the navigation of the ship.[70] The Committee of Independent Experts has maintained its opinion that, contrary to the view of the British Government, these remaining offenses were inconsistent with Article 1(2).[71] The Committee's opinion, it is submitted, is correct. For example, the persistent and willful failure of a cook to prepare meals on

---

[64]The Act remains in force in Ireland and has been found to fall short of Art. 1(2) in respect to that contracting party. C VI 7 (Ireland).

[65]C III 7–8 (U.K.).

[66]Merchant Shipping Act 1970, sec. 31.

[67]Id. at sec. 29.

[68]Merchant Shipping Act 1974, sec. 19(3).

[69]Merchant Shipping Act 1979, sec. 45(2), amending the 1974 Act, sec. 28.

[70]Merchant Shipping Act 1970, sec. 30, as amended by sec. 19 of the Merchant Shipping Act 1974. The offense does not apply to fishing vessels and persons serving in them. Merchant Shipping Act 1970, sec. 95(1)(a).

[71]C VI 8. (U.K.); C VII 8 (U.K.).

time would be an offense under the 1970 Act (sec. 30) without necessarily endangering the safety of the ship and scarcely merits criminal punishment.

In addition, the Committee of Independent Experts has ruled that the requirement of the Merchant Shipping Act 1970[72] by which seamen deserting from certain foreign ships in a British port may be arrested and returned on board is contrary to the Charter.[73] The Committee of Independent Experts noted that this ruling could affect nationals of the other contracting parties serving on board merchant ships; the law, though "virtually never applied," was, therefore, contrary to Article 1(2). The provision is based upon reciprocal arrangements with other states, including five parties to the Charter—Austria, Denmark, the F.R.G., Italy, and Norway.[74] The law of these states presumably contains comparable provisions that are equally in breach of Article 1(2).

The Committee of Independent Experts has applied the same approach to the meaning of "forced labor" to restrictions upon persons working on board civil aircraft and has found Italy in violation of Article 1(2) in this respect.[75] The other instance of forced labor that the Committee of Independent Experts has found also concerns Italy. Under the Italian Criminal Code, a "public servant or other person responsible for a public service may be sentenced to penal servitude in the event of unwarranted refusal or failure to perform, or unwarranted delay in performing the duties of his office or service or in the event of any interruption or abandonment of the service with the intent to disturb its regularity or having the effect of so doing."[76] The Committee of Independent Experts has found this to be in violation of Article 1(2) in view of the fact that criminal liability was not limited, as Article 31 of the Charter would allow, to cases "where the refusal, failure, delay or interruption would endanger public security or order" and that "public servants" and other persons "responsible for a public

---

[72]Merchant Shipping Act, 1970, sec. 89. It was not repealed by the 1974 Act.

[73]C IV 10 (U.K.). No criminal offense is committed by the deserter: he is simply returned. See now C VII 8 (U.K.).

[74]See, e.g., the Merchant Shipping (Foreign Deserters) (F.R.G.) Order 1958, [1958] 1 STAT. INST. 1414 (No. 142), which implements sec. 89 as far as the F.R.G. is concerned, and which is based on the Consular Convention, signed July 30, 1956, United Kingdom–Federal Republic of Germany, 1959 Gr. Brit. T.S. No. 2 (Cmnd. 607), 330 U.N.T.S. 233.

[75]C VII 8 (Italy).

[76]C IV 7–8 (Italy). The above passage is a summary by the CIE of Arts. 328, 331, and 333 of the Italian Criminal Code.

service" extended beyond persons concerned with essential services to, for example, officials of public savings banks, employees of transport companies, and tourist officers.[77] The Committee of Independent Experts has reached a different conclusion when applying Article 31 to restrictions upon members of the armed forces. In its view, "the peculiar status of the military may justify penal sanctions for breach of a voluntary engagement without constituting a breach of the prohibition of forced labour."[78]

While agreeing with the Committee of Independent Experts' approach to the meaning of "forced labor" for the purposes of Article 1(2), the Governmental Committee has expressed the opinion that the Committee of Independent Experts has been "too stringent and theoretical" in its treatment of the cases of "forced labor" that it has found "given that the offences mentioned were virtually non-existent and that the regulations concerned had fallen into disuse."[79] Although the Governmental Committee may well be correct in stating that the laws that the Committee of Independent Experts has called in question are not often enforced in practice, their presence may nonetheless affect the conduct of persons subject to them, thus justifying the Committee of Independent Experts' concern at their continued existence.[80]

Discrimination in Employment. The Committee of Independent Experts has stated that Article 1(2) imposes an obligation upon states to "eliminate all forms of discrimination in employment."[81] The Preamble to the Charter, which states

[77]C IV 8 (Italy).

[78]C I 15. In the fourth cycle, the CIE accepted the U.K. position concerning members of the armed forces as consistent with the Charter. On the position of "boy soldiers," which had given rise to the "Boy Soldiers" Case, 1968 Y.B. EUR. CONV. ON HUMAN RIGHTS 562 (Eur. Comm'n of Human Rights), under Art. 4 of the ECHR, note 1 *supra,* the CIE

> noted that the consent of the parents is compulsory for minors under 17½ years of age, that they are free to leave during the first six months of training, and that at the age of 18 they may decide the length of their permanent engagement which, taking into account the raising of the compulsory school-leaving age to 16, will at most be six years, and in most cases, four years.

C IV 10 (U.K.).

[79]GC IV 5.

[80]For the CIE's continued insistence that they be repealed, see C V 6 and C V 6–7 (Italy).

[81]*Compare* C III 8 *with* C I 15.

that "the enjoyment of social rights should be secured without discrimination on grounds of race, colour, sex, religion, political opinion, national extraction or social origin," supports this interpretation and indicates at least some of the kinds of discrimination that are prohibited.[82] The Preamble to the Charter refers to "national extraction" and not to nationality.[83] The distinction is important; states are not prepared to accept a general prohibition of discrimination between their nationals and aliens in their law or practice. It is important to note that the Charter applies *ratione personae* only to the nationals of contracting parties.[84] It is only such nationals, therefore, who must not be discriminated against in employment for reasons of "national extraction." Other kinds of discrimination that are not mentioned in the Preamble but that, arguably, might come within Article 1(2) are discrimination based upon youth or old age. So far, the Committee of Independent Experts has concentrated in the application of Article 1(2) mainly upon discrimination against women.[85]

Employment in this context means public and private employment. A state must ensure that discrimination in either kind of employment is not required by its law. Ireland was found to be in violation of Article 1(2) during the first three cycles when its law prohibited married women from employ-

---

[82]*Cf.* the definition in the ILO Discrimination (Employment and Occupation) Convention 1958, Art. 1(1), note 29 *supra:*

For the purpose of this Convention the term "discrimination" includes: (a) any distinction, exclusion or preference made on the basis of race, colour, sex, religion, political opinion, national extraction or social origin, which has the effect of nullifying or impairing equality of opportunity or treatment in employment or occupation; (b) such other distinction, exclusion or preference which has the effect of nullifying or impairing equality of opportunity or treatment in employment or occupation as may be determined by the Member concerned after consultation with representative employers' and workers' organisations, where such exist, and with other appropriate bodies.

[83]*Cf. id.,* ECHR, note 1 *supra,* Preamble and Art. 14; International Convention Against All Forms of Racial Discrimination, Art. 1, *opened for signature* Mar. 7, 1966, 1969 Gr. Brit. T.S. No. 77 (Cmd. 4108); 660 U.N.T.S. 195; and ICESR, Art. 2(2), note 29 *supra.* The term "national origin" is used instead of "national extraction" in some of these treaties. *See also* McKean, *The Meaning of Discrimination in International and Municipal Law,* 44 BRIT. Y.B. INT'L L. 177 (1970).

[84]*See* Wiebringhaus, *Le Champ d'Application "Ratione Personae" de la Charte Sociale Européenne,* in LIBRO-HOMENAJE AL PROFESOR LUIS SELA SAMPIL OVIEDO 525 (1970).

[85]*But see* the CIE's doubts about the F.R.G.'s 1979 Regulations requiring undertakings of fidelity to the Constitution by candidates for the civil service (possible discrimination because of political opinions). C VII 6 (F.R.G.).

ment in the civil service.[86] Exceptions are allowed in the case of laws protecting women from heavy manual labor or excluding them from "combat appointments" in the armed forces.[87] In fact, these exceptions are required for states accepting Article 8(4).[88]

Article 1(2) does not make it obligatory for contracting parties to enact legislation prohibiting discrimination by private employers. Legislation may, of course, help, but it is neither necessary nor, by itself, sufficient. The objective is the absence of discrimination in fact. What Article 1(2) means is that "positive, practical steps be taken" to eliminate such discrimination as actually exists.[89] The Committee of Independent Experts' practice concerning the U.K. supports this interpretation. In the first cycle, the U.K. was found in violation of Article 1(2) because, by its own admission, sex discrimination in employment did exist in the U.K.[90] In its second report, the U.K. indicated a number of practical steps that were being taken to improve the situation, including specifically instructing labor exchange officials not to discriminate by sex and action by the Youth Employment Service and by schools to encourage girls to take up jobs traditionally thought to be only for men. The report also commented generally upon changing attitudes in industry and in the community and upon the relatively low level of sex discrimination in employment that continued to exist. On the basis of this information, and without any express, general prohibition of sex discrimination in employment in law of the sort later adopted in the U.K. Sex Discrimination Act

[86]C I 166 (Ireland), C II 4 (Ireland), C III 9 (Ireland). The prohibition resulted from Civil Service Regulation Act 1956, sec. 10, and Civil Service Commissioners Act 1956, sec. 16(2)(c). These provisions were repealed by the Civil Service (Employment of Married Women) Act 1973. A similar ban on the employment of married women in local authority posts was terminated by the Local Government (Declaration of Qualifications) Order 1973.

[87]The CIE has not found the Swedish Workers Protection Act of Jan. 3, 1949, as amended in 1962, which prohibits women from manual work underground in mines or quarries, to be in violation of the Charter. (Sweden has not accepted Art. 8[4].) Nor has it questioned the Swedish regulations concerning the employment of women in the armed forces whereby women may not take "combat appointments." Both of these prohibitions were reported by Sweden in the second cycle in which Sweden was found to comply with Art. 1(2) as far as discrimination in employment was concerned. C II 4 (Sweden).

[88]On the consistency of such paternalistic legislation with women's rights, see note 489 *infra*.

[89]C I 16 (Italy).

[90]C I 16 (U.K.).

1975, the Committee of Independent Experts accepted that the U.K. complied with the Charter.[91] A further question in this area is whether proof of the existence of particular instances of discrimination in employment covered by Article 1(2), regardless of steps taken to eradicate it, would mean that a party has not "effectively" protected the right to employment in the sense of Article 1(2). The wording used by the Committee of Independent Experts in the first cycle, indicating that parties had to take steps to "create a situation which really ensured complete equality of treatment,"[92] might suggest that it would. This would be inconsistent with the Committee of Independent Experts' approach to the undertakings in Part II generally as far as a requirement imposed upon a state to control the de facto situation is concerned and is scarcely realistic. Discrimination in private employment in particular is likely to continue to some extent despite the most vigorous efforts of the state to prevent it.

The Appendix to the Charter states that Article 1(2) "shall not be interpreted as prohibiting or authorising any union security clause or practice." A "closed shop" arrangement whereby a worker must be a member of a trade union or a particular trade union is, therefore, not discrimination that a contracting party must take steps to prevent. As in the case of the International Labor Organization Right to Organise and Collective Bargaining Convention 1949,[93] Article 1(2) of the Charter takes no stand on the legality of the "closed shop."[94] The diversity of approaches on this question in the legal systems of the members of the Council of Europe made this impossible.[95] In other respects, discrimination based upon trade union membership is contrary to Article 1(2).[96]

The Committee of Independent Experts has ruled that Article 1(2) contains an obligation to "provide appropriate education and training" without discrimination.[97] Clearly this is important; the absence of discrimination in the employment of

---

[91]C II 5 (U.K.). *Cf.* C VII 9 (U.K.) (religious or political discrimination).

[92]C I 16 (Italy).

[93]ILO Right to Organise and Collective Bargaining Convention 1949, Art. 1, note 29 *supra. See* the commentary to INT'L LAB. CODE, Art. 691 n. 17 & 871.

[94]*See* G. LYON-CAEN, DROIT SOCIAL INTERNATIONAL ET EUROPÉEN 85 (1976). (1969). *See also* note 314 *infra.*

[95]*See Kahn-Freund, supra* note 62, at 138–39. *But see* note 314 *infra.*

[96]C VI 6 (Cyprus). It is also contrary to Art. 5. *See* note 334 *infra.*

[97]C I 15.

qualified or trained candidates is meaningless if there is discrimination in the provision of facilities to obtain the necessary qualifications or training. For this reason, the Committee of Independent Experts has been concerned to obtain information about access to apprenticeships for women.[98]

So far, the Committee of Independent Experts has emphasized access to employment. Equally important is discrimination in matters of promotion, dismissal, etc. Discrimination in these respects also comes within Article 1(2).[99] Sex discrimination in the area of pay is dealt with in Article 4(3).[100]

Commenting upon the discrimination aspect of Article 1(2) for the first time, the Governmental Committee stressed in its fourth *Report* that the "exercise of freedom of engagement by an employer when choosing from candidates who have the same basic qualifications for a particular job should not in itself be regarded as an act of discrimination"; it is the "abuse of this freedom by unfair discrimination" that contravenes Article 1(2).[101] The absence of criticism of the Committee of Independent Experts' jurisprudence concerning discrimination suggests that that jurisprudence is consistent with the Governmental Committee's concept of "unfair discrimination."

Article 1(2) applies to the self-employed.[102]

Article 1(3): Employment Services

By Article 1(3), the contracting parties undertake to "establish or maintain free employment services for all workers." The "employment services" required are essentially services for the placement of workers in employment;[103] they are not expected to offer vocational guidance. The Committee of Independent Experts has accepted that they may be provided by private employment agencies.[104] This is a surprising reading of the wording to "establish or maintain," but one that may be suited

---

[98]C III 9 (Italy).

[99]*See* Question F, Art. 1(2) of the Report Form for Art. 21. On the interpretative value of the Report Form, see note 763 *infra*.

[100]*See* note 237 *infra*. The acknowledgment by the CIE in the fourth cycle of the phasing out of pay discrimination against female local government clerical workers in Ireland was presumably made under Art. 1(2), (*see* C IV 7 [Ireland]), because Ireland had reported it under Art 1(2) and has not accepted Art. 4(3).

[101]GC IV 5.

[102]C I 8.

[103]C I 167 (Ireland).

[104]C I 167 (Ireland), C III 10 (Ireland), C III 9 (Austria).

to the traditions of some contracting parties without necessarily affecting the quality of the services provided. The services must be "free." In the case of both public and private services, therefore, the cost must be borne by the state or in some other way that does not involve charging the person seeking employ ment[105] or the employer. Thus, the U.K. has been found in violation of Article 1(3) because employers must pay a charge for the public employment services provided in the U.K. for the placement of certain categories of workers.[106] In the opinion of the Committee of Independent Experts it followed from the text of Article 1(3) and the need to ensure that the employer did not pass this expense on to the employee that no charge should be made for the use of the service by an employer.[107]

Employment services must be available for "all workers." This includes women,[108] workers of all ages,[109] workers in all sectors of the economy (including agriculture[110] and domestic service[111]), and workers in all parts of the country.[112] Discrimination is prohibited on the ground of race or on any other ground listed in the Preamble of the Charter.[113] Article 1(3) does not apply to the self-employed.[114]

The Committee of Independent Experts has interpreted Article 1(3) as meaning that the services required must be "properly operated."[115] Every employment service should accordingly keep statistics on the age and sex of applicants and of persons for whom employment is found. This the Committee regards as "necessary to any effective employment policy."[116]

---

[105]The workers' delegates to the TC were particularly concerned that workers should not have to use fee-charging private agencies. REC PROC TC 194.

[106]Most recently, C VII 10 (U.K.). The requirement applies to the placement of staff by the Professional and Executive Recruitment Service. The GC appears to read Art. 1(3) as requiring free services for workers only. GC VII 6.

[107]C IV 10.

[108]C III 10 (Italy).

[109]C III 10 (Denmark), (Ireland), C IV 12 (Norway).

[110]C III 10 (Italy).

[111]Id., C IV 12 (Italy).

[112]C I 16, C II 180 (Cyprus), C III 10 (Ireland).

[113]The question of discrimination on ethnic grounds arose in connection with Cyprus and the availability of public employment services for Greek and Turkish Cypriots. On the receipt of further information, the CIE found no violation of Art. 1(3) in this regard. C II 180 (Cyprus), C III 9 (Cyprus).

[114]C I 8.

[115]C I 16.

[116]C IV 11 (Denmark).

Employment services must also be supervised "in collaboration with both sides of industry."[117] Such collaboration may be at local or national level as necessary.[118] This requirement was met by the U.K., for example, by providing information about the role of the National Joint Advisory Council, the local employment committees attached to employment exchanges, and other tripartite bodies.

Article 1(4): Vocational Guidance, Training, and Rehabilitation
By Article 1(4), the contracting parties undertake "to provide or promote vocational guidance, training and rehabilitation." This is a curious provision in that it contains obligations which are found again and in more detail later in the Charter in Articles 9 (the right to vocational guidance), 10 (the right to vocational training), and 15 (the right to rehabilitation). The Committee of Independent Experts has described the obligations in Article 1(4) as "identical" to the ones in these later Articles.[119] Elsewhere, however, the Committee has stated, correctly, it is believed, that compliance with Article 1(4) does not mean *eo ipso* compliance with Articles 9, 10, and 15.[120] The obligation in Article 1(4) is different from, and less exacting than, those later in the Charter, but precisely what it entails is difficult to say. The jurisprudence of the Committee of Independent Experts is not extensive. Eight of the ten states that have submitted reports during the first seven cycles of implementation have accepted all of the provisions of Articles 9, 10, and 15.[121] In *Conclusions I,* the Committee of Independent Experts indicated that these states need not report on Article 1(4) and that their position concerning the guarantees covered by it would be considered in the application of Articles 9, 10, and 15.[122] As a result, the Committee of Independent Experts has examined the reports of only two states (Cyprus and the F.R.G.) on Article 1(4) and, until the sixth cycle, examined these only insofar as they concern the parts of Articles 9, 10,

[117]C I 16. *See* ILO Employment Service Convention 1948, Arts. 4 & 5, note 29 *supra.*
[118]C III 9 (Austria).
[119]C I 16.
[120]C II 6. The reverse is true. *See* C VII 11 (Denmark, etc.).
[121]*See* Appendix I.
[122]C I 16, C II 181 (Cyprus). *Contra* C VII 11 (Austria, U.K.).

and 15 that have not been accepted by them. The Committee considered its approach to the relationship between Articles 1(4) and Articles 9, 10, and 15 again in the sixth cycle. There the F.R.G. was found to be in violation of Article 1(4) when it was found to have infringed two of the paragraphs of Article 10 that it had accepted, but it is not clear whether this was because of the seriousness of the breaches of Article 10 or because, contrary to the view above, any breach of any provision of Articles 9, 10, and 15 is a breach of Article 1(4).[123]

Article 1(4) applies to the self-employed.[124]

Article 2: The Right to Just Conditions of Work[125]

Whereas the title to Article 2 is very generally phrased, the five undertakings it contains are concerned only with hours of work and holidays—matters which, as the Committee of Independent Experts has stated, "were among the original concerns of the labour movement and among the early standards established by international labour law."[126] The provision of safe and healthy working conditions and of fair remuneration are treated separately in Articles 3 and 4 respectively. Although there is also no express equivalent in the Charter to the right to "leisure" found in the International Covenant on Economic, Social and Cultural Rights,[127] the undertakings in Article 2 are, in effect, concerned with it. Article 2 applies to children and young persons, although some of its provisions are effectively replaced by the stricter provisions of Article 7.[128] The whole of Article 2 is subject to Article 33 of the Charter and may therefore be complied with by showing that "the great majority of the workers concerned" are treated in accordance with it is as a result of legislation, collective agree-

---

[123]C VI 10 (F.R.G.). C VII 11 (Austria, U.K.) suggest the latter.

[124]C I 8.

[125]*Compare* UDHR, Arts. 23(1) & 24, note 7 *supra*, and ICESR, Art. 7(d), note 29 *supra*, *with* Art. 2(1), ILO Forty Hour Week Convention (ILO Convention No. 47), *adopted* June 22, 1935, 271 U.N.T.S. 199; in respect to Art. 2(3), ILO Holidays with Pay Convention (Revised) (ILO Convention No. 132), *adopted* June 24, 1970, and ILO Seafarers Annual Leave with Pay Convention (ILO Convention No. 146), *adopted* Oct. 29, 1976; in respect to art. 2(5), ILO Weekly Rest (Industry) Convention (ILO Convention No. 14), *adopted* Nov. 17, 1921, 38 U.N.T.S. 187, and ILO Weekly Rest (Commerce and Offices) Convention (ILO Convention No. 106), *adopted* June 26, 1957, 325 U.N.T.S. 279.

[126]C I 17.

[127]ICESR; Art. 7(d), note 29 *supra*.

[128]*Compare* Arts. 2(1) and 7(4) *with* Arts. 2(3) and 7(7) and Arts 2(4) and 7(10).

ments, or otherwise.[129] Article 2 would not appear to apply to the self-employed.[130]

Article 2(1): Reasonable Working Hours

By Article 2(1), the contracting parties undertake "to provide for reasonable daily and weekly working hours, the working week to be progressively reduced to the extent that the increase of productivity and other relevant factors permit." No precise number of hours is mentioned. During the drafting of the Charter, the Consultative Assembly pressed strongly for a reference in Article 2(1) to the forty-hour week as an ultimate objective.[131] The Social Committee of the Committee of Ministers rejected this proposal, preferring the more flexible text that was finally adopted. In its view, although member states were working toward a lowering of working hours, a precise commitment to a forty-hour week would be a mistake; it might be that the forty-hour week, although a meaningful goal when the Charter was being drafted, would later prove to have been unduly modest.[132] Events have already shown the wisdom of the approach adopted.

Applying Article 2(1), the Committee of Independent Experts has established that the concept of "reasonable . . . working hours" is not an absolute one. "What would be thought reasonable under the Charter varied from place to place and from time to time, depending on productivity and other factors."[133] The Committee of Independent Experts has, therefore, not tried to lay down a particular number of daily or weekly hours that might be considered "reasonable" in all cases. Its treatment of individual cases does, however, give some indication of what Article 2(1) requires. A forty-five-hour week for "the great majority of the workers" in Norway was found to be acceptable in the first cycle of implementation.[134] In contrast, the sixty-hour week worked in Italy and

[129]E.g., by custom or administrative measures.

[130]*See* GC IV 7. On the application of the Charter to the self-employed, see C I 8.

[131]For the final text proposed by the CA, see Eur. Consult. Ass., 11th Sess., Doc. No. 1035 (1959), Art. 2(1). The ILO Forty Hour Week Convention 1935, note 125 *supra*, states the principle of the 40-hour week.

[132]See Deprez, *Droit à des Conditions de Travail Equitable, Droit à l'Orientation Professionelle, Droit à la Formation Professionelle* 7, paper presented to the Brussels Colloquium on the European Social Charter, Institut d'Etudes Europeénnes (1976).

[133]C I 18.

[134]*Id.* (Norway). *Cf.* C V 13 (France): average working week of 42 hours satisfactory.

Ireland during the first and second cycles respectively was found to be contrary to the Charter.[135] The Committee of Independent Experts has emphasized weekly rather than daily hours of work in its *Conclusions*. The national reports of the contracting parties indicate that an eight- or nine-hour day is normal.[136] One other guideline which the Committee of Independent Experts has suggested is that it is relevant to consider the level of unemployment in a state. The higher it is, the lower the Committee of Independent Experts will expect the number of hours worked by any particular person to be.[137] Article 2(1) applies to all employed workers, including family workers in agriculture.[138]

Article 2(1) has been characterized by the Committee of Independent Experts as "dynamic" because of the commitment that the contracting parties make to reduce the working week "progressively . . . to the extent that the increase of productivity and other relevant factors permit."[139] As to the level to which the working week should ultimately be reduced in accordance with Article 2(1), the Committee of Independent Experts has noted "that there are limits to change in this direction, particularly in connection with the fixing of the length of the working week," and pointed out that "the current tendency for the five-day, forty-hour week to become general is already giving rise to new social problems, such as those of the use of leisure time, etc."[140]

On the question of leisure, the Committee of Independent Experts has expressed its concern that a consequence of the limitation of normal working hours in accordance with Article 2(1) may be that instead of enjoying more leisure, a worker volunteers for overtime or takes a second job.[141] While acknowledging its lack of competence to act to prevent him doing this, the Committee of Independent Experts has ex-

---

[135]*Id.* (Italy); C II 7 (Ireland). In the case of Italy, the 60 hours consisted of 48 plus 12 hours of compulsory overtime. Required overtime counts as a part of the hours worked for the purposes of Art. 2(1). C I 18 (Italy). The finding against each of these states was reversed in later cycles on evidence of shorter working weeks (and taking into account Art. 33). C IV 15 (Ireland) and C V 13 (Italy) (provisionally).

[136]For the view that weekly and daily hours of work must each be reasonable, see Deprez, *supra* note 132, at 6.

[137]C I 18, C II 7 (Ireland).

[138]C III 12 (Ireland).

[139]C I 17. On "dynamic" provisions, see note 27 *supra*.

[140]C I 18.

[141]C III 12.

pressed the opinion that where it happens "the protection originally intended was thus rendered futile."[142] The Committee of Independent Experts' concern in this respect seems somewhat misplaced. Subject to considerations of health and safety, a worker should be free to use his spare time as he wishes. As the Governmental Committee has noted, "although adequate pay can certainly make it unnecessary for the worker to look for overtime or for a second job, it is equally sure that the people concerned have more complex motives than the mere wish to earn more."[143] As far as second jobs are concerned, the national reports submitted in the first seven cycles indicate that only one of the five contracting parties then bound by Article 2(1) limits the freedom of workers to take them.[144]

Article 2(2): Public Holidays with Pay

By Article 2(2) the contracting parties undertake "to provide for public holidays with pay." In an interpretation adopted during the drafting of the Charter, the Committee of Ministers stated "It is understood that this provision would not cover *all* public holidays, but only days for which the worker would have been paid, had they not been holidays."[145] "Pay" is presumably a worker's usual basic pay.[146] Article 2(2) does not specify how many public holidays should be provided. In the first seven cycles, the Committees of Independent Experts found that all eight of the contracting parties which had accepted Article 2(2) complied with it, with public holidays ranging from six to seventeen a year. Presumably, public holidays should not count as part of the minimum of two weeks' annual holiday guaranteed separately in Article 2(3).[147] Presumably also, in exceptional cases a person can be required to work on a day that is designated as a public holiday in the state in which he is employed.[148]

[142]C IV 15.

[143]GC IV 6.

[144]Under Art. 2(3), F.R.G. Working Hours Code, the total number of hours worked on different jobs must not exceed eight hours a day altogether.

[145]CM (61) 95 rev., 2.

[146]*Cf.* Deprez, *supra* note 132, at 8.

[147]ILO Holidays with Pay Convention (ILO Convention No. 52), Art. 2(3), *adopted* June 24, 1936, 40 U.N.T.S. 137.

[148]E.g., ventilation or safety officers in mines. *Cf.* ILO Hours of Work (Coal Mines) Convention (Revised) (ILO Convention No. 46), Art. 6(1), *adopted* June 21, 1935 (Cmd. 5033).

Article 2(3): Annual Holidays with Pay

By Article 2(3), the contracting parties undertake "to provide for a minimum of two weeks annual holiday with pay."[149] Most of the states that have accepted this provision do not provide this for every worker but comply on the basis of Article 33.[150] It is contrary to Article 2(3) for a worker to be allowed by law, by collective agreement, or otherwise to waive his annual two weeks' holiday even though he might be entitled to additional remuneration for doing so.[151] This does not prevent payments being made to an employee when his employment terminates in respect to holidays that have accrued and that he has not taken.[152] Article 2(3) does not prohibit a restriction by which "a certain period of employment be required for acquiring the right to holiday with pay."[153] Thus it is permissible to require a worker to be employed for a qualifying period of twelve months before he is eligible for an annual holiday.[154] So far, the Committee of Independent Experts has left open two questions of interpretation of Article 2(3), viz., whether sick leave that is taken during a period that would normally be a holiday counts toward a person's entitlement of two weeks' annual holiday[155] and whether an employee can be required to take all of his holiday at once or whether he must be allowed to divide it into two or more periods.[156] As to the second of these questions, the rules of treaty interpretation suggest that the first interpretation is correct; although the English text is ambiguous, the French text[157] clearly supports this interpretation.[158]

[149]The CA, like the workers' delegates to the TC, proposed three weeks. Eur. Consult. Ass., 11th Sess., Doc. No. 1035 (1959), Art. 12(3), but the CMSC rejected this proposal at its Ninth Session, April 1960. The Parliamentary Assembly has recommended that the Charter be revised to guarantee four weeks' annual holiday. Recommendation 839, TEXTS ADOPTED, September 1978.

[150]The F.R.G. complies with it regardless of Art. 33. Its Wage Earners Minimum Holidays Act of Jan. 8, 1963, sec. 3, guarantees a minimum of 15 working days holiday for all workers and 18 days for workers over 35.

[151]C I 170, GC IV 6. Austria, C IV 16, and Ireland, C II 8, C III 14, and C IV 17, were found in violation of Art. 2(3) on this ground. The finding against Austria was reversed on proof that Austrian law had been misunderstood. C V 12.

[152]C I 170.

[153]Interpretation adopted by the CM during the drafting of the Charter, CM (61) 95 rev., 2.

[154]C I 20.

[155]*Id.*

[156]C I 170.

[157]"Un congé payé annuel de deux semaines."

[158]The question was raised (but not answered) in the case of Austria in the third cycle. C III 13 (Austria).

Article 2(4): Holidays and Hours in Dangerous or Unhealthy
  Occupations

By Article 2(4), the contracting parties undertake "to provide for additional paid holidays or reduced working hours for workers engaged in dangerous or unhealthy occupations as prescribed." This provision is closely related to Article 3 of the Charter concerning safe and healthy conditions of work.[159] The wording "as prescribed" leaves states "a certain amount of latitude in the choice of occupations to be classed as dangerous or unhealthy," but the supervisory organs at Strasbourg may review the choice made by a state and rule against it if it does not include occupations that are "manifestly dangerous or unhealthy."[160] These include quarrying, mining, and other underground work;[161] the handling of explosives, asbestos, radioactive substances, and toxic chemicals;[162] employment in the merchant navy, aerial naviagation, and road transport;[163] and such work as steelmaking,[164] the extraction of peat,[165] the slaughtering and preparation of meat,[166] and shipbuilding.[167] The obligation in Article 2(4) is to "provide for additional paid holidays or reduced working hours." It is not complied with by increasing a worker's pay in recognition of the dangerous or unhealthy nature of his employment.[168] Nor is it met by a policy of reducing the hazards involved in dangerous or unhealthy occupations without at the same time increasing holidays or reducing hours.[169] In the case of a worker employed on work involving exposure to ionizing radiation or a similar hazard, the Governmental Committee has suggested that it would be consistent with Article 2(4) to put him on other work rather than reduce his working hours; this contrasts with the

---

[159]*Cf.* C IV 18.
[160]C II 9.
[161]C I 20 (U.K.).
[162]C IV 29 (Italy).
[163]C IV 18, 19 (Austria, Italy).
[164]C VI 14 (Italy).
[165]C V 16 (Ireland).
[166]*Id.*
[167]*Id.*
[168]C III 14 (Austria).
[169]C III 15 (Ireland). Without disagreeing, the GC has suggested that the CIE should concentrate on eliminating risks rather than reducing hours. GC IV 6. In response, the CIE has confirmed its position that Art. 2(4) requires the reduction of hours. C V 16. *See also* C V 16 (Austria) and C VI 13 (Austria).

position of the worker employed on heavy work who suffers fatigue.[170]

Article 2(5): Weekly Rest Periods
By Article 2(5), the contracting parties undertake "to ensure a weekly rest period which shall, as far as possible, coincide with the day recognised by tradition or custom in the country or region concerned as a day of rest." The "rest period" need, as the text implies, be only of one day's duration.[171] In accordance with "tradition or custom" in the states that are parties to the Charter, it will normally fall on a Sunday. The reference to "tradition or custom in the country or region concerned" may place immigrant or other minority group workers at a disadvantage if it is assumed that a part of the purpose of the day at rest is to allow a worker to practice his religion.[172] It is contrary to the Charter for a worker to be able to forgo his "weekly rest period" for a lump sum by way of compensation.[173]

Article 3: The Right to Safe and Healthy Working Conditions[174]
The field of application of the right to safe and healthy working conditions, which is a long-established right in interna-

---

[170]GC IV 6.

[171]The CA has proposed a weekly rest period of at least 36 consecutive hours, Eur. Consult. Ass., 11th Sess., Doc. 1035 (1959), Art. 2, but the CMSC found this unacceptable at its Ninth Session, April 1960.

[172]*Cf.* Deprez, *supra* note 132, at 10. The guarantee of freedom of religion in Art. 9 of the ECHR, note 1 *supra,* may be of assistance to such persons in some cases. *See* Art. 32.

[173]C I 172 (Ireland), C II 11 (Ireland).

[174]*Cf.* UDHR, Art. 23(1), note 7 *supra,* and ICESCR, Art. 7(b), note 29 *supra. Cf.* in respect to Art. 3(1), ILO White Lead (Painting) Convention (ILO Convention No. 13), *adopted* Nov. 19, 1921, 38 U.N.T.S. 175, ILO Protection Against Accidents (Dockers) Convention (Revised) (ILO Convention No. 32), *adopted* Apr. 27, 1932, 39 U.N.T.S. 103 (Cmd. 4115), ILO Safety Provisions (Building) Convention (ILO Convention No. 62), *adopted* June 23, 1937, 40 U.N.T.S. 333, ILO Radiation Protection Convention (ILO Convention No. 115), *adopted* June 22, 1960, 431 U.N.T.S 41, 1963 Gt. Brit. T.S. No. 41 (Cmnd. 2058), ILO Guarding of Machinery Convention (ILO Convention No. 119), *adopted* June 25, 1963, 532 U.N.T.S. 159, ILO Hygiene (Commerce and Offices) Convention (ILO Convention No. 120), *adopted* July 8, 1946, 560 U.N.T.S. 201, ILO Maximum Weight Convention (ILO Convention No. 127), *adopted* June 28, 1967 (Cmnd. 3765), and ILO Benzene Convention (ILO Convention No. 136), *adopted* June 23, 1971 (Cmd. 4706); in respect to Art. 3(2), ILO Labour Inspection Convention (ILO Convention No. 81), *adopted* July 11, 1947, 57 U.N.T.S. 3 (Cmd. 7437), and ILO Labour Inspection (Agriculture) Convention (ILO Convention No. 129), *adopted* June 25, 1969 (Cmnd. 4526); in respect to Art. 3(3), ILO Convention Nos. 13, 115, 119, 120, 127, and 136 (for details, see this note *supra*).

tional labor legislation, has been widened in recent years as a result of the "technical advances and increasing mechanisation manifest in every branch of activity."[175] The Committee of Independent Experts emphasized its continued importance in the fifth cycle:

> . . . generally speaking, despite considerable progress in preventive measures, increasing automation of the production process and the creation of bodies responsible for safety and health in firms, the number of industrial accidents was still very high. Apart from the humanitarian aspect, which was difficult to quantify but still very important, the Committee wished to recall the social and economic repercussions of this phenomenon, expressed in the cost to the community of each case of industrial injury, loss of capital in the form of knowledge, infrastructures required for the physical rehabilitation and social and economic re-integration of workers, etc.[176]

Article 3 applies to all sectors of the economy: to manufacturing industry, to mining and quarrying, to commerce and transport (including shipping), and to agriculture. Conditions on oil rigs are also covered.[177] Article 3 applies to moral as well as physical safety and health,[178] although the Committee of Independent Experts has not as yet emphasized this aspect of it. The guarantees in Article 3 are supplemented, as far as children and young persons and women are concerned, by those in Articles 7 and 8 respectively.

The Committee of Independent Experts and the Governmental Committee disagree on the question whether Article 3 applies to the self-employed. Although both start from the premise that the undertakings in Part II apply to the self-employed unless the context indicates otherwise,[179] the Committee of Independent Experts considers that Article 3 does apply to them

---

[175]C II 12.

[176]C V 19. The Parliamentary Assembly has recommended that Art. 3 be revised to emphasize that "the working environment should be satisfactory taking into account the nature of the work and the social and technical development of society." Recommendation 839, Texts ADOPTED, September 1978.

[177]Cf. notes 782 & 846 infra.

[178]The CA had proposed an express reference in the Chapter to "physical and moral safety." Eur. Consult. Ass., 11th Sess., Doc. No. 1035 (1959), Art. 3. The CMSC rejected this proposal at its Ninth Session, April 1960, but did so on the understanding that the word "safety" in the final text could be interpreted in a broad sense, so as to include moral elements.

[179]See C I 8.

and the Governmental Committee considers that it does not. Referring to Article 3(2) in particular,[180] the latter argues that it "implies the existence of an employer or other person able to assume responsibility for ensuring conditions of safety and health at work and against whom the workers could bring a claim in case of breach or against whom the state could take action for failure to provide safe and healthy working conditions."[181] The Committee of Independent Experts argues in respect to Article 3 as a whole that, contrary to the view of the Governmental Committee, it is possible to impose a duty of self-protection upon the self-employed person and that there is no difficulty in having him replace the employer in this respect.[182] As far as the state's supervisory obligation under Article 3(2) is concerned, allowance can be made, in the opinion of the Committee, where necessary for any special problems that exist because of lack of cooperation by the self-employed person and for other difficulties of inspection.[183] In addition, the level of inspection required can be related to the high or low risk involved in an occupation. The Committee of Independent Experts also argues in terms of the purpose of Article 3: a person's place of work is not likely to be less dangerous or unhealthy for himself or others because he is self-employed.[184] It is, moreover, arbitrary to distinguish between the self-employed and the employed where, as is sometimes the case, they are employed in the same work.[185] The Committee of Independent Experts' view would seem preferable as being consistent with the general presumption that the Charter applies to the self-employed. In practice, this disagreement is not as important as it might seem because of the view taken by the Governmental Committee of the position of workers in agricul-

---

[180]The GC concerned itself only with Art. 3(2), this being the part of Art. 3 that presents the most difficulties for states if Art. 3 does apply to the self-employed. Clearly the same interpretation must be adopted in respect to all three paragraphs of Art. 3.

[181]GC II 10–11 (the Danish representative dissenting) and GC IV 7.

[182]C IV 21. *See also* C II 12 and C III 17.

[183]With regard to agriculture in particular, the CIE has stressed "the diversity of ways in which safety in the area of agricultural workers may be assured"; a system of inspection which, it has acknowledged, would be very difficult to operate was not the only answer. The GC has mentioned what it called "consumer protection" techniques—safety devices, the control of chemicals, etc.—as an alternative to a system of inspection. GC II 11.

[184]C IV 21.

[185]C III 17. This might be true, for example, on a building site.

ture, which has presented the most difficulties. In its opinion, most independent farmers can be regarded as employers since they are assisted by their family or employees. Article 3 then applies to them as employers, and the question whether it applies to the self-employed does not arise.[186]

Article 3(1): The Issue of Safety and Health Regulations

By Article 3(1), the contracting parties undertake "to issue safety and health regulations." Regulations must be issued concerning all areas of the economy.[187] They must be issued by the state; it is not sufficient to show that regulations have been issued by a private organization or employer.[188] The Committee of Independent Experts has claimed competence under Article 3(1) to assess the adequacy of regulations in certain respects. It has stated, for example, that regulations concerning transport should control such matters as driving hours and vehicle safety features.[189] Although Article 3(1) does not have a "dynamic" character,[190] regulations must keep abreast of new technical developments.[191] The Committee of Independent Experts has sought accident statistics as one measure by which to judge the adequacy of regulations.[192]

Article 3(2): Enforcement of Regulations

By Article 3(2), the contracting parties undertake "to provide for the enforcement of such regulations by measures of supervision." There are two aspects of this requirement. First, there must be an adequate system of inspection, which may be a public or a private one,[193] covering the entire state's territory and all sectors of its economy.[194] Accordingly, the Committee

---

[186]GC II 11.

[187]C I 22 and 173. Ireland and Italy remain in default of Art. 3(1) for this reason. C VI 15 (Ireland) and C VI 16 (Italy).

[188]C III 18 (Ireland).

[189]C III 18 (Ireland).

[190]As to which, see C II 59.

[191]C III 17. The CIE has drawn attention to the fact that newly introduced chemical and other products and equipment may pose dangers to industrial and agricultural workers which are not recognized until it is too late. The CIE has called for a study of the situation. C V xvii.

[192]C III 17–19.

[193]C IV 25 (F.R.G.). The system of supervision partly by private "professional organisations" and partly by the state that existed in the F.R.G. was held permissible, although the CIE expressed doubts as to whether it is effective. C IV 25 (F.R.G.).

[194]C I 23 (Denmark, Norway, U.K.). This includes shipping, in respect to which there should be an inspection system operating on board. C I 23 (Norway).

of Independent Experts has sought details from states concerning the numbers of labor inspectors (including medical labor inspectors) and the frequency and methods of inspection.[195] Second, there must be adequate civil and criminal sanctions in law, and these must be effectively enforced.[196] Whereas the Committee of Independent Experts asked for information about civil remedies available against the employer in the first cycle, it has more recently emphasized criminal sanctions,[197] although apparently regarding either as sufficient provided that the overall level of sanctions is adequate.[198] In the opinion of the Committee of Independent Experts, a violation of Article 3(1) means a violation of Article 3(2) *eo ipso*.[199] The Governmental Committee disagrees with this reading. In its opinion, a contracting party may comply with Article 3(2) if it has some regulations—though not sufficient to comply with Article 3(1)—and it supervises "such regulations" effectively.[200] This cannot be correct. "Such regulations" must be regulations complying with Article 3(1).

Article 3(2) overlaps with the requirement of "a system of labour inspection" in Article 20(5).[201]

Article 3(3): Consultation with Employers and Workers Organizations
By Article 3(3), the contracting parties undertake "to consult, as appropriate, employers' and workers' organisations on measures intended to improve industrial safety and health." Article 3(3) requires states to establish machinery for consultation between governments on the one hand and employers and workers organizations on the other[202] and to undertake such consultation when the need arises ("as appropriate").[203] The term "consultation" means the seeking of advice "at either national, regional, local, or possibly enterprise level."[204] In applying Article 3(3), the Committee of Independent Experts

[195]C III 19 (Austria), C III 19 (Cyprus), C IV 26 (Italy).

[196]C I 23.

[197]C IV 25 (F.R.G.); C IV 26 (Italy).

[198]In the third cycle, it asked the F.R.G. for information about measure of "civil and/or criminal liability." C III 19 (F.R.G.).

[199]*See, e.g.,* C IV 25 (Cyprus).

[200]GC IV 7.

[201]As to which, see note 13 *supra*.

[202]C II 15 (Norway). Contrast Art. 6(1) which is concerned with consultation between workers and employers. *See* note 340 *infra*.

[203]C I 23, C I 174, C VI 19 (U.K.).

[204]C I 23.

has sought information about the level and frequency of consultation[205] and about procedures followed when consultation takes place.[206] "Measures" include legislative measures.[207] So far, no state has been found in violation of this provision.

Article 4: The Right to a Fair Remuneration[208]
The right to a fair remuneration is "the essential corollary of the first three fundamental rights of the Social Charter,"[209] viz., the right to work, the right to just conditions of work, and the right to safe and healthy working conditions. These "would stand in danger of losing much of their meaning without an effective guarantee of the right to fair remuneration, which constitutes one of the basic economic objectives of human activity."[210]

The final unnumbered paragraph of Article 4[211] has been interpreted by the Committee of Independent Experts to mean that a contracting party may leave the realization of the rights recognized in paragraphs (1) to (4), as well as compliance with the undertaking in paragraph (5), to collective bargaining, but that if such bargaining fails, the contracting party is under an obligation to intervene.[212] This interpretation,

[205]C I 24 (Norway, Denmark, Italy), C I 174 (F.R.G., Ireland).

[206]See, e.g., C I 24 (Norway, Denmark, Italy). In the fifth cycle, the CIE made a request for further information on the extent and frequency of consultations. C V 23.

[207]C III 21 (Cyprus).

[208]Compare UDHR, Art. 23(2) and (3), note 7 supra, and ICESCR, Art. 7(2), note 29 supra, with Art. 4(1), ILO Minimum Wage–Fixing Machinery Convention (ILO Convention No. 26), adopted June 16, 1928, 39 U.N.T.S. 3, ILO Minimum Wage–Fixing Machinery (Agriculture) Convention (ILO Convention No. 99), adopted June 28, 1951, 172 U.N.T.S. 159, and ILO Minimum Wage—Fixing Convention (ILO Convention No. 131), adopted June 22, 1970; in respect to Art. 4(2), ILO Hours of Work (Industry) Convention (ILO Convention No. 1), adopted Nov. 28, 1919, 38 U.N.T.S. 17, and ILO Hours of Work (Commerce and Offices) Convention (ILO Convention No. 30), adopted June 28, 1930, 39 U.N.T.S. 85; in respect to Art. 4(3), ILO Equal Remuneration Convention (ILO Convention No. 100), adopted June 29, 1951, 165 U.N.T.S. 303; and in respect to Art. 4(5), ILO Protection of Wages Convention (ILO Convention No. 95), adopted July 1, 1949, 138 U.N.T.S. 225.

[209]C I 25.

[210]Id.

[211]This reads: "The exercise of these rights shall be achieved by freely concluded collective agreements, by statutory wage-fixing machinery, or by other means appropriate to national conditions."

[212]Although this interpretation has been adopted by the CIE in its examination of Art. 4(3) only, it must logically apply to the other parts of Art. 4 also. The unnumbered paragraph refers to the "rights in Art. 4, which could accordingly be read as excluding the undertaking in para. 5 since only the undertakings in paras. 1–4 are expressed in terms of "rights." This paragraph could, however, be phrased in terms of a right also, and it seems likely that it is intended to be covered.

which has been questioned by certain contracting parties, is considered further below in discussing Article 4(3).

Article 4(1): Adequate Remuneration

By Article 4(1), the contracting parties undertake "to recognise the right of workers to a remuneration such as will give them and their families a decent standard of living."

The Committee of Independent Experts has experienced great difficulty in applying this provision. This was particularly so during the early cycles. The main problem has been that the concept of a "decent standard of living" is extremely elusive. The Committee quickly established that it is a relative one, varying in meaning from state to state according to local economic and social conditions.[213] But it was not until the fifth cycle that the Committee settled upon the criterion it has since followed in deciding what it otherwise means. Relying upon a Council of Europe study,[214] the Committee decided to adopt a "decency threshold" approach, by which any wage that is excessively lower than the national average wage cannot be taken as being sufficient to permit a decent standard of living in the society concerned.[215] Adopting the precise figure suggested by the Council of Europe study, the Committee quantified the lowest permissible wage as 68% of the national average. If the wages paid in a sector of the economy of a contracting party fall below this level, they are not such as to provide a "decent standard of living" in the sense of Article 4(1). Thus, for example, in the sixth cycle, the U.K. was found to be in breach of the Charter because the "salaries paid to certain female workers ... in several branches (in particular, textiles, clothing, distribution, and catering) remained well under 68% ... of the average national salary."[216] The Committee of Independent Experts has stressed that in applying this test it is concerned with the lowest wages actually paid in a sector of the economy and not

---

[213]C II 16 and GC IV 8. It is not variable within a state; a contracting party is expected to take measures to redress imbalances. C IV 31 (U.K.). The GC has also argued that it is "dependent on individual attitudes" so that the contracting parties "cannot be blamed" where "people whose wants or desires are fairly modest ... opt for less demanding forms of work and consequently earn less." GC IV 8.

[214]J. DALOZ, METHODS OF DEFINING "DECENT REMUNERATION" (Council of Europe 1977). The CIE also referred to a similar 1976 OECD study. C V 25.

[215]C V 25–26.

[216]C VI 23–34 (U.K.).

the average wage paid in that sector.[217] The 68% "decency threshold" test is, however, not necessarily conclusive. Although it is not met, the wage may nonetheless be such as to provide a "decent standard of living" when certain "weighting factors" are taken into account. These include "substantial social benefit payments; family and housing subsidies; educational and cultural subsidies; tax concessions; an excessive widening of income distribution; and an effort on the part of the government of a country to ensure sustained progress in the social field for workers."[218] In the case of the first four of the "factors" mentioned in this list, the question is not the extent to which they raise wages that fall below the "threshold" level, but whether they affect the ratio between those wages and wages in more highly paid sectors of the economy.[219] As far as government efforts to "ensure sustained progress in the social field for workers" are concerned, presumably these may tilt the balance in favor of a contracting party in a marginal case. The effect of "an excessive widening of income distribution" is not clear. Generally, recourse to the "weighting factors" provides the means for avoiding the effects of a rigid application of the Committee's 68% rule.

The "decency threshold" approach that the Committee of Independent Experts has adopted, which has received a mixed response from the Governmental Committee,[220] has the advantage that the data upon which its application depends are, as the Committee of Independent Experts has indicated, "easy to use," "few in number," and "relatively easy for all governments to collect."[221] All that is needed is the national average wage and the lowest wage actually paid in the various sectors of the economy.[222] The approach also means that state A may be in breach of Article 4(1) when state B is not, even though the wages in all sectors of state A's economy compare

[217]*See, e.g.,* C VI 21 (Denmark). If the average wage in a sector, etc., is below 68% there is no need to look further to consider the lowest wage actually paid. *See* C VI 21 (Austria).

[218]C V 26.

[219]C VI 21 (Austria).

[220]*See* GC VII 6. Earlier, the GC had stated that "the principal duty" of the contracting parties under Art. 4(1) was "to ensure the fair operation of a free collective bargaining system." GC IV 8.

[221]C V 26. The GC questions the last of these assertions. GC VII 6.

[222]Nonetheless, the CIE has stated that, as in earlier cycles (see C IV 32 [U.K.]), it would like to "learn of statistical studies on family budgets which can still be helpful although they are not essential" for its "decency threshold" approach. C V 26.

favorably with comparable wages in the economy of state *B*. The Committee of Independent Experts' approach thus emphasizes equality of income distribution rather than the amount of income paid. It is not surprising, therefore, that the three Nordic states—Denmark, Norway, and Sweden—are the only ones that have been found to comply fully with Article 4(1) in accordance with this approach.[223]

The undertaking in Article 4(1) does not extend to all members of society, just to workers and their families.[224] Whether a worker's family should be supportable at the required level solely on the basis of the pay which the head of the household earns from one job or whether other pay coming into the home should be taken into account is not clear. The Committee of Independent Experts would seem to incline toward the former view.[225] Article 4(1) applies to the self-employed. Although the Governmental Committee argues otherwise,[226] its wording and context would not seem to be such as to rebut the presumption that this is so.[227] It cannot be met by showing that the "great majority" of workers or the average worker receives sufficient remuneration since Article 33 does not apply.[228]

Finally, there is the question of the steps a contracting party must take to comply with Article 4(1), i.e., to "recognise the right" to sufficient remuneration. In the first cycle, the Committee of Independent Experts stated that a contracting party should "take appropriate measures to ensure a decent standard of living,"[229] without giving any indication of what it thought these measures might be. Recently, the Committee of Independent Experts has looked mostly to results rather than measures taken and has found contracting parties in breach of Article 4(1) simply on the basis that the "decency threshold" test of 68% is not met. The measures taken by a state are

[223]The F.R.G. has been found to comply with Art. 4(1) provisionally. C VI 23 (F.R.G.); C VII 24 (F.R.G.). Denmark was found to comply fully with Art. 4(1) in the sixth cycle, but to be in breach in the seventh: C VII 23 (Denmark).

[224]For criticism of Art. 4(1) on this score, see Schoetter, *La Charte Sociale Européenne: Considérations Critiques*, 1966 REVUE DE L'INSTITUT DE SOCIOLOGIE 109, 113. There is no definition of a "family" for the purpose of Art. 4(1). *Cf.* note 729 *infra*.

[225]C I 8.

[226]GC IV 8.

[227]On the application of Part II of the Charter to the self-employed generally, see C I 8.

[228]On Art.33, see note 21 to Chapter IV *infra*.

[229]C I 26.

relevant only in any consideration of the effect of the Committee of Independent Experts' "weighting factors."

Article 4(2): Remuneration for Overtime Work

By Article 4(2), the contracting parties undertake "to recognise the right of workers to an increased rate of remuneration for overtime work, subject to exceptions in particular cases." The premise underlying this provision is that overtime work requires increased effort.[230] Overtime work normally means "work . . . performed outside or in addition to normal working hours."[231] The precise definition "differs slightly from one country to another."[232] Thus, night work and shift work at night are treated as overtime in some contracting parties.[233] So far, the Committee of Independent Experts has not developed an autonomous Charter meaning of overtime work. The phrase "increased rate of remuneration" is a very general one. An arrangement by which workers are paid time and a quarter for overtime work on weekdays and time and a half or double time on Sundays and public holidays has been found acceptable by the Committee of Independent Experts.[234] The International Labor Organization conventions on the subject require the rate of pay for overtime work to be not less than $1\frac{1}{4}$ times the usual rate.[235] Article 4(2) makes provision for "exceptions in particular cases." This exception was intended to allow for special classes of workers and for special situations; by the former were meant personnel in certain responsible jobs who did not normally receive overtime payments and, by the latter, special cases of urgency similar to those allowed in International Labor Organization conventions.[236] Overtime

[230]C I 28.

[231]*Id.*

[232]*Id.*

[233]*Id.*

[234]C II 18 (F.R.G.).

[235]Hours of Work (Industry) Convention 1919, Art. 6(2), note 208 *supra*, and Hours of Work (Commerce and Offices) Convention 1930, Art. 7(4), note 208 *supra*.

[236]This was the understanding of the CMSC, which introduced this wording at its Ninth Session in April 1960. The cases referred to would seem to be those—accident, force majeure, etc.—in which the limitations on hours of work imposed by the ILO conventions mentioned may be suspended, note 235 *supra*. See Arts. 3 & 5 of those conventions respectively. What is curious is that these ILO conventions require rates of pay to be paid in such cases (see Arts. 6 and 7 of the conventions respectively) contrary to the apparent understanding of the CMSC.

by domestic staff may be compensated for by additional leave instead of extra pay.[237]

Article 4(3): Equal Pay

By Article 4(3), the contracting parties undertake "to recognise the right of men and women workers to equal pay for work of equal value." This is undoubtedly one of the most important provisions of the Charter. Discrimination between men and women in employment has long existed in job opportunities, conditions of employment, and pay. Article 1(2) deals with discrimination in respect of the first two of these, Article 4(3) deals with pay. Such discrimination takes two forms: (i) pay differentials between men and women doing the same work and (ii) unequal payment for equivalent work. In requiring "equal pay for work of equal value," as opposed to "equal pay for equal work," Article 4(3) prohibits both forms of discrimination. It is analogous in this respect to the International Labor Organization Equal Remuneration Convention 1951[238] and contrasts with the 1966 International Covenant on Economic, Social and Cultural Rights,[239] which applies only to "equal work." The significance of this difference in wording, which was well understood when the Charter was drafted,[240] is illustrated by the experience of the European Communities. Whereas the Treaty of Rome refers only to equal pay for "equal work,"[241] this requirement has been intentionally broadened in the practice of the Communities so that it is now one of equal pay for "the same work or work done to which equal value is attributed."[242]

In accordance with the above interpretation, the Committee of Independent Experts has ruled that a contracting party must satisfy two requirements to comply with Article 4(3): (1) it must show that equal pay for equal work is guaranteed within its jurisdiction "in law and in fact," and (2) it must

---

[237]C I 28.

[238]ILO Equal Remuneration Convention 1951, Art. 1(b), note 208 *supra.*

[239]ICESCR, Art. 7(a) (1), note 29 *supra. See,* however, U.N. General Assembly Declaration on the Elimination of Discrimination Against Women 1967, Art. 10(1)(b), G.A. Res. 2263, 22 U.N. GAOR Supp. (No. 16) at 35, U.N. Doc. A/6880 (1967).

[240]This appears from the discussion at the TC. REC PROC TC 201.

[241]Art. 119.

[242]Directive 75/117 on the Approximation of the Laws of Member States Relating to the Application of the Principle of Equal Pay for Men and Women, 18 O.J. Eur. Comm. (No. L 45) 19 (1975).

provide "evidence that it has taken adequate steps, the nature of which is left to the State's own judgment, to equalise remuneration for work of comparable value."[243] The first of these requirements concerns equal pay for the same work and is the easier of the two requirements to comply with. The second requirement concerns equal pay for work of equal value. This raises the complicated question of job evaluation. The "adequate steps" expected of a contracting party must consist primarily of the establishment of "objective criteria" (the details of which are left to the contracting party) for evaluating work.[244]

The Governmental Committee has been critical of the Committee of Independent Experts' insistence upon the establishment of objective criteria for job evaluation. In the fourth cycle it suggested the following alternative approach:

> Regarding the universal application of job evaluation recommended by the Committee of Independent Experts, the Committee emphasized that it is very difficult to establish objective criteria and to draw comparisons between firms. The Committee noted that several European States have adopted or are considering adopting legislative provisions giving women workers who consider themselves discriminated against the right to put their case before a tribunal, or a special commission, which will decide whether it is well founded or not, possibly after consultation with a body qualified to make an assessment of the individual case. A measure of this kind would seem to be more appropriate and less costly than starting a series of lengthy evaluations covering all branches of work and the whole of a country.[245]

The Committee of Independent Experts has not responded directly to this suggestion in its later *Conclusions*. If, as the Governmental Committee agrees,[246] Article 4(3) requires equal pay for work of equal value (as well as the same pay for the same work), it is difficult to see how the tribunal or commission to which the Governmental Committee refers can help a state comply with Article 4(3) without the guidance of the "objective criteria for evaluating work." The Governmental Committee's suggestion is concerned with the procedure for

---

[243]C III 26. The CIE had earlier set a stricter standard (in law and in fact) for the second requirement. C I 28.

[244]*See, e.g.*, C III 27 (Austria), C VI 26 (Sweden).

[245]GC IV 9. *See also* GC VII 7.

[246]*Id.*

enforcing the right to equal pay, not with its meaning. The Committee of Independent Experts has, with the support of the Parliamentary Assembly,[247] continued to insist upon a job evaluation approach, although it recognizes the difficulties that a state may encounter in introducing one. For this reason, in acknowledgment of the efforts made by the Italian authorities, the Committee was prepared to accept in the fifth cycle that Italy provisionally complied with Article 4(3) even though it had achieved only a partial system of job evaluation by then.[248] In the same cycle, the Committee of Independent Experts commented generally that job evaluation "is in the embryonic stage, and is always restricted to certain sectors of the economy or even to a few firms in the industrial sector." "In many cases," it added, "the branches of the economy in which women workers hold most or all of the jobs are not covered."[249] In later cycles, the Committee of Independent Experts has been somewhat more sanguine, noting that "some progress had been made."[250]

The Committee of Independent Experts has, as is implied above, interpreted the final unnumbered paragraph of Article 4[251] as meaning that a state is free to leave compliance with Article 4(3) to private collective bargaining in the first place but that, if this fails, the state must act itself.[252] This interpretation was challenged during the first cycle of implementation by the states that had then accepted Article 4(3).[253] In their opinion,[254] the obligation under Article 4(3) is the same as that for states under the International Labor Organization Equal Remuneration Convention 1951,[255] which does not require the

[247]Eur. Consult. Ass., 31st Sess., Doc. No. 4371, at 8 (1979).

[210]C V 32 (Italy).

[249]C V xviii.

[250]C VI xv; C VII xvi. For criticism of Art. 4(3), see Vogel-Polsky, *The Right of Employed Women to Equal Pay and to Protection,* Working Paper for the Strasbourg Symposium on the European Social Charter 1977, CE Doc. AS/Coll/Charte 4-E at 13.

[251]This is *quoted in* note 211 *supra.*

[252]C II 8.

[253]The F.R.G., Italy, Norway, and Sweden.

[254]*See* GC I 5, 38, 43. *Cf.* Mme. Bergeren, Eur. Consult. Ass. Deb. 25th Sess. 298 (Sept. 26, 1973). The Parliamentary Assembly agrees with the CIE. *Supra note 247, at 7.*

[255]Art. 2 of the Convention reads:

(1) Each Member shall, by means appropriate to the methods in operation for determining rates of remuneration, promote and, insofar as is consistent with such mehtods, ensure the application of all workers of the principle of equal remuneration of men and women workers for work of equal value.

contracting parties to intervene directly if collective bargaining proves inadequate. The Governmental Committee has since adopted the same restricted view of a contracting party's obligation.[256] The Committee of Independent Experts has maintained its position.[257] It has, correctly it is believed, distinguished the Charter obligation from that in the International Labor Organization Convention on two grounds: first, the Charter contains "an explicit undertaking to recognise this right, whereas under the International Labour Organization Convention the states merely undertake to promote the application of the principle of equal pay for work of equal value"; second, the principle is to be promoted under the International Labor Organization Convention only "insofar as this is consistent with the methods in operation, for determining rates of remuneration," whereas the Charter obligation is "absolute."[258]

As will be apparent, Article 4(3) has proved to be an exacting provision, particularly since Article 33 does not apply.[259] It was only in the course of the seventh cycle of supervision that a majority of the seven states that have accepted it had been found to comply with Article 4(3), either provisionally or in full.[260]

Article 4(4): Reasonable Notice

By Article 4(4), the contracting parties undertake "to recognise the right of all workers to a reasonable period of notice for termination of employment." This provision was included in Article 4 and not Article 2 (just conditions of work) because the purpose of requiring notice is essentially to ensure that a worker is guaranteed his wages for a reasonable period while he is looking for another job.[261] In deciding whether a period of notice is "reasonable," the Committee of Independent Experts applies a criterion of fairness, primarily by reference to length of service.[262] The Committee also takes into account

(2) This principle may be applied by means of—
(a) national laws or regulations;
(b) legally established or recognised machinery for wage determination:
(c) collective agreements between employers and workers; or
(d) a combination of these various means.

[256] GC IV 9.

[257] C V 31; C VII xvi.

[258] C II 18.

[259] On Art. 33, see note 21 to Chapter IV *infra*.

[260] *See* C VII 26–28.

[261] This was the understanding of the CMSC at its Ninth Session, April 1960.

[262] C IV 35.

"the progressive character of the Charter"[263] so that, as elsewhere in the Charter,[264] the length of notice may be expected to increase in time. A good indication of what is a "reasonable period of notice" for the moment can be found in the Committee of Independent Experts' assessment of the U.K. position. In the U.K., most employees are entitled to a minimum period of notice of discharge from employment.[265] Employees are entitled to one week's notice after four weeks' employment, increasing to two weeks' notice after two years' employment. Thereafter, they are entitled to an extra week's notice for each further year of employment up to twelve years. An employee with twelve or more years of employment is entitled to twelve weeks' notice. The Committee of Independent Experts found that this complied with Article 4(4) save insofar as employees with less than two years' employment were concerned. The Committee felt that although "a very short period of notice could be justified during the initial or probationary period of employment," more than one week's notice was required thereafter.[266] It appears from this that a minimum of two weeks' notice for all established employees after their first few weeks of employment is necessary to comply with Article 4(4). The Appendix to the Charter provides that Article 4(4) does not prohibit "immediate dismissal for any serious offence." There is no definition of the term "serious offence." It is clear from its terms that Article 4(4) does not extend to the self-employed.[267]

By the end of the seventh cycle, only three—France, Norway and, provisionally, Sweden—of the six states that had reported on Article 4(4) had been found to comply with it.[268]

Article 4(5): Deduction from Wages

By Article 4(5), the contracting parties undertake "to permit deductions from wages only under conditions and to the extent prescribed by national laws or regulations or fixed by collective agreements or arbitration awards." Although this wording could be read as allowing a state complete discretion

---

[263]*Id.*
[264]*See* Pugsley, note 25 *supra.*
[265]Employment Protection (Consolidation) Act 1978, sec. 49(1).
[266]C VI 26 (U.K.).
[267]C I 8.
[268]C VII 29–30. The GC has criticized the CIE's strict approach. GC VII 7.

to make or allow deductions, it is to be interpreted as allowing it to do so only if the deductions do not run counter to the essential elements of the right of the worker "to receive his wages in full."[269] The Committee of Independent Experts has not found countries reporting deductions from wages for taxation, social insurance, trade union contributions, money paid by an employer for housing or food, money due for damage to an employer's property, or for alimony to be in violation of the Charter.[270] A deduction will be permitted under Article 4(5) only if it is authorized in one of the ways indicated (i.e., "prescribed by national law," etc.) A deduction that is otherwise within the terms of Article 4(5) will not be consistent with it if it is provided for only in an individual contract of employment or by some other means not listed in Article 4(5).[271] The nature of the undertaking in Article 4(5) ("deductions from wages") indicates that it does not apply to the self-employed.[272] The Appendix to the Charter reads: "It is understood that a Contracting Party may give the undertaking required in this paragraph if the great majority of workers are not permitted to suffer deductions from wages either by law or through collective agreements or arbitration awards, the exceptions being those persons not so covered." This was inserted at the suggestion of the U.K.[273] because of the limited scope of the U.K. Truck Acts 1831–40, which do not apply to nonmanual workers or to domestic workers.[274] In contrast with Article 33,[275] the Appendix refers to the "great majority

[269]C I 30.

[270]On deductions made by employers for a loan to an employee, see C VI 27 (Italy).

[271]C V 35 (Italy).

[272]On the application of Part II to the self-employed, see C I 8.

[273]CMSC, Ninth Session, April 1960.

[274]Evidence that the reason for the U.K.'s suggestion was the existence of the U.K. Truck Acts is found in the British records concerning the drafting of the Charter. The CIE found the U.K. to be in violation of Art. 4(5) in the second cycle and called for the extension of the Truck Acts to other workers. C II 21 (U.K.). In the Third U.K. Report, at 46, the U.K. rejected this suggestion. It pointed out that although in law deductions could be made from the wages on nonmanual or domestic workers contrary to Art. 4 (5) (in the absence of the Appendix), in practice deductions were not made from the salaries of nonmanual workers and their interests were well protected by trade unions. In the fourth cycle, the CIE changed its ruling from "non-compliance" to "no decision" pending the receipt of information concerning Northern Ireland on the basis of which it could apply the exception allowed by the Appendix. C IV 37 (U.K.). The ruling was changed to one of compliance in the fifth cycle. C V 34 (U.K.).

[275]Note 259 *supra*.

of workers" and not the "great majority of the workers concerned." Whereas Article 4(5) does not apply to the self-employed, this difference in wording supports the view that they ought to be taken into account with employed workers in applying the exception allowed by the proviso.[276] Presumably, the "great majority" should have the same meaning here as it has in Article 33, viz., approximately 80%.[277]

Article 5: The Right to Organize[278]
With Article 6, Article 5 is one of the two key provisions of the Charter in the field of labor relations. Article 5 reads:

> With a view to ensuring or promoting the freedom of workers and employers to form local, national or international organisations for the protection of their economic and social interests and to join those organisations, the Contracting Parties undertake that national law shall not be such as to impair, nor shall it be so applied as to impair, this freedom. The extent to which the guarantees provided for in this Article shall apply to the police shall be determined by national laws or regulations. The principle governing the application to the members of the armed forces of these guarantees and the extent to which they shall apply to persons in this category shall equally be determined by national laws or regulations.[279]

Article 5 provides guarantees for "workers and employers." The following account is limited to the position of workers; the right of employers to organize, although important, does not present any great difficulty.[280] The self-employed are

[276]The weakness of such a "textual" interpretation, however, is that there are several textual differences that can be shown to have been unintentional. *See* the French text of Art. 15(2), and text accompanying note 714 *infra*.

[277]Note 259 *supra*.

[278]*Cf.* UDHR, Art. 23(4), note 7 *supra;* ICESCR, Art. 8, note 29 *supra*, ECHC, Art. 11, note 1 *supra;* Freedom of Association and Right to Organize Convention (ILO Convention No. 87), *adopted* July 9, 1948, 68 U.N.T.S. 17, and ILO Right to Organise and Collective Bargaining Convention 1949, note 29 *supra*. On Art. 5 generally, see Zacher, *The Right to Organise and the Right to Take Collective Action under Article 5 and Article 6, Paragraph 4, of the European Social Charter*, Working Paper for the Strasbourg Symposium on the European Social Charter 1977, CE Doc. As/Coll/Charte 3-E.

[279]The introductory wording to Art. 5 differs from that which introduces each of the other Articles in Part II in that it reads "ensuring *or* promoting." (Emphasis added.) This would not appear to be significant; it would not seem to affect the nature of the undertaking in Art. 5 that "national law shall not be such as to impair. . . ."

[280]*Cf.* Report of the CE, Int'l Lab. Conf., 58th Sess., Report III (Part 4A), at 20–21 (1973).

protected as well as employed workers.[281] No special provision is made for civil servants; they are entitled to the full range of guarantees in Article 5.[282] Cyprus was in breach in the sixth cycle for this reason.[283] The only workers not protected by Article 5 are the armed forces and, to some extent, the police.[284] A state may prohibit its armed forces from organizing themselves altogether;[285] it may limit the freedom of the police to organize provided that the freedom is left intact in its essentials. That the Charter draws a distinction between the armed forces and the police is evidenced by the separate treatment of them in sentences two and three of Article 5. The nature of the distinction then appears from the different wording of the two sentences. Whereas the third expressly gives to states a discretion to decide whether "the principle" of freedom to organize should apply to the armed forces, the second only permits them to decide upon the "extent" to which that principle should apply to the police; by implication the freedom of the police to organize is guaranteed in its essentials.[286] This interpretation, which is confirmed by the *travaux préparatoires*

[281]On the application of Part II to the selfemployed, see C I 8.

[282]C I 31. This is subject to the effect of Art. 31(1). Art. 5 goes further than Art. 11 of the ECHR, note 1 *supra*, in this respect. The CM had initially intended that civil servants should be placed in the same special category as members of the armed forces. Later it accepted the proposal of the CA, Eur. Consult. Ass., 11th Sess., Doc. No. 1035 (1959), Art. 5, that they should be afforded full protection. The U.K. had been particularly anxious to exclude civil servants because they lacked the right to organize in Northern Ireland. This ceased to be the case with the Trade Union (Northern Ireland) Act 1958.

[283]C VI 29 (Cyprus). Ruling now reversed. C VII 31 (Cyprus).

[284]These terms—the "armed forces" and the "police"—can be taken to apply only to military and police personnel and not to include civilians working for the armed forces or the police. This is the ILO interpretation of comparable wording in ILO Freedom of Association and Right to Organise Convention 1948, note 278 *supra*. Statement by the ILO representative at the Ninth session of the CMSC, April 1960.

[285]An ILO study suggests that in fact the armed forces are allowed to organize in at least half of the states parties to the Charter which reported during the first six cycles. ILO, FREEDOM OF ASSOCIATION AND COLLECTIVE BARGAINING 15 n.8, Int'l Lab. Conf., 58th Sess., Report III (Part 2), (1973).

[286]This distinction appears from the English text; it is even clearer in the French text ("Le principe de l'application de ces garanties . . ."), which was the original one. Art. 9 of the ILO Freedom of Association and Right to Organise Convention, note 278 *supra*, uses the wording "the extent to which" in respect of both the armed forces and the police. It was understood when that Convention was drafted that a state would be free to prohibit either or both from organizing entirely on the basis of this wording. INT'L Lab. CODE arts. 685 n.9 & 864.

of the Charter,[287] has been adopted by the Committee of Independent Experts.[288] When Italy indicated that its law[289] did not allow the police to organize at all, the Committee of Independent Experts proposed that a recommendation be made suggesting that Italy change its law "to recognise the principle of trade union freedom for members of the police force."[290]

The extent to which a contracting party may limit the freedom of the police to organize consistent with Article 5 has been the subject of dispute. In the third cycle, the Committee of Independent Experts stated that:

> ... legislation or regulations which:
> (i) forbid policemen to set up their own trade union or to join a trade union of their own choice
> (ii) oblige policemen to join a trade union imposed by statute
> are contrary to the Charter because they effectively completely suppress the freedom to organise.[291]

In accordance with this interpretation the Committee of Independent Experts has found the U.K. to be in violation of the Charter.[292] In the U.K., policemen may not establish their own trade union; there is instead a body established and regulated by statute—the Police Federation—which they are obliged to join.[293] The U.K. has challenged the view that this arrangement infringes the Charter. While agreeing that it does not ensure the police the full right to organize guaranteed in Article 5, the U.K. has argued that the right is sufficiently granted

---

[287]The distinction was argued for by France at the Ninth Session of the CMSC, April 1960, and the text was altered to include it.

[288]C I 31.

[289]*See* C I 32 (Italy).

[290]*Id.* In the sixth cycle, the CIE stated that steps were being taken by Italy to bring its practice concerning the police more closely into line with Art. 5. C VI 31 (Italy).

[291]C III 30.

[292]*See*, most recently, C VII 32 (U.K.). *See also* the CIE's ruling against Ireland concerning its police representative bodies. C II 23 (Ireland). These constitute an a fortiori case in the sense that not only are they (i) established by statute and (ii) the only organizations of a trade union kind the police are allowed, but they also consist of representatives elected by the police from among their number; not every policeman is a member. The CIE will consider new Irish legislation in the eighth cycle. C VII 32 (Ireland). For a defense of the U.K. position, see Dame Joan Vickers, Eur. Consult. Ass. Deb. 25th Sess. 296–97 (Sept. 26, 1973).

[293]There are in fact two Police Federations, one for England and Wales and one for Scotland. Senior officers do not belong to the Police Federations, but have their own statutory organizations.

in its law to satisfy the requirements of that provision. The
better view is that of the Committee of Independent Experts.
To require workers to join a particular trade union—one,
moreover, the constitution and membership of which is determined by the state—is not to limit the freedom to organize but
to deny it entirely. An example of a restriction upon the freedom of the police to organize which would comply with the
Charter might be a rule by which the police are free to form
or join a trade union provided that it is composed exclusively
of policemen.[294] This would be an important restriction but
would not deny the freedom to organize entirely.

The Governmental Committee has taken a different view
from that of the Committee of Independent Experts. Although it agrees that the right of the police to organize may
not be denied entirely, it considers that a state is allowed more
"latitude" in the imposition of restrictions than the Experts
have been prepared to concede. In the opinion of the Governmental Committee, if "the police were able to express themselves collectively through one or more democratically organised bodies, there was no call for criticism."[295] Applying this
approach, the Governmental Committee has concluded that
none of contracting parties criticized by the Experts in respect
to the police are in breach of Article 5.

Article 5 guarantees the rights of foreign workers who are
nationals of contracting parties to the Charter as well as those
of nationals. Accordingly, France has been found in breach of
Article 5 because "foreign workers are not eligible for administrative or managerial functions in the trade union to which
they belong, until they have worked for a period of five years
in France" and because "the proportion of foreign workers
among trade union members exercising administrative or
managerial functions cannot exceed one-third."[296] The Committee of Independent Experts rejected the French argument
that the first limitation could be justified because it was necessary for persons performing administrative or managerial
functions to acquire knowledge and experience of French

[294]Such a rule has been found to violate Art. 5 as applied to civil servants who are
not subject to any restrictions under Art. 5. See C VI 29 (Cyprus).
[295]GC V 6. Contrast the opinion of the European Trade Union Confederation
which agrees with the CIE. GC V 18.
[296]C VI 30 (France).

trade union life.[297] As to the second limitation, the Committee was concerned that it could affect the representativeness of trade unions in areas of employment in which migrant labor was extensive.[298]

Article 5 protects the freedom of workers to form and join "organisations for the protection of their economic and social interests." It is here referring to, and indeed offering a definition of, trade unions.[299] Although legal interests are not mentioned, it could not have been the intention to exclude from Article 5 organizations that act for their members in legal as well as economic and social matters, as trade unions usually do.[300] Nor are organizations that engage in political activities necessarily outside Article 5; such activities are too common within member states of the Council of Europe to be contrary to the Charter. Provided that the primary purpose of an organization remains the protection of its members' economic and social interests, it comes within Article 5. It may be, however, that the note of caution struck by the International Labor Organization in its 1952 Resolution Concerning the Independence of the Trade Union Movement[301] is relevant: "When trade unions . . . decide to establish relations with a political party or to undertake constitutional political action as a means towards the advancement of their economic and social objectives, such political relations or actions should not be of such a nature as to compromise the continuance of the trade union movement or its social and economic functions, irrespective of political changes in the country."

Article 5 protects the freedom of workers "to form . . . and to join" organizations for the protection of their economic and

[297]*Id.* The CIE was influenced by the fact that no such limitation existed for foreign workers from European Communities countries.

[298]*Id.*

[299]*Cf.* ILO Freedom of Association and Right to Organise Convention 1948, Art. 10, note 278 *supra,* which refers to "organisations" and which defines these as "any organisation of workers or of employers for furthering and defending the interests of workers or of employers." The ICESCR, Art. 8, note 29 *supra,* and the ECHR, Art. 11, note 1 *supra,* use the term "trade union."

[300]Legal interests are, in any event, indirectly economic or social interests.

[301]ILO PROCEEDING, Int'l Lab. Conf., 583 35th Sess. (1952). The ILO has taken the view in the application of the ILO Freedom of Association and Right to Organise Convention 1948, note 278 *supra,* that political activity by trade unions is permissible subject to the qualification implicit in its 1952 Resolution. ILO, FREEDOM OF ASSOCIATION AND COLLECTIVE BARGAINING 46, note 285 *supra.*

social interests. The freedom ranges beyond the establishment, dissolution, and membership of trade unions to other
organizational matters (the election of officers, the management of funds, the conduct of meetings, etc.)[302] and to their
effective functioning also. As to the last of these, the Committee of Independent Experts has held that an impairment of
the freedom of a trade union to engage in collective bargaining[303] or to hold meetings[304] is a breach of Article 5. It has
not considered the right to take collective action, including the
right to strike, to be within Article 5.[305] This may be because
there is clear evidence in the *travaux préparatoires* that when
the right to strike was moved from Article 5 (where it was at
one point) to Article 6, the understanding was that it would
then be protected only by Article 6.[306] Insofar as the Committee of Independent Experts has found that Article 5 has a
functional, as well as an organizational, aspect, it is presumably relying upon the fact that the freedom guaranteed is that
of workers to form and join "organisations for the protection
of their economic and social interests." An organization cannot be "for the protection" of these interests in any real sense
unless it is free to engage in such activities as are necessary for
the attainment of those interests.[307]

The freedom protected by Article 5 is to form or join "local,
national or international" organizations. Workers must, therefore, be free to organize at whichever of these levels they wish.
A state cannot insist that organizations be locally or nationally

---

[302]*Cf.* Kahn-Freund, *Labour Relations and International Standards—Some Reflections on the European Social Charter*, in 1 Miscellanea W. J. Ganshof Van der Meersch 131, 142 (1972).

[303]C III 31 (Ireland), C IV 39, C IV 40 (Ireland).

[304]C III 30 (Austria), C IV 39 (Austria). This is consistent with the 1970 Interna-
tional Labour Conference Resolution Concerning Trade Union Rights in which the
Conference resolved that trade union rights are robbed of their significance if they
cannot be exercised within a framework in which basic civil liberties are protected.
Resolution VIII, ILO Resolutions Adopted by the Int'l Lab. Conf. at its 54th
Sess. (1970).

[305]The F.R.G. has been found to be in breach of Art. 6(4) because it does not allow
its established civil servants (*Beamte*) to strike (*see* note 319 *infra*) but has not been
found to be in violation of Art. 5 as well. *See,* however, the CIE's question to Sweden
about the Schmidt and Dahlstrom Case, 1976 Y.B. Eur. Conv. on Human Rights 485
(Eur. Court of Human Rights).

[306]This occurred at the meeting of the CA's Social Committee in September 1958.

[307]*Cf.* National Union of Belgian Police Case, 57 I.L.R. 262, 279 (Eur. Court of
Human Rights 1975), on the interpretation of Art. 11 of the ECHR, note 1 *supra*.

based.[308] It must also allow national trade union organizations to join international organizations in accordance with Article 5.[309]

By Article 5, the contracting parties undertake "that national law shall not be such as to impair, nor shall it be so applied as to impair," the freedom to form and join a trade union. In the opinion of the Committe of Independent Experts, this undertaking contains both a negative and a positive obligation:

> The implementation of the first obligation requires the absence, in the municipal law of each Contracting State of any legislation or regulation or any administrative practice such as to impair the freedom of employers or workers to form or join their respective organisations. By virtue of the second obligation the Contracting State is obliged to take adequate legislative or other measures to guarantee the exercise of the right to organise, and in particular to protect workers' organisations from any interference on the part of employers.[310]

In accordance with the first of these obligations, a contracting party must not prohibit any worker or group of workers, apart from members of the armed forces, from forming or joining a trade union or, subject to Article 31, suspend or dissolve one.[311] Nor must it compel workers to join a trade union by law.[312] To this extent, the freedom to form and join a trade union includes the freedom not to do so.[313] As far as private compulsion is concerned, the Committee of Independent Experts has left open the possibility that a state may be in breach of Article 5 in some cases in which its law authorizes a "closed shop" agreement.[314] Workers who form or join a trade

[308]*Cf.* Kahn-Freund, *supra* note 302, at 142.

[309]C II 184 (Cyprus), C III 31 (Cyprus), C IV 39 (Cyprus). *Cf. id.* at 143.

[310]C I 31.

[311]C III 30 (Austria), C IV 29 (Austria).

[312]C III 30. The compulsory nature of membership of the Police Federation was one of the features of U.K. law found to violate Art. 5 in the case of the police. C II 22 (U.K.), C III 30 (U.K.).

[313]Contrast the ILO Freedom of Association and Right to Organise Convention 1948 (ILO Convention No. 87), note 278 *supra*, which does not guarantee the freedom not to form or join a trade union. *See* ILO, FREEDOM OF ASSOCIATION AND COLLECTIVE BARGAINING 33, note 285 *supra*.

[314]C VII 32 (U.K.). The CIE referred to the Young, James, and Webster cases, Eur. Court H.R. Series A, Vol. 44, Judgment of Jan. 13, 1981, in which it was held that although Art. 11 ECHR does not generally prohibit the "closed shop," U.K. law was in breach of it insofar as it made a "closed shop" agreement lawful as against

union must be free in law to form or join one "of their own choosing."[315] Thus Cyprus has been found to be in violation of Article 5 because civil servants are only allowed to join a trade union composed exclusively of civil servants.[316] Although a trade union may impose membership requirements at its discretion, it seems likely that a contracting party may legislate to prevent the exclusion of an individual on discriminatory grounds contrary to the terms of the Preamble of the Charter or on other unreasonable grounds.[317] Similarly, it seems likely that a contracting party may exercise control over the organization and functioning of trade unions in other respects in the interests of individual members. It has been argued that it may, for example, regulate elections and the management of funds to this end.[318]

Compulsory registration of trade unions does not in itself "impair" the freedom to form and join a trade union; it is permissible provided that there is "adequate administrative and jurisdictional [sic] protection against abuse of the power to refuse to register a trade union."[319] Presumably a system in which registration is voluntary but which makes registration a condition of the grant of privileges and immunities necessary to a trade union's functioning does not impair trade union freedom either if the same safeguards are provided.[320] The Committee of Independent Experts applied reasoning like this in ruling on the voluntary system of negotiating licenses in Ireland. Under Irish law, a trade union must obtain a negoti-

---

employees already in post. In *Conclusions VII,* the CIE asked the U.K. for information about its "closed shop" legislation, indicating that it would be likely to adopt a similar interpretation of Art. 5. This was so despite evidence in the *travaux préparatoires* showing that the policy written into the Appendix to the Charter concerning Art. 1(2), *see* note 95 *supra,* was to apply to the Charter as a whole. See the discussion at TC, REC PROC TC 194, and the report of the Ninth Session of the CMSC, April 1960. *See also* Professor Zanetti's dissenting opinion, C VII 113 (U.K. in breach of Art. 5); Zanetti, *Droit à une Rémunération Equitable, Droit Syndical, Droit de Négociation Collective* 9–11, paper for the Brussels Colloquium on the European Social Charter, Institut d'Etudes Européennes (1976). Kahn-Freund, *supra* note 302, at 138–39, points out that the "closed shop" issue exemplifies the conflict between the human rights and collective aspects of the right to organize.

[315]C II 22.

[316]C II 184 (Cyprus).

[317]*Cf.* Kahn-Freund, *supra* note 302, at 140.

[318]*Cf. id.*

[319]C II 184 (Cyprus). *Cf.* Kahn-Freund, *supra* note 302, at 140.

[320]On the voluntary certification procedure in U.K. law, see O. KAHN-FREUND, LABOUR AND THE LAW 215–220 (2d ed. 1977).

ating license before it can engage in collective bargaining.[321] In the first cycle, the Committee of Independent Experts stated that the system would comply with the Charter if the issue of a license was "subject to the fulfillment of objective conditions which can be reviewed by an independent and impartial authority."[322] Having found that these requirements were met in the second cycle,[323] it learned for the first time in the third cycle that a license is issued only if the applicant trade union has 500 or more members and if it deposits a prescribed sum which increases with the size of its membership but which is at least £5,000.[324] The Committee of Independent Experts found that both of these requirements were in violation of Article 5.[325] Each amounted to a substantive—as opposed to a formal—limitation which, given the importance of collective bargaining among trade union activities, was a violation of Article 5.[326] Both restrictions were justified by Ireland in its Fourth Report by reference to the large number of trade unions in Ireland[327] and the need to reduce the number of them with negotiating rights in a particular case. It further explained the deposit requirement on the ground that a trade union should have adequate funds to provide services for its members. The Committee of Independent Experts, which clearly did not think that these arguments brought the case within Article 31, maintained its ruling.[328] As far as the 500 membership requirement is concerned, this was so even though a trade union with less than 500 members might obtain a declaration from the Irish High Court which would be binding on the Government to the effect that it would not be

---

[321]Sec. 6, Trade Union Act 1941. There are certain groups with "excepted body" status which can negotiate without a license. See Trade Union Act 1941, sec. 6, and Trade Union Act 1942, sec. 2. The CIE has found the arrangements concerning these groups of workers to be in breach of Art. 5 in other respects. C VI 30 (Ireland).

[322]C I 179 (Ireland).

[323]C II 22 (Ireland).

[324]The deposit ranges from £5,000 for unions with 500 to 2,000 members to £15,000 for unions with more than 39,000 members.

[325]C III 31 (Ireland).

[326]Cf. the criticisms of minimum member requirements by the ILO in applying the ILO Freedom of Association and Right to Organise Convention 1948, note 278 supra. ILO, FREEDOM OF ASSOCIATION AND COLLECTIVE BARGAINING 27, note 285 supra.

[327]The Report stated that there were over 400,000 workers organized in almost 100 unions with, for example, 21 unions representing 11,000 workers in one concern and 12 representing 700 in another.

[328]C IV 39 (Ireland).

against the public interest for a license to be granted to it in its particular case.[329] The Committee of Independent Experts' ruling on this requirement would appear harsh in view of this possibility.[330] In contrast, its view that a deposit requirement would only be permissible "if the payment demanded covered only minimal administrative costs"[331] is reasonable. In the sixth cycle, the Committee of Independent Experts discovered further requirements that it considered infringed Article 5, viz., "that a period of 18 months must elapse between notification of the intention to apply for the license and presentation of the formal application, and that proof be furnished that upon the expiry of that period, the number of members is still higher than the required minimum."[332] These requirements were held to impede the activities of trade unions contrary to Article 5.

The second, positive obligation under Article 5 is "to take adequate measures to guarantee the exercise of the right to organise, and in particular to protect workers' organisations from any interference on the part of employers."[333] The Charter is here concerned with interference in the form of discrimination by employers against workers in the areas of recruitment, dismissal, promotion, etc., because of trade union membership or activities.[334] As in the case of other provisions in the Charter where the obligation upon a contracting party is to control the conduct of private persons,[335] the emphasis in the practice of the Committee of Independent Experts has been upon what actually happens. Thus a contracting party need not make such discrimination illegal in order to comply with Article 5 if it can satisfy the Committee of Independent

---

[329]Trade Union Act 1941, sec. 6.

[330]In the sixth cycle, the CIE maintained its ruling in the absence of any judicial precedents interpreting "public interest." C VI 30.

[331]C IV 39.

[332]C VI 30 (Ireland).

[333]ILO Right to Organise and Collective Bargaining Convention 1949, Art. 1, note 29 *supra*, ILO Termination of Employment Recommendation 1963 (ILO Recommendation No. 119), *adopted* June 23, 1963 *printed in* ILO, CONVENTIONS AND RECOMMENDATIONS, 1919–66, at 1060 (1966); ILO Workers Representatives Convention 1971 (ILO Convention No. 135), *adopted* June 23, 1971, 1974 Gr. Brit. T.S. No. 30 (Cmd. 5612); and ILO Workers Representatives Recommendation 1971 (no. 143). Discrimination in employment because of trade union activities is also contrary to Art. 1(2). *See* note 96 *supra*.

[334]C I 32 (Italy, Sweden). *Cf.* ECHR, Art. 11, note 1 *supra*, as interpreted in A. 4125/69, 1971 Y.B. EUR. CONV. ON HUMAN RIGHTS 198 (Eur. Comm'n of Human Rights).

[335]*Cf., eg.,* Art. 1(2), note 89 *supra*.

Experts that it is not a serious problem.[336] Even if such legislation is adopted, it will not constitute an "adequate measure" if there is evidence to suggest that it is ineffective. An interesting example of a violation of the second obligation in Article 5 was the former provision in Swedish law[337] by which an employer was permitted to include in a contract of employment with a foreman a clause prohibiting him from joining the same trade union as workers under his supervision. The reason for this exception was that the foreman was thought to represent the employer. The Committee of Independent Experts found this provision to be a technical violation of Article 5 because it allowed an employer to limit, albeit with the employee's consent, the latter's freedom to join a trade union. The Committee of Independent Experts did not, however, recommend that Sweden alter its law on this point because the violation was not a "serious" one.[338]

Article 6: The Right to Bargain Collectively[339]

Article 6(1): Joint Consultation
By Article 6(1), the contracting parties undertake "to promote joint consultation between workers and employers." This un-

---

[336]*Cf.* the approach adopted in applying ILO Right to Organise and Collective Bargaining Convention, note 89 *supra. See* ILO, FREEDOM OF ASSOCIATION AND COLLECTIVE BARGAINING 66, note 285 *supra.* In the first cycle the U.K. was found to comply with Art. 5 although it lacked such legislation. C I 33 (U.K.). The First U.K. Report stated that its trade unions were sufficiently strong not to require protection of this sort. After the first cycle, protection was introduced by law by the Industrial Relations Act 1971 (since repealed) and, now, the Employment Protection (Consolidation) Act 1978, secs. 23 & 58. There is often considerable difficulty in showing that refusal to employ, dismissal, etc., are attributable to trade union membership or activities. As the ILO has pointed out, "the effectiveness of any legal protection against acts of anti-union discrimination depends, to a large extent, on the machinery which exists for its implementation and the remedies and sanctions which are available." ILO, FREEDOM OF ASSOCIATION AND COLLECTIVE BARGAINING 87, note 285 *supra.*

[337]Act Respecting the Right of Association and the Right to Collective Bargaining of Sept. 11, 1936, sec. 3 as amended in 1940. *See* F. SCHMIDT, THE LAW OF LABOUR RELATIONS IN SWEDEN 143, Appendix 3 (1962) (text of Act). The provision was repealed in 1976. *See* KAHN-FREUND, *supra* note 320, at 170.

[338]C II 23 (Sweden). The CIE characterized the provision as "technically" a breach of Art. 5 but nonetheless found that Sweden complied with its obligations under Art. 5. In doing so, it would seem to have confused the existence and seriousness of a breach.

[339]The UDHR and the ICESCR do not contain provisions on the right to collective bargaining. *Compare* in respect to Art. 6(4), on the right to strike, ICESCR Art. 8, note 29 *supra. Cf.* in respect to Art. 6(2), ILO Right to Organise and Collective Bargaining Convention 1949, note 29 *supra.*

dertaking deals with consultation between workers and employers; it does not concern consultation between the government on the one hand and workers and employers on the other.[340] "Consultation" means consultation on all matters of common interest, including "productivity, efficiency, industrial health, safety and welfare."[341] It means, as the Committee of Independent Experts has stressed, consultation "on terms of equality."[342] The Committee of Independent Experts has taken the view that adequate consultation must be promoted "at all levels."[343] This reading seems too strict. There is clear evidence that the intention was to require the promotion of adequate consultation, but to leave it to the contracting parties to decide in accordance with national law and practice whether such consultation should be at national or local levels or both.[344] But Article 6(1) can be complied with by arrangements for consultation between workers and employers in which government representatives participate.[345]

Article 6(1) does not provide a "real right" to consultation; the only obligation is to "promote" consultation, as the European Court of Human Rights has pointed out.[346] Although the Committee of Independent Experts has stated that a contracting party is "bound to take steps" to promote joint consultations,[347] it seems that if adequate consultation occurs as a result of private arrangements made by employers and workers without government assistance, a state need but keep a weather eye on the situation.[348] This is consonant with the object and purpose of collective bargaining, which would not

[340]C I 35, C IV 43. The text was changed at the TC to make this clear. REC PROC TC 204. Contrast Art. 3(3) of the Charter.

[341]C I 35.

[342]C IV 43. The CIE emphasized the wording "*joint* consultation" or, in the French text, "*consultation paritaire.*" (Emphasis added.)

[343]C II 25 (Ireland). C IV 43.

[344]The wording "both on the level of the understanding and on the industrial and the national level" was omitted by the CMSC at its Fifth Session, July 1957, for this reason.

[345]C V 41.

[346]National Union of Belgium Police Case, 57 I.L.R. 262, 279 (Eur. Court of Human Rights 1975).

[347]The difference in wording between Art. 6(1) ("promote") and Art. 6(2) ("promote, where necessary and appropriate") has not been interpreted as being significant in this respect. *Contra* note 356 *infra.*

[348]Norway was found to comply with Art. 6(1) almost entirely because of the 1966 Basic Agreement Between the Norwegian Employers Association and the National Federation of Trade Unions (as amended in 1969). C I 35, C II 25.

be furthered by unnecessary state intervention. Where consultation is unsatisfactory, however, the intransigence of workers and employers does not excuse a contracting party of its obligation to take steps to improve it. In its Fourth Report, Italy asserted that it could do little to promote consultation in the face of the determined opposition of the trade unions. Italian trade union policy, it argued, was confrontation, not consultation, so that consultation procedures already existing were not used. The Committee of Independent Experts took the view that this situation could not relieve Italy of its obligations under the Charter and asked for further information.[349]

Article 6(1) applies to all employed persons; as its terms indicate, it does not apply to the self-employed.[350] In the case of public employees whose employment is governed by law and not by a contract of employment, Article 6(1) requires that machinery should exist for consultation between them and the Government, as employer, in the drafting of the relevant legislation or regulations.[351] Public employees whose employment is governed by a contract of employment are covered by Article 6(1) in the same way as private employees.

Article 6(2): Machinery for Voluntary Negotiations

By Article 6(2), the contracting parties undertake "to promote, where necessary and appropriate, machinery for voluntary negotiations between employers or employers' organisations and workers' organisations, with a view to the regulation of terms and conditions of employment by means of collective agreements."[352] This means (i) that employers and workers must, "in accordance with legislation or industrial practice," be "at liberty to conclude collective agreements"[353] and (ii) that a state must "actively promote the conclusion of such agreements if their spontaneous development is not satisfactory

---

[349]C IV 44 (Italy). In the fifth cycle, the GC commented generally that "it has to be recognised that action by government is limited, and that it depends for its effectiveness on the willingness of labour and management to accept it." GC V 7.

[350]On the application of Part II to the self-employed see C I 8.

[351]C III 35 (F.R.G.).

[352]The French text of Art. 6(2) differs from that of Art. 6(1) and (3) by using the word "promouvoir" instead of "favouriser." This would not seem to indicate a difference in meaning.

[353]C I 35. In the preceding paragraph on the same page, the CIE would appear to insist that a state legislate to this effect, but it would seem that Art. 6(2) may be complied with in this respect just on the basis of custom, as the passage quoted in the text above indicates.

and, in particular, ensure that each side is prepared to bargain collectively with the other."[354] As the European Court of Human Rights has indicated, Article 6(2) does not provide "a real right" to have a collective agreement concluded; it affirms instead "the voluntary nature of collective bargaining and collective agreements."[355] The qualifying words "where necessary and appropriate" are to give governments some discretion in cases where satisfactory machinery already exists or where other measures, such as statutory wage fixing machinery, are more appropriate than voluntary negotiating machinery.[356]

To determine whether satisfactory voluntary negotiating machinery exists, the Committee of Independent Experts has called upon states to provide a full account of their system of collective bargaining with statistics indicating the extent of its application.[357] On the basis of such information, the Committee of Independent Experts found, for example, that the U.K. complied with Article 6(2) because approximately 65% of its work force was covered by collective agreements, which indicated the satisfactory functioning of its system of collective bargaining.[358] Compliance with Article 6(2), however, presupposes "the guarantee of a complete freedom to organise."[359] For this reason, the Committee of Independent Experts found the "negotiating license" system in Irish law contrary to Article 6(2).[360]

As with Article 6(1), public employees are protected by Article 6(2) mutatis mutandis. Whereas the ordinary procedures of collective bargaining cannot apply in the case of public

[354]Id.

[355]Swedish Engine Drivers Union Case, 58 I.L.R. 19, 32–33 (Eur. Court of Human Rights 1976).

[356]REC PROC TC 205.

[357]C I 35.

[358]C II 26 (U.K.).

[359]C IV 46 (Ireland).

[360]C III 35 (Ireland), C IV 46 (Ireland), C VI 36 (Ireland). The "negotiating license" system is considered, text accompanying note 321 infra, in connection with Art. 5. Quaere whether a registration system of a kind that conflicts with Art. 5 (see note 319 supra) would also violate Art. 6(2). The CIE found the system of voluntary registration of trade unions under the U.K. Industrial Relations Act 1971 to be compatible with Art. 6(2). C III 35 (U.K.). Similarly, it found the position concerning the recognition of trade unions by employers in the U.K., particularly in the nationalized industries and in respect to white-collar workers, satisfactory. C I 36 (U.K.) and C II 26 (U.K.).

employees whose employment is subject in some degree to regulation by law instead of by contract of employment, public employees can and must be consulted in the preparation of the laws and regulations that govern their employment.[361]

Article 6(3): Machinery for Conciliation and Voluntary Arbitration
By Article 6(3), the contracting parties undertake "to promote the establishment and use of appropriate machinery for conciliation and voluntary arbitration for the settlement of labour disputes." The "machinery" referred to may be established "by legislation, collective agreements, or industrial practice."[362] A state is not obliged to act to establish or promote the use of conciliation and arbitration procedures where satisfactory machinery is already operating privately.[363] In the opinion of the Committee of Independent Experts, Article 6(3) is concerned only with procedures for the settlement of labor disputes arising "within the framework of collective bargaining, i.e. the purpose of which is to resolve the disputes which can arise at the time of the negotiation and conclusion of collective agreements."[364] The Committee has supported this limited reading by reference to the introductory wording to article 6 as a whole ("With a view to ensuring the effective exercise of the right to bargain collectively . . ."). Exceptionally the Governmental Committee reads Article 6(3) more widely than the Committee of Independent Experts. In the former's opinion, it applies to "all labour disputes which may be the matter of, or arise in connection with, collective bargaining,"[365] whether the bargaining concerns the negotiation of a collective agreement or not. The Governmental Committee's interpretation

---

[361]C II 34 (F.R.G.), C IV 52 (F.R.G.), C IV 45 (Austria).

[362]C I 37.

[363]C V 45. If satisfactory conciliation procedures established by collective agreements exist, there is no need for the state to intervene to establish arbitration procedures. C I 137. In the CA, an attempt to have the words "voluntarily accepted" (as the idea behind the term "voluntary" was then expressed) deleted because they might prevent a state from introducing compulsory arbitration where the public interest required it to settle a dispute was defeated without discussion. EUR. CONSULT. ASS. DEB. 11TH SESS. at 667 (Jan 19, 1960). The proposal would seem to have been misguided. Whereas Art. 6(3) requires voluntary arbitration, it does not prohibit compulsory arbitration. *See also* Vogel-Polsky, *L'Article 6 de la Charter Sociale Européenne*, 1966 REVUE DE L'INSTITUT DE SOCIOLOGIE 83, 96–97.

[364]C V 45, 46 (Italy).

[365]GC V 8.

would seem the natural interpretation of the text and more in keeping with the object and purpose of the Charter.[366]

So far, no state has been found in violation of this provision.

Article 6(4): The Right to Take Collective Action

By Article 6(4), the contracting parties "recognise the right of workers and employers to collective action in cases of conflicts of interest, including the right to strike, subject to obligations that might arise out of collective agreements previously entered into." From the standpoint of the worker, Article 6(4) is a landmark in international labor law. It represents the first occasion on which the right to strike has been expressly recognized by a treaty in force.[367] The right to strike is stated to be one of the forms that "collective action" by workers may take. Others presumably include a ban on overtime, "working to rule," etc. As far as employers are concerned, "collective action" includes the "lockout."[368] This interpretation has been questioned by Italy,[369] under whose law a lockout is illegal unless it follows an illegal strike and which has been found because of this to be in violation of Article 6(4).[370] The right to strike is specifically mentioned in Article 6(4); its equivalent, the lockout, is not. It might be inferred from this textual evidence that the latter is not guaranteed, but, as the Committee of Independent Experts has pointed out, "the lockout is the principal, if not the only, form of collective action which employers can take in defense of their interests"[371] and should therefore be regarded as being included in Article 6(4) in order to give the wording "collective action" some meaning insofar as it applies to employers. The *travaux préparatoires* of

---

[366]It is also more in keeping with the CIE's own approach to Art. 6(4). *See* C IV 50 (F.R.G.).

[367]ICESCR, Art. 8, note 29 *supra*, which entered into force in 1976, also expressly recognizes the right. It is impliedly recognized by ILO Freedom of Association and Right to Organize Convention 1948, note 278 *supra*. *See* ILO FREEDOM OF ASSOCIATION AND COLLECTIVE BARGAINING 6, note 285 *supra*. On the position under ECHR, Art. 10, note 1 *supra*, see the Schmidt and Dahlstrom Case, note 305 *supra*. The Parliamentary Assembly has recommended that Art. 6(4) be strengthened to protect the right to strike further. Recommendation 839, TEXTS ADOPTED, September 1978.

[368]C I 38.

[369]*See* GC II 13–14.

[370]C II 29 (Italy), C III 38 (Italy). Similarly, France has been found to be in breach of Art. 6(4) because a lockout is only permitted by its law in response to an unlawful strike, or to maintain "order and security," or in a case of force majeure. C VI 39 (France).

[371]C I 38.

the Charter support the Committee of Independent Experts' interpretation.[372] There need not, however, be legislation protecting the right of employers to lockout their workers.[373]

The right to take collective action is "subject to obligations that might arise out of collective agreements previously entered into."[374] A second restriction upon the scope of the right is implicit in the wording "conflicts of interest." The Committee of Independent Experts has understood this wording to exclude cases of "conflicts of rights."[375] "Rights" mean legal rights—in particular, those in issue in "cases of disputes concerning the existence, validity or interpretation of a collective agreement, or its violation, for example, through action taken during its currency with a view to its revision."[376] Each of the above restrictions applies only to legal systems in which collective agreements are binding in law. The latter applies notwithstanding the terms of the collective agreement; the fact that the agreement purports to permit collective action in disputes concerning the legal rights of the parties does not mean that a state is obliged by Article 6(4) to refrain from rending such action illegal.[377] Collective action taken in connection with the conclusion of new collective agreements is, however, within Article 6(4).[378]

Certain other restrictions upon the right to resort to collective action that are not expressly indicated in Article 6(4) are permitted where they constitute a regulation, rather than a

---

[372]At the TC, the employers' delegates had sought to introduce the right to a lockout into the text of Art. 6(4) but were successfully opposed by the workers' delegates. REC PROC TC 207. Later, however, the matter was raised again by the CMSC at its 11th Session, December 1960, and it was there agreed that although the right to a lockout would not be specifically mentioned, it was to be implied from the wording "collective action." L.E. TROCLET, ELÉMENTS DE DROIT SOCIAL EUROPÉEN 103 (1963), points out that a lockout is usually by one employer and hence is not "collective action." Even so, the travaux préparatoires make it clear that it is recognized by Art. 6(4).

[373]C II 187 (Cyprus). Although the GC agreed that the right to lockout workers was included in the Charter, it considered that Italy and France were not in breach of Art. 6(4) because their "regulations did not forbid a lockout." GC V 9. The European Trade Union Confederation took the (unconvincing) view the the right to lockout workers is not included in Art. 6(4) because it is not expressly mentioned. GC V 18.

[374]Cf. C II 28 (F.R.G.).

[375]C I 38.

[376]Id. Thus the CIE found Sweden, whose law prohibits strikes in such cases (Act Respecting Agreements of June 22, 1928, sec. 4, as amended in 1945) and which regards collective agreements as legally binding, to be complying with Art. 6(4). C I 40 (Sweden). Cf. the ruling concerning Denmark. C I 40 (Denmark).

[377]C I 38.

[378]C I 183.

limitation, of the right or where they can be justified by Article 31.[379] Thus, the prohibition of collective action during a "cooling-off" period is permissible because it does not "impose a real restriction of the right to collective action" but "merely regulates the exercise thereof."[380] For the same reason, a state may require a secret ballot of the workers concerned in favor of a strike as a condition of its legality.[381] Strikes for political purposes may be prohibited because they are "obviously quite outside the purview of collective bargaining."[382] Legislation for the compulsory settlement of conflicts of interest where resort to collective action by either party might "expose the national economy to serious danger" is permitted on the basis of Article 31.[383] Strikes undertaken for "immoral" reasons may also be prohibited under Article 31.[384] It is not clear whether the same Article ("the rights and freedoms of others") permits the denial in common law systems of the immunity from civil and criminal law liability which is vital to the effective exercise of the right to take collective action. Although it might be inferred from the Committee of Independent Experts jurisprudence that it does,[385] such an interpretation would seriously undermine the

[379]To make this clear as far as strikes are concerned, the following section was added to the Appendix to the Charter. "It is understood that each Contracting Party may, insofar as it is concerned, regulate the exercise of the right to strike by law, provided that any further restriction that this might place on the right can be justified under the terms of Art. 31." On the interpretation of this wording, see Bleckmann, *supra* note 10, at 394 n.23. *See also* on the permissibility of restrictions on collective action under Art. 6(4), the Schmidt and Dahlstrom Case, note 305 *supra*. The case leaves open the question whether the right to strike is guaranteed by the ECHR, Art. 11, note 1 *supra*.

[380]C I 38.

[381]C II 187 (Cyprus). *Cf.* Bleckmann, *supra* note 10, at 374.

[382]C II 27. *Cf.* Bleckmann, *supra* note 10, at 402, who also suggests that a strike to strengthen the position of a trade union is not protected.

[383]C I 38. Norway, for example, passed laws in 1966 referring four disputes to compulsory arbitration because of their consequences for the economy. These were reported to the CIE and have not been questioned.

[384]C II 28 (F.R.G.). It is not clear what a strike for an "immoral" reason would be.

[385]This is to be inferred from the CIE's assessment of Ireland's position. Whereas the CIE ruled that Ireland was in breach of Art. 6(4) when it was under the mistaken impression that a negotiating license was necessary for a trade union to be able to strike (see C I 185 [Ireland]), it has made no such ruling in respect to the situation which does exist. As Ireland explained in its Second and Third Reports, that position is that registered trade unions without a negotating license, workers for non-profit-making organizations, and workers not organized in the form of trade unions may go on strike but lack the immunities of the Trade Disputes Act 1906 if they do. An interesting question is whether the refusal of unemployment or supplementary benefit to a worker on strike or his dependents conflicts with Art. 6(4). For the U.K. law on the matter, see H. CALVERT, SOCIAL SECURITY LAW 146–77, 421 (2d ed. 1978).

guarantee in Article 6(4). It is, of course, permissible to impose civil or criminal liability for resorting to collective action that is otherwise illegal under a contracting party's law when that action takes a form not recognized by Article 6(4).[386]

The Committee of Independent Experts has found several kinds of restriction upon the right to strike to be contrary to Article 6(4). Prohibiting strikes on the ground that they are not organized by a trade union is contrary to Article 6(4).[387] So too is a prohibition of strikes that are not for the purpose of concluding a collective agreement.[388] The Committee of Independent Experts has also taken the view that a law by which a strike terminates the contract of employment is "in principle" contrary to Article 6(4) as a restriction upon the right to strike. It has, however, looked beyond the law to the reality of the situation: "If in practice those participating in a strike are, after its termination, fully reinstated and if their previously acquired rights, e.g., as regards pension, holidays, and seniority in general, are not impaired, the formal termination of the contracts of employment by the strike does not, in the opinion of the Committee, constitute a violation of the Charter."[389] The Committee of Independent Experts has insisted upon convincing evidence that persons participating in a strike are reinstated with their acquired rights unaffected and that they can enforce these rights at law.[390] Commenting on the Committee of Independent Experts' approach, the Governmental Committee has observed: "The Committee noted that in general practice contracts were not broken, either because it was specified by statute or in case-law or because re-employment was the normal practice (sometimes even provided for in collective agreements), and considered that it would be difficult to reconcile the right to strike with the breaking of a work contract, although Article 6 does not expressly give workers the right to be re-employed."[391]

In contrast with Article 5, Article 6(4) lists no restriction ra-

---

[386]C I 39.

[387]C II 28 (F.R.G.), C IV 50 (F.R.G.), C V 50 (F.R.G.), C VI 40 (F.R.G.), C VI 41 (Sweden). *Contra* Bleckmann, *supra* note 10, at 402–03. The F.R.G. has been found to be in violation of Art. 6(4) in this respect.

[388]The F.R.G. has been found to be in breach of Art. 6(4) on this basis also. CII 28 (F.R.G.). *See, however,* the reassessment of the position in West German Law in C V 50 (F.R.G.) and C VI 39–40 (F.R.G.). *See also* C VI 41 (Sweden).

[389]C I 39.

[390]*See, e.g.,* C V 47 (Denmark), C V 51 (Ireland), C VI 38 (Denmark).

[391]GC V 8.

tione personae upon the right to strike or to engage in collective action of any sort. Even so, it was understood during the drafting of the Charter that certain categories of workers could be restricted or prohibited in the exercise of the right to strike in accordance with Article 31,[392] and this interpretation has been adopted by the Committee of Independent Experts.[393] These categories consist mostly[394] of public servants, including civil servants and others. They include workers in essential services (e.g., gas and electricity),[395] "member of the police and armed forces, judges, and senior civil servants."[396] Whereas it is permissible to treat public servants as a whole differently (and generally more restrictively) from private employees, it is contrary to Article 6(4) to prohibit all public servants from striking because not all of them do work to which Article 31 would apply.[397] For the same reason, all established civil servants cannot be prohibited from striking. Accordingly, the Committee of Independent Experts has found the F.R.G. in violation of Article 6(4) because the *Beamte* (the West German established civil service)[398] are not allowed to strike.[399] Although the ruling has

[392]This was understood to be so when the part of the Appendix to the Charter that concerns Art. 6(4) was being discussed in the CM in March 1961.

[393]C I 38.

[394]Merchant seamen have been listed also. C I 38.

[395]C I 38. In the U.K., it was a criminal offense for gas, water, and electricity workers to strike. Conspiracy and Protection of Property Act 1875, sec. 4, and Electricity (Supply) Act 1919, sec. 31. These provisions were repealed by the Industrial Relations Act 1971, sec. 133.

[396]C I 39. It was a criminal offense for merchant seamen to strike in the U.K. under the Merchant Shipping Act 1894, secs. 220, 221, 225. The U.K. reported upon the Act in the First U.K. Report, at 46, but was not found in contravention of Art. 6(4). C I 39 (U.K.). The offense has since been repealed. Merchant Shipping Act 1970, sec. 100. It still applies in Ireland under the 1894 Act.

[397]C I 39, C III 36. *See,* however, the dissenting opinion of Mr. Zanetti. C IV 132 (F.R.G.). *See also* Zanetti, *supra* note 314, at 15. *Quaere* whether the prohibition of the right to strike of U.K. postal workers (Post Office Act 1953, sec. 58 [delaying postal packets a crime]) or the restrictions placed upon Registrars of Births, Marriages, and Deaths in the U.K. (*see* 896 PARL. DEB. H.C. [5th ser.] 1878–83 [1975]) are consistent with Art. 6(4).

[398]On the position of the *Beamte* in West German law, see O. KAHN-FREUND, THE RIGHT TO STRIKE: ITS SCOPE AND LIMITATIONS (Council of Europe), 1974, paras. 49, 51, 62.

[399]C I 184–85 (F.R.G.), C II 28 (F.R.G.), C III 37 (F.R.G.), C IV 56 (F.R.G.), C V 49 (F.R.G.), C VI 39 (F.R.G.). Professor Zanetti dissented from this finding in the fourth cycle. C IV (F.R.G.). Denmark, whose civil servants may not strike either, has also been found to be in breach of Art. 6(4). C V 47 (Denmark), C VI 38 (Denmark). Norway, whose senior civil servants only are prohibited from striking, has been found to comply with the Charter. C I 40 (Norway). Austria, whose civil servants may not strike, has not accepted Art. 6(4). The Netherlands has accepted Art. 6(4) except insofar as it applies to civil servants.

been challenged by the F.R.G.[400] and the Governmental Committee,[401] the Committee of Independent Experts' interpretation of Article 6(4) that led to it would appear to be correct. Article 31 allows restrictions that "are necessary in a democratic society for the protection of the rights and freedoms of others or for the protection of public interest, national security, public health, or morals." It is difficult to accept that a prohibition of the right to strike of all established civil servants qualifies under this wording. It is relevant in this connection, as the Committee of Independent Experts has pointed out,[402] that members of the *Beamte* often do the same work as members of the *Angestellte* (the nonestablished civil service), who do have the right to strike, and that the established civil services in many other contracting parties are not prohibited from striking.[403] The Committee's view is supported by the *travaux préparatoires* of the Charter. It was agreed by the Committee of Ministers that Article 31 "would permit a Government to take measures depriving *certain categories* of functionaries and other persons employed in the public service" of the right to strike.[404] The question is an important one for the F.R.G. The inability of the *Beamte* to strike is a fundamental feature of its tradition of service. Quite apart from the Social Charter, however, it is one that has in recent years been the subject of controversy, with the trade unions wanting to modify a tradition which they feel to have become anachronistic. In *Conclusions VII*, the Committee stated that, although it maintained its view, it would not "revert to the matter [of the F.R.G.'s compliance with Article 6(4) on this point] again."[405]

---

[400]GC I 11. An argument by the F.R.G. that civil servants were not "workers" for the purposes of Art. 6(4) was rejected by the CIE. C III 36, 37. *See*, in support of the F.R.G. position generally, Bleckmann, *supra* note 10, at 401.

[401]By a majority, the GC considered that the CIE's opinion that the right to strike could not be denied to all civil servants "was hardly tenable." GC V 9. The majority took the view that "Article 31 [*see* note 11 of Chapter IV] should be given a wide interpretation, although in the view of some delegations too flexible an interpretation of Art. 31, generally speaking, would distort the aim of the Charter." *Id.*

[402]C IV 48–49 (F.R.G.).

[403]*See* KAHN-FREUND, *supra* note 398, paras. 21–37. Note in particular that the *fonctionnaire*, whose position is very like that of the *Beamte*, is allowed to strike (although subject to restrictions) in French law. *See* KAHN-FREUND, *supra* note 320, at 235. On the meaning of "necessary in a democratic society" in Art. 31, *see* note 11 of Chapter IV.

[404]CM/Del./Concl. (61) 96, *quoted in* GC II 14. Emphasis added.

[405]C VII 39 (F.R.G.). This was because of the declaration made by the F.R.G. on the matter before signature. See note 61 of Chapter IV.

Article 7: The Right of Children and Young Persons to Protection[406]

Article 7 protects children and young persons primarily (though not entirely) in employment. It overlaps with several earlier provisions in the Charter that protect workers generally. Clearly, the stricter standards of Article 7 apply to children and young persons where this is so. Where Article 7 does not apply, the earlier provisions can be taken to protect children and young persons as well as adults. Article 7 does not overlap with Article 17 (the right of mothers and children to protection). In addition to the largely different subject matter

[406]*Cf.* ICESCR, Art. 10(3), note 29 *supra. Cf.* in respect to Art. 7(1), ILO Minimum Age (Sea) Convention (Revised) (ILO Convention No. 58), *adopted* Oct. 24, 1936, 40 U.N.T.S. 205, ILO Minimum Age (Industry) Convention (Revised) (ILO Convention No. 59), *adopted* June 22, 1937, 40 U.N.T.S. 217, ILO Minimum Age (Non-Industrial Employment) Convention (Revised) (ILO Convention No. 60), *adopted* June 22, 1937, 78 U.N.T.S. 181, ILO Minimum Age (Fishermen) Convention (ILO Convention No. 113), *adopted* June 19, 1959, 413 U.N.T.S. 148, and ILO Minimum Age Convention 1973 (ILO Convention No. 138), *adopted* June 26, 1973 (Cmnd. 5829); in respect to Art. 7(2), ILO White Lead (Painting) Convention 1921, note 174 *supra*, ILO Minimum Age (Trimmers and Stokers) Convention (ILO Convention No. 15), *adopted* Nov. 11, 1921, 38 U.N.T.S. 203, ILO Conventions Nos. 59 and 60 (*see* Art. 7[1] *supra*), ILO Safety Provisions (Building) Convention 1937, note 174 *supra*, ILO Convention No. 115 (*see* Art. 7[1] *supra*), ILO Minimum Age (Underground Work) Convention (ILO Convention No. 123), *adopted* June 22, 1965, 610 U.N.T.S. 79, ILO Benzene Convention 1971, note 174 *supra,* and ILO Convention No. 138 (*see* Art. 7[1] *supra*); in respect to Art. 7(3), ILO Mimimum Age (Agriculture) Convention (ILO Convention No. 10), *adopted* Nov. 16, 1921, 38 U.N.T.S. 143, 1964 Gr. Brit. T.S. No. 1 (Cmnd. 2227), ILO Convention No. 60 (*see* Art. 7[1] *supra*), ILO Night Work of Young Persons (Non-Industrial Occupations) Convention (ILO Convention No. 79), *adopted* Oct. 9, 1946, 78 U.N.T.S. 227, and ILO Convention No. 138 (*see* Art. 7[1] *supra*); in respect to Art. 7(7), ILO Holidays with Pay Convention (Revised) 1970, note 125 *supra;* in respect to Art. 7(8), ILO Night Work of Young Persons (Industry) Convention (ILO Convention No. 6), *adopted* Nov. 28, 1919, 38 U.N.T.S. 93 (Cmd. 627), ILO Convention No. 79 (*see* Art. 7[3] *supra*), and ILO Night Work of Young Persons (Industry) Convention (Revised) (ILO Convention No. 90), *adopted* July 10, 1948, 91 U.N.T.S. 3; in respect to Art. 7(9), ILO Conventions Nos. 13, 115, and 136 (*see* Art. 7[2] *supra*), ILO Medical Examination of Yough Persons (Sea) Conventions (ILO Convention No. 16), *adopted* Nov. 11, 1921, 38 U.N.T.S. 217 (Cmd. 1612), ILO Medical Examination (Seafarers) Convention (ILO Convention No. 73), *adopted* June 29, 1946, 214 U.N.T.S. 233, ILO Medical Examination of Young Persons (Industry) Convention (ILO Convention No. 77), *adopted* Sept. 19, 1946, 78 U.N.T.S. 197, ILO Medical Examination of Young Persons (Non-Industrial Occupations) Convention (ILO Convention No. 78), *adopted* Sept. 19, 1946, 78 U.N.T.S. 213, and ILO Medical Examination of Yound Persons (Underground Work) Convention (ILO Convention No. 124), *adopted* June 23, 1965, 614 U.N.T.S. 239, 1967 Gr. Brit. T.S. No. 70 (Cmnd. 2753).

In its 1972 Resolution on the Protection of Young Persons at Work, CM Res. (72) 4, the CM of the CE recommended that member states take into account the principles in Art. 7 of the Charter.

of the two provisions, Article 7 is concerned with children from school age onwards, whereas Article 17 is concerned with children of preschool age.[407]

Article 7(1): Minimum Age of Employment
By Article 7(1), the contracting parties undertake "to provide that the minimum age of admission to employment shall be 15 years, subject to exceptions for children employed in prescribed light work without harm to their health, morals or education." The undertaking applies to all categories of work, including agricultural and domestic work.[408] The setting of fifteen as the minimum age of employment has proved to be ambitious. Only three states—Italy, Sweden and France—have reported on Article 7(1), and none have been found to comply with it.[409] Under Italian law, the minimum age of employment is generally fifteen; fourteen-year-olds may be employed in agriculture, in domestic work, and in light work in other nonindustrial activities. The Committee of Independent Experts' finding against Italy is based on the fact that not all kinds of agricultural and domestic work necessarily fall within the proviso to Article 7(1) ("subject to exceptions for children in prescribed light work without harm to their health, morals or education"). Moreover, there was evidence showing that employment of persons under fifteen in agricultural jobs that could not be regarded as "light work" was fairly common practice.[410] It was also doubtful whether all of the kinds of nonindustrial occupations listed as "light work" for the purposes of Italian law could be so regarded within the terms of the proviso to Article 7(1).[411] The Committee of Independent Experts found confirmation of its opinion that Article 7(1) was

[407]C I 42.

[408]C I 42 (Italy), C V 55.

[409]*See* C VII 41–42. The GC has suggested that one reason for the small number of states accepting Art. 7(1) was that "it was not clearly specified whether certain forms of vocational training were to be considered as training or as employment." GC V 10. It has also criticized the CIE for being "over-meticulous in their attitude to certain points, often going further than the Charter requires." GC VII 9.

[410]C I 42 (Italy), C III 39 (Italy).

[411]C IV 53 (Italy). "Light work" for the purposes of Italian law includes office work, errand boy work, and work in shops, restaurants, and hairdressers. The CIE has stated that the work which children under 15 are permitted to do "must be laid down in a limitative list." C V 55. The GC disagrees: "Such a list would be difficult to draw up, would be bound to prove incomplete and would require periodic review." GC V 10.

not being complied with by ILO statistics showing that 80,000 children under fifteen were in employment in Italy.[412] In the case of France, the Committee of Independent Experts considered that the law on the employment of children in family businesses was not compatible with the Charter.[413] Sweden was in breach in respect of work done within the employer's household and of employment within the family.[414]

Article 7(1) applies to part-time, as well as to full-time, employment. However, in both regards, it neglects to specify a minimum age for employment of children.

Article 7(2): Minimum age of Employment in Dangerous or Unhealthy Occupations

By Article 7(2), the contracting parties undertake "to provide that a higher minimum age of admission to employment shall be fixed with respect to prescribed occupations regarded as dangerous or unhealthy." By "higher minimum age" is meant higher than fifteen.[415] Precisely what age is not indicated.[416] Presumably, it may differ depending on the occupation and the worker's sex.[417] The term "prescribed occupations" suggests that a contracting party is given some discretion to determine which occupations are to be treated as dangerous or unhealthy. But, as with other provisions of the Charter with similar wording,[418] this is subject to the restriction that Article 7(2) cannot be limited so that it would fail to apply to work that is manifestly dangerous or unhealthy. The Committee of Independent Experts acted on this basis when rejecting the argument of the F.R.G. that Article 7(2) had no application to employment in the areas of commerce, transport, the hotel trade, and catering; in its view "certain activities carried out in these sectors were beyond all doubt dangerous and unhealthy."[419]

---

[412]C VII 42 (Italy).

[413]C VII 41 (France).

[414]C VII 42 (Sweden).

[415]C I 186.

[416]The CA, following the proposal of the workers' delegates to the TC, had proposed that a minimum age of 18 be set (Eur. Consult. Ass., 11th Sess., Doc. No. 1035 [1959], Art. 7[4]), but this proposal was rejected by the CMSC at its Ninth Session, April 1960, as too rigid.

[417]Regarding restrictions on occupation according to sex, see Art. 8(4) (b), note 514 *infra*.

[418]*See, e.g.,* Art. 2(4), note 159 *supra*.

[419]C III 39 (F.R.G.).

Article 7(3): Employment of Schoolchildren

By Article 7(3), the contracting parties undertake "to provide that persons who are still subject to compulsory education shall not be employed in such work as would deprive them of the full benefit of their education." As the Committee of Independent Experts has indicated, "the aim of this provision is primarily that of permitting children and young persons to draw the full beneficial effects from compulsory school attendance and of ensuring that any occupational activity exercised outside school hours does not have an adverse effect on such compulsory education."[420] The extent of this undertaking will vary from one contracting party to another according to the age when schooling ceases to be "compulsory." In most of the contracting parties schooling is compulsory to the age of fifteen or sixteen. For those parties in which compulsory schooling ends at fifteen or less, Article 7(3) overlaps fully with Article 7(1) in its control of children under the school-leaving age who do part-time work out of school. In such cases, Article 7(1) contains a fuller guarantee since it refers to "health" and "morals" as well as education.[421] Where the age at which compulsory schooling ends is higher than fifteen Article 7(3) continues to apply to children still subject to such schooling after Article 7(1) has ceased to do so. Article 7(3) does not apply to children who remain at school after it has ceased to be compulsory to do so; Article 7(1), however, continues to apply to such children in respect of any part-time work that they may do where the compulsory school-leaving age is less than fifteen.

To comply with Article 7(3), states must prohibit by law the employment of schoolchildren contrary to its terms.[422] Schoolchildren may be allowed to work outside school hours[423] provided that the work is "light work" of a kind specifically defined by law[424] and is limited to a reasonable number of hours. The Committee of Independent Experts has held that legislation whereby a schoolchild may work not more than two hours

---

[420]C V 57.

[421]This assumes that the wording "without harm to their . . . education" in Art. 7(1) is not narrower than the wording "as would deprive them of the full benefit of their education" in Art. 7(3).

[422]C II 31.

[423]C I 43.

[424]Norway was found to be in breach of Art. 7(3) because its law did not list in detail the kinds and hours of permitted light work. C V 59 (Norway).

a school day on "light work" is satisfactory.[425] In contrast, it has found three hours of work on a school day plus six to eight hours on other weekdays to be excessive.[426] In the opinion of the Committee of Independent Experts, no exception may be allowed for children who are members of the employer's family. It was because an exception is made for such children in respect to domestic employment and employment in agriculture that the F.R.G. was found to be in violation of Article 7(3) in the early cycles.[427]

The Governmental Committee has challenged the Committee of Independent Experts' interpretation of Article 7(3) in two respects. First, it has questioned the Committee of Independent Experts' insistence upon the need for a statutory list of permissible "light work":

> It was doubtful whether a statutory conception of "light work" was an adequate way of resolving the problems which arose when the minimum age of admission to employment was lower than the school leaving age, which was the specific situation covered. It was obvious that only limited categories of easy tasks could be permitted, commensurate with the age and the degree of physical, emotional and intellectual development of the young people in question. It had also to be recognised that scientific and technical progress had considerably modified the notion of light work and that any definition of such work where it existed must be continually brought up to date. Moreover, it was a subjective notion and for that reason, the Committee felt that it should not be introduced. An important consideration was to place appropriate limits on the daily or weekly time during which young people usually aged 14, 15 and even 16 could be employed.[428]

Second, it has argued that Article 7(3) is not concerned with work done in the absence of a contract of employment because of the problem of enforcement: "When young persons

---

[425]C III 41 (U.K.).

[426]C IV 54 (Austria). The CIE has also held that employment for periods of up to 25 hours a week is excessive (C II 32 [U.K.]). Similarly, Northern Irish bylaws which permitted children under 15 to work for 27 hours a week and children over 15 to work for 37 hours were in breach of the Charter. C VI 49 (U.K.).

[427]C I 187 (F.R.G.). The ruling was reversed by the CIE in C VI 46 (F.R.G.). Sweden has been found in breach because there is no legislative protection in Sweden for children working in their own homes. C VI 47 (Sweden); C VII 45 (Sweden).

[428]GC III 7. *See also* GC VII 9.

worked as members of a family, especially on domestic and farm work, the particular conditions in which that work was effected were such that international provisions aimed at protecting young workers could not be applied in practice. It was therefore difficult, if not impossible, to exercise supervision without threatening personal freedom."[429] In its opinion, a contracting party should be regarded as complying with Article 7(3) if it "took measures to secure school attendance" and "controlled the employment," necessarily part-time, of young people under the school-leaving age but over the minimum age of employment.[430] The Committee of Independent Experts did not comment upon the Governmental Committee's interpretation of Article 7(3) in *Conclusions IV*. It has implicitly rejected it by continuing to apply the interpretation that it had developed earlier.[431]

Article 7(4): Hours of Work of Persons Under Sixteen
By Article 7(4), the contracting parties undertake "to provide that the working hours of persons under 16 years of age shall be limited in accordance with the needs of their development, and particularly with their need for vocational training." Article 7(4) is concerned with the employment of children under sixteen who have left school. If the school-leaving age is sixteen, it is redundant. For a contracting party that has accepted Article 7(1) as well and whose school-leaving age is under sixteen, Article 7(4) will apply mainly to fifteen-year-olds. The number of hours that a person under sixteen may work, consistent with Article 7(4), will be less than that permitted for adults under Article 2(1).[432] Thus a forty-hour week of eight hours a day, which would be consistent with Article 2(1), is excessive,[433] unless time is allowed off during working hours for vocational study.[434] The Committee of Independent Experts has concentrated upon the "vocational training" of

[429]*Id.* And see GC V 11.
[430]*Id.*
[431]*See*, most recently, C VII 43–45.
[432]*See* note 132 *supra.*
[433]C IV 57 (Italy), C VI 50 (F.R.G.).
[434]*See* C IV 57 (Italy). The F.R.G. was held to comply with Art. 7(4) because time was allowed off during an eight-hour day (*quaere* a 40-hour week) for vocational training. C I 187 (F.R.G.), C I 32 (F.R.G.), C III 42 (F.R.G.), C IV 57 (F.R.G.). *See also* C III 42 (Ireland), C IV 56 (Ireland).

young workers; it has not referred to any other aspect of "their development."[435]

Article 33 applies to Article 7(4) so that it is complied with by showing that the "great majority of the workers concerned"—in this case workers under sixteen—benefit from its terms.[436] The application of Article 33 means that, despite the wording "to provide that," which has been held to require legislation in the case of Article 7(3),[437] this undertaking may be met by legislation or by collective agreements or other means.[438]

Article 7(5): Fair Wages or Allowances for Young Workers and Apprentices

By Article 7(5), the contracting parties undertake "to recognise the right of young workers and apprentices to a fair wage or other appropriate allowances." The Committee of Independent Experts has applied Article 7(5) by relating the wage paid to young workers and apprentices to that paid to adults doing the same job. Accordingly, it has required national reports to contain "*quantified* particulars of the wages and allowances *actually* paid, *including minimum rates,* to young workers and apprentices respectively in all sectors of the economy, and of the minimum wages paid to adults in the corresponding trades."[439] This information must concern wages paid in all parts of a state's territory.[440] Regarding young workers who are not apprentices, the Committee of Independent Experts has stated: ". . . there is not really any basic reason for not paying the same wage for the same output. However, it is not unthinkable that certain reductions may be justified, allowing for the fact that the needs of young workers are less than those of adults. Nevertheless, such reductions must not be too substantial and ought to be for a

---

[435]The wording "particularly" or "in particular" in the Charter (which is paralleled by *notamment* or, as here, *plus particulièrement* in the French text) is understood to have its ordinary meaning of "especially" and not as indicating the whole of the meaning of the general phrase it follows. This view is supported in the case of Art. 7(10) and Art. 13(1) by the *travaux préparatoires. See* the commentary to these provisions, notes 479 and 647 respectively *infra. Cf. also* Nielsen Case, 1961 Y.B. EUR. CONV. ON HUMAN RIGHTS 490, 548 (Eur. Comm'n of Human Rights).

[436]On Art. 33 *see* note 259 *supra.*

[437]*See* note 422 *supra.*

[438]See C VII 46 and GC VII 10 on the statistical evidence required.

[439]C VI 52 (France). *Cf.* C I 44 and C V 65 (Italy).

[440]*See, e.g.,* C V 63 (Austria).

limited time."[441] Applying this approach, the Committee of Independent Experts has found that a difference "approaching 30%" between wages paid to workers aged eighteen to twenty and the earnings of adult workers for the same work is excessive.[442] With regard to apprentices, the Committee of Independent Experts has said: "... the value of the training given ought obviously to be taken into account, but ... after two or three years' vocational training an apprentice was fitted to render services such that one could hardly go [on] considering him as an apprentice."[443] Wages ranging between one-third and two-thirds of the average wage for adults depending on the year of apprenticeship are probably sufficient.[444] Wages during the third year of an apprenticeship that are only 30% of the wages paid to an adult are inadequate.[445] The wording "other appropriate allowances" was included because in some states apprentices receive "allowances" (in the form of money) instead of wages.[446] Article 33 does not apply so that the necessary level of wages or allowances must be paid to all workers.

Article 7(5) states no upper age limit to the concept of "young workers." National reports have shown wage scales based upon ages up to and including the age of twenty-two without attracting comment by the Committee of Independent Experts. The Committee of Independent Experts has, however, not mentioned any age greater than twenty in its *Conclusions*.[447] An upper age limit must exist for "apprentices" since Article 7 generally applies to "young persons."

Article 7(6): Vocational Training During Working Hours
By Article 7(6), the contracting parties undertake "to provide that the time spent by young persons in vocational training during the normal working hours with the consent of the meployer shall be treated as forming part of the working day." This undertaking applies to apprentices and other young workers.[448] No indication of an upper age limit is given here

---

[441]C II 33. *Contra* GC VII 10 (CIE approach generally "unsuitable").

[442]C IV 58 (U.K.). *See also* C IV 58 (Norway) and C VI 52 (F.R.G).

[443]C II 33. *See also* C II 34 (Ireland).

[444]C III 44 (Norway). Allowances at a level less than this are not sufficient. C VI 52 (F.R.G.).

[445]C IV 57 (F.R.G.).

[446]*See* the comment of the employers' delegates to the TC. REC PROC TC 210.

[447]C IV 58 (U.K.).

[448]*Cf.* Art. 10(4) (c) regarding vocational training for adults.

either. Article 33 applies so that the obligation may be met by showing that "the great majority" of young persons benefit in the manner indicated, whether by legislation, collective agreements, or otherwise.[449] At the end of the sixth cycle, the Committee of Independent Experts had been unable to reach a decision in respect of three[450] of the six contracting parties that had then accepted Article 7(6). In each case, the difficulty had been the lack of statistical information of the kind necessary to apply to Article 33. Of the other three contracting parties, the F.R.G.[451] and Ireland[452] had been found to comply with the undertaking, while Italy had not.[453] In Italy, although all workers were by law[454] granted "certain facilities, such as paid or unpaid leave, to complete their education or vocational training," only apprentices were treated in accordance with the specific requirements of Article 7(6), and they did not constitute "the great majority" of young workers.

The Committee of Independent Experts has understood the wording "shall be treated as forming part of the working day" as meaning both that the young person is to be paid for the time spent away from work and that his working day is not to be extended to make up for the hours lost.[455] The Governmental Committee has taken a different view.[456] In its opinion, although legislation, collective agreements, or private arrangements may provide for an employer to pay a worker for his time off, all that Article 7(6) requires is that the working day be not extended. A similar disagreement has concerned the wording "with the consent of the employer." In the opinion of the Committee of Independent Experts, this is not to be read as meaning that the employer can be allowed to refuse permission; it must be taken instead as indicating only that he may within reason be permitted to set the time and the conditions for the exercise of the right to release.[457] The Governmental Committee again disagrees.[458] In its opinion, Article

---

[449]*See* note 259 *supra*
[450]Reduced to one (France) in the next cycle. C VII 48–49.
[451]C I 188 (F.R.G.).
[452]C VI 55 (Ireland).
[453]C VI 55 (Italy).
[454]Act No. 300 of May 20, 1970.
[455]C V 67.
[456]GC V 11.
[457]C V 67.
[458]GC V 12. Neither argument is repeated in GC VII 10.

7(6) requires only that a young person who is released must not have his working day lengthened. Although neither view on either question is inevitable, that of the Committee of Independent Experts on each is the more in keeping with the object and purpose of the Charter.

Article 7(7): Three Weeks' Annual Holiday with Pay for Persons Under 18

By Article 7(7), the contracting parties undertake "to provide that employed persons of under 18 years of age shall be entitled to not less than three weeks' annual holiday with pay." This undertaking adds an extra week to the guarantee of two weeks' annual holiday with pay for adult workers in Article 2(3).[459] The ruling made in connection with that undertaking preventing the waiver of holidays in return for more pay[460] can be taken to apply to Article 7(7). Presumably, it is permissible to require a young worker to be employed for a qualifying period before being entitled to an annual holiday.[461] As in the case of Article 2(3), the Committee of Independent Experts has not indicated whether sick leave that is taken during a period that would normally be a holiday counts toward a person's annual holiday in two or more parts. The Committee of Independent Experts has interpreted Article 7(7) to mean that a person under eighteen is entitled to holidays per year equal to three full working weeks.[462] A person employed on a six-day-week basis, for example, is entitled to an eighteen working-day holiday. Article 33 applies to Article 7(7); therefore, parties can demonstrate compliance by showing that the "great majority" of employed persons under eighteen are treated in accordance with Article 7(7) as a result of legislation, collective agreements, or otherwise.[463]

Article 7(8): Prohibition of Night Work of Persons Under 18

By Article 7(8), the contracting parties undertake "to provide that persons under 18 years of age shall not be employed in

---

[459]*See* note 149 *supra*. Acting on the proposal of the workers' delegates to the TC, the CA suggested four weeks (Eur. Consult. Ass., 11th Sess., Doc. No. 1035 [1959], Art. 7[9]), but the CMSC agreed to only three at its Ninth Session, April 1960.

[460]*See* note 151 *supra*.

[461]*Cf.* Art. 2(3),note 154 *supra*.

[462]C I 45.

[463]*See* note 259 *supra*.

night work with the exception of certain occupations provided for by national laws or regulations." Article 7(8) is to be read in the light of the Appendix to the Charter, which states: "It is understood that a contracting party may give the undertaking required in this paragraph if it fulfills the spirit of the undertaking by providing by law that the great majority of persons under 18 years of age shall not be employed in night work." The Committee of Independent experts has given little indication of its interpretation of this provision. Here, as elsewhere, the proviso in respect of "certain occupations provided for by national laws or regulations" is to be read as giving only a limited discretion to states.[464]

Article 7(9): Regular Medical Examination of Persons Under 18
By Article 7(9), the contracting parties undertake "to provide that persons under 18 years of age employed in occupations prescribed by national laws or regulations shall be subject to regular medical control." "Regular medical control" means periodic medical examination on a continuing basis.[465] For example, a law which provides that a young person must have a medical examination before beginning employment and a second examination before the end of the first year of employment but which fails to require further medical examination at reasonable intervals up to the age of eighteen does not comply with the Charter.[466] Medical examinations must be held at reasonable intervals; an interval of two years between the examinations of young seamen has been held to be contrary to Article 7(9).[467] Examinations must be compulsory; a law making them optional would not comply with the Charter.[468] It is probable that they should also be free. A state must provide for medical examinations "in occupations prescribed by national laws or regulations."[469] The Governmental Committee

[464]*Cf.* note 160 *supra.*

[465]C II 37.

[466]C VI 57 (F.R.G.). Whereas the French and English authentic texts of Art. 7(9) have the meaning of "regular" adopted by the CIE, the official, but unauthentic, German translation—*regalmässig*—could have that meaning or could mean medical control "according to prescribed rules." *Contra* C VII 51 (F.R.G.).

[467]C II 46 (Sweden). The information concerning Sweden on this point in C II 37 appears to have been erroneous.

[468]C IV 61.

[469]At the TC, the workers' delegates had proposed that all workers under eighteen should be within Art. 7(9), but this proposal was rejected by the employers' delegates and some government delegates as unnecessary and impracticable. REC PROC TC 212.

has taken the view that this wording gives states complete freedom to draw up their own lists of occupations necessitating regular medical inspection.[470] The Committee of Independent Experts has thought otherwise and, as with similarly worded provisions of the Charter,[471] has insisted upon reviewing the "prescribed occupations" in order to give the undertaking meaning. Commenting upon the Third West German Report, which gave information only in respect to occupations involving contact with dangerous substances, the Committee of Independent Experts held that Article 7(9) required coverage of a greater number of occupations than this.[472] In the sixth cycle, the U.K. was found to comply with Article 7(9) by providing information on inspections in mining and seafaring and in certain hazardous processes and industries.[473] The Committee of Independent Experts has insisted that reports contain a full list of "prescribed occupations."[474]

Article 7(10): Protection of Children and Young Persons Against Physical and Moral Dangers

Under Article 7(10), the contracting parties undertake "to ensure special protection against physical and moral dangers to which children and young persons are exposed, and particularly against those resulting directly or indirectly from their work." Article 7(10) has been interpreted by the Committee of Independent Experts as covering "all physical and moral dangers to which children and young people are exposed, *whether or not such dangers are a result of their work*"[475] (emphasis added). Accordingly, the Committee of Independent Experts has asked for "the fullest possible information on measures specifically designed to protect the physical and moral health of children and young persons in the family, at school and in society as a whole as well as in the world of work, from the age at which they are required to attend school until the age at which they become adults"[476] The Governmental Committee

[470]GC V 13.
[471]*Cf.* Art. 7(8), note 160 *supra.*
[472]C III 46 (F.R.G.).
[473]C VI 58 (U.K.). The U.K. has reported on various statutory regulations concerning, e.g., lead processes, diving, carcinogenic substances, radiation, and work in compressed air.
[474]C VI 58 (U.K.).
[475]C I 47.
[476]C V 73.

has accepted the Experts' interpretation of Article 7(10) in this regard.[477] At first sight, this appears to be a surprising reading in that the remainder of Article 7 is concerned with the position of the child or young person in employment and Article 7 is set in that part of the Charter which is concerned predominantly with employment. The wording "particularly" (*notamment* in the French text), indicates, however, that although emphasis is placed upon them, "dangers . . . resulting directly or indirectly from . . . work" are not the only dangers covered by Article 7(10).[478] The *trauvaux préparatoires* support this conclusion.[479]

Regarding dangers at work, the requirement of "special protection" against physical danger is met by showing the existence of special safeguards tailored to the needs of children and young persons concerning such matters as the lifting of heavy objects and the cleaning of machinery.[480] In this respect, Article 7(10) supplements Article 3. Moral dangers at work may be sufficiently guarded against by provisions prohibiting the employment of children or young persons in such places as betting shops, clubs, and race tracks.[481]

Dangers outside of work are numerous and varied, and the Committee of Independent Experts has been satisfied with evidence that a state has taken some steps in some areas to protect the young. Thus, the U.K. was found to comply with Article 7(10) when it reported on its legislation relating to the sale of intoxicating liquor to young persons[482] and the admission of young persons to places of public entertainment.[483] Prompted by the mention of the drug problem in the U.K.'s

[477]GC V 13.

[478]*Cf.* note 435 *supra*.

[479]Art. 7(10) was added by the CA after the TC (Eur. Consult. Ass., 11th Sess., Doc. No. 1035 [1959], Art. 7[12]). In the debate upon Doc. No. 1035, one member of the Assembly, Mr. Weiss (Austria), understood it as including dangers to be encountered "during spare time on the streets, in cinemas, in radio and television, in penny dreadfuls and illustrated papers." EUR. CONSULT. ASS. DEB. 11TH SESS. 656 (Jan. 19, 1960).

[480]*see, e.g.,* in English law, Children and Young Persons Act 1933, sec. 18 (heavy objects), and Offices, Shops and Railway Premises Act 1963, sec. 18 (cleaning machinery).

[481]*See, e.g.,* in English law, Betting, Gaming, and Lotteries Act 1963, sec. 21, and the Home Office Model Bylaws.

[482]Licensing Act 1964, sec. 168.

[483]Third U.K. Report, at 72.

Third Report,[484] the Committee of Independent Experts asked for "more details of specific measures taken in order to protect young people against the dangers of drug consumption."[485] It has also asked for further details from Austria about its police force specializing in the protection of young people on which Austria had volunteered information in its Second Report.[486] It should be stressed, however, that a state is not obliged to act to afford "special protection" under Article 7(10) unless there is evidence of a need to do so and a problem of sufficiently general proportions to require it.[487]

Article 8: The Right of Employed Women to Protection[488]

Article 8 is paternalistic, or protective, in its approach. An interesting question is whether, with the progress of women's liberation, some parts of it (particularly Article 8[4]) may be out-of-date.[489] The diversity in social background of the member states of the Council of Europe makes this true of some member states but not others.

[484]*Id.* at 75. Its Government's reference in the Sixth U.K. Report to criminal laws protecting the young against sexual offenses was also regarded as relevant by the CIE. C VI 60 (U.K.).

[485]C III 47 (U.K.).

[486]C IV 62 (Austria). *Cf.* its request for information about the social services and educational facilities available. C VI 60 (Norway).

[487]This interpretation was agreed upon by the CM. CM (61) 95 rev., 2.

[488]*Cf.* UDHR, Art. 25(2), note 7 *supra,* and ICESCR, Art. 10(2), note 29 *supra. Cf.* ILO Maternity Protection Convention (Revised) (ILO Convention No. 103), *adopted* June 28, 1952, 214 U.N.T.S. 321; in respect to Art. 8(1), ILO Social Security (Minimum Standards) Convention 1952 (ILO Convention No. 102), note 16 *supra;* and in respect to Art. 8(4), ILO Night Work (Women) Convention (ILO Convention No. 4), *adopted* Nov. 28, 1919, 38 U.N.T.S. 67, ILO Night Work (Women) Convention (Revised) (ILO Convention No. 41), *adopted* June 19, 1934, 40 U.N.T.S. 33, ILO Underground Work (Women) Convention (ILO Convention No. 45), *adopted* June 21, 1935, 40 U.N.T.S. 63, and ILO Night Work (Women) Convention (Revised) (ILO Convention No. 89), *adopted* July 9, 1948, 81 U.N.T.S. 147.

[489]*Cf.* GC V 14. Art. 8 was discussed in these terms in the CA at the drafting stage, with the paternalistic approach which was finally preferred finding its supporters and opponents. Mrs. Weber and Mr. Gloerfelt-Tarp, EUR. CONSULT. ASS. DEB. 11TH SESS. 640 and 670–71 (respectively) (Jan. 19, 1960). See more recently, the following statement by Dame Joan Vickers: "Another reason for revision of and amendment to the Charter is [Article 8] . . . if women are anxious to be equal, they should not have special privileges of protection, and if they retain them they will find that it militates against giving them equal rights." EUR. CONSULT. ASS. DEB. 26TH SESS. 296 (Sept. 26, 1973). The PA has recommended that Art. 8 be amended to abandon its paternalistic approach. Recommendation 839, TEXTS ADOPTED, September 1978. It has been argued that Art. 8 is also outdated in the maternity protection it provides. *See* Vogel-Polsky, *supra* note 250, at 15.

As its terms indicate, Article 8 does not apply to self-employed women.[490] It draws no distinction between married and unmarried mothers.

Article 8(1): Maternity Leave and Pay

By Article 8(1), the contracting parties undertake "to provide either by paid leave, by adequate social security benefits or by benefits from public funds for women to take leave before and after childbirth up to a total of at least 12 weeks." This undertaking imposes two obligations upon the states accepting it: the first is to provide by law that employed women are entitled to a minimum of twelve weeks of maternity leave, and the other is to ensure that they have sufficient funds to take it.[491]

Regarding the first obligation, the Committee of Independent Experts has insisted that the right to twelve weeks' maternity leave must be guaranteed by legislation; it is not enough that a right "of such capital importance" be recognized by custom or in collective agreements.[492] The required legislation must make maternity leave "compulsory for a part, at least, of the 12 week period."[493] The Committee of Independent Experts has approved laws that require the employee to take all of her leave.[494] The question whether leave is compulsory or not is an important one where maternity pay or benefits are not equivalent to the wage or salary the women would receive at work. It is not clear whether the twelve weeks must be for a certain period before or after the birth or whether this is a matter to be left to the state or for the state to leave to the woman.[495] What is clear is that a state may not insist that a woman has worked with the same employer for twelve months

---

[490]C I 50, C II 38, C III 48.

[491]*Cf.* Arts. 3 and 4, ILO Maternity Protection Convention (Revised) 1952, note 488 *supra*. Both the CIE (C I 50, C II 38, C III 48) and the GC (GC II 15 and GC V 13) have adopted the twofold interpretation indicated.

[492]C III 48, C IV 65–66. The U.K. has challenged the ruling of the CIE on this point, GC II 27. The U.K. position was supported by Lord Selsdon (U.K.), Eu. Consult. Ass. Deb. 27th Sess. 81–82 (Apr. 22, 1975). *See also* C V 76 (Ireland).

[493]C V 76 (Sweden). The CIE does not state how long.

[494]*See* The Austrian Maternity Protection Act 1957, secs. 3 & 5, and the Italian Act No. 1204 of Dec. 30, 1971. These were approved in C III 48–49.

[495]In the CA, one member assumed that the period was for six weeks before and six weeks after the birth, Mrs. Weber, Eur. Consult. Ass. Deb. 11th Sess. 646 (Jan. 19, 1960); another (Mrs. Cullen [U.K.]) spoke (at the Sept. 1958 meeting of the CA's Social Committee) of eight weeks before and four weeks after.

to be eligible for maternity leave.[496] It would seem reasonable, however, to allow some length of service requirement in the case of women who are already pregnant when taking up employment for the first time or after a gap in employment.

The second obligation in Article 8(1) is to provide financial security "either by paid leave, by adequate social security benefits or by benefits from public funds." The International Labor Organization Maternity Protection Convention (Revised) 1952[497] permits only the second and third of these alternatives; it does not allow the state the option of placing the burden upon the employer because that might cause an employer to discriminate against female employees and create difficulties in obtaining payments.[498] The level of payments or benefits is stated in only very general terms in Article 8(1), which refers to "adequate social security benefits" and then simply to "benefits from public funds." It seems reasonable to suppose that despite the difference in wording the requirement in respect to both kinds of benefits is that they be "adequate," i.e., sufficient to ensure that the employed woman may take maternity leave with financial security.[499] The payment to be made by an employer in the case of "paid leave" should be adequate in the above sense also. It need not, however, be full pay. The Committee of Independent Experts found the level of state benefits during the first seven cycles to be adequate in most cases.[500] A maternity benefit of 80% of the normal wage has been found to comply with Article 8(1).[501]

---

[496]Sweden was found to be in violation of Art. 8(1) in the second cycle because its law contained such a requirement. C II 39 (Sweden), C III 49 (Sweden), C IV 66 (Sweden). Cf. C VI 62 (U.K.), where the requirement in U.K. Employment Protection Act 1975, sec. 35(2)(b), of two years' continuous employment with the same employer for entitlement to full maternity pay and allowances was found to be in breach of Art. 8(1). The CIE has commended Sweden in respect to another provision in its law whereby both the mother and the father are entitled to seven months' parental leave in the event of childbirth. C IV 66 (Sweden).

[497]Art. 4, note 488 *supra.*

[498]*The European Social Charter and International Labour Standards,* 84 INT'L. LAB. REV. 354, 368 (1961). A proposal by the CA to omit the "paid leave" alternative in the Charter, EUR. CONSULT. ASS. DEB. 11TH SESS. 668–69 (Jan. 19, 1960), was rejected by the CMSC at its Ninth Session, April 1960. In most cases payment is made out of state benefits.

[499]The wording "benefits from public funds" was added separately at a later state (*see* EUR. CONSULT. ASS. DEB. 11TH SESS. 668–69 [Jan. 19, 1960]) from the wording "adequate social security benefits."

[500]*But see,* most recently, C VII 53 (Ireland); C VII 54 (U.K.).

[501]C III 49 (Italy).

Article 8(2): Dismissal During Maternity Leave

By Article 8(2), the contracting parties undertake "to consider it as unlawful for an employer to give a woman notice of dismissal during her absence on maternity leave or to give her notice of dismissal at such a time that the notice would expire during such absence." There is no link between Article 8(1) and Article 8(2). Article 8(2) may be complied with even though the period during which a woman is entitled to be absent on maternity leave is less than the twelve weeks required by Article 8(1).[502] Article 8(2) does not contain an absolute prohibition upon the dismissal of an employed woman during the periods indicated. The purpose is to protect her from discrimination on grounds of pregnancy. If, therefore, an employer dismisses her for some other good reason, such as misconduct, the termination of the employer's business, or the expiration of the contract of employment, during those periods, Article 8(2) is not violated.[503] Article 8(2) is expressed in terms of actual "absence on maternity leave" and not in terms of the period of leave to which the woman is entitled.

Article 8(2) applies to all forms of employment. It is because their law does not protect female domestic servants adequately or at all that two of the only three states that have accepted this paragraph of Article 8—Austria and Italy—have been found to be in breach of it.[504] Under Austrian law, female domestic servants are not protected from dismissal between the end of the fifth month of pregnancy and childbirth;[505] Italian law offers no protection and the relevant collective agreement does not cover all of these servants.[506]

It was suggested in the Consultative Assembly during the drafting of the Charter that in some cases it would be inappropriate for a woman to continue in employment if she were expecting a baby or had had an illegitimate child.[507] Article 8(2) makes no concession to such an argument; it does not,

[502]C VI 63 (Austria).

[503]C I 51, GC V 14.

[504]Italy: C I 51, C II 39, C III 49, C IV 67, C V 77, C VI 63, C VII 55. Austria: C III 49, C IV 66, C V 77, C VI 63, C VII 54. Art. 8(3) does not permit exclusion of certain categories of worker as does Art. 7, ILO Maternity Protection Convention (Revised) 1952 (note 488 *supra*), C IV 67 (Austria). The third state that has accepted Art. 8(2)—France—complies with it. C VII 55 (France).

[505]C V 77 (Austria), C VI 63 (Austria).

[506]C V 77 (Italy), C VI 63 (Italy).

[507]Mr. Hughes-Hallett, EUR. CONSULT. ASS. DEB. 11TH SESS. 661 (Jan. 19, 1960).

however, prevent notice being given to a woman immediately following her return to work.[508]

Article 8(3): Feeding Time for Nursing Mothers

By Article 8(3) the contracting parties undertake "to provide that mothers who are nursing their infants shall be entitled to sufficient time off for this purpose." The Committee of Independent Experts has found that two rest periods of thirty minutes or one rest period of an hour during the working day meets this requirement.[509] Rest periods must be treated as hours of work and remunerated accordingly.[510] Article 8(3) applies to all employed women, including domestic workers, family workers, and women working at home.[511]

Article 8(4): Employment of Women in Certain Occupations

By Article 8(4) the contracting parties undertake "(a) to regulate the employment of women workers on night work in industrial employment" and "(b) to prohibit the employment of women workers in underground mining, and, as appropriate, on all other work which is unsuitable for them by reason of its dangerous, unhealthy, or arduous nature." In contrast with the remainder of Article 8, Article 8(4) is not concerned with maternity. Article 8(4) requires that states "regulate" the employment of women on night work. It applies only to "industrial employment."[512] This term excludes nonindustrial employment in industry.[513] Article 8(4)(b) is stricter in that it requires states to "prohibit" the employment of women in "underground mining," etc.[514] In the equally authentic French text of the Charter, "underground mining" reads "des travaux de sous-sol dans les mines," which seems to prohibit all under-

---

[508]*Quaere* whether the prohibition of discrimination in employment in Art. 1(2) would apply.

[509]C I 191 (F.R.G.). Italian law allows two rest periods of half an hour each if the employer has provided a *crèche* or nursing room or of one hour each where he has not done so. In the latter case, the mother is entitled to leave the premises. C I 51 (Italy).

[510]GC V 14. *Cf.* C III 49 (Austria). *Cf.* Art. 5(2), ILO Maternity Protection Convention (Revised) 1952, note 488 *supra*.

[511]C III 50 (Italy), C IV 67 (Italy).

[512]A CA proposal that Art. 8(4) apply to all night work was rejected by the CMSC at its Ninth Session, April 1960, because it was discriminatory against women (a view expressed by the Danish and Swedish Governments).

[513]C I 192, GC V 14.

[514]The rules concerning discrimination against women in access to employment in Art. 1(2) must be read subject to Art. 8(4).

ground work, not just mining work (as the English text suggests). This difference in wording became important in the sixth cycle when the Committee of Independent Experts considered a change in U.K. law which allowed women to work in mines as doctors, nurses, etc.[515] The Experts adopted the more limited meaning of the English text when finding that the U.K. complied with the Charter.[516] Such interpretation is in accord with present thinking on sex equality.

Article 9: The Right to Vocational Guidance
Article 9 reads: "With a view to ensuring the effective exercise of the right to vocational guidance, the Contracting Parties undertake to provide or promote, as necessary, a service which will assist all persons, including the handicapped, to solve problems related to occupational choice and progress, with due regard to the individual's characteristics and their relation to occupational opportunity: this assistance should be available free of charge, both to young persons, including school children, and to adults."

Article 9, which was the first treaty provision in force in international labor law guaranteeing the right to vocational guidance,[517] is an essential supplement to Article 1 of the Charter protecting the right to work.[518] Vocational guidance is "the service which assists all persons to solve problems related to occupational choice . . . with due regard to the individuals's characteristics and their relation to occupational opportunity."[519] To comply with Article 9, a contracting party must ensure that such a service is provided for all persons in need of it, including schoolchildren and students as well as adults.[520] Particular attention should be paid to the handicapped. Guidance may be provided through private organizations or pub-

---

[515]*See* Sex Discrimination Act 1975, sec. 21.

[516]C VI 65 (U.K.). The CIE referred to the wording of the ILO Underground Work (Women) Convention 1935 (note 488 *supra*) in support of its interpretation. Note 488 *supra*.

[517]The right to vocational guidance is not specifically protected in the UDHR or the ICESCR. It is, however, implied in provisions on the right to work (UDHR Art. 23, note 7 *supra*, and ICESCR, Art. 6, note 29 *supra*). *Cf.* ILO Human Resources Development Convention (ILO Convention No. 142) *adopted* June 23, 1975, 1978 Gr. Brit. T.S. No. 17 (Cmd. 7086). *See also* the ILO Vocational Guidance Recommendation 1949.

[518]Art. 9 in fact overlaps with Art. 1(4) and is more exacting. *Cf.* note 120 *supra*.

[519]C IV 69.

[520]C I 53.

licly, although in each case it must be free. The wording "as necessary" underlines the fact that the greater the degree of unemployment, the greater the obligation to provide vocational guidance.[521]

Beyond this, it is difficult to say what is required by Article 9. Some indication is given by the experience of Italy, whose vocational guidance system was held to fall short of Article 9 in certain respects in the fourth cycle.[522] Where the Committee of Independent Experts has acknowledged the progress that has been made in the guidance provided for handicapped young persons seeking work, it found that Italy did not entirely satisfy Article 9 as far as vocational guidance facilities for other young persons and for adults are concerned. The Committee of Independent Experts reversed this finding in the fifth cycle in the light of the efforts being made to improve the guidance offered.[523] In making this and other rulings or criticisms,[524] the Committee of Independent Experts has been guided by such factors as the numbers of school-leavers, etc., assisted,[525] the size and qualifications of the staff providing the service,[526] and, particularly, the amount of public funds allocated to vocational guidance.[527] Both the Committee of Independent Experts and the Governmental Committee have stressed the particular importance of vocational guidance at a time of economic recession.[528] The Governmental Committee elaborated upon this point in a very helpful passage in its fourth *Report:*

> It is clear that well-contrived vocational guidance can smooth the transition from the educational system to the working world; and this is especially important in the current economic situation. It seems likely that more adequate guidance given in the recent past might have alleviated the present employment situation which is characterised by large numbers of young persons, including

[521]*Id.*

[522]C IV 70.

[523]C V 79 (Italy). This favorable ruling was renewed, provisionally, in the sixth cycle, but with doubt being expressed about the low number of young persons being assisted. C VI 67 (Italy).

[524]See, e.g., the criticism of the low percentage of schools in which vocational guidance personnel were available in Ireland. C II 51 (Ireland).

[525]C III 52 (U.K.).

[526]C I 53 and C III 52 (U.K.).

[527]C I 53.

[528]C IV 69 and GC IV 9.

graduates, looking for their first job and many unemployed young people who are unable to obtain employment because they lack qualifications. It might also have helped to correct certain unbalances in the labour market.

Where vocational guidance systems are inadequate to meet current requirements, governments have a duty to improve them, in some cases it may be necessary to remodel them completely. In the opinion of the Committee such action should be taken with the help of those concerned, notably both sides of industry and the education authorities.[529]

Article 10: The Right to Vocational Training

Article 10 was the first international treaty provision to guarantee the right to vocational training.[530] As in the case of vocational guidance, both the Committee of Independent Experts and the Governmental Committee have emphasized its special importance at a time of economic recession.[531] The Committee of Independent Experts has also stressed that at such times priority in vocational training should be given to young persons, who are particularly hit by unemployment.[532] Article 33 applies to the whole of Article 10; it may be complied with, therefore, by information showing that "the great majority" of workers are treated in accordance with its terms, whether by legislation, collective agreements, or otherwise.[533]

Article 10 applies to the self-employed, so far as relevant.[534]

Article 10(1): Technical and Vocational Training

By Article 10(1), the contracting parties undertake "to provide or promote, as necessary, the technical and vocational training of all persons, including the handicapped, in consultation with

---

[529]GC IV 9–10.

[530]The right to vocational training is not specifically protected in the UDHR or the ICESCR. It is covered to some extent in their provisions on the rights to work (UDHR, Art. 23[1], note 7 *supra*, and ICESCR, Art. 6, note 29 *supra*) and to education (UDHR, Art. 26, note 7 *supra*, and ICESCR, Art. 13, note 29 *supra*). *Cf.* the ILO Human Resources Development Convention 1975, note 517 *supra*. Plans for vocational training are an important part of the European Communities Social Policy. Treaty of Rome, Art. 128. *See also* K. LIPSTEIN, THE LAW OF THE EUROPEAN ECONOMIC COMMUNITY 304–05 (1974).

[531]C I 55 and GC IV 10.

[532]C IV 71.

[533]*See* note 259 *supra*.

[534]*See, e.g.,* C VI 74 (U.K.), concerning Art. 10(3). *See also* the reference to legal education (Art. 10[2]). C III 55.

employers' and workers' organisations, and to grant facilities for access to higher technical and university education, based solely on individual aptitude."

The first of the two distinct parts to this undertaking is to "provide or promote" technical and vocational training. The wording "provide or promote" allows for the provision of training by the state or privately. The requirement of "Consultation with employers' and workers' organisations" was included to ensure that such state action as is taken is in touch with the real needs of economic and social life. Contracting parties have experienced little difficulty in complying with this part of Article 10(1).

Article 10(1) also requires that contracting parties "grant facilities for access to higher technical and university education, based solely on individual aptitude." Despite its general wording, this requirement only concerns access to "technical and vocational training." Thus, it applies to university education only in respect to access to vocational courses, such as courses in engineering, medicine, law, and agriculture. This limited reading of Article 10(1) follows from the scope of Article 10 as a whole and from the *travaux préparatoires* of the Charter.[535] In its early cycles, it was not clear whether the Committee of Independent Experts was acting on this interpretation or whether it regarded Article 10(1) as guaranteeing access to higher education generally;[536] more recently, its comments have been limited to vocational training.[537] Concerning the substance of Article 10(1), the Committee of Independent Experts has stressed its emphasis upon making access to

[535]The second part of the undertaking in Art. 10(1) was added at the suggestion of workers' delegates to the TC. REC PROC TC 216. When it was pointed out by the F.R.G. and U.K. Government representatives that the CA had decided not to include an article on the right to education (*see* note 1021 *infra*), the workers' delegates replied that the intention was only to provide for access to higher education establishments for vocational training relevant to employment in industry. Although the F.R.G. and the U.K. again expressed doubts later at the Ninth Session of the CMSC, April 1960, these two states did not press their objections, and the CMSC adopted the workers' delegates' proposal. Bearing in mind the CM decision to omit the right to education, it must have done so on the basis of the workers' delegates' explanation of their proposal.

[536]The CIE's *Conclusions* contain statements phrased in terms of access to higher education generally (*see, e.g.,* C I 55), and several states have been asked to submit general information on university access. *See, e.g.,* C I 56 (U.K.) and C II 42 (U.K.). Sweden, however, was found to comply with Art. 10(1) on the basis of its First Report, which only gave information about vocational university education. C I 56 (Sweden).

[537]C VI 69–70.

higher education "more democratic."[538] To comply with the requirement, a contracting party must provide for admission to higher technical and university education for purposes of technical and vocational training on the basis "solely" of "individual aptitude." It must also take steps to realize the educational principle involved by providing "facilities" in such forms as financial assistance to all students to take up places in higher education offered to them; "a reasonable level of educational fees"; and "enough establishments."[539] It would not, however, seem to be necessary to provide a place for every qualified candidate.[540]

Both parts of the undertaking apply to all workers, including the handicapped.[541] The F.R.G. has been found to in breach of Article 10(1) because of the "severe restrictions" imposed on young foreigners (including nationals of other contracting parties, who are protected by the Charter) in the availability of vocational training assistance.[542] The limitation "as necessary" can be taken to apply to both parts also.[543]

Article 10(2): Apprenticeships and Other Arrangements for Training Young Persons

By Article 10(2), the contracting parties undertake "to provide or promote a system of apprenticeship and other systematic arrangements for training young boys and girls in their various employments." Article 10(2) spells out what might be implied in Article 10(1) concerning young persons. The apprenticeship facilities required by Article 10(2) "should not be purely empirical or aim solely at manual training but should be conceived in broad terms and comprise full, coordinated and systematic training."[544] Article 10(2) does not, however, prevent states "from making arrangements aimed at gradually

---

[538]C I 55.

[539]*Id.* The GC disagrees (financial aid required only by Art. 10(4). GC VI 9).

[540]The U.K. has been found to comply with Art. 10(1) (C II 42) although, as it has reported, university places are competitive in the U.K.

[541]The fact that the second part was added later and the generally slipshod nature of the drafting of the Charter suggests that the reference to the "handicapped" only in the first part of the undertaking is not to be taken as overriding an interpretation which is more consonant with the purpose of the Charter. The CIE has understood the handicapped to be covered by both parts of the undertaking. *See* C II 43, C III 54 (Norway).

[542]C VI 70 (F.R.G.). Cf. the negative finding in C VII 60 (U.K.).

[543]*See* the argument, note 541 *supra*.

[544]C I 57.

replacing apprenticeship by more institutionalised vocation training."[545] Such flexibility, in fact, is allowed by the wording "other systematic arrangements." As with Article 10(1) and (3), the wording "provide or promote" in Article 10(2) allows a state to meet its obligation by state action or by promoting private apprenticeship and other systems of training.[546] In contrast with Article 10(1) and (3), the obligation in Article 10(2) is not limited by the words "as necessary." The obligation applies to the training of young persons "in their various employments." It thus applies to the training of commercial and clerical workers as well as industrial workers.[547] It also applies to the "compulsory periods of partial [sic] experience forming part of the training of, for example, students in medicine, dentistry, law and education, whether in the course of their university education or after."[548]

In the sixth cycle, the F.R.G. was found to be in breach of Article 10(2) (as well as Article 10[1]) because of the restrictions it had imposed on the access of young foreigners to vocational training. In particular, it had totally excluded those entering the F.R.G. after a certain date and imposed restrictions on others related to the length of their parents' residence and employment in the F.R.G. These, the Experts thought, were restrictions that "constituted a differentiation that could not be considered compatible with the Charter."[549]

Article 10(3): Training Facilities for Adults

By Article 10(3), the contracting parties undertake:

to provide or promote, as necessary:
(a) adequate and readily available training facilities for adult workers;
(b) special facilities for the re-training of adult workers needed as a result of technological development or new trends in employment.

As in the case of Article 10(2), Article 10(3) contains an undertaking—in this case in respect to adults[550]—which might be

[545]Id.
[546]Id.
[547]C III 55 (U.K.).
[548]C III 55.
[549]C VI 71 (F.R.G.). Cf. C VII 61 (F.R.G.) (Austria). But cf. GC VII 11.
[550]The age at which "young boys and girls" or "young persons" become adults is not indicated.

implied in Article 10(1). It imposes an obligation upon states
to provide the facilities themselves or to promote their provision privately by industry. A certain discretion is contained in
this obligation, as indicated by the phrase "as necessary." The
number of unemployed in each case is therefore relevant; a
state that has a large number of unemployed has a greater
obligation than one that does not.[551] Article 10(3) requires that
"adequate" facilities be provided.[552] It does not mention training women who wish to start or restart work after raising a
family.[553] Presumably Article 10(3)(a) applies in such cases. By
West German law, trained and untrained workers must have
been employed for three or six years respectively to be eligible
for vocational training assistance. The Committee of Independent Experts has found this to be consistent with the Charter
upon learning that periods of occupational activity in other
contracting parties are taken into account in applying this
rule.[554]

Article 10(4): Encouragement of the Full Use of Facilities
By Article 10(4), the contracting parties undertake:

> to encourage the full utilisation of the facilities provided by ap-
> propriate measures such as:
> (a) reducing or abolishing any fees or charges;
> (b) granting financial assistance in appropriate cases;
> (c) including in the normal working hours time spent on supple-
>   mentary training taken by the worker, at the request of his
>   employer, during employment;
> (d) ensuring through adequate supervision, in consultation with
>   the employers' and workers' organisations, the efficiency of
>   apprenticeship and other training arrangements for young
>   workers, and the adequate protection of young workers gen-
>   erally.

[551]C I 58 (Italy), C II 44 (U.K.).

[552]On this ground, Italy and the U.K. were found in violation of the Charter in the
first two cycles (C I 58 [Italy, U.K.], C II 43 [Italy], C II 44 [U.K.]). These findings
have since been reversed. C IV 74 (Italy, U.K.).

[553]*Cf.* Fuks, *Les Dispositions de la Charte Européenne à la Lumière des Revendications des
Syndicats Belges,* 1966 REVUE DE L'INSTITUT DE SOCIOLOGIE 29, 48.

[554]C VI 73 (F.R.G.). It had earlier stated that while "the application of such measures to the nationals of the state concerned might in certain circumstances and under
certain conditions, be considered as compatible with the Charter, they could, in the
committee's opinion, create major difficulties in respect of foreign workers." C V 84
(F.R.G.).

National reports indicate that the granting of "financial assistance in appropriate cases" is the "measure" that states have most commonly taken. Article 10(4) has caused little difficulty in practice.

Article 11: The Right to Protection of Health[555]
Article 11 contains undertakings that cover an extremely wide field and are "of a very general kind."[556] One consequence of their general nature is considerable overlapping between the three paragraphs. This led the Committee of Independent Experts to treat them together in the first cycle. It has since treated them under separate headings, and this approach is adopted in following commentary.

Commenting upon Article 11 as a whole, the Committee of Independent Experts noted in the first cycle that in the contracting parties generally the "organisation of preventive care does not always appear to be advanced as that of curative treatment."[557] It thought this to be particularly true

(a) in the field of mental illness, though this appears to be a problem of increasing importance in European countries;
(b) in respect of vaccination and the control of epidemics which, perhaps because of the decrease in epidemic diseases, no longer appear to occupy a sufficient place in the thinking of the governments.[558]

The Committee of Independent Experts also considered that the "special effort needed for the care of old people, bearing in mind that the proportion of old people in the population is on the increase, is still generally insufficient."[559]

In the fourth cycle, the Committee of Independent Experts expressed its concern about the effect upon health of "the recrudescence of certain epidemic and venereal diseases, as

---

[555]*Cf.* ICESCR, Art. 12, note 29 *supra.* There is no ILO convention concerned with the protection of health generally; there are conventions (e.g., those listed under Art. 3, note 174 *supra*) protecting health in employment. On Art. 11, see Heuskin, *Le Droit à la Protection de la Santé dans la Charte Sociale Européenne,* 1966 REVUE DE L'INSTITUT DE SOCIOLOGIE 65. The PA has recommended that Art. 11 be revised to require regular checks on all workers. Recommendation 839, TEXTS ADOPTED, Sept. 1978.
[556]C I 59.
[557]C I 60.
[558]*Id.*
[559]*Id.*

well as the appearance of hitherto unknown or unrecognised diseases, such as viral hepatitis."[560] It also emphasized "the importance, at the present time, of iatrogenic diseases, often caused by the common misuse of medicines, and of new risks to consumers resulting from the composition and processing of certain foods, household products and other everyday articles."[561] In each case, appropriate remedial and preventive action was called for. More recently, the Committee of Independent Experts has been particularly concerned with environmental pollution.

Article 11(1): Removal of the Causes of Ill Health
By Article 11(1), the contracting parties undertake "to remove as far as possible the causes of ill-health." In the opinion of the Committee of Independent Experts, a state can be taken to comply with this undertaking if it provides evidence of the existence of a medical and health system comprising the following elements:

1. Public health arrangements making generally available medical and para-medical practitioners and adequate equipment consistent with meeting its main health problems. Such arrangements must ensure:
   (a) proper medical care for the whole population;
   (b) the prevention and diagnosis of disease.
2. Special measures to protect the health of mothers, children and old people.
3. General measures aimed in particular at the prevention of air and water pollution, protection from radio-active substances, noise abatement, food control and environmental hygiene, and the control of alcoholism and drugs.
   . . . .
6. The bearing by collective bodies of all, or at least a substantial part, of the cost of the health services.[562]

As this extract indicates, the range of Article 11(1) is immense. Lately, the Committee of Independent Experts has stressed the need to provide for the elderly and the mentally ill and to

---

[560]C IV 75.
[561]*Id.*
[562]*Id.* This is part of a passage from *Conclusions* I in which the CIE lists the requirements of Art. 11 as a whole. The above extract would seem to apply to Art. 11(1) in particular; it also has application in part to Art. 11(2) and (3) as well.

control environmental pollution.[563] It has also attempted to confirm that a contracting party's medical and health system is adequately financed, organized, and operated.[564] Regarding industrial medicine, the Committee of Independent Experts has emphasized that it not only concerns treatment and control of occupational diseases but "also cover[s] problems concerning the adjustment of individuals to their occupational surroundings, accident prevention, etc."[565] The provision of a satisfactory school health system is required by Article 11(1) as well as by paragraphs (2) and (3).[566]

Article 11(2): Health Education

By Article 11(2), the contracting parties undertake "to provide advisory and educational facilities for the promotion of health and the encouragement of individual responsibility in matters of health." Article 11(2) specifically requires what seems to be only implied by Article 11(1),[567] viz., the provision of "a system of health education."[568] In assessing whether an adequate system exists, the Committee of Independent Experts has tried to establish the amount of funds that a state sets aside for this purpose.[569] It has sought information about health education in school curricula[570] and insisted upon a satisfactory school health service.[571] It has also asked about advisory services for other age groups[572] and about measures taken to inform the population of the effects of drugs.[573] In *Conclusion I*, the Committee of Independent Experts was generally critical of the provision made for health education: "with a few exceptions, health education remains fragmentary and is not sufficiently systematically organised, bearing in mind the part it can play in the prevention and treatment of disease."[574]

---

[563]*See* C V 87–88, C VI 77–78.
[564]C IV 77 (U.K.).
[565]C III 58.
[566]C III 58 (Cyprus).
[567]*See* Question E, Art. 11(1), Report Form for Art. 21 reports.
[568]C I 59.
[569]*See, e.g.,* C II 46 (Denmark), C III 60 (Denmark), C IV 77 (Denmark).
[570]C III 59 (Austria).
[571]C III 59 (Cyprus).
[572]C III 60 (Italy).
[573]C III 60 (Norway).
[574]C I 60.

Article 11(3): Prevention of Epidemics, etc.
By Article 11(3), the contracting parties undertake "to prevent as far as possible epidemic, endemic and other diseases." In applying this undertaking, which overlaps with those in Article 11(1) and (2), the Committee of Independent Experts has sought to ensure that a contracting party has an adequate vaccination program.[575] This need not require compulsory vaccination if it can be shown that a voluntary scheme works satisfactorily.[576] It has also insisted upon a comprehensive school health service at primary and secondary levels.[577] Although the Committee of Independent Experts has requested information about regular medical checks for the population at large, it does not appear that the Committee of Independent Experts considers that medical checks are essential.[578] A number of contracting parties have been asked to provide information about measures that they take (apart, presumably, from vaccination) to control the spread of serious epidemic diseases.[579]

Article 12: The Right to Social Security[580]
The Charter is one of several treaties adopted under the auspices of the Council of Europe that guarantee social security rights. The first were the European Interim Agreement on Social Security Schemes Relating to Old Age, Invalidity and

[575] *See, e.g.,* C II 46.
[576] The U.K. was found to comply with Art. 11(3) on this basis after reporting on its program of voluntary vaccinations in the third cycle (Third U.K. Report, 117). C III 60 (U.K.). *See also* C III 60 (Austria).
[577] C I 198 (Ireland), C II 46 (Ireland), C III 60 (Ireland), C IV 79 (Ireland). School health services are also required under Art. 11(1) and (2). It is likely that they have been emphasized under Art. 11(3) in the case of Ireland because that state has not accepted Art. 11(1) and (2).
[578] C III 60 (Cyprus), C IV 78 (Cyprus).
[579] *See, e.g.,* C IV 79 (Denmark).
[580] *Cf.* UDHR, Art. 22, note 7 *supra,* and ICESCR, Art. 9, note 29 *supra. Cf.* in respect to Art. 12(1), (2), and (3), ILO Social Security (Minimum Standards) Convention 1952, note 16 *supra;* in respect to Art. 12(1), ILO Employment Injury Benefits Convention (ILO Convention No. 121), *adopted* July 8, 1964, 602 U.N.T.S. 259, ILO Invalidity, Old Age and Survivors Benefits Convention (ILO Convention No. 128), *adopted* June 29, 1967, 699 U.N.T.S. 185, and ILO Medical Care and Sickness Benefits Convention (ILO Convention No. 130), *adopted* June 25, 1969 (Cmnd. 4526); and in respect to Art. 12(4), ILO Equality of Treatment (Social Security) Convention (ILO Convention No. 118), *adopted* June 28, 1962, 494 U.N.T.S. 271. The PA has proposed that Art. 12 be revised to provide "basic social security and old age pensions for all." Recommendation 839, TEXTS ADOPTED, September 1978.

Survivors and Protocol[581] and the European Interim Agreement on Social Security Other than Schemes for Old Age, Invalidity and Survivors and Protocol,[582] which were signed in 1953. These, which remain in force, require a contracting party to treat the nationals of other contracting parties equally with its own under its social security law. They were followed by the Social Charter in 1961 and by the European Code of Social Security and Protocol[583] in 1964. Both the Code and its Protocol were based upon the International Labor Organization Social Security (Minimum Standards) Convention 1952.[584] The Code spells out a comprehensive set of social security standards. The Protocol improves upon it by requiring higher benefits and care and the acceptance of more undertakings for ratification. Finally, the European Convention on Social Security and Supplementary Agreement[585] were adopted in 1972. The Convention replaces, for the parties to it, the 1953 Interim Agreements. Although more ambitious, it is similar to these agreements in ensuring equality of treatment of nationals by contracting parties (and also of refuges and stateless persons) in social security matters. The Convention takes into account regulations adopted by the European

[581]European Interim Agreement on Social Security Schemes Relating to Old Age, Invalidity and Survivors and Protocol, *signed* Dec. 11, 1953, 1955 Gr. Brit. T.S. No. 40 (Cmd. 9510), 218 U.N.T.S. 211. The Agreement and Protocol entered into force on July 1, 1954, and Oct. 10, 1954, respectively. Sixteen of the 21 member states of the CE are parties. The exceptions are Austria, Liechtenstein, Malta, Portugal, and Switzerland.

[582]European Interim Agreement on Social Security Schemes to Old Age, Invalidity and Survivors and Protocol, *signed* Dec. 11, 1953, 1955 Gr. Brit. T.S. No. 41 (Cmd. 9511), 218 U.N.T.S. 153. The information in the preceding note applies to this Agreement and Protocol as well.

[583] European Code of Social Security and Protocol, *opened for signature* Apr. 16, 1964, 1968 Gr. Brit. T.S. No. 10 (Cmnd. 3871), 648 U.N.T.S. 235. The Code and Protocol entered into force on Mar. 17, 1968. The Code has been ratified by the following 13 states: Belgium, Denmark, the F.R.G., Greece, Ireland, Italy, Luxembourg, the Netherlands, Norway, Sweden, Switzerland, Turkey, and the U.K.; the Protocol has been ratified by Belgium, the F.R.G., Luxembourg, the Netherlands, Norway, and Sweden.

[584]Note 16 *supra*. Sixteen of the 21 members of the CE are parties to this Convention, the exceptions being Cyprus, Liechtenstein, Malta, Portugal, and Spain.

[585]European Convention on Social Security and Supplementary Agreement, *done* Dec. 14, 1972, Europ. T.S. No. 78. The Convention and Supplementary Agreement entered into force on Mar. 1, 1977. The following members of the CE have ratified them: Austria, Luxembourg, the Netherlands, Portugal, and Turkey.

Communities[586] and the International Labor Organization Equality of Treatment (Social Security) Convention 1962.[587]

The European Interim Agreements and the European Code of Social Security and Protocol, the latter of which were in preparation at the same time as the Charter, presented a problem for the drafters of the Charter. Whereas it was not practicable or desirable for detailed texts on social security of the sort found in or projected for these specialists texts to be included, the Charter could scarcely claim to be a balanced or comprehensive statement of social rights if it completely failed to protect the right to social security. The solution chosen was to include a text protecting it in general terms, leaving it to the specialist texts to spell out the details.[588] The result is that the Charter has only a secondary role with aspect to social security insofar as the parties to it are also parties to the Interim Agreements or the Code. This is particularly true of the Code, which, unlike the European Interim Agreements (or the 1972 Convention), has its own system of implementation.[589]

One final introductory point concerns the meaning of "social security." This is a term that is not defined in the Charter.[590] The International Labor Organization Social Security (Minimum Standards) Convention and the European Code of Social Security are divided into nine Parts, which are concerned in turn with medical care, sickness benefits, unemployment benefits, old-age benefits, employment injury benefits, family benefits, maternity benefits, disability benefits, and survivors' benefits. This list probably also indicates the kinds

---

[586]For a full account of the action taken by the European Communities under Arts. 51 and 118 of the Treaty of Rome to secure the social security rights of migrant workers and to harmonize national social security legislation within the Communities, see P. WATSON, SOCIAL SECURITY LAW OF THE EUROPEAN COMMUNITIES (1980).

[587]See note 580 supra.

[588]The same problem was seen to exist in the drafting of the ICESCR in respect to the ILO Social Security (Minimum Standards) Convention 1952, note 16 supra. See U.N. Docs. E/CN.4/SR.220, at 11, and E/CN.4/SR. 221, at 4. The same solution was adopted. See ICESCR, Art. 9, note 29 supra.

[589]See note 54 of Chapter I.

[590]Cf. Art. 9 of the ICESCR, note 29 supra, which also lacks a definition. The inclusion of a definition in the ICESCR was considered but not pursued because it was thought to present too many difficulties. See the references in note 588 supra. M. Cassin (France) stated in the UNCHR that social security "should be interpreted in its broad sense as embracing not only individual social security, but also family allowances and the other means of social protection covered by Article 23(3) of the Universal Declaration of Human Rights." U.N. Doc. E/CN.4/SR.220, at 12.

of care and benefits covered by Article 12 of the Charter. A question which arose in the third cycle was whether the "social pension" payable under Italian law to certain persons over sixty-five who have no income of any kind or whose income does not exceed a certain amount came within Article 12. Although clearly containing elements in common with social assistance for persons in need, the Committee of Independent Experts ruled that it was a social security benefit in the form of an old-age pension, so that it did come within Article 12.[591]

Article 12 (1): Establishment of Maintenance of a System of Social Security

By Article 12 (1), the contracting parties undertake "to establish or maintain a system of social security." While it is difficult to be specific about what is required by this "very general provision,"[592] it follows from the progressively more difficult nature of tne undertakings in the first three paragraphs of Article 12 and from the specific content of Article 12(2) that a state may comply with Article 12(1) by meeting the requirements for ratification of the International Labor Organization Social Security (Minimum Standards) Convention or the European Code of Social Security.[593] Although Article 12(1) operates, therefore, at a fairly modest level, the experience of Cyprus indicates that it is not entirely devoid of meaning. In the second and third cycles, the Committee of Independent Experts concluded that it could not decide that Cyprus complied with the undertaking: "Although there was social insurance legislation providing benefits covering certain risks, there were substantial gaps in it and many benefits were so low as to warrant serious doubt as to whether the measures in force could be termed as social security system."[594] Since Cyprus had indicated that new and more comprehensive legislation was being prepared, the Committee of Independent Experts

---

[591]*See* note 638 *infra.* As this case illustrates, Art. 12 applies to noncontributory benefits as well as contributory ones. *Cf.* Laroque, *Droit à la Sécurité Sociale, Droit à l'Exercise d'une Activité Lucrative sur le Territoire des Autres Parties Contractantes, Droits des Travailleurs Migrants et de Leurs Familles à la Protection et à l'Assistance,* paper presented to the Brussels Colloquium on the European Social Charter, Institut d'Etudes Européennes (1976). See also the similar ruling in C VII 74 (France).

[592]C I 62.

[593]*See* note 598 *infra.*

[594]C III 62 (Cyprus). *See also* C II 191 (Cyprus).

delayed its rulings until that legislation was in force. By the end of the fourth cycle, the legislation[595] was in force and the Committee of Independent Experts was able to rule that Cyprus complied with the Charter. Although "some risks (benefits in kind for sickness and maternity and family benefits) were still not covered," taken as a whole it could be regarded as "a genuine system of social security."[596] It appears, therefore, that a "system" may be said to exist in the sense of Article 12(1) even though there is no provision at all for care or benefits in respect to one or more of the kinds listed in the nine Parts of the International Labor Organization Social Security (Minimum Standards) Convention or the European Code of Social Security. It would have been possible for the Committee of Independent Experts to have insisted upon coverage at some level, though not that required for ratification of each of the kinds of care or benefits protected by these treaties, for Article 12 (1) to be complied with. It has adopted a less stringent approach in accepting that a "system" exists when care or benefits are provided in respect to most, but not all, of the areas covered by them.

Article 12(2): Minimum Permissible Level of a Social Security System
By Article 12(2), the contracting parties undertake "to maintain the social security system at a satisfactory level at least equal to that required for ratification of International Labour Organization Convention (No. 102) Concerning Minimum Standards of Social Security." It was intended originally that the "level"[597] required for compliance with Article 12(2) should be that required for ratification of the European Code of Social Security. Unfortunately, the Code ran into difficulties and its final text had not been adopted by the time that the Charter was signed in 1961. As a result, it was decided to make the required level that necessary to ratify the International Labor Organization Social Security (Minimum Standards) Convention.[598] The switch lowered the standard ex-

---

[595]Social Insurance Law No. 106 of 1972.

[596]C IV 81 (Cyprus). *See also* Laroque, *supra* note 591, at 1.

[597]The word "level" in Art. 12(2) is used in a more general sense—including the kinds and duration of care and benefits as well as the level at which each is provided—than that in which it is used in the commentary to Art. 12(1).

[598]The incorporation by reference of the detailed standards of an existing text was considered preferable to a requirement formulated in extremely general terms, which is all that the Charter would otherwise have been able to offer.

pected of contracting parties. Whereas the undertakings in the Code are based upon those in the ILO Convention and are not substantially different from them, a state has to accept more undertakings in order to ratify the Code than it does to ratify the ILO Convention. To become a party to the ILO Convention, a state must accept three of its nine parts,[599] including at least one of the Parts dealing with unemployment benefits, old-age benefits, employment injury benefits, disability benefits, and survivors' benefits.[600] To become a party to the Code, a state must accept at least six of the same nine Parts, although for this purpose the Part concerning medical care counts as two Parts and the Part concerning old-age benefits counts as three. The Code also covers all workers without exception, whereas a state does not have to apply the ILO Convention to seamen and sea fishermen to ratify it.[601]

Nine of the eleven parties that have accepted Article 12(2) are parties to the International Labor Organization Social Security (Minimum Standards) Convention.[602] These parties are unlikely to be found in violation of Article 12(2) if they have been found to comply with their obligations under the ILO Convention for the relevant period under the ILO reporting system; similarly, if the ILO Committee of Experts finds that they do not satisfy the number of Parts of the ILO Convention needed for ratification of it, it is unlikely that the Committee of Independent Experts would decide otherwise.[603] Although a party has been found to be in violation of an undertaking in the ILO Convention by ILO Committee of Experts, it may still be found to comply with Article 12(2) if it has accepted more Parts of the Convention than is necessary for ratification.[604] This occurred in the case of Sweden in the first cycle.[605] In the case of a party to the Charter not also party to the ILO Convention, so that its law and practice are not subject to examina-

---

[599]*See* note 590 *supra.*

[600]Art. 2. Acceptance of the ILO Employment Injury Benefits Convention 1964, note 580, *supra,* counts as acceptance of Part VI of the ILO Social Security (Minimum Standards) Convention 1952, note 16 *supra.* ILO Employment Injury Benefits Convention 1964, Art. 29, note 580 *supra.*

[601]ILO Social Security (Minimum Standards) Convention 1952, Art. 77, note 16 *supra.*

[602]Cyprus and Spain are the exceptions.

[603]*Cf.* C I 62 and C VI 82 (Austria).

[604]C I 62.

[605]C I 62 (Sweden).

tion by the ILO Committee of Experts, the Committee of Independent Experts must apply the ILO Convention itself. This occurred when the Committee found Cyprus in violation of Article 12(2).[606]

When, very reluctantly, it was agreed to replace the requirements of ratification of the projected European Code of Social Security by those of the International Labor Organization Social Security (Minimum Standards) Convention 1952 as the basis for compliance with Article 12(2), the Committee of Ministers of the Council of Europe agreed that when the Code was eventually adopted, it would be desirable to consider amending the Charter to implement the original intention.[607] Although the Code has been in existence for over ten years, no steps have yet been taken to amend the Charter along these lines.

Article 12(3): Progressive Improvement of the Social Security System
By Article 12(3), a contracting party undertakes "to endeavour to raise progressively the system of social security to a higher level." This provision is unique in Part II in that the obligation is only to "endeavour" to do something. The distinction was important in the case of Denmark in the third cycle. There was no improvement in the Danish social security system during the years 1970–71 to which the cycle related, but considerable improvements had been made as a result of legislation adopted in 1972. Since preparatory work for this legislation had been done during the period being reported upon, the Committee of Independent Experts found that Denmark had complied with Article 12(3) during that period because it had then been "endeavoúring" to improve its social security system, although the improvements did not materialize until later.[608] The distinction also would be relevant in a time of economic stringency when a state was prevented from acting during the cycle reported upon for economic reasons.

In most cases, the Committee of Independent Experts has been able to find sufficient evidence of actual improvements to make a determination regarding Article 12(3). In doing so, the Committee has been prepared to accept as sufficient im-

---

[606]C II 191 (Cyprus), C III 63 (Cyprus), C IV 82 (Cyprus).
[607]CM (61) 95 rev., 2.
[608]C III 63 (Denmark). *See also* C I 63 (Italy).

provement in respect to just one kind of benefit or care provided that the improvement is substantial. For example, Italy was found to comply with Article 12(3) during the third cycle because there had been a great deal of improvement in the field of maternity coverage.[609] The benefit paid to women wage earners during maternity leave had been increased to 80% of earnings; hospital care for childbirth had been made free; and maternity benefits had been extended to women farmers and tenant farmers.

In the same cycle, the Committee of Independent Experts took note of a Committee of Ministers' resolution[610] adopted in the course of implementing the European Code of Social Security in which Norway was asked to provide further information concerning a change in its national insurance law[611] in order to establish whether it involved a lowering of standards. The Committee of Independent Experts did not make any determination on the law's compliance with Article 12(3) pending Norway's response to the Committee of Ministers' Resolution.[612] In the fourth cycle, the Committee of Independence Experts noted that the 1970 law had been repealed and that Norway's law, as altered, had been found to comply with the European Code and the International Labor Organization Social Security (Minimum Standards) Convention by the competent supervisory organs; in these circumstances, and in view of improvements in Norway's social security law in other respects, the Committee of Independent Experts found that Norway complied with Article 12(3).[613] The case raised, but did not answer, the question whether the lowering of social security standards in one respect must indicate a violation of Article 12(3) even though improvements have occurred in other respects and the overall picture is one of improvement.[614] It is submitted that a party should be held to comply with Article 12(3) if there is overall improvement.

In looking for improvement, the Committee of Independent Experts has asked states to supply information on increases in the cost of living on the ground that an increase in

[609]C III 64 (Italy).
[610]CM Resolution (73) 11.
[611]Act No. 67 of June 19, 1970, amending the National Insurance Act 1966.
[612]C III 64 (Norway).
[613]C IV 83 (Norway).
[614]See also C IV 84 (Sweden).

benefits which only keeps pace with increases in the cost of living does not constitute an improvement.[615] The Committee of Independent Experts took this into account in the third cycle in its ruling that Ireland complied with Article 12(3).[616] Ireland had reported that social security benefits had been increased between 28% and 54% while the cost of living had risen only 19.5%.

Another requirement for compliance under Article 12(3) is that the level of improvement surpass that required for ratification of the International Labor Organization Convention.[617] Just as compliance with Article 12(2) was intended to depend on reaching the level necessary for ratification of the projected European Code of Social Security, so compliance with Article 12(3) was intended to depend on a state's progressive raising of its social security system to the higher level necessary for ratification of the projected Protocol to the Code.[618] When the Protocol failed to materialize by the time that the Charter was adopted, the proposed reference to it, like the reference to the Code in Article 12(2), was deleted.[619] It is reasonable to suppose that it was still intended that Article 12(3) should build upon Article 12(2) and that, in the light of the final version of the latter, the undertaking in Article 12(3) means that a state, in its first report, should demonstrate that it is taking steps to improve upon the level required for ratification of the ILO Convention and will continue to do so thereafter. One consequence of reading Article 12(3) in this manner is that compliance with Article 12(3) hinges upon compliance with Article 12(2).[620] A state may, of course, comply with Article 12(3) without accepting Article 12(2)[621] if it meets the standards set by the latter.

The requirement that the level of the social security system

---

[615]C I 200. In Oct. 1957 an ad hoc working party of the CMSC rejected a proposal that Art. 12 contain a fifth paragraph requiring that the level of social security benefits be adjusted to take account of inflation. It did so not because of what it would require but because such an undertaking was already contained in the projected European Code of Social Security.

[616]C III 64 (Ireland).

[617]C III 63. C II 190 (Cyprus) is ambiguous on this point.

[618]The CMSC agreed at its Sixth Session in Nov. 1957 that a statement to this effect should be included in the Appendix to the Charter.

[619]96th Meeting of the Ministers' delegates, Mar. 22, 1961.

[620]C II 192–93 (Cyprus), C III 65 (Cyprus), C IV 82 (Cyprus), C III 63 (Austria), C IV 83 (Austria).

[621]Ireland was the only state in this position during the first six cycles. It has been found to comply with Art. 12(3).

be "progressively" raised has led the Committee of Independent Experts to characterize Article 12(3) as a "dynamic" undertaking,[622] so that a party is required to provide evidence of further improvement or "endeavour" in every reporting cycle. The Committee of Independent Experts has so far shown no sign that it regards the undertaking of Article 12(3) as finite.[623] During the Charter's drafting, the Committee of Ministers suggested that when the Protocol to the proposed Code came into being, the Charter should be amended to revert to the original intention that Article 12(3) should require states, at the most, to reach the level set by the Protocol.[624] This suggests that the text as it stands does not contain such a limitation. However, there may well be limitations inherent in the concept of the right to social security as reflected in the thinking of Western European states that are members of the Council of Europe.

Article 12(4): Equal Treatment for Nationals of Other Contracting Parties in Social Security Matters
By Article 12(4), the contracting parties undertake:

> to take steps, by the conclusion of appropriate bilateral and multilateral agreements, or by other means, and subject to the conditions laid down in such agreements, in order to ensure:
> (a) equal treatment with their own nationals of the nationals of other Contracting Parties in respect of social security rights, including the retention of benefits arising out of social security legislation, whatever movements the persons protected may undertake between the territories of the Contracting Parties;
> (b) the granting, maintenance and resumption of social security rights by such means as the accumulation of insurance or employment periods completed under the legislation of each of the Contracting Parties.

Subparagraph (a) incorporates the principle of equality of treatment of nationals of contracting parties. Subparagraph (b) is concerned with the recognition by one contracting party

---

[622] C I 62. As to "dynamic" undertakings generally, see note 27 *supra*.

[623] See, e.g., its treatment of the reports of the F.R.G., which display a very high level of attainment. C I 200 (F.R.G.), C II 47 (F.R.G.), C III (F.R.G.), and C IV 83 (F.R.G.).

[624] CM (61) 95 rev., 2. *Cf.* the view of the CM expressed on a similar question concerning Art. 12(2). *See* note 607 *supra*. The GC concludes from this that attainment of the level set by the Protocol only is required. GC VII 11.

of attainments qualifying a person for social security rights under the legal system of another.

Article 12(4) applies to the nationals of all of the contracting parties to the Charter; it is not limited to nationals of those contracting parties that have accepted this undertaking. It applies to all such nationals, whether or not they lawfully reside or work regularly within the territory of the contracting party concerned.[625] The requirements of both subparagraphs may be met "by the conclusion of appropriate bilateral and multilateral agreements, or by other means." "Other means" include legislative or other unilateral action by a contracting party.[626] The national reports on Article 12(4) show that a large number of bilateral social security agreements have been concluded between parties to the Charter. The relevant multilateral agreements are the 1953 European Interim Agreements on Social Security,[627] the International Labor Organization Equality of Treatment (Social Security) Convention 1962,[628] and the 1972 European Convention of Social Security.[629] There are also the regulations of the European Communities concerning social security for migrant workers within the Communities.[630]

In the third cycle, the Committee of Independent Experts distinguished between subparagraphs (a) and (b) in two respects. First, it stated that whereas subparagraph (a) could be complied with by international agreements or national action, subparagraph (b) could only be implemented by the former. This was so despite the fact that the wording "by other means" applied to both subparagraphs. In the Committee's view, "the solution to the problem posed by the transfer of entitlements from one legal system to another could only be achieved by

[625]Appendix to the Charter.

[626]The words "or by other means" were introduced at the suggestion of the U.K. at the Seventh Session of the CMSC, February 1958, to allow unilateral legislative action; it would cover, for example, any arrangements made in the special situation of Northern Ireland by which Irish nationals might be entitled to social security benefits in Northern Ireland.

[627]Notes 581 & 582 *supra*. All of the parties to the Charter are parties to the Interim Agreements except Austria.

[628]Note 580 *supra*. Eight of the parties to the Charter—Denmark, the F.R.G., France, Ireland, Italy, Netherlands, Norway, and Sweden—are parties.

[629]Note 585 *supra*. Only two parties to the Charter—Austria, and the Netherlands—are parties to the Convention.

[630]*See* note 586 *supra*. Seven of the parties to the Charter—Denmark, the F.R.G., France, Ireland, Italy, Netherlands, and the U.K.—are European Communities members.

means of bilateral or multilateral agreements."[631] Second, the Committee applied a stricter standard to subparagraph (a) than to subparagraph (b) insofar as it described the former as "an undertaking by each contracting party to *ensure* equal treatment" and the latter as one only to "*endeavour* to enable" migrant workers to retain their rights.[632] It followed from this, the Committee stated, that subparagraph (a) was complied with only if "equality between a country's own nationals and those of other contracting parties is effectively safeguarded under national legislation," whereas all that was required under subparagraph (b) was that "adequate efforts are made to conclude and implement international agreements whereby migrants' rights are maintained or restored.[633] Thus, under subparagraph (a), a contracting party had, by international agreements or national law, to provide at once for equality of treatment for the nationals of all of the other contracting parties and, so far as this was done by international agreements, to ensure that the agreements were effective in national law.[634] Under subparagraph (b) "adequate efforts" only needed to be taken to achieve both of these ends. Again, this is a difference in treatment of the two subparagraphs that does not follow the language of the text, which uses the same word—"ensure"—in each. In the seventh cycle, the Experts applied a more relaxed standard for subparagraph (a) (agreement not needed if no migration between the two parties; active negotiation of agreement sufficient for provisional compliance) and a stricter one for subparagraph (b) (agreements required in all cases), while still insisting that the latter can only be complied with by international agreements.[635] The Committee has not referred since the third cycle to the requirement that any international agreement that is relied upon (whether in compliance with subparagraph [a] or [b]) should be incorporated into national law.

Applying subparagraph (a), the Committee of Independent Experts has found infringements of the principle of equality of treatment in several cases. A Norwegian law, entitling only

<hr />

[631] C III 64.

[632] *Id.* Emphasis added.

[633] C III 65.

[634] *Cf.* C I 63 (Denmark, Norway), C II 48 (Denmark, Ireland, Norway).

[635] See C VII 73–74. The above statement is inferred from a somewhat obscure text. It would be helpful for the CIE to reformulate its position generally. The GC has commended the CIE's new approach to subparagraph (a). GC VII 11.

Norwegian citizens to disablement and survivors' benefits while resident abroad, has been found to violate the Charter.[636] Although the Committee of Independent Experts was prepared to take into account the fact that the competent authority (the National Insurance Institute) had been instructed within the existing law to allow the benefits in question to be paid to foreigners resident abroad where they are nationals of parties to the 1953 European Interim Agreements on Social Security, this was not sufficient because one party to the Charter—Austria—was not a party to the Interim Agreements. Curiously, no violation would have been found if neither Norwegian nor foreign nationals could have received the benefits in question abroad. This was the position under Irish law regarding the payment of family allowances; although foreigners might suffer more frequently than nationals, there was equality in law and, thus, compliance with Article 12(4).[637] A second case concerns Italy. Under Italian law, a "social pension" is available to Italian citizens resident in Italy over the age of sixty-five who have no income or limited income below a certain ceiling. The pension infringes Article 12(4) (a) because it is not available to nationals of other contracting parties resident in Italy.[638]

An exception is allowed to the principle of equality of treatment in the case of residence requirements. The Appendix to the Charter states: "The words 'and subject to the conditions laid down in such agreements' in the introduction to this paragraph are taken to imply *inter alia* that with regard to benefits which are available independently of any insurance contribution a Contracting Party may require the completion of a prescribed period of residence before granting such benefits to nationals of other Contracting Parties."[639] The exception applies to both subparagraphs of Article 12. It would permit, for example, the U.K. to impose a residence requirement in respect to the national health service, whose availability is not

[636]C III 66 (Norway). Ruling reversed on new facts. C VII 74 (Norway).

[637]C I 201 (Ireland).

[638]C III 65, C VII 74 (Italy). On the classification of the pension as a social security benefit, see note 591 *supra.*

[639] The wording of Art. 12 and the Appendix suggests that it applies only where a state complies with Art. 12 on the basis of an international agreement and not solely on the basis of unilateral legislative or other action. This is probably a drafting error. When "by other means" was added at a late stage, the remainder of the introductory text was not altered. *See supra* note 584, at 115.

dependent upon the payment of any insurance contribution. It is not clear whether conditions other than residence contributions may be imposed. The English text of the Appendix to the Charter states that the "conditions" in Article 12 are *"inter alia"* concerned with residence, implying that other kinds of conditions may be imposed. The French text differs and is to the effect that only residence conditions are permitted.[640] The latter interpretation is preferable as being more consonant with the object and purpose of the Charter.

Article 13: The Right to Social and Medical Assistance[641]

When Article 13 was drafted, an effort was made to "break away from the old idea of assistance, which was bound up with the dispensing of charity."[642] In particular, an attempt was made to eradicate the stigma attached to public assistance, which has both marked the recipient and prevented proper fulfillment of its purpose. This effort is noticeable in the language used in the text ("persons without adequate resources" instead of "the poor" and "want" instead of "poverty").[643] It is also evident from the undertaking in Article 13(2), which is intended to "eradicate . . . any remnants of social and political discrimination against persons receiving assistance."[644]

Article 13(1): Social and Medical Assistance of Persons in Need
By Article 13(1), the contracting parties undertake "to ensure that any person who is without adequate resources and who is unable to secure such resources either by his own efforts or from other sources, in particular by benefits under a social

---

[640]The French text approved at the 96th Meeting of Ministers' Deputies, Mar. 22, 1961, had read "comme significant notamment que," which has a meaning comparable to that in the final English text. Subsequently, in a way not apparent from the *travaux préparatoires*, but possibly to conciliate Italy which had wanted to strengthen the protection afforded to migrant workers by Art. 12(4), "notamment" was omitted.

[641]The right to social assistance is not specifically guaranteed in the UDHR or the ICESCR. To some extent, it is protected by the provisions concerning the rights to social security (UDHR, Art. 22, note 7 *supra*, and ICESCR, Art. 9, note 29 *supra*), to an adequate standard of living (UDHR, Art. 25[1], note 7 *supra*, and ICESCR, Art. 11, note 29 *supra*) and to health (ICESCR, Art. 12, note 29 *supra*).

[642]C I 64.

[643]*Cf. id.* and Bourlard, *Droit à l'Assistance Sociale et Médicale, Droit au Bénéfice des Services Sociaux, Droit des Personnes Physiquement ou Mentalement Diminuées à la Formation Professionelle et à la Réadaptation Professionelle et Sociale*, 2, paper presented to the Brussels Colloquium on the European Social Charter, Institute d'Etudes Européennes (1976).

[644]C I 64.

security scheme, be granted adequate assistance, and, in case of sickness, the care necessitated by his condition." Although the Committee of Independent Experts has not defined expressly the phrase "without adequate resources," its assessment of national reports suggests that a person comes within Article 13(1) when he lacks sufficient resources to provide for the necessities of life, as determined by reference to the prevailing cost and standard of living within the contracting party concerned. It has also insisted that a contracting party have in its law a "criterion by which 'want' is assessed."[645] The F.R.G., for example, complies with Article 13(1) by the provision of means tests that relate a person's income and other available assets to the cost of living. In contrast, Italy has been found to violate it because of the lack of provision of any such objective criteria in its law.[646]

Assistance need only be given where a person without adequate resources "is unable to secure such resources either by his own efforts or from other sources, in particular by benefits under a social security scheme." It is clear from the *travaux préparatoires* that "in particular" (*notamment*) does not mean that "benefits made under a social security scheme" are the only "other sources" to which an indigent person may be expected to have recourse before a contracting party must provide him with social assistance; he may, inter alia, be expected to seek assistance from his near relatives.[647] It would not seem that a person who is on strike is "unable to secure . . . resources . . . by his own efforts." There is, therefore, no obligation to allow him social assistance (as distinct from social security).[648]

Subject to the rule concerning the scope of the Charter *ratione personae*,[649] "any person" who meets the requirements on eligibility is entitled to assistance. The imposition of residence

---

[645]C I 66.

[646]C I 66 (Italy), C II 67 (Italy).

[647]At the TC, the workers' delegates proposed a change of wording which would have meant that an indigent person could not be required to have recourse to his family before being eligible for social assistance. REC PROC TC 222. Although it was supported later by the CA, (Art. 13, Eur. Consult. Ass., 11th Sess., Doc. No. 1035), the proposal was rejected by the CMSC at its Ninth Session, April 1960, because it wanted to leave it open to a state to impose that requirement.

[648]Whether such a refusal violates Art. 6 of the Charter, see note 385 *supra*.

[649]*See* Wiebringhaus, *Le Champ d'application "Ratione Personae" de la Charte Sociale Européenne,* in LIBRO-HOMENAJE AL PROFESOR LUIS SELA SAMPIL OVIEDO, *passim* (1970).

or place of birth requirements is impermissible. This question arose in examination of a British law concerning the Isle of Man. Supplementary benefits are not available to anyone living in the Isle of Man unless the applicant was born there or has lived there for ten (formerly five) years.[650] The reasons were explained in the Third British Report as follows: "In the summer months there is a large influx of workers, mainly from other parts of the United Kingdom for the holiday trade for the Island, and it is considered that without the imposition of the birth or residence qualification many of these workers might stay on in the Island as unemployed in the off season. The regulations are thus regarded as purely practical measures intended to regulate the economy of the Island and not as discrimination against any particular type or nationality of workers."[651] The Committee of Independent Experts rejected this explanation and ruled that the U.K. was in violation of Article 13(1).[652]

In the opinion of the Committee of Independent Experts, Article 13(1) creates a "subjective right" (*droit subjectif*): a party to the Charter must provide in its law a right to assistance for persons within Article 13 which they can enforce before a court or tribunal.[653] The U.K., for example, has been held to meet this requirement by providing that a person may apply for supplementary benefits to the Ministry of Social Security and may appeal a negative decision or a condition attached to benefits to an independent appeal tribunal.[654] In contrast, Italy has been found to be in violation of Article 13(1) inter alia because its law does not provide these kinds of procedures except in certain particular contexts.[655] The Governmental

---

[650]National Assistance (Isle of Man) Act 1951, sec. 22(6), as amended. C VI 88 (U.K.).

[651]Third U.K. Report, at 119.

[652]C III 67 (U.K.). In the sixth cycle, the CIE noted that eligibility for social assistance in Northern Ireland was dependent upon five years' residence and found the U.K. to be in breach of Art. 13(1) because of this also. C VI 88 (U.K.). Art. 12(4) does not apply because there is no discrimination based upon nationality.

[653]C I 65. This is different from saying that Art. 13(1) is self-executing (which it is not). *See* note 68 of Chapter IV.

[654]C I 66 (U.K.), C II 49 (U.K.).

[655]C I 66 (Italy), C II 49 (Italy), C III 67 (Italy), C IV 87 (Italy). Art. 38 of the Italian Constitution provides that every citizen unable to work and without the means of subsistence has the right to maintenance and to social assistance. This has been interpreted by the Italian courts as stating a principle and not as creating a "subjective right."

Committee disagrees with the Committee of Independent Experts' interpretation of Article 13(1) in this respect. In its opinion, the contracting parties must "take steps to ensure that persons in need are granted appropriate assistance, but this does not necessarily imply the existence of a subjective right to such assistance."[656] This would appear the better interpretation.[657] Nothing in the wording of Article 13(1) distinguishes it from other provisions of Part II that have been held not to generate subjective rights. Provided adequate steps are taken to assist persons in need, Article 13(1) would appear to be complied with whether or not the indigent person has a legally enforceable right.

The "assistance" to which a person is entitled may be in cash or in kind; the national reports show that it is almost always in the form of cash. The assistance given must be "adequate." This term is not defined in the Charter;[658] in practice, the Committee of Independent Experts appears to have acted on the basis that it should be sufficient to allow the person concerned to provide for the necessities of life in accordance with the prevailing cost and standard of living in the contracting party concerned. In order to assess the adequacy of benefits, the Committee of Independent Experts has asked for the provision of figures indicating public expenditure on public assistance.[659] In cases of sickness, a person must be provided with "the care necessitated by his condition" regardless of his ability to pay.[660]

Article 13(2): Nondiscrimination Against Persons in Receipt of Social and Medical Assistance

By Article 13(2), the contracting parties undertake "to ensure that persons receiving such assistance shall not, for that reason, suffer from a diminution of their political and social

[656]GC III 7.

[657]*Contra* Bourlard, *supra* note 643, at 2. Art. 14(1) is the other provision that has been held by the CIE to create a "subjective right," *see* C I 70 (Sweden, U.K., Denmark, Italy).

[658]The definition in Art. 2(2) of the European Convention on Social and Medical Assistance 1953 is not very helpful. European Convention on Social and Medical Assistance, *signed* Dec. 11, 1953, 1955 Gr. Brit. T.S. No. 42 (Cmd. 9512), 218 U.N.T.S. 255.

[659]C I. 66. The Committee has also asked for information about private expenditure by charities and other bodies; the national reports show that such bodies provide assistance to persons in need of cash and in kind on a considerable scale.

[660]C I 202 (Ireland).

rights." The Committee of Independent Experts has understood "political and social rights" to include the right to vote in an election, to hold public office, and to be admitted to the public service.[661] These are "political" rights; all of the rights in the Charter would presumably be "social" rights in the sense of Article 13(2), although there is no indication that any exact equivalence was intended.[662] Alternatively, the distinction between economic and social rights[663] might apply. The Committee of Independent Experts has also adopted the view that Article 13(2) is only violated where there is an "express statutory provision" limiting a person's "political or social rights."[664] Until 1972, Ireland was in violation of Article 13(2) because a person in receipt of public assistance was not allowed to be a member of a local authority (whose function it is to grant public assistance) within twelve months of receipt.[665] Otherwise, the national reports show that Article 13(2) has been complied with in the first seven cycles.

Article 13(3): Advice and Personal Help in Case of Want
By Article 13(3), the contracting parties undertake "to provide that everyone may receive by appropriate public or private services such advice and personal help as may be required to prevent, to remove, or to alleviate personal or family want." The Committee of Independent Experts has emphasized that inclusion of the "prevention" of want in Article 13(3) indicates that Article 13 is "progressive in that it binds the states accepting it to set up an effective system of assistance, but also to ensure that such assistance gradually becomes unnecessary, until it completely disappears—the ultimate aim."[666] The wording of Article 13(3) is very general and could mean that the undertaking provides that advice and help is available to "everyone," whether in want or not. The Committee of Independent Experts has understood it to apply to person "without, or liable to be without, adequate resources."[667] Regarding

[661]C I 67, C I 203 (Ireland).
[662]For rights not included in the Charter which might be thought to qualify, *see* notes 1020–37 *infra*.
[663]*See* note 13 of Chapter I.
[664]C I 67.
[665]This was so under the Local Government (Application of Enactment) Order 1898, Art. 12, which was repealed by the Local Elections Act 1972.
[666]C I 64.
[667]C I 64.

the removal or alleviation of existing want, "advice" may be given concerning such matters as the availability of housing, social benefits, and social welfare services. "Personal help" may take such forms as those reported upon in the First U.K. Report, viz., home nursing; cleaning help, meals services, day centers or clubs, holidays and outings, and transport facilities for hospital visits for elderly people; and day nurseries.[668] Concerning the prevention of future want, "advice" on employment and educational opportunities and on such matters as birth control is relevant. Article 13(3) refers to "personal and family want." As far as "family want" is concerned, it overlaps with Article 16, which protects the right of the family to social, legal, and economic protection.[669] The obligation of a contracting party is "to provide" advice or help "by appropriate public or private services." It may, therefore, be carried out either by the establishment of public bodies able to give advice or help or by allowing and, if need be, encouraging (by tax allowance, grants,[670] etc.) private bodies to do so, or by a combination of both. The national reports indicate that in practice advice and help are mainly provided through public bodies, although voluntary organizations also play an important part.

The relationship between Article 13(3) and the more general provision in Article 14 protecting the right to benefit from the social welfare services is considered below.[671]

Article 13(4): Equality of Treatment
By Article 13(4), the contracting parties undertake "to apply the provisions referred to in paragraphs 1, 2 and 3 of this Article on an equal footing with their nationals to nationals of other Contracting Parties lawfully within their territories, in accordance with their obligations under the European Convention on Social and Medical Assistance, signed at Paris on 11th December 1953."[672] A contracting party undertakes the

[668]First U.K. Report, at 141–42.
[669]*See* note 680 *infra*.
[670]Citizens' Advice Bureaux in the U.K., for example, are often given financial assistance by local authorities, and the National Citizens' Advice Bureaux Council receives a central government grant. First U.K. Report, at 141.
[671]*See* note 688 *infra*.
[672]Note 658 *supra*. The Convention entered into force on July 1, 1954. A Protocol to the Convention, note 658 *supra*, which was adopted at the same time as the Convention, extends it to refugees.

obligation contained in this provision in respect to the nationals of every contracting party to the Charter, whether or not those parties have accepted Article 13, or any part of it, and whether or not they are parties to the European Convention on Social and Medical Assistance.[673] The undertaking applies to nationals of another contracting party "lawfully within" territory of the contracting party concerned. This is a *lex specialis,* recognized by the Appendix to the Charter, derogating from the normal, narrower rule as to the scope of the Charter, *ratione personae,* by which it applies only to nationals of other contracting parties who are "lawfully resident or working regularly within" the territory of the contracting party concerned.[674] For Article 13(4), the requirement is lawful presence, not residence or place of regular work.[675]

Equal treatment must be granted by the contracting parties "in accordance with their obligations under the European Convention on Social and Medical Assistance." The primary obligation for a party to that Convention is to ensure that the nationals of other parties to the Convention who are "lawfully present" in its territory and who are "without sufficient resources" are "entitled equally with its own nationals and on the same conditions to social and medical assistance."[676] In principle, a contracting party must provide such assistance and not repatriate the indigent person. By the Convention, a contracting party is not entitled to repatriate a national of another party to the Convention "on the sole ground that he is in need of assistance,"[677] unless the following conditions are met:[678]

(a) The provisions of Article 6(a) notwithstanding, a Contracting Party may repatriate a national of another Contracting Party resident in its territory on the sole ground mentioned in Article 6(a) if the following conditions are fulfilled:
(i) the person concerned has not been continuously resident in the territory of that Contracting Party for at least five years if he entered it before attaining the age of 55 years, or for at least ten years if he entered it after attaining that age;
(ii) he is in a fit state of health to be transported; and
(iii) has no close ties in the territory in which he is resident.

[673]C V 97, 98 (Denmark, France), C VII 78 (France). Cf. GC VII 12.
[674]*See* note 32 of Chapter IV.
[675]*Cf.* Art. 12(4). *And see* C II 51 (Norway).
[676]European Convention on Social and Medical Assistance, Art. 1, note 658 *supra.*
[677]*Id.* Art. 6.
[678]*Id.* Art. 7.

(b) The Contracting Parties agree not to have recourse to repatriation except in the greatest moderation and then only where there is no objection on humanitarian grounds.

(c) In the same spirit, the Contracting Parties agree that, if they repatriate an assisted person, facilities should be offered to the spouse and children, if any, to accompany the person concerned.

A contracting party that repatriates the national of another party must bear the cost of repatriation.[679]

At present, all but three of the parties to the Charter are parties to the 1953 Convention.[680] For the parties to both, the reference to the Convention is intended as a safeguard. In its absence, they would be required by Article 13(4) to afford equal treatment in the application of the earlier paragraphs of Article 13 without qualification. In contrast, the Convention allows the repatriation of foreigners in need in some cases[681] and allows parties to make reservations.[682] The purposes of referring to the Convention was to incorporate into the undertaking in Article 13(4) the qualifications upon equal treatment provided for in the Convention or added in the case of a particular state by reservation. The wording "obligations" was used to incorporate such reservations to the Convention as had been made.[683]

[679]*Id.* Art. 8.

[680]The exceptions are Austria, Cyprus, and Spain. The 16 parties to the Convention are Belgium, Denmark, France, the F.R.G., Greece, Iceland, Ireland, Italy, Luxembourg, Malta, the Netherlands, Norway, Portugal, Sweden, Turkey, and the U.K. The Protocol has been ratified by 15 states: the above 16, less Malta.

[681]Note 678 *supra.*

[682]European Convention on Social and Medical Assistance, Arts. 2(b) & 16(b), note 658 *supra.*

[683]Two parties to the Convention that are also parties to the Charter—the F.R.G. and the U.K.—have made reservations. The F.R.G. reservation reads:

Where the German legislation referred to in Annex 1 provides for special subsidies and training in order to enable an individual to set up in business or start a career or for purposes of vocational training, and where such subsidies exceed the scope of assistance covered by this Convention, the Government of the Federal Republic of Germany may accord, but will not be bound to accord, such special subsidies to the nationals of other Contracting parties.

The U.K. reservation reads:

Her Majesty's Government reserve the right to free themselves from their obligation under Article 1 in respect of any person who may be repatriated by virtue of the provisions of Article 7 but who fails to take advantage of the facilities offered for his repatriation (including free transport to the frontier of his country of origin).

In the case of the U.K., the reservation is intended to cover repatriation across the border in Ireland. Nonetheless, the U.K. has been found in breach of Art. 13(4) in respect of the residence requirements for social assistance in Northern Ireland and in the Isle of Man. C VII 79 (U.K.).

Concerning parties to the Charter that are not party to the Convention, the Appendix to the Charter clarifies a point left uncertain in the text of Article 13(4), viz., that parties can accept Article 13(4) without becoming parties to the Convention. Two states—Austria and Spain—have, in fact, done so.[684] They may do so "provided that they grant to nationals of other Contracting Parties a treatment which is in conformity with the provisions of the said Convention."[685] In their case the question of reservations does not arise and they must comply with "the provisions" of the Convention as a whole. They may, of course, ratify the Convention subject to a reservation and thereby reduce the extent of their undertaking under Article 13(4).

The only question of substance that has arisen under Article 13(4) has, in fact, been repatriation. The Committee of Independent Experts has stated that it would be "quite incompatible with the provisions of the Charter" to repatriate such a person solely because he was in need.[686] This is correct, although the effect of the reference to the 1953 Convention in Article 13(4) is to incorporate the quite considerable qualification upon this principle that the Convention allows.

Article 14: The Right to Benefit from Social Welfare Services
Article 14 protects the right to benefit from social welfare services. For the purposes of the Charter, these services are "services which use 'methods of social work' and 'contribute to the welfare and development of both individuals and groups in the community, and to their adjustment to the social environment."[687] They consist of the whole range of social welfare services that are associated with the welfare state in Western Europe.

Although Article 14 and Article 13(3) overlap, they also contain substantial differences. *Ratione personae*, Article 14 is general in its application, whereas Article 13(3) applies only to the indigent. In respect to the services within their purview, Article 14 applies to any action taken to facilitate the development

---

[684]C III 69 (Austria). Earlier, the CIE had stated as a general proposition that in order to comply with Art. 13(4) a party to the Charter had to have ratified the Convention. C I 68. This did not take into account the Appendix to the Charter.

[685]Appendix to the Charter.

[686]C IV 91 (Denmark). *See also* C V 97 (Denmark).

[687]C I 69.

of individuals and their adjustment to society, while Article
13(3) is limited to services providing assistance in the form of
"advice and personal help." Clearly, a contracting party may
comply with Article 13(3) without necessarily complying with
Article 14.[688] The Committee of Independent Experts has also
held that noncompliance with Article 13(3) does not necessarily mean noncompliance with Article 14.[689] It has taken this
view presumably on the basis that a contracting party's actions
may be sufficient to "promote or provide" social welfare services as a whole to comply with Article 14(1)[690] even though
they may be insufficient in the particular area covered by Article 13(3).

In the opinion of the Committee of Independent Experts,
the very wide scope of Article 14 indicates that the two undertakings which it contains are "dynamic" in the sense of the
Committee of Independent Experts' understanding of that
concept: "This implies . . . that, beyond a certain level of social
development, what the state must do, in order to conform to
the provisions of Article 14, is to promote the establishment of
services providing advice and individual help rather than to
encourage the granting of material assistance. Article 14 may
therefore be considered as dynamic in its implications, since
the social welfare services for which it provides are designed
to keep on increasing and broadening their action."[691] As a
result, contracting parties are under an obligation to continue
to seek improvement, cycle by cycle, in the development of
their social welfare services.[692]

Although Article 14 is potentially one of the most forward-
looking of the Articles in Part II,[693] contracting parties have
experienced little difficulty in complying with it. Such problems as have arisen have been in the provision of sufficient
information for the Committee of Independent Experts to
make a decision on compliance with either of the undertakings therein.[694]

---

[688]C I 65, 69.

[689]C I 65.

[690]It is primarily Art. 14(1) that is relevant.

[691]C I 69. On "dynamic" provisions, see note 27 supra.

[692]But quaere whether Art. 14 is any more "dynamic" than, for example, Art. 11,
which is not so characterized by the CIE.

[693]Cf. Bourland, supra note 643, at 6.

[694]See, e.g., C IV 93–95.

Article 14(1): Provision or Promotion of Social Welfare Services

By Article 14(1), the contracting parties undertake "to promote or provide services which, by using methods of social work, would contribute to the welfare and development of both individuals and groups in the community, and to their adjustment to the social environment." Article 14(1) may be complied with by the provision of public services or the promotion of private ones. In the opinion of the Committee of Independent Experts, it establishes a "subjective right" (*droit subjectif*) so that services must be available as a matter of legal right enforceable in the courts.[695] Although this interpretation has not been challenged by the Governmental Committee (because no contracting party has yet been found to violate Article 14[1]), it is questionable for the same reason that the Committee of Independent Experts' comparable finding of a "subjective right" in Article 13(1) is questionable.[696]

One measure that the Committee of Independent Experts has used in gauging compliance with Article 14(1) with respect to public services has been "the number of personnel employed in the various sectors of social services and the amounts allocated to these services."[697] Some further indication of what level and kind of services will satisfy Article 14(1) is found in the experience of the U.K., which was ruled to be in compliance on the basis of the account of its public and private social welfare services given in its First Report. It described the public services that it provides in respect to health and medicine (e.g., school health services, home nursing, health visiting, etc.), social security (e.g., reception centers for persons without a settled way of life), probation, children (e.g., child care, fostering, adoption, day nursing), the mentally handicapped or ill (e.g., provision of mental welfare officers, training centers, residential accommodation), the physically handicapped (e.g., day centers, aid, and equipment), and the elderly (e.g., cleaning help, meals, day centers). Regarding the promotion of private services, the U.K. reported on the link between public and private services provided by the National Council of Social Services, "which brings together most of the principal voluntary

[695]C I 70 (Sweden, U.K., Denmark, Italy).
[696]*See* note 653 *supra*.
[697]C III 72 (U.K.).

agencies for consultation and joint action, either as a whole or in groups of those concerned with particular aspects."[698]

Article 14(2): Encouragement of Private Participation in Social Welfare Systems

By Article 14(2), the contracting parties undertake "to encourage the participation of individuals and voluntary or other organisations in the establishment and maintenance of such services." In considering a contracting party's compliance with this undertaking, the Committee of Independent Experts has not insisted that the required participation be "systematically promoted"; it has considered it sufficient that "some encouragement" be given in appropriate cases.[699] Norway, for example, has been found to comply with Article 14(2) although its Report indicated it had no deliberate policy directed toward encouraging private individuals to participate in social service work. It had, however, stated that in some cases voluntary organizations performing social work are given public financial support.[700] In addition, certain Norwegian local authorities have in recent years, as a part of organized social welfare schemes, used the services of individuals by arranging for neighbors, relations, and others to be paid to carry out such jobs as nursing and washing for persons in need of such assistance.

Article 15: The Right of Physically or Mentally Disabled Persons to Vocational Training, Rehabilitation, and Social Resettlement[701]

In *Conclusions I*, the Committee of Independent Experts explained the purpose of Article 15 as follows:

> For a long time aid to the handicapped was classed together with aid to the aged; since the Second World War aid to handicapped

[698]First U.K. Report, at 144.

[699]C IV 95 (Norway).

[700]This is stated in the Third Norwegian Report. *Cf.* C III 73, where the CIE asked for information from the U.K. about the level of subsidies granted by public authorities to voluntary organizations.

[701]There is no equivalent to Art. 15 in the UDHR or the ICESCR. The provisions concerning the right to work in each (UDHR, Art. 23[1], note 7 *supra*, and ICESCR, Art. 6, note 29 *supra*), cover the same ground in more general terms. There is no ILO convention precisely in point. *See* however, the ILO Human Resources Development Convention, note 517 *supra*, and the ILO recommendations referred to in note 703 *infra*.

persons has developed on separate lines, under the influence of Anglo-Saxon legislation. Traditional assistance policies are now out of date and in legislation the emphasis regarding this category of persons has shifted to vocational training and rehabilitation, the reintegration with society. The overriding purpose is that such persons shall be enabled to work and be independent. The Charter in Articles 9 and 10, raises the right of physically or mentally disabled persons to training, vocational rehabilitation and social resettlement to the level of a separate social right. Such a right is inconceivable in the absence of means for bringing it into effect, and the Charter therefore incorporates some of the provisions already contained in relevant ILO recommendations.[702]

The International Labor Organization recommendations referred to are the Vocational Training (Adults) Recommendation 1950 (Recommendation 88) and the Vocational Rehabilitation (Disabled) Recommendation 1955 (Recommendation 99).[703] Article 15(1) and (2) enact the proposals of these recommendations except for "the fact that the Charter is somewhat less categorical regarding the provision of employment for physically disabled persons than the corresponding provisions of the 1955 Recommendation."[704]

Article 15 overlaps with several other Articles of the Charter. Article 1(4) is concerned with the "vocational guidance, training and rehabilitation" of all persons, including the disabled. This general provision is supplemented by Article 9, which protects the right to vocational guidance of all persons "including the handicapped," and by Article 10, which protects the right to vocational training of all persons, again "including the handicapped." The function of Article 15 is to emphasize the special needs of the disabled by assembling them in a single provision protecting a separate social right.

Article 15 applies to the "physically or mentally" disabled, although there is some doubt as to whether Article 15(2) extends to the latter.[705] The Committee of Independent Experts has been concerned to establish a common Charter meaning

---

[702]C I 72.

[703]These are printed in ILO, CONVENTIONS AND RECOMMENDATIONS 1916–66 at 781, 858 (1966).

[704]The European Social Charter and International Labour Standards, 84 INT'L LAB. REV. 354, 373 (1961).

[705]C I 208 (F.R.G.) and GC IV 11.

of the term "disabled" by which the achievements of the contracting parties might be judged.[706]

Article 15(1): Provision of Training Facilities
By Article 15(1), the contracting parties undertake "to take adequate measures for the provision of training facilities, including, where necessary, specialised institutions, public or private." In determining whether a state complies with this undertaking the Committee of Independent Experts has looked to the nature and amount of the training facilities that a state provides for the different kinds of disabled persons, including persons who are blind, deaf, spastic, lacking a limb, mentally ill, or subnormal. Ireland and Norway were found to be in violation of Article 15(1) in the first cycle because of the very small number of persons who were undergoing training.[707] Further information led the Committee of Independent Experts to change its conclusions concerning Norway in the second cycle.[708] When the Third Irish Report "indicated that special measures had been taken and new *ad hoc* institutions had been created,"[709] the Committee of Independent Experts found that Ireland had provisionally complied with Article 15(1) also.[710] It is clear from these two cases that although the undertaking in Article 15(1) is very generally worded, it does have some substance.[711]

Article 15(2): Placement of Disabled Persons
By Article 15(2), the contracting parties undertake "to take adequate measures for the placing of disabled persons in employment, such as specialised placing services, facilities for sheltered employment and measures to encourage employers to admit disabled persons to employment." The Committee of Independent Experts and the Governmental Committee have

---

[706]One definition which the CIE has impliedly accepted is that in U.K. Disabled Persons (Employment) Act 1944, sec. 1. C I 73 (U.K.).

[707]C I 207 (Ireland), C I 73 (Norway), C I 207 (Norway).

[708]C II 54 (Norway).

[709]C III 75 (Ireland).

[710]*Id.* The finding is no longer provisional. C VII 84 (Ireland).

[711]*See also* the ruling against the U.K. in the seventh cycle because rehabilitation and training facilities for the physically and mentally disabled were not open to nationals of other contracting parties to the Charter unless they were EEC nationals. C VII 84 (U.K.).

taken the view that Article 15(2) applies to both the physically and the mentally handicapped.[712] This is clearly consistent with the English text ("disabled persons"), which can be construed as an abbreviated form of the phrase "physically and mentally disabled persons" used elsewhere in the text and title of Article 15. In contrast, the French text—"personnes *physiquement diminuées*"[713]—is equally clearly more limited. The object and purpose of the Charter support the wider interpretation taken from the English text, as do the *travaux préparatoires*.[714]

As far as the substance of the undertaking in Article 15(2) is concerned, three measures that may be taken are indicated in a nonexhaustive list in its text: the establishment of specialized placement services, the provision of facilities for sheltered employment, and measures to encourage employers to admit disabled persons to employment.[715] Some indication of the approach taken by the Committee of Independent Experts in determining whether a contracting party has adopted sufficient measures to comply with Article 15 is indicated by the sort of information that it has sought from contracting parties. It has asked for figures indicating the numbers and percentages of employable disabled who have returned to ordinary employment or have been provided sheltered employment[716] and has asked whether states have legislation obliging employers to take a certain percentage of disabled worker or to take back employees who have become disabled at work,[717] although it has not insisted upon such legislation.[718] Finally, the Committee of Independent Experts has sought information on the role played

[712]C I 208 (F.R.G.) and GC IV 11.

[713]Emphasis added.

[714]*Cf.* Bourlard, *supra* note 643, at 9. The title and introductory wording of Art. 15 were at one stage in the drafting expressly limited in both language texts to the "physically disabled." They were changed by the CMSC at its Ninth Session, April 1960, in both the English and French texts to their present wording to include the mentally disabled. The English text of Art. 15(2) was changed in the same way to achieve the same result. *Id.* It seems likely that the absence of any change to the French text of Art. 15(2) was accidental.

[715]The Parliamentary Assembly has recommended the addition of a third paragraph to Art. 15 giving the disabled the right to a properly planned place of work. Recommendation 839, TEXTS ADOPTED, September 1978.

[716]C I 73, C III 75 (Austria).

[717]C I 73 (Sweden, Norway), C I 208 (Ireland). An example of the first kind of legislation is U.K. Disabled Persons (Employment) Act 1944, sec. 9.

[718]Ireland, for example, has been found to comply with Art. 15(2) although it lacks legislation of either kind. C III 76 (Ireland).

by private organizations and the coordination of their work with that of the public services.[719]

Article 16: The Right of the Family to Social, Legal, and Economic Protection[720]

Article 16 reads: "With a view to ensuring the necessary conditions for the full development of the family, which is a fundamental unit of society, the Contracting Parties undertake to promote the economic, legal and social protection of family life by such means as social and family benefits, fiscal arrangements, provision of family housing, benefits for the newly married, and other appropriate means." By Article 16, the contracting parties undertake to "promote the economic, legal and social protection of family life." They do so with a view not, as in the case with all of the other undertakings in Part II, to ensuring the effective exercise of any right but "to ensuring the necessary conditions for the full development of the family." That this is not a significant difference is supported by the heading to Article 16 and the relevant paragraph in Part I of the Charter, which refer to the "right of the family to social, legal and economic protection."

The Committee of Independent Experts has explained its understanding of Article 16 as follows:

> This Article must be seen in conjunction with a number of other provisions in the Charter, such as Articles 14 and 17, that aim rather to give scope to the individual in our highly developed society, than to remedy a need, as Article 13 does. All these provisions are clearly founded on the idea that, since the industrial revolution and the social upheavals it produced, the modern state has had to take on certain new tasks and, in particular, as provided in Article 16, to create the living conditions necessary to give the family its full scope. The traditional affirmation of the family as the fundamental unit of society is maintained in Article 16, which however adds the idea that family welfare cannot henceforth be left to individual effort, as in the liberal epoch. Acceptance of these principles led the authors of Article 16 to lay down in it an obligation to implement a true family which was intended to operate in those fields where the needs of families become

[719]C II 55 (Ireland).
[720]Cf. UDHR, Art. 25(1), note 7 supra, ICESCR, Art. 10, note 29 supra, and ECHR, Art. 8, note 1 supra.

particularly pressing because of the restricted means they have available to meet them.

In the Committee's opinion a family policy of this sort must take the form of diversified action planned in harmony with and as a supplement to existing arrangements for assistance and social security.[721]

Some indication of the action expected of a contracting party is indicated by the examples given in the text of Article 16—the provision of "social and family benefits," etc.—and by the following general request for information made by the Committee of Independent Experts in the first cycle:

> The Committee observed, in examining the reports, that in view of the vast field covered by Article 16 as indicated above, it would not be able to judge whether or not a Contracting State that had accepted the Article complied with its undertakings unless that state provided in its report sufficient information on the various sectors concerned, in particular on the national system of family benefits, alleviation of certain expenses in favour of families, social and cultural amenities available to them, arrangements for their participation in the safeguarding of their interests, legal protection for the family, particularly in cases of material disputes, provision of family housing and the economic and social situation of families in national terms.[722]

Of the kinds of action, or "means," listed in Article 16, the Committee of Independent Experts has so far been particularly concerned with the level of family benefits[723] and assistance in the form of loans, etc., in respect to housing.[724] The list in Article 16 is not, however, an exhaustive one.[725] The Committee of Independent Experts added to it in the fourth cycle when it stressed the need, as a result of the increasing number of mothers going out to work, for the provision of day-care facilities for children, particularly sick children.[726] As

[721]C I 75.

[722]Id.

[723]C I 209 (Ireland).

[724]CIV 102 (Norway).

[725]Art. 16 is tautologous in this respect; having introduced a list of the kinds of action that may be taken by "by such means as," it ends by "and other appropriate means."

[726]C IV 101. The PA has recommended that Art. 16 be revised to require the provision of paid leave financed from public funds for parents to look after their children. Recommendation 839, TEXTS ADOPTED, September 1978.

far as "legal" protection is concerned, the Committee of Independent Experts has asked to be kept informed of developments in the law concerning the legal status of children[727] and of husbands and wives.[728] Article 16 contains no definition of the "family." Whether, for example, it includes the one-parent family—or whether this comes only within Article 17, as far as mothers and children are concerned—is not clear.[729] Relying, presumably, upon the Preamble to the Charter, the Committee of Independent Experts has interpreted Article 16 as incorporating "the principle of equality of treatment between men and women." In particular, it has suggested that a provision by which "a couple is entitled to the family income supplement only if the *man* is in full-time work" could be in breach of the Charter.[730]

So far, one has the impression that the Committee of Independent Experts is feeling its way in its interpretation of Article 16. It covers a "vast field"[731] and does so in extremely general wording which could be given a very extensive meaning or emphasized in certain directions and not in others. Whether it will be a "Cinderella" provision or whether it will grow into a commitment of some substance remains to be determined. No state has yet failed to comply with it.

[727]C IV 101 (Austria). There is an overlap in this respect with Art. 17 of the Charter and Art. 8 of the ECHR, note 1 *supra*. In the Marckx Case, 58 I.L.R. 561, 578–79 (Eur. Court of Human Rights 1979), the European Court of Human Rights indicated that the guarantee of "respect for family life" in Art. 8 of the ECHR, note 1 *supra*, meant (i) negatively, that the state should abstain from interfering in a person's family life (subject to Art. 8[2]) and (ii) positively, "that when the state determines in its domestic legal system the regime applicable to certain family ties such as those between an unmarried mother and her child, it must act in a manner calculated to allow those concerned to lead a normal family life."

[728]C IV 101 (Austria), referring in particular to the succession rights of spouses and to the law concerning community of goods.

[729]In the Marckx Case, note 727 *supra*, the European Court of Human Rights understood the guarantee of "respect for family life" in Art. 8 of the ECHR, note 1 *supra*, as drawing no distinction between the legitimate and the illegitimate family, so that both were protected. Accordingly, it held that a one-parent family (of mother and illegitimate child) was protected by Art. 8. In doing so, it referred, inter alia, to the Committee of Ministers' 1970 Resolution on the Social Protection of Unmarried Mothers and Their Children. CM Res. (70) 15.

[730]C V 111 (U.K.), C VI 103 (U.K.). This was the position in the U.K. before the Social Security Act, 1980. C VII 88 (U.K.).

[731]C I 75.

Article 17: The Right of Mothers and Children to social and
  Economic Protection

Article 17 reads: "With a view to ensuring the effective exercise
of the right of mothers and children to social and economic
protection, the Contracting Parties will take all appropriate and
necessary measures to that end, including the establishment or
maintenance of appropriate institutions or services." Article 17
draws no distinction on grounds of legitimacy; all mothers and
children are covered by it.[732] Moreover, it gives no indication of
the meaning of "children" in terms of their age. The Committee
of Independent Experts has suggested that Article 17 applies
only to children of preschool age when distinguishing between
Articles 17 and 7.[733] Insofar as it also has suggested that Article
17 applies to the legal status of children born out of wedlock,[734] it
seems that it can apply into adulthood where appropriate. It is
not clear from the text whether Article 17 is concerned with the
protection of mothers and children only in their relations with
each other, or whether there are, to some extent at least, two
separate concepts of the protection of mothers and the protection of children. The practice of the Committee of Independent
Experts suggests that the latter is the case.

The contracting parties agree to "take all appropriate and
necessary" measures of protection. It follows from this wording that a state action is not necessary to the extent that private sources provide assistance to mothers and children.[735] According to the text of Article 17, the "measures" to be taken
include "the establishment or maintenance of appropriate institutions or services." For this purpose, "institutions" include
homes, nurseries, etc.; "services" include guidance, advice, assistance, etc.[736] Other measures may be taken also, as indicated
in the following general statement by the Committee of Independent Experts of what national reports should contain:

---

[732]C I 77. Cf. the wording of paragraph 17 of Part I. The PA has recommended
that Art. 17 be revised by replacing "mother" by "parents." Recommendation 839,
TEXTS ADOPTED, September 1978.

[733]See note 407 supra.

[734]See note 745 infra.

[735]C I 77 (Italy).

[736]"Services" were added to "institutions" during the course of the drafting at the
suggestion of the U.K. in the CMSC, to indicate that measures other than the provision of physical facilities, such as homes, might be sufficient. Seventh Session, CMSC,
February 1958. The U.K. was particularly concerned that this addition be made
because it did not provide physical facilities for mothers.

In view of the very general character of Article 17, the Committee wished to make it clear that it expected to find in the government reports adequate information on general arrangements for the social and economic protection of mothers and children, economic assistance available to mothers before and after confinement, procedures for the establishment of paternity and maternity, maintenance arrangements for illegitimate children, guardianship, custody, the legitimation and inheritance rights of illegitimate children, the protection of unmarried mothers, the system of guardianship for orphans, the protection of homeless children, the measures taken in regard to adoption, and the treatment of juvenile delinquents.[737]

The Committee of Independent Experts has stated in more detail elsewhere what it considers Article 17 requires in certain of the above areas. Regarding the protection of unmarried mothers, it has stated that "the mere absence of unjust discrimination against unmarried mothers did not amount to 'ensuring the effective exercise of the right of mothers and children to social and economic protection' and . . . that special measures were necessary, such as the institution of services of guidance and assistance including financial assistance."[738] Applying this approach in the third cycle, the Committee of Independent Experts found Ireland to be in breach of Article 17.[739] Although unmarried mothers were treated equally wth married mothers in respect to social security benefits, maternity leave, and maternity care, this did not suffice in the absence of special protective measures of the kind indicated in the passage quoted above. The Committee of Independent Experts maintained this ruling in the fourth cycle.[740] Although Ireland had introduced a weekly allowance for unmarried mothers who kept their children, the amount was not sufficiently large to permit a change in the ruling.[741] With regard to the protection of mothers during pregnancy, the Committee of Independent Experts has stated that "the basic principle in this field is that mothers before and after confinement should be in a position of medical and financial secu-

[737]C I 77. *Cf.* C III 80.
[738]C III 80.
[739]C III 82 (Ireland).
[740]C IV 104 (Ireland).
[741]The CIE has not referred to this aspect of Art. 17 when continuing to find Ireland in breach of it in its more recent *Conclusions. See* C V 113 (Ireland) and C VI 105 (Ireland).

rity."[742] For a while Ireland was found to violate Article 17 in this respect also because not all mothers were eligible for maternity grants or allowances, although a mother without adequate resources was entitled to free medical care during confinement and for a certain time thereafter.[743] In the case of homeless children "the basic objective . . . should be to provide such children with the nearest possible approximation to a normal home environment."[744]

As to children born out of wedlock, the Committee of Independent Experts has stated:

a. while it might not be possible at the present time for such children to be treated before the law in exactly the same way as other children, a State, whose legislation manifestly discriminated against the first group of children, could not be held to satisfy its obligations under Article 17;

b. besides ensuring as near as possible equality of treatment, the State should also take such measures as are necessary and appropriate for the protection of children born out of wedlock, in view of their special needs.[745]

The main problem that has arisen in connection with children born out of wedlock has concerned inheritance to property. Three states—Austria, Ireland, and the U.K.—are in violation of the Charter because of their law in this area. Under Irish law,[746] an illegitimate child may succeed to his mother's property on her intestacy only if there are no surviving legitimate children of the mother. The Committee of Independent Experts has considered this to be a limitation "so restrictive as to seem almost punitive."[747] U.K. law during the first two cycles was identical to that of Ireland on this matter so that the U.K. was also found to be in violation of Article 17.[748] Although this restriction upon inheritance rights was later abolished by legislation for most of the U.K.,[749] it remains intact in the Isle of

---

[742]C III 80.

[743]C III 82, C IV 104. Maternity grants were available on the basis of a mother's national insurance payments or those of her husband; maternity allowances were available on the basis of the mother's payments only.

[744]C III 80.

[745]Id.

[746]Legitimacy Act 1931, sec. 9. Cf. A. SHATTER, FAMILY LAW IN THE REPUBLIC OF IRELAND 33 (1977).

[747]C III 81 (Ireland).

[748]C I 77 (U.K.) and C II 57 (U.K.).

[749]Family Law Reform Act 1969, sec. 14; Law Reform (Miscellaneous Provisions) (Scotland) Act 1968, sec. 4; Family Law Reform (NI) Order 1977, Art. 2, S.I. 1977 No. 1250 (NI 17).

Man, so that the Committee of Independent Experts has not altered its ruling for the U.K.[750] In the fourth cycle, the Committee of Independent Experts also ruled that "in the current state of society and of ideas about society reflected in law and regulations in the member states of the Council of Europe, a born-out-of-wedlock child cannot be regarded as enjoying adequate economic and social protection if he has no claim to inherit the estate of the father whose paternity has been established."[751] Austria was held to be in violation of Article 17 because its law did not sufficiently permit inheritance in such a case.[752]

This last instance of the Committee of Independent Experts' practice is of particular interest since it confirms what the Committee of Independent Experts had indicated earlier in the passage quoted above, viz., that Article 17 does not require absolute equality between children born in and out of wedlock. The matter is to be governed instead by the standards reflected in the law of states that are members of the Council of Europe. In recent years, these standards have consistently moved toward reducing or eliminating discrimination.[753] One question raised by this trend which has not been commented upon yet by the Committee of Independent Experts in its *Conclusions* is the relationship between Articles 16 and 17 in this respect. There is a need to define the family, an issue which the Committee of Independent Experts has yet to consider under Article 16.[754]

A basic first question, however, is whether Article 17 applies to the law concerning children born out of wedlock at all. The question is prompted by a difference in wording between Articles 16 and 17 of the Charter. Whereas the former refers to the "economic, *legal* and social protection"[755] of the family, the

----

[750]C VII 91 (U.K.).

[751]C IV 104 (Austria).

[752]*Id.* Under Austrian law, an illegitimate child has a right to the estate of his intestate father only in the absence of legitimate issue. C VI 105 (Austria).

[753]*See* European Convention on the Legal Status of Children Born Out of Wedlock 1975, *done* Oct. 15, 1975, 1976 Gr. Brit. Misc. No. 2 (Cmnd. 6358), Europ. T.S. 85. The Convention has so far been ratified by Austria, Cyprus, Denmark, Luxembourg, Norway, Portugal, Sweden, Switzerland, and the U.K. In the Marckx Case, note 727 *supra*, the European Court of Human Rights adopted the same approach.

[754]*See* note 729 *supra*.

[755]Emphasis added.

latter refers only to the "social and economic protection" of mothers and children. In the opinion of the Governmental Committee, the absence of a reference in Article 17 to "legal" protection means that "the existence of certain differences in legal status between children born out of wedlock and children born in wedlock should not be the deciding factor in concluding whether or not a contracting party was fulfilling its undertaking. . . ."[756] Although accepting that "the rapid and progressive elimination of any discrimination between various categories of children should be included in a contracting party's programme for social protection," the Governmental Committee "nevertheless felt that the problems arising from family law and from the law of inheritance did not enter into the sphere of Article 17."[757] The Committee of Independent Experts has rejected this interpretation:

> The Committee thought it was difficult to separate the social and economic protection of mothers and children from the legal provisions governing their situation; objectives of social policy in their regard could not be achieved without taking account of the rights granted to the persons protected and of the duties of those called on to ensure this protection.
>
> In this field, as in others, the law is not only the mirror of economic and social facts, but governs them through the way it regulates relationships in this area.
>
> It follows that, generally speaking, it is not possible to disregard the legal position of the mother and her child in establishing the extent of the social and economic protection on which they may call and in assessing the trends within the states in one important sector of the social policy which is the very object of Article 17 of the Charter.
>
> Clearly, if there happened to be any measures of legal protection which had no economic and social implications, the Committee would have to ignore them, but it very much doubted that such measures could exist. In any case as regards all the points raised in Conclusions III, in particular the right of succession and the position with regard to its family of a child born out of wedlock, it was quite certain that social considerations were overriding. As a result, the Committee stood by its previous verdict on this point.[758]

[756]GC III 8.
[757]*Id.*
[758]C IV 103.

The Committee of Independent Experts' claim that it is not possible to divorce the law from its economic and social consequences, which has been supported by the Parliamentary Assembly,[759] is clearly correct. This applies, however, to its impact upon family life (Article 16) as well as to the position of mothers and children (Article 17) so that it does not answer the question of the significance of the presence of "legal" in Article 16 and its absence in Article 17. The *travaux préparatoires* show that the drafters were not unaware of this obvious difference in wording; they do not, however, indicate what, if anything, it was intended to exclude from Article 17 and include in Article 16.[760] In one sense, all measures of protection, including those specifically mentioned in Article 17, are measures of "legal" protection in that they are based upon law or upon the exercise of administrative discretion authorized by law. In another sense, "legal" protection can be understood as meaning only access to the courts and such ancillary rights (legal aid, etc.) which make it effective. Between these two extremes is the view that "legal" protection relates to the personal rights that an individual has in the law of contract, tort, property, family law, inheritance, etc. There is evidence to suggest that at least one of the drafting states understood the concept in this last and quite common sense.[761] The most probable explanation is that there was no consensus of opinion on the matter; certainly if there was, it is not apparent. What is interesting is that the Report Form approved by the Committee of Ministers on the basis of which contracting parties draft their reports contains questions under Article 17

[759]*See* para. 20, Eur. Parl. Ass., 27th Sess., Doc. No. 3592 (1975). *Cf.* Kojanec, *Droit au Travail, Droit de la Famille à une Protection Sociale, Juridique et Economique, Droit de la Mère et de l'Enfant à une Protection Sociale et Econonique,* 5–6, paper presented to the Brussels Colloquium on the European Social Charter, Institut d'Etudes Européennes (1976).

[760]The reference to the "legal" position was inserted in Art. 16 at a late stage after the Ninth Session of the CMSC in April 1960. It was inserted either by that Committee or by the CM. A contemporaneous proposal to alter the text of Art. 17 so that it also would refer to "legal" protection was made and withdrawn without any reason for the proposal or the withdrawal being recorded.

[761]The British Government records of the drafting of the Charter contain a memorandum in which it is understood that "legal" protection in Art. 17 would relate to disabilities in law (e.g., in the law of inheritance) to which a person born out of wedlock might be subject. Whether the private opinion of one of the signatories to a multilateral treaty carries much weight in the interpretation of the treaty is doubtful; it is the consensus of opinion of the drafting states as a whole that counts. *See* A. McNair, The Law of Treaties 421 (2d ed. 1961).

on the legal position of children born out of wedlock.[762] This is an instance of subsequent practice on the part of the signatory states (and others) that can be taken into account in the interpretation of the Charter.[763] It supports the view that, whatever else may be included, the particular question of the legal position of children born out of wedlock is one covered by Article 17. It is true, of course, that this is a matter dealt with by Article 8 of the European Convention on Human Rights[764] and by the European Convention on the Legal Status of Children Born Out of Wedlock 1975.[765] The three treaties are not, however, mutually exclusive.

Article 18: The Right to Engage in a Gainful Occupation in the Territory of Other Contracting Parties

Article 18 is concerned with employment in the territory of a contracting party. It is not concerned with entry, whether for employment or other purposes.[766] Article 18 is thus the equivalent of Chapter IV of the European Convention on Establishment 1955[767] (headed "gainful occupation") and not of Chapter I of that Convention (headed "entry, residence and expulsion").[768] This limitation upon Article 18 presents no problem for nationals of parties to the Charter who are also members of the European Communities.[769] In addition, a person whose national state is a party to the European Convention on Establishment as well as to the Charter is helped by the fact that a party to that Convention must "facilitate," without being obliged to permit, "the entry into its territory by nationals of the other parties for the purpose of temporary visits."[770]

[762]Report Form, 69.

[763]*Cf.* Kojanec, *supra* note 759, at 4.

[764]*See* Marckx Case, note 727, *supra.*

[765]*See* note 54 of Chapter 1.

[766]Appendix to the Charter. *See also, e.g.,* C III 85 (Sweden).

[767]European Convention of Establishment (with Protocol), *done* Dec. 13, 1955, 1971 Gr. Brit. T.S. No. 1 (Cmnd. 4573), 529 U.N.T.S. 141.

[768]There is no provision in the Charter guaranteeing a right of entry (for nationals or others) into the territory of a contracting party. The right of a state's nationals to enter its territory for any purpose is protected by Art. 3(2) of the Fourth Protocol to the ECHR, *signed* March 20, 1952, 1954 Gr. Brit. Misc. No. 6 (Cmd. 6309), 590 U.N.T.S. 300.

[769]On freedom of movement and the right of establishment in Communities law, see K. LIPSTEIN, *supra* note 530, at 84–88, 142–45, and T. HARTLEY, EEC IMMIGRATION LAW (1979).

[770]European Convention on Establishment, Art. 1, note 767 *supra.* *See also* Art. 10 and secs. II(a) and V(a) of the Protocol to the Convention, note 767 *supra.* The

In the case of nationals of parties to the Charter that do not come within either of the above categories, there is no obligation to admit them.[771]

The existence of the detailed provisions of Chapter IV of the European Convention on Establishment presented the same problem during the drafting of the Charter for Article 18 as the existing and proposed European treaty law on social security had for Article 13.[772] Whereas the solution adopted in the case of Article 13 was to incorporate the detailed standards of European (and International Labor Organization) social security treaty law into the Charter by reference, there was little inclination to do the same in the case of Article 18. Although the inspiration of the Establishment Convention is apparent in one or two respects, Article 18 contains a distinct set of undertakings that are essentially different from those of the Establishment Convention. Whereas that Convention spells out particular standards of treatment of migrant workers that are based on the idea of equality of treatment with national workers, Article 18 does not.[773] Thus, paragraph (1) requires that existing regulations, whatever their content, be applied liberally, and paragraphs (2) and (3) require that the existing regulations, whatever they are, be simplified, etc., or liberalized respectively.

One further fact that should be mentioned concerning the European Convention on Establishment is that it has its own system of reports. This is based upon a Standing Committee composed of government officials. In view of its independence of the Charter system and the different content and approach of the Convention and the Charter, it is perfectly possible that a contracting party to both might be found to be in violation of the "gainful occupation" provisions of one but not of the other.

Article 18 applies *ratione personae* to nationals of the contracting parties; it does not apply to nationals of other states.[774]

Appendix to the Charter states that Art. 18(1) and para. 18 of Part I "do not prejudice the provisions of the European Convention on Establishment." The following eight parties to the Charter are also parties to the Establishment Convention: Denmark, the F.R.G., Ireland, Italy, Netherlands, Norway, Sweden, and the U.K.

[771]Subject, that is, to any treaties of friendship, etc., to the contrary.

[772]*See* note 588 *supra.*

[773]*Contrast* the position concerning the Charter and the European Code of Social Security, note 583 *supra.*

[774]C I 79.

Although, with the exception of paragraph (4), this limitation is not apparent from the text of Article 18, or from the general provision as to the scope of the Charter *ratione personae* in the Appendix,[775] which is stated not to apply to Article 18, the title to Article 18 suggests this. It also is evident from the *travaux préparatoires*[776] that Article 18 was intended to have the same scope as Paragraph 18 in Part I, which applies only to nationals of the contracting parties.[777] Article 18 creates an obligation for parties that accept it, or a part of it, vis-à-vis the nationals of all other contracting parties whether the latter states have accepted Article 18, or any part of it, or not.[778] Article 18 applies to refugees in accordance with the general rule in the Appendix to the Charter.[779] Article 18 also applies to the self-employed.[780] Although the wording of Article 18(3) and, to a lesser extent, Article 18(2) can be read as suggesting otherwise, it is clear from the *travaux préparatoires* that the self-employed were intended to be protected by Article 18 as a whole.[781]

"Territory" has been understood by the Committee of Independent Experts to include for the purposes of Article 19 oil rigs located on the continental shelf adjacent to the metropolitan territory of a contracting party, whether within its territorial waters or beyond it.[782] This is a permissible interpretation and one that can also be applied to Article 18. An oil rig may be regarded as a part of a state's territory for jurisdictional purposes if stationed within its exclusive economic zone or on its continental shelf.[783]

[775]*See* note 649 *supra*.

[776]The title to Art. 18 ("The rights to engage in a gainful occupation in the territory of other Contracting Parties") and its introductory wording ("With a view . . . undertake") were introduced in place of other wording in the 96th meeting of the Ministers' Deputies in March 1961 on a proposal of the Directorate of Legal Affairs of the CE for the specific purpose of bringing Art. 18 into line with para. 18 in this respect.

[777]*See* the Appendix to the Charter, para. 1.

[778]The CIE left this question open in *Conclusions I*, at 79, and has not returned to it since. Its practice in respect to Art. 18 is consistent with the sense of the text above.

[779]*See* note 649 *supra*.

[780]*Cf.* Laroque, *supra* note 591, at 5.

[781]The order of the paragraphs of Art. 18 was altered at the Seventh Meeting of the CMSC in February 1958 to make this clear at the suggestion of Belgium. Somewhat confusingly, Belgium had earlier successfully pressed an ad hoc working party of the CMSC to limit Art. 18 to wage earners.

[782]*See* note 846 *infra*. Presumably, a contracting party's ships and aircraft are also covered.

[783]*See* U.N. Convention on the Law of the Sea 1982, Arts. 60(2) & 80, U.N. Doc. A/CONF. 62/122; 21 I.L.M. 1261 (1982).

The Committee of Independent Experts has characterized paragraphs (1) to (3) of Article 18 as "dynamic."[784] Whereas paragraphs (2) and (3) of Article 18 can clearly be seen thus, this is not true of paragraph (1). It is submitted that the requirement is "to apply existing regulations in a spirit of liberality" at once and that the criterion of a "liberal" application of the regulations is a constant rather than a progressive one. So far as Article 18 is "dynamic," there is a limit to what is required of contracting parties. As the Committee of Independent Experts has stated, "a contracting state cannot be required to report further progress in every biennial report, if the liberal spirit in which existing rules are applied, the simplicity of formalities and the liberal nature of the regulations are already such that the state in question can be regarded as completely satisfying the undertakings entered into."[785] The progress that can be expected in a particular cycle is also dependent upon economic conditions.[786]

In Paragraph 18 in Part I, which parallels Article 18, the right of the nationals of one party to engage in a gainful occupation in the territory of another is said to be a right "on a footing of equality with the nationals of the latter." There is no express national treatment requirement in Article 18.[787] In the light of Paragraph 18, however, the Committee of Independent Experts has suggested that the "letter and spirit of Article 18 mean that the situation of nationals of States bound by the Charter should gradually become as far as possible like that of nationals." Whereas it is difficult to find anything in the "letter" of Article 18 to support this conclusion, it is reasonable, in the light of the objective set in Paragraph 18, to judge the "spirit of liberality" in which existing regulations are applied and what can be required of states by way of simplifying formalities, reducing charges, and liberalizing regulations by reference to the treatment that is afforded to nationals.[788] There is no requirement, however, that a contracting party should treat nationals of other contracting parties better than it treats nationals of third states.

Paragraph 18 of Part I has also proved significant because

[784]C II 59. As to the meaning of "dynamic," see note 27 of Chapter I.
[785]Id.
[786]C III 84, GC III 8. Cf. GC VII 13. See also Laroque, supra note 591, at 5.
[787]C II 60.
[788]See also the commentary to Art. 18(3), note 812 infra.

of the exception that it allows in respect to "restrictions based upon cogent economic or social reasons."[789] This has been read into Article 18 by the Committee of Independent Experts and applied by it in considering whether certain restrictions upon the employment of aliens are permissible under Article 18(1), (2), and (3). Given that Paragraph 18 is stating an objective which may go beyond the specific terms of the obligation in Article 18 and can be taken not to fall below its requirements, this is a reasonable interpretation. The same result would obtain, however, by the application of Article 31, which allows restrictions to Article 18 (as well as Paragraph 18) based, inter alia, upon "public interest" or *ordre public*.[790] Applying the exception borrowed from Paragraph 18, the Committee of Independent Experts has held that "economic or social reasons might justify restricting the employment of aliens to specific types of jobs in certain occupational and geographic sectors."[791] They could not justify, however, restrictions upon employment that distinguished between the nationals of different contracting parties or that gave better treatment to nationals of noncontracting parties than they gave to nationals of some or all contracting parties. Thus, Ireland was found to be in violation of Article 18(2) in the third cycle, despite its evident employment difficulties, because it applied more liberal rules to the employment of British and Commonwealth nationals, some of whom were not even nationals of a contracting party, than it applied to nationals of other contracting parties.[792] In the fourth cycle, the Committee of Independent Experts found the U.K. to be in violation of Article 18(2) because of the rules concerning the issue of work permits to nonpatrials (other than nationals of European Communities members) under the Immigration Act of 1971.[793] It considered that there were no "economic or social reasons" that could justify these "considerably more stringent restrictions."[794] Bearing in mind the racial aspects to this legislation,[795] this is one instance in which "social" reasons

[789]This wording is taken from European Convention on Establishment 1955, Art. 10, note 767 *supra*.

[790]*See also* the commentary to Art. 18(3), note 812 *infra*.

[791]C II 60.

[792]C III 85 (Ireland), C IV 109 (Ireland). *See also* C III 86 (U.K.).

[793]C IV 111 (U.K.).

[794]*Id.*

[795]*See* I. MacDonald, The New Immigration Law 14–15 (1972).

were relevant as well as economic ones.[796] The Committee of Independent Experts has acknowledged that "economic or social reasons" may be particularly pressing in times of economic recession such as those experienced by the contracting parties in the years reported upon (1972–73) in the fourth cycle.[797] This is in accord with the statement made by the Governmental Committee interpreting Article 18 in the third cycle:

> 41. In Part I, it is clearly specified that nationals of a Contracting Party have the right to engage in a gainful occupation in the territory of any one of the others on a footing of equality with nations "subject to restrictions based on cogent economic or social reasons." These reasons, which may be of a persistent character in some States or exist intermittently in others, are usually the same as those described in the biennial reports with reference to Article 1, paragraph 1, so that it should not be necessary to repeat them with reference to Article 18. They must be realistically assessed by each government in relation to its economic situation and the problems it has to face. In any case, only the government concerned can decide if and when restrictions should be introduced or relaxed.
>
> 42. It would seem natural, if and when the economic situation makes a crisis appear imminent, to act in such a way as to limit its adverse effects. It is with this end in mind that Contracting Parties may reasonably limit the numbers of foreign workers. In this context, the Committee would wish to emphasise that national reports have shown that the governments of Contracting Parties have adopted a particularly liberal attitude in this matter and have frequently regularised the status of persons present on their territory. Such an attitude is nevertheless influenced by the economic climate; and regulations may necessarily be applied more strictly during periods of recession or crisis. The Committee however expects that the Governments of Contracting Parties will not have recourse to the restrictions mentioned in paragraph 18 of Part I without taking full account of the aim set out in Article 18 of Part II.[798]

The approach of the Governmental Committee differs from that of the Committee of Independent Experts, however, in one important respect. Whereas the Governmental Committee

---

[796]U.K. Government records show that the U.K. also had in mind under the heading of "social reasons" during the drafting of the Charter the situation where an alien is refused a renewal of his permit because he proves to be an unsatisfactory worker.

[797]C IV 107.

[798]GC III 8.

is of the opinion that "only the government concerned can decide if and when restrictions should be introduced or relaxed," the Committee of Independent Experts clearly does not take this view and has questioned the measures taken by a number of contracting parties. It has been critical, for example, of Denmark for not granting any work permits during part of the fourth cycle to foreigners, including nationals of contracting parties, unless they were nationals of members of the European Communities or Nordic States. Since the number of nationals of contracting parties other than such states seeking work permits was likely to be small (only Austrian and Cypriot nationals were concerned), the Committee of Independent Experts "found it hard to accept that economic arguments could justify such restrictive provisions in their case."[799] The correct approach, it is believed, is that contracting parties are answerable to the supervising authorities who have the final decision on the question whether there are good economic or social reasons to justify the action taken, but that a "margin of appreciation" doctrine applies.[800] Provided the contracting parties submit in their reports the necessary information allowing the supervisory organs to take a decision— and the onus is upon the contracting party to provide this information—the latter should only find against them if there is no doubt in their minds that the action cannot be justified on economic or social grounds.

In all seven cycles, the Committee of Independent Experts has treated compliance with Article 18(1), (2), and (3) under one heading. This is the only case in which it has consistently not treated compliance with particular paragraphs of Part II separately.[801] Although the obligations in the first three paragraphs are not easy to distinguish, the Committee of Independent Experts has managed to do so in some of its comments, and it is proposed to follow this approach in the following pages.

Article 18(1): Liberal Applications of Existing Regulations
By Article 18(1), the contracting parties undertake "to apply existing regulations in a spirit of liberality." Article 18(1) is

---

[799]C IV 108 (Denmark). *Cf.* C VI 110 (Denmark).

[800]*Cf.* that which applies in the interpretation of the ECHR; *see* Ireland v. U.K., 58 I.L.R. 190, 278–79 (Eur. Court of Human Rights 1978).

[801]It treated the three paragraphs of Art. 11 together in the first cycle but has distinguished between them since.

concerned, therefore, with administrative practice rather than the law. A party may comply with Article 18(1) even though it has very strict rules about the employment of aliens in law[802] provided that these rules allow some administrative discretion and this is exercised generously.[803] Thus, the U.K. was found to comply with Article 18(1) because its admittedly strict rules concerning the taking of employment, the renewal of work permits, and the lifting of restrictions were applied "in a distinctly liberal spirit."[804] The percentage of successful applications for work permits is a good indication of a liberal or nonliberal spirit.[805] Whether the imposition of restrictions upon employment is subject to Article 18(1) or Article 18(3) will depend on whether they are subject to administrative discretion or required by law. In the former case, Article 18(1) applies; in the latter case, the question is one of liberalizing the law in the sense of Article 18(3). Although this distinction is not always drawn in the practice of the Committee of Independent Experts,[806] it seems that it follows from the wording of the two provisions. One consequence is that more can be expected from the outset of a contracting party whose law leaves a lot of discretion to its administrative authorities than it can of a party which has detailed rules.

Article 18(2): Simplification of Regulations and Reduction of Abolition of Charges

By Article 18(2), the contracting parties undertake "to simplify existing formalities and to reduce or abolish chancery dues and other charges payable by foreign workers or their employers." The Committee of Independent Experts has characterized this undertaking as "dynamic," although there is, as the Committee of Independent Experts has recognized, clearly a limit to what can be done in respect to both the simplification of regulations

---

[802]The term "regulations" in Art. 18(1) is to be read generally so as to include any legal rule, whether its source is legislation, delegated legislation, or case law.

[803]*Cf.* Laroque, *supra* note 591, at 5.

[804]C III 86 (U.K.).

[805]*See, e.g.,* C III 85 (Ireland). The CIE has expressed satisfaction in cases where the contracting party has reported that over 90% of applications are successful, although the percentage of successful applications may be due to the liberality of the regulations themselves. The GC has questioned the CIE's reliance on the numbers of working permits issued or refused each year because "the number of permits issued depended on the period of validity of the permits and gave no indication of the actual numbers of migrant workers accepted in any one year." GC V 14.

[806]*See, e.g.,* C III 83.

and the reduction or abolition of charges.[807] As far as the latter is concerned, "charges" include charges for work permits or other documents or a tax upon the import of a worker's tools.[808] Small administrative charges for work permits and other documents have been held to be consistent with the Charter[809] as has a deposit that a worker must leave with the Austrian authorities to cover the cost of his return rail fare.[810] If, as is true of almost all of the contracting parties, no dues or charges are payable, there can be no question of their reduction and Article 18(2) is necessarily complied with.

It is not easy to draw a clear distinction between the obligation in Article 18(2) and that in Article 18(3) "to liberalise . . . regulations governing the employment of foreign workers." As the Committee of Independent Experts has stated, "if these two paragraphs undoubtedly differ, they also overlap in some respects in that simplication of formalities is normally indicative of a liberalisation of regulations, and conversely the latter is hard to achieve without simplifying the formalities."[811] Where a contracting party accepts both undertakings, the borderline between them is not very important; where, as in the case of Austria, it accepts only one, it is. It appears that the essential distinction between the two is that Article 18(2) is concerned with the procedural rules governing the employment of migrant workers, whereas Article 18(3) is concerned with substantive restrictions that may be imposed upon such employment. On this interpretation, Article 18(2) concerns such matters as the documentation and charges required for work permits. On the other hand, Article 18(3) concerns the grounds for allowing a work permit or a change of employment and any substantive restrictions imposed in each case

---

[807]Cf. note 27 supra. It was agreed by the CM during the drafting of the Charter that no further action need be taken under Art. 18(2) "where existing formalities are already simple." CM (61) 95 rev., 3.

[808]C III 80 (U.K.). Cf. Annex III, ILO. Migration for Employment Convention (Revised) (ILO Convention No. 97), adopted July 1, 1949, 120 U.N.T.S. 71.

[809]C III 83 (Austria). The CM agreed that this "undertaking in respect of other charges does not preclude the imposition of nominal charges to meet direct administrative costs involved." CM (61) 95 rev., 3. In the sixth cycle, the CIE noted the high cost of an Austrian visa and asked Austria whether it intended to waive, or at least reduce, the charge made for migrant workers from other contracting parties. C VI 109 (Austria).

[810]C IV 107 (Austria). The deposit must be paid only if the worker's country of origin is very far away.

[811]C III 83 (Austria).

(e.g., limitations upon the duration or scope of the kind of employment permitted).

In the seventh cycle, five parties—France, F.R.G., Ireland, Sweden, and the U.K.—were found to be in breach of Article 18(2).[812]

Article 18(3): Liberalization of Regulations

By Article 18(3), the contracting parties undertake "to liberalise, individually or collectively, regulations governing the employment of foreign workers."[813] Article 18(3) does not require contracting parties to comply at once in their law with a particular standard of liberality. Article 18(3) is a "dynamic" provision, the essence of which, in this case, is continual improvement to a certain level after which the obligation is to maintain the status quo.[814] The Committee of Independent Experts has identified a number of restrictions that need to be absent or eliminated before that level has been reached and before, therefore, a contracting party's obligation to show overall[815] improvement in each cycle ceases.[816] These are restrictions limiting work permits to particular jobs;[817] restrictions preventing workers from changing their job in the first year of employment, at least where the restriction prevents changes in the same occupation in the same geographic area;[818] restrictions requiring a work permit to be obtained before entry into the country;[819] restrictions requiring a per-

[812]C VII 93–97.

[813]This text had read, in an early 1959 Secretariat version, "individually or collectively *within the framework of appropriate international organisations.*" The final text is broader.

[814]Despite occasional statements by the CIE that can be interpreted to mean that it is applying a particular standard of liberality in Art. 18(3) (e.g., C III 84 [Ireland]), the general statements by the CIE in *Conclusions II,* at 60 and 61, suggest that this is not so except in the sense that there is a standard of liberality which, when reached, does not have to be improved upon further.

[815]Regression in a particular respect is permissible if there is an overall improvement in the cycle. C IV 110 (Sweden).

[816]Restrictions may exist in law or in practice. Insofar as they result from practice, they are relevant to Art. 18(1) and to the requirement of "a spirit of liberality" in that provision.

[817]C II 60, C III 83, C III 84 (Ireland). *Cf.* Laroque, *supra* note 591, at 6.

[818]C III 84 (Denmark), C II 85 (Sweden). In the fifth and sixth cycles the CIE found against the U.K. partly because of the "rule whereby a migrant worker (other than a European Communities national) must remain in the same type of employment during the first four years of his residence in the U.K." C VI 115 (U.K.). *Cf.* C VI 111 (France) (migrant worker restricted in choice of job and location for first four years).

[819]C III 83, C III 84.

son who wishes to change his job to apply for a permit in the same way as he applied for the permit for the first job;[820] and a "requirement that an alien may not apply for a vacancy if there is a national applicant."[821] A complete ban on the granting of work permits to nationals of other contracting parties or to the members of the family of such persons already holding work permits has also been held to be contrary to Article 18(3).[822] Restrictions generally should be relaxed or abolished as the worker's length of employment in the contracting party increases.[823]

The Governmental Committee has questioned whether certain of the restrictions that the Committee of Independent Experts has criticized might in fact benefit foreign workers so that their existence, rather than their absence, is indicative of a "liberal" approach. In its third *Report,* it stated:

> The Committee felt obliged to point out that certain measures which might appear to restrict the freedom to aliens to engage in a gainful occupation, in fact assured them of better social protection by defending them against undesirable practices and misleading publicity. For example, the restriction of the exercise of a gainful occupation to foreigners who were in possession of a work permit or, where appropriate, to those whose intention of seeking employment was known before their entry into the national territory, and, consequently, the refusal to permit employers to recruit foreigners who have entered the territory illegally or as "false tourists," could be considered as measures to combat clandestine immigration, to check the activities of smugglers of foreign labour and finally to afford justice to those whose applications has been made in due form and who were waiting their turn.[824]

On the question of a restriction by which a person is not allowed to take employment unless this has been agreed before he enters the country, the Governmental Committee

---

[820]*See* C III 86 (U.K.).

[821]C V 117 (Denmark), C VI 110 (Denmark). Cyprus, which has not accepted Art. 18, has a restriction of this kind. *See* note 913 *infra.* Note that the Charter permits the reservation of certain occupations for nationals. *See* note 14 of Chapter IV.

[822]C VI 111 (France). *Contra* C VII 94 (France). *Cf.* the ruling against the F.R.G. under Art. 18(1) and (3). C VI 112 (F.R.G.). *Cf.* the ruling against the F.R.G. under Art. 18(1) and (3). C VI 112 (F.R.G.). *But cf.* C VII 95 (F.R.G.).

[823]C II 60.

[824]GC III 9. See the remarks of the International Confederation of Free Trade Unions (ICFTU), which did not "entirely agree" with the GC on this point. GC III, Appendix III.

agreed that "it was not desirable that regulations should be applied so rigidly as to totally and permanently prevent any foreigner lawfully resident in the territory of a Contracting Party for a considerable time from ever being able to take up a gainful occupation solely on the ground that any work permit had invariably to be obtained *before* arrival."[825] In its opinion, "the implementation of such provisions called for some flexibility on the part of the competent authorities, though only the latter were competent to decide whether the reasons for a belated demand justified derogation of the regulation."[826] The Governmental Committee also commented upon the Committee of Independent Experts' criticism of regulations "restricting work permits to a given sector or stipulating that a foreign worker's first contract should require him to work for a set period in a given job for the same employers."[827] The Governmental Committee stressed that "measures of this kind were primarily designed to protect the worker."[828] It added that "the breaking of a contract (which is not as frequent as is supposed) did not generally result in the obligatory return of the worker to his country of origin. In accordance with the principle of equal treatment, he was normally free to look for new employment and if he were unable to obtain it immediately he had the right to unemployment benefits under the prescribed conditions."[829]

It is not clear how far contracting parties are required to go in treating the nationals of other contracting parties equally with their own. As noted earlier,[830] the Committee of Independent Experts has suggested in respect to Article 18 as a whole that "the situation of nationals of states bound by the Charter should gradually become *as far as possible* like that of nationals."[831] The phrase "as far as possible" clearly means that absolute equality of treatment is not essential.[832] This also follows from the interpretation of Article 31 adopted by the

[825]GC III 9.
[826]*Id.*
[827]*Id.*
[828]*Id.*
[829]*Id.*
[830]*See* note 788 *supra.*
[831]C II 60.

[832]*Cf.* the meaning of "as far as possible" in Art. 19(6) of the Charter, note 945 *infra.*

Committee of Ministers during the drafting of the Charter, by which certain occupations may be reserved to nationals.[833]

Article 18(4): The Right of Nationals to Leave the Country for Employment

By Article 18(4), the contracting parties "recognise the right of their nationals to leave the country to engage in a gainful occupation in the territories of the other Contracting Parties." All of the contracting parties which have accepted Article 18(4) have been found in compliance. Such restrictions as exist which affect departure for employment purposes have been held to be justified on grounds of "public interest" under Article 31. Thus, the restrictions in Austrian law whereby a national will not be allowed a passport if, inter alia, it is reasonably suspected that he wishes to avoid a criminal prosecution or sentence or that his residence abroad would endanger national security were considered justified on this ground.[834]

Article 19: The Right of Migrant Workers and Their Families to Protection and Assistance[835]

Whereas Article 18 is concerned with access to employment, Article 19 focuses upon other kinds of assistance for migrant workers who already have jobs or who are looking for them. It covers emigrant and immigrant workers and protects members of their families as well as themselves. In the case of immigrant workers, it calls to some extent for preferential treatment, not just equality of treatment with nationals.[836]

---

[833]*See* note 14 of Chapter IV.

[834]C III 86. The second of the above restrictions is more accurately regarded in the terms of Art. 31 as being justified on grounds of "national security." The restriction reported by Italy in its First Report by which a national may be refused permission to leave if he has not met his military service obligations can be taken to be within Art. 31 also.

[835]The UDHR and the ICESCR contain no provisions on the treatment of migrant workers. *Cf.*, in respect to Art. 19(1),(2),(4),(5),(7),(9), ILO Migration for Employment Convention (Revised) 1949, note 808 *supra,* and ILO Migrant Workers (Supplementary Provisions) Convention (ILO Convention No. 143), *adopted* June 24, 1975 (Cmnd. 6674). For the extensive European Communities law on migrant workers, *see* K. LIPSTEIN, *supra* note 530, at 84–128, and D. WYATT AND A. DASHWOOD, THE SUBSTANTIVE LAW OF THE EEC Chaps. 13 & 14 (1980). The PA has recommended that Art. 19 be strengthened. Recommendation 839, TEXTS ADOPTED, September 1978.

[836]C I 81, C V 123. *Cf.* Laroque, *supra* note 591, at 8.

Most of the undertakings in Article 19 are modeled upon the International Labor Organization Migration for Employment Convention (Revised) 1949.[837] Some are based upon, or parallel, undertakings in the European Convention on Establishment 1955.[838] For parties that are also members of the European Communities, some of the undertakings in Article 19 coexist with those in Communities law.[839] The Council of Europe has added to Article 19 by the 1977 European Convention on the Legal Status of Migrant Workers.[840]

Article 19 applies to the nationals of the contracting parties; it does not apply to the nationals of other states.[841] It applies to the former differently from one paragraph to another so that in some cases the national must be "lawfully within" the territory of the contracting party concerned, in others "lawfully residing within" or "permitted to establish himself in" that territory, and in yet others does not have to be there at all. Its nonapplication to nonnationals of contracting parties follows from the limited wording of the equivalent Paragraph 19 of Part I of the Charter and is consistent with the scope of Article 18[842] and the other provisions of Part II also.[843] Article 19 applies to refugees in accordance with the general rule in the Appendix to the Charter.[844] It applies to the self-employed for those contracting parties that accept Article 19(10) to this effect.

The Committee of Independent Experts has understood Article 19 as applying to migrant workers on oil rigs located on the continental shelf adjacent to a contracting party's metropolitan territory in the North Sea and to do so whether the oil rig is within the contracting party's territorial sea or not.[845] It appears permissible to regard such rigs as a part of a state's territory for the jurisdictional purposes of the Charter.[846]

---

[837]Note 808 supra. This has since been supplemented by the ILO Migrant Workers (Supplementary Provisions) Convention 1975, note 835 supra.

[838]Note 767 supra.

[839]See the references in note 835 supra.

[840]European Convention on the Legal Status of Migrant Workers, done Nov. 24, 1977, Europ. T.S. No. 93.

[841]C I 81. Cf. Laroque, supra note 591, at 8.

[842]Cf. the (clumsy) introductory wording common to Arts. 18 & 19.

[843]See the rule ratione personae applying to Part II generally, note 649 supra.

[844]See note 649 supra.

[845]C IV 113.

[846]Cf. note 782 supra in respect to Art. 18.

Article 19(1): Services to Assist Migrant Workers: Action to Prevent Misleading Propaganda

By Article 19(1), the contracting parties undertake in respect to migrant workers "to maintain or to satisfy themselves that there are maintained adequate and free services to assist such workers, particularly in obtaining accurate information, and to take all appropriate steps, so far as national laws and regulations permit, against misleading propaganda relating to emigration and immigration." Article 19(1) applies to emigrant and immigrant workers.[847] It obliges a contracting party (1) to ensure the existence of services to assist migrant workers coming into its territory and (2) to take steps to prevent misleading propaganda or information being given about emigration and immigration. Both obligations are taken, almost word for word, from the equivalent provisions of the International Labor Organization Migration for Employment Convention (Revised) 1949.[848]

The first obligation requires contracting parties to provide the necessary services themselves or to "satisfy themselves" that they are provided privately. In practice, a combination of public and private assistance is common.[849] Services must be provided both before and after migration and must be "adequate and free." Their adequacy is to be determined by their ability to meet the demands placed upon them and by the kind of assistance provided. The assistance should consist of "accurate information," preferably in the worker's mother language,[850] about employment prospects and conditions and about other matters that will concern a migrant, for example, housing, education, and health facilities.[851] The obligation is not limited to the giving of information; it includes also the giving of advice and the receipt of complaints.[852] In general

[847]C I 81, 82, C II 195. In the case of immigrant workers, it does not seem to matter where they migrate from so long as they are nationals of a contracting party.

[848]*See* note 808 *supra.* Arts. 2 & 3 respectively. *See also* the Annexes to the ILO Migration for Employment Convention (Revised) 1949, note 808 *supra,* and the Migration for Employment Recommendation (Revised) 1949.

[849]In Austria, for example, a federal Migration Officer (*Wanderungsamt*) provides guidance in respect to emigration; government employment offices, the Austrian Trade Union Federation, and other public and private bodies offer assistance in respect to immigration.

[850]C I 213 (F.R.G.).

[851]C II 195 (Cyprus), C III 87 (Cyprus).

[852]This was understood during the drafting of Art. 2, ILO Migration for Employment Convention (Revised) 1949, note 808 *supra,* upon which Art. 19(1) is based. 32 ILC RP 579–80.

terms, it includes "all the services of advice and assistance to migrant workers except those covered by the more specific provisions of paragraphs 2–9" of Article 19.[853] Assistance in the form of housing, for example, comes within Article 19(4).[854] Equality of treatment with nationals in the provision of services is not the test of compliance with Article 19(1); what is expected are measures related to the special needs of the migrant.[855]

A contracting party does not need to ensure that the required services exist in respect to immigration to and from all other contracting parties; it is sufficient that they are appropriate to the prevailing patterns of emigration and immigration. This was the view finally taken by the Committee of Independent Experts in the case of Ireland. In its First Report, Ireland had indicated that there was very little immigration into Ireland by nationals from other contracting parties and that virtually all of the emigration from Ireland to other contracting parties was to the U.K. No public services were provided for intending emigrants or immigrants; there were, however, about forty private emigrant bureaus spread throughout the country providing a free advisory service to intending emigrants to the U.K. or elsewhere, although it was geared particularly to emigration to the U.K. In the first cycle, the Committee of Independent Experts rejected Ireland's argument that it was not required to have services for the nationals of all contracting parties; adequate services were needed for Irish workers who might want to work in a contracting party other than the U.K. and for persons who wished to immigrate to Ireland from contracting parties generally.[856] This approach was confirmed by a general statement in the second cycle in which the Committee of Independent Experts "reaffirmed that a contracting party could not be released from obligations entered into under the Charter by reason of the reduced volume of migratory movements affecting it."[857] In the same cycle, however, it found that Italy had complied with Article 19(1) although it had provided no infor-

[853]C IV 114 (F.R.G.).

[854]*See* note 918 *infra.*

[855]C I 82 (Norway). An example of the sort of service particularly appropriate for migrant workers is that provided by the network of advice centers established by the West German Confederation of Trade Unions which give advice on questions of labor law and social insurance. C IV 114 (F.R.G.).

[856]C I 213 (Ireland).

[857]C II 195. *Cf.* C II 208.

mation about services for immigrant workers coming to Italy because their numbers were minimal.[858] In the third cycle, the Committee of Independent Experts was prepared to view the Irish situation more generously. Ireland had reported that the Employment Agencies Act 1972, which provides for measures combating misleading advertising concerning, inter alia, emigration and immigration, had been enacted and that a booklet for foreign immigrant workers giving information and advice about social services, taxation, etc., had been produced. On the basis of these developments the Committee of Independent Experts concluded provisionally that Ireland complied with Article 19(1) in view of the small number of immigrants into Ireland and the fact that the large majority of emigrants went to the U.K.; it added that "if significant changes in the volume of immigration or in the orientation of the emigration occurred this might lead to the revision of the position because such changes would imply the obligation for Ireland . . . to create true services for the aid of immigrants and emigrants."[859] The same more flexible approach, which gains support from the wording "*adequate* . . . services,"[860] is apparent in the fourth cycle, in which the Committee of Independent Experts noted in the case of Italy that the number of migrant workers lawfully in Italy had risen and was "though still small, no longer insignificant" and that it had information that there was "clandestine immigration" into Sicily.[861] It asked Italy to "keep it informed of the situation," implying that more might be expected of Italy under Article 19(1) in the light of these developments. In fact, Italy later reported to the satisfaction of the Independent Experts that the immigration in question was not from contracting parties to the Charter.[862]

The use of the term "propaganda" in the second obligation is misleading since it has nothing to do with activities commonly associated with a Minister of Propaganda. Instead, it is concerned with information about employment and other prospects and conditions that might mislead intending migrant workers, particularly that given by employers and employment agencies. The U.K., for example, has complied with

[858]C II 63 (Italy).
[859]C III 89 (Ireland). *See* C VI 117 (Ireland) (full compliance).
[860]Emphasis added.
[861]C IV 114 (Italy).
[862]C V 124 (Italy).

Article 19(1) by reporting on: (1) section 14 of the Trade Descriptions Act 1968, which makes it a criminal offense for a person in the course of any trade or business to make false or misleading statements concerning, inter alia, employment placement and related services, and (2) its practice of investigating any complaints by a migrant worker that he has been misled.[863] Austria has been found to comply with this obligation as far as emigration is concerned by laws prohibiting the giving of advice for reward on matters of emigration especially in respect of conditions of life, work, and residence in foreign countries and by the active program of advice operated by the Federal Ministry of the Interior for intending emigrants. Although Austria has no comparable laws or programs in respect to immigration, the Committee of Independent Experts accepted that the lack of evidence of dishonest recruitment practices and the existence of a pre-entry work permit system, by which work permits are given only in the case of proven job offers and which acted as a disincentive to misleading propaganda, were sufficient.[864] Although Article 19(1) refers to "propaganda relating to emigration and immigration" without qualification, this is to be read in the present context as being limited to misleading information that might affect a person intending to migrate for employment purposes to the territory of a contracting party. The wording "so far as national laws and regulations permit" makes allowance for constitutional or other laws in the law of the contracting parties protecting freedom of speech.[865] It does not permit laws that substantially limit or undermine the obligation to control misleading propaganda.[866] As in the case of the first

---

[863]Second U.K. Report, at 149, C II 63 (U.K.), C III 87 (U.K.), C IV 114 (U.K.).

[864]C IV 113 (Austria).

[865]*Cf.* the comment by the U.K. in the drafting of Art. 3 of the ILO Migration for Employment Convention (Revised) 1949. 32 ILC RP 580. A workers' delegate to the TC suggested that the wording should be interpreted as relating "solely" to the liberty of the press. REC PROC TC 224.

[866]Italy suggested at the TC that the wording meant "within the framework of and according to the methods prescribed by national laws and regulations." REC PROC TC 224. During the drafting of Art. 3 of the ILO Migration for Employment Convention (Revised) 1949, note 808 *supra*, a similarly worded amendment proposed by Italy with the intention of avoiding the possibility that the wording "so far as national laws and regulations permit" might allow substantial inroads upon the obligation that Art. 3 of the Convention contained attracted considerable sympathy but was not adopted because it presented difficulties in other respects. 32 ILC RP 580.

obligation in Article 19(1), the wording "appropriate" measures supports an interpretation that looks to the existing patterns of migration when determining what steps need to be taken.

Article 19(2): Assistance to Migrant Workers in Respect to Their Journey

By Article 19(2), the contracting parties undertake in respect to migrant workers "to adopt appropriate measures within their own jurisdiction to facilitate the departure, journey and reception of such workers and their families, and to provide, within their own jurisdiction, appropriate services for health, medical attention and good hygenic conditions during the journey." Like Article 19(1), Article 19(2) imposes obligations upon contracting parties in respect to both emigrant and immigrant workers.[867] Like Article 19(1) also, it imposes two distinct obligations, which are again taken in substance from the International Labor Organization Migration for Employment Convention (Revised) 1949.[868]

The first obligation is to "adopt appropriate measures within their own jurisdiction to facilitate the departure, journey and reception" of migrant workers and, where appropriate, "their families."[869] It applies to organized migration and to migration by individuals.[870] By "jurisdiction" is meant "territorial jurisdiction."[871] Some indication of what are "appropriate" measures is probably to be found in the meaning of the same term in the International Labor Organization Migration for Employment Convention (Revised) 1949.[872] There they are stated to

[867]*See further* on the scope of Art. 19(2) in this respect, the commentary on Art. 19(1).

[868]Arts. 4 & 5 of the ILO Migration for Employment Convention (Revised) 1949, note 808 *supra. See also* the Annexes to the ILO Convention and the Migration for Employment Recommendation (Revised) 1949.

[869]The Charter does not require a party to admit the family of a migrant worker with him. There is an obligation to "facilitate . . . the reunion" of a migrant worker and his family. Art. 19(6). Presumably Art. 19(2) applies when the members of a migrant worker's family migrate at a different time from the worker.

[870]C I 214 (F.R.G.), C IV 115.

[871]This was the meaning of the same term recorded in Art. 5 of the ILO Migration for Employment Convention (Revised) 1949, note 808 *supra*, 32 ILC RP 582. It can be taken to have the same meaning in Art. 4, *id.*, which is the source of this part of Art. 19(2). Aircraft, ships, and oil rigs of a state's registration or located within its exclusive economic zone or on its continental shelf are within its "jurisdiction." *Cf.* notes 782 & 783 *supra*.

[872]*Id.* Art. 4 and Annexes I (Art. 6) and II (Art. 7).

include the simplification of administrative formalities; the provision of interpretation services; any necessary assistance during an initial period in the settlement of the migrants and their families; and the safeguarding of the welfare of migrants and their families during the journey, particularly on board ship. The Migration for Employment Recommendation (Revised) 1949, which supplements the Convention but which is not binding, is more detailed. It lists as "appropriate" measures the provision of adequate food and clothing on arrival where necessary, the provision of vocational training so as to enable the migrant to obtain the qualifications necessary for employment in the country of immigration, and the provision of access to schools for migrants and members of their families.[873] It also suggests that migrants and their families should be assisted in obtaining access to recreation and welfare facilities and that special facilities of these kinds should be available to them during the initial period of settlement.[874]

The Committee of Independent Experts has been particularly concerned with the "reception" of immigrant workers. For this purpose, it has taken the period of "reception" to be "the time of arrival and the period immediately following, that is to say during the weeks in which immigrant workers and their families find themselves in a particularly difficult position."[875] By "reception," the Committee of Independent Experts has understood assistance both in respect to the placement and integration of migrants in employment and in overcoming initial problems such as lack of immediate accommodation, illness, or shortage of money.[876] It has asked for information about schooling facilities for the children of migrant workers.[877] Advice and information generally for migrants have been treated as coming within Article 19(1);[878] it seems likely that they come within Article 19(2) as far as the "reception" period is concerned.[879] As far as medical "reception" is con-

[873]Id. Art. 10.

[874]Id. Art. 11.

[875]C IV 115.

[876]C IV 116 (F.R.G.). See also C III (F.R.G.). In contrast, it was agreed during the drafting of the ILO Migration for Employment Convention (Revised) 1949, note 808 supra, that financial assistance was not required under Art. 4 of that Convention, which parallels the obligation being discussed. 32 ILC RP 579–80.

[877]C IV 117 (U.K.).

[878]See note 852 supra.

[879]Cf. C IV 117 (Norway).

cerned, in the fourth cycle the Committee of Independent Experts noted that in Austria provision was made for a compulsory examination of immigrant workers upon arrival to ensure that they were free from disease and otherwise healthy.[880] The Committee of Independent Experts found this provision alone insufficient to comply with the undertaking in Article 19(2), which was intended to provide medical reception facilities for migrants and their families "with their interests in mind."[881] The U.K. has reported that "reliance was placed on employers to ensure the social aspects of the reception of migrant workers and their families" and that "special official reception arrangements had not proved necessary."[882] The Committee of Independent Experts accepted that this situation complied with the Charter provided that the U.K. could confirm that "where the employer's or private arrangements at the point of arrival broke down or where emergencies or special problems arose, appropriate assistance was in fact made available."[883]

Apart from particular forms that assistance might take, the Committee of Independent Experts has stressed the importance of treating persons in transit with humanity. In the first cycle, it complained that the reports submitted "related almost exclusively to purely administrative measures and as often as not made no reference to the social and human aspect of the problem which, in the Committee's view, is of capital importance."[884]

The second obligation imposed upon contracting parties is "to provide, within their own jurisdiction, appropriate services for health, medical attention and good hygienic conditions during the journey." As in the case of the first obligation, "jurisdiction" can be taken to refer to territorial jurisdiction. The obligation applies only "during the voyage"; it relates, that is, "only to journeys by migrant workers, and/or their families, between the country of origin and that of destination," and hence "does not oblige the contracting states . . . [to take any] . . . measures either before or after such journeys."[885] It

---

[880]C IV 115 (Austria.

[881]*Id.* Austria has since provided further information to the satisfaction of the CIE. C VI 118 (Austria).

[882]C IV 117 (U.K.).

[883]*Id.*

[884]C I 83.

[885]The comparable provision (Art. 5) of the ILO Migration for Employment Convention (Revised) 1949, note 808 *supra*, requires the maintenance of "appropriate

applies to both publicly and privately arranged collective recruitment of labor.[886] It cannot for practical reasons apply to
migrant workers who make their own travel arrangements; in
such cases, the need for reception facilities in accordance
with the first obligation in Article 19(2) is consequently "all
the greater."[887]

As in the case of Article 19(1), in assessing compliance with
Article 19(2), the Committee of Independent Experts has taken
into account the actual patterns of emigration and immigration
between the contracting parties for employment purposes. The
lower the level of immigration or emigration, the less that is
expected of a contracting party.[888] If emigration or immigration is, as in the case of emigration from Ireland, almost entirely to or from a particular contracting party, the measures
and services required may be judged accordingly.[889] If the pattern of migration changes, so will the Committee of Independent Experts' expectations.[890] This interpretation of Article
19(2) is supported by the wording "*appropriate* measures" and
"*appropriate* services."[891] As in the case of Article 19(1) also, the
Committee of Independent Experts has stressed that compliance with Article 19(2) normally requires special measures and
services for migrant workers beyond those that are provided
for nationals; equality of treatment is not sufficient.[892] Article
19(2) as a whole goes further than the equivalent European
Communities provisions, which, insofar as they concern the
actual migration of a worker and his family, require only that
the children of migrant workers be allowed access to schooling,
apprenticeships, and vocational training on the same footing as
nationals.[893]

---

medical services" (a) to ascertain whether migrants are in reasonable health on departure and on arrival and (b) to ensure that they "enjoy adequate medical attention and
good hygenic conditions *at the time of departure, during the journey and on arrival in the
territory of destination.*" (Emphasis added).

[886]C IV 115.

[887]*Id.*

[888]C II 64 (Italy), C IV 116 (Italy), C III 89 (Ireland), C IV 116 (Ireland), C IV 116
(Cyprus).

[889]C III 89 (Ireland). *See also* C IV 116 (Cyprus).

[890]C IV 116 (Cyprus).

[891]Emphasis added.

[892]C III 88 (Cyprus).

[893]Art. 12, Regulation 1612/68 on Freedom of Movement for Workers Within the
Community, 11 J.O. COMM. EUR. (No. L 257) 2 (1968).

Article 19(3): Cooperation Between Social Services

By Article 19(3), the contracting parties undertake "to promote co-operation, as appropriate, between social services, public and private, in emigration and immigration countries."[894] Article 19(3) is paralleled to some extent by the arrangements in the European Communities for matching job offers and applications and for cooperation in facilitating free movement and employment of workers.[895]

By "social services" are meant not only employment services but "all public or private organisations which [facilitate] . . . the life of emigrants and their families, their adjustment to their new environment and their relations with members of their families who [have] . . . remained in their country of origin."[896] The F.R.G. was found to comply with Article 19(3) as a result of arrangements whereby the West German organizations responsible for assisting foreign workers, which are private (although financed to a large extent by the state), send social workers to the countries from which migrant workers come—particularly, among the present parties of the Charter, Italy—to establish and develop contacts with public authorities and private organizations there.[897] Sweden has satisfied its requirements through its use of International Social Services (ISS).[898] The Swedish Board of Health and Welfare keeps in touch with developments in other contracting parties through ISS publications and seminars and deals with individual cases in which migrant workers require assistance as a result of communication through ISS with equivalent social service organizations in other contracting parties.[899] The Board deals with about 500 cases annually through ISS in this way. One common situation in which such cooperation is useful is that of the migrant worker who leaves his family at home and fails to send back money or needs to be contacted for some other family reason. Another is that of the migrant worker who has

---

[894] Art. 7 of the ILO Migration for Employment Convention (Revised) 1949, note 808 *supra*, overlaps with Art. 19(3) to a small extent.

[895] Arts. 15–31, Regulation 1612/68, note 893 *supra*.

[896] C III 91 (Ireland). *See also* C IV 117 (Austria).

[897] C I 215 (F.R.G.).

[898] C II 66 (Sweden). But see the CIE's doubts in C V 129 (Sweden) and C VI 120 (Sweden).

[899] *See* GC I 47, reprinted in a revised form as an Appendix to the Second Swedish Report.

returned home and has to recover unpaid wages or otherwise needs to settle his affairs in the state in which he was employed.

In the third cycle, Ireland argued that the wording "as appropriate" in Article 19(3) meant that it was for each contracting party—and not for the supervising authorities—to decide what steps should be taken to promote cooperation. The Committee of Independent Experts rejected this interpretation. In its view, "the words 'as appropriate' should be understood as applying not to the undertaking as such but to the ways of implementing it, co-operation being organised 'as appropriate' either between public services or between private services, or between both of them, depending on the structure of the social services in the countries concerned."[900] The words "as appropriate" also support the Committee of Independent Experts' opinion that existing patterns of migration may be taken into account in applying Article 19(3).[901] Cyprus, for example, was found to comply with Article 19(3) almost entirely on the basis of evidence of cooperation between Cypriot and U.K. social services.[902]

Although the obligation is to promote cooperation between social services "in emigration and immigration countries" without qualification, it follows from the context of Article 19(3) that each contracting party is expected to promote cooperation only between social services "established on its own territory or on that of other Contracting States."[903]

Article 19(4): Equal Treatment in Respect of Employment, Trade Unions and Accommodation

By Article 19(4), the contracting parties undertake in respect to migrant workers "to secure for such workers lawfully within their territories, insofar as such matters are regulated by law or regulations or are subject to the control of administrative authorities, treatment not less favourable than that of their own nationals in respect of the following matters: (a) remuneration and other employment and working conditions; (b) membership of trade unions and enjoyment of the benefits of

[900]C II 90–91 (Ireland).
[901]C IV 118 (Cyprus).
[902]C IV 118 (Cyprus). In 1973, 206 emigrants went to the U.K.; 8 to other European countries.
[903]C III 91 (U.K.).

collective bargaining; (c) accommodation." Article 19(4) is modeled closely upon the International Labor Organization Migration for Employment Convention (Revised) 1949.[904] The contracting parties' undertaking extends to nationals of other contracting parties who are "lawfully within their territory." A worker is "lawfully within" a party's territory if he has entered that territory in accordance with its laws and also if his continued presence is in accordance with them; this is likely to require the existence of valid residence and work permits.[905] The Committee of Independent Experts has interpreted "territory" as including oil rigs.[906] The undertaking in Article 19(4) exists only insofar as the matters dealt with by it "are regulated by law or regulations or are subject to the control of administrative authorities" of a contracting party.[907] Thus, no state is obligated to enact legislation that makes the prohibited kinds of discrimination illegal; the position is, instead, that its laws must not discriminate and that its officials must not do so either in the exercise of any discretion that they have in law.[908] As is true in respect to Article 19(1) and (2), the Committee of Independent Experts has taken account of the pattern of migration in assessing compliance with Article 19(4). Thus Italy, whose nationals emigrate to other contracting parties in large

[904]ILO Migration for Employment Convention, Art. 6(1)(a) (Revised) 1949, note 808 *supra. See also* ILO Migration for Employment Recommendation (Revised) 1949, and ILO Migrant Workers (Supplementary Provisions) Convention, Art. 10, 1975, note 835 *supra.*

[905]The wording "lawfully within" is used also in Art. 19(5) and (7). As to the distinction between "lawfully within" and "permitted to establish himself within" (Art. 19[6]) and "lawfully residing within" (Art. 19[8]), see notes 940 & 994 *infra.*

[906]C VI 121 (F.R.G., Norway). *See also* note 845 *supra.*

[907]The worker's delegates to the TC sought to replace the second part of this wording—"are subject to the control of administrative authorities"—by the wording "by collective agreements." The proposal was opposed by a U.K. delegate because the supervision of such agreements was not a matter for the state. REC PROC TC 224. It was explained by a U.K. delegate to the TC that the words "or are subject to the control of administrative authorities," which are taken from Art. 6, ILO Migration for Employment Convention (Revised) 1949, note 818 *supra,* had been inserted to cover matters such as the allocation of public housing by local authorities. REC PROC TC 224.

[908]C II 67. The CIE's statement that "it is not enough for a government to prove that no discrimination exists in law alone but that it is obliged to prove in addition that no discrimination is practised in fact" (C III 92) can be read as referring to discrimination practiced by public officials. But *quaere* whether the CIE's questioning of Sweden about de facto discrimination (*see, e.g.,* C IV 122 [Sweden], C VI 122 [Sweden]) is consistent with this approach, or whether the CIE is asking for state action controlling private discrimination? C VII 102 (Sweden) suggests the latter.

numbers to work but to which very few nationals of other parties emigrate, has been found to comply with Article 19(4) on the basis of information that would have been insufficient if provided by a party such as the F.R.G. which receives a large number of immigrant workers.[909]

Article 19(4) requires equal treatment, first, in respect to "remuneration and other employment and working conditions." "Other employment and working conditions" have been interpreted by the Committee of Independent Experts as including arrangements for training and promotion.[910] Grants and allowances paid under transfer schemes to workers who move to different areas in the U.K. to take up work have also been considered to come within Article 19(4), either under the same heading or that of "remuneration."[911] Some further indication of what is required by Article 19(4) may be found in Article 6 of the Migration for Employment Convention (Revised) 1949.[912] This requires equality of treatment in respect to "remuneration, including family allowances where these form part of remuneration, hours of work, overtime arrangements, holidays with pay, restrictions on home work, minimum age for employment, apprenticeship and training, women's work and the work of young persons." Article 19(4) is not concerned with access to employment, which is the subject of Article 18 of the Charter. Cyprus, for example, has been found to comply with Article 19(4) although by its law an employment permit may not be granted to an alien when there is a suitably qualified Cypriot applicant.[913] In the fourth cycle, the Committee of Independent Experts indicated that Article 19(4) requires equality of

[909]C II 67 (Italy), C IV 120 (Italy).

[910]C III 92 (F.R.G., Ireland, Italy). In this connection the CIE has commented upon or asked for information about language instruction for migrant workers. C IV 120 (F.R.G.), C IV 122 (Sweden).

[911]C III 94 (U.K.). The U.K. has been found to be in breach of Art. 19(4) because access to Government training schemes is not available to migrant workers on terms of full equality with U.K. nationals. C VII 103 (U.K.). *But see* GC VII 13.

[912]*Cf. also* European Convention on Establishment 1955, Art. 17(1), note 767 *supra*.

[913]C IV 119 (Cyprus). Although the position in Cypriot law referred to in the text is not expressly commented upon in *Conclusions IV*, it had been indicated in the Cypriot Report for the fourth cycle in response to a question put by the CIE during the third cycle (*see* C III 92 [Cyprus]). *See*, however, the CIE's ruling against France because of its residence permit system. C VI 121 (France). By this system, work permits allowing a person to obtain employment in any part of France were available only upon four years' residence in France. This inevitably discriminated against nationals of other contracting parties. *Quaere* whether such permits concern "employment and working conditions" in the sense of Art. 19(4).

treatment in respect to redundancy. It did so when stressing the importance of equality of treatment for migrant workers in respect to employment at a time of economic recession such as was being experienced by most contracting parties during that cycle. In this connection, it calls upon the parties concerned to "take specific action to avoid discrimination to the extent that an increase of the level of unemployment is likely to have a particular impact upon" migrant workers.[914]

Article 19(4) requires, second, equal treatment in respect to "membership of trade unions and enjoyment of the benefits of collective bargaining." This requirement is identical to that in Article 6 of the International Labor Organization Migration for Employment Convention (Revised) 1949.[915] France has been found to be in breach of Article 19(4) because of restrictions upon the exercise of certain administrative and managerial functions in French trade unions by immigrant workers.[916]

Article 19(4) requires, finally, equal treatment in respect to "accommodation."[917] It is this requirement, which concerns the accommodation of migrant workers and members of their family insofar as the latter are allowed entry, that has, because of the "prime importance"[918] of accommodation for them, attracted most of the Committee of Independent Experts' attention.[919] The U.K. was for several cycles found to be in violation of this part of Article 19(4) in respect to both Northern Ireland and the Isle of Man.[920] In Northern Ireland, immigrant workers who were nationals of contracting parties other than members of the European Communities and who were not "key workers" or who did not fall within certain other limited categories were only eligible for public housing if they were born in Northern Ireland or had lived in the U.K.

---

[914]C IV 119.

[915]Note 808 *supra. Cf.* Art. 8, Regulation 1612/68 of the European Communities, note 893 *supra.*

[916]C VI 121 (France). Another question that has been raised has been whether membership of certain trade unions in the U.K. is restricted to U.K. nationals. C III 93 (U.K.), C IV 122 (U.K.), C V 132 (U.K.), C VI 122 (U.K.). Although certain British trade unions (e.g., the British Airline Pilots Association) do exclude aliens (*see* B. HEPPLE, RACE, JOBS AND THE LAW 53–54 [2d ed. 1970]), this is not a matter regulated by law so that Art. 19(4) does not apply.

[917]*Cf.* ILO Migration for Employment Convention (Revised) 1949, Art. 6(1)(a), note 808 *supra.*

[918]C I 84.

[919]*Cf.* C IV 125 (Austria).

[920]*See,* most recently, C VI 122 (U.K.).

for seven years immediately prior to the date of the proposed occupation.[921] A similar rule still exists in the Isle of Man, where a ten-year residential qualification applies to any person not born in the island, whatever his nationality.[922] In neither of these cases was the Committee of Independent Experts prepared to accept, either under Article 19(4) taken by itself or as read in conjunction with Article 31, the British argument that the requirement was necessitated by a shortage of public housing.[923] The ruling against the U.K. was reversed in *Conclusions VII* on receipt of information that this residential qualification had been abandoned in Northern Ireland. The Committee of Independent Experts has also agreed now that the ruling in respect to the situation in the Isle of Man is mistaken in that, unlike that in Northern Ireland, it does not involve a discrimination based upon nationality. A U.K. national not born in the Isle of Man is discriminated against as much as a national of any other contracting party not born there.[924]

The requirement in Article 19(4) is concerned not only with the allocation of public housing but also with access to private housing. A restriction in law upon the acquisition or renting of accommodation by a migrant worker would be contrary to Article 19(4).[925] So, too, would discrimination in the eligibilty requirements for public loans or other public assistance for house purchase purposes.[926] A restriction on the location of a migrant worker's residence would also infringe it.[927] An interesting case is that of Cyprus. Under Cypriot law, an alien must obtain permission from the Council of Ministers before he can acquire real estate. In the third cycle, the Committee of Independent Experts found that this did not conflict with Article

---

[921]Housing Selection Scheme of the Northern Ireland Housing Executive. Fourth U.K. Report, at 145.

[922]Isle of Man Board of Social Security Act 1970, sec. 8(1), as amended.

[923]C IV 122–23 (U.K.).

[924]C VII 103 (U.K.).

[925]*Cf.* C IV 121 (Norway). A restriction on the acquisition of real property by a migrant worker for a purpose other than accommodation would not violate Art. 19(4).

[926]C III 92 (Italy). A requirement that a foreign worker should have worked in a state for two years to be eligible for a grant for the construction of family housing is contrary to Art. 19(4). C I 215 (F.R.G.).

[927]C VI 121 (F.R.G.) (exclusion of migrant workers from areas of high immigrant population).

19(4) because the Council has, in practice, exercised its power on the basis that permission is not refused to "*bona fide* foreigners" who are buying land for residential purposes.[928] There is, nonetheless, unequal treatment in that an alien, including an immigrant worker, has to apply for permission when a national does not have to do so. For this reason, this law seems a violation of Article 19(4). The fact that Article 19(4) imposes only a negative obligation, one not to discriminate in its law or practice, not one to act to prevent private discrimination, is particularly limiting in the case of housing.[929] It is in this field, above all, that positive state action to require equality of treatment on the part of private landlords and to assist migrant laborers (e.g., by requiring employers to find housing for employees whom they recruit abroad) would be helpful.

Since Article 19(4) is an equality of treatment provision, it contains no requirement as to the level or kind of "accommodation" for immigrant workers unless the national law contains such a requirement for nationals. Article 19(6) supplements Article 19(4) in this respect.[930]

Article 19(5): Equal Treatment in Respect to Taxation[931]
By Article 19(5), the contracting parties undertake in respect to migrant workers "to secure for such workers lawfully within their territories treatment not less favourable than that of their own nationals with regard to employment taxes, dues or contributions payable in respect of employed persons." In practice, this undertaking has caused little difficulty because taxation and social security contributions in the contracting parties are based upon residence, not nationality.[932] Charges imposed upon migrant workers for work permits, etc., to cover administrative costs are not prohibited; this was acknowledged during the drafting of the Charter when it was pointed out that they are impliedly recognized by Article 18(2).[933]

[928]C III 94 (Cyprus).
[929]Note 908 *supra*. Note, however, the questioning of Sweden referred to there.
[930]*See* note 958 *infra*.
[931]*Cf.* ILO Migration for Employment Convention (Revised) 1949, Art. 6(1)(c), note 808 *supra*, upon which Art. 19(5) is based, and ILO Migration for Employment Recommendation (Revised) 1949.
[932]*Cf.* Laroque, *supra* note 591, at 11. A special tax upon employers of migrant workers might infringe Art. 19(5), C IV 124 (F.R.G.).
[933]CMSC, Seventh Meeting, February 1958.

Article 19(6): Reunion of the Families of Migrant Workers

By Article 19(6), the contracting parties undertake "to facilitate as far as possible the reunion of the family of a foreign worker permitted to establish himself in the territory."[934] This improves upon the International Labor Organization Migration for Employment Convention (Revised) 1949, which contains no such undertaking. "The later ILO Migrant Workers (Supplementary Provisions) Convention 1975, however, provides (Article 12) that a party '*may* take all necessary measures . . . to facilitate the reunification of the families of all migrant workers legally residing in its territory'" (emphasis added). Article 19(6) falls short of the European Communities rules on the subject, which accord rights of admission and employment to members of the family (widely defined) of migrant workers.[935] Article 19(6) is a watered-down version of a text which, as proposed by the Consultative Assembly, required states to grant migrant workers "the right to be accompanied or joined by their families" and "to facilitate," without qualification, "the reunion of their families."[936]

The Appendix to the Charter reads: "For the purpose of this provision, the term 'family of a foreign worker' is understood to mean at least his wife and dependent children under the age of 21 years."[937] Italy, with support from some other states, attempted to have this definition drafted more widely so as to include the husband of a working woman and handicapped children over the age of twenty-one. Although this attempt was unsuccessful, the members of the Committee of Ministers agreed unanimously that they "would in practice be willing to give sympathetic consideration to deserving cases in the categories referred to . . . viz., the husbands of working women and dependent children over the age of 21 but

---

[934]*See* Art. 19(6), Kojanec, *Reunion of the Families of Migrant Workers,* Working Paper for the Strasbourg Symposium on the European Social Charter 1977, CE Doc. AS/Coll/Charte 5-E. The English text of Art. 19(6) is out of step with the rest of Art. 19 in referring to a "foreign worker" instead of a "migrant worker." This would not seem to be significant; the French text of Art. 19(6) reads "travailleur migrant," the term used uniformly throughout Art. 19. "Foreign worker" is also used in Art. 18.

[935]Arts. 10 & 11, EEC Regulation 1612/68, note 893 *supra.*

[936]Art. 19(4) of the Draft Charter submitted by the CA to the CM with Opinion 32, TEXTS ADOPTED, September 1959.

[937]As the CIE has pointed out, although the age of majority has been reduced below 21 in some contracting parties, this does not affect Art. 19(6) since the Appendix expressly refers to 21. C V 133. *See also* C VI 123–24 (Austria); C VII 106 (U.K.).

handicapped."[938] This would still exclude dependent parents or other relatives. A "wife" must clearly be a wife in law. It is not clear whether "dependent children" must be children of the existing wife or whether they may be (i) children of a former wife or (ii) illegitimate. If they may be other than the children of the existing wife, the question of the meaning of "dependent" becomes particularly important. Although the wording of the Appendix is such as to exclude the husband of a female migrant worker, the Committee of Independent Experts has interpreted it to include her "children."[939] In doing so, it has relied upon the fact that the Charter applies equally to male and female workers unless the wording or context indicates otherwise.

Article 19(6) extends only to the family of a worker who is "permitted to establish himself in the territory" of a contracting party. This wording differs from that in other parts of Article 19, which requires only that a person be "lawfully within" or "lawfully residing within" the territory of a contracting party for the undertaking to apply.[940] The Committee of Independent Experts has not interpreted this difference in wording as indicating any distinction between Article 19(6) and the other undertakings in Article 19 *ratione personae*.[941] That there is some distinction, and that Article 19(6) is narrower in terms of the workers who come within it, must surely be the case, particularly since the difference in wording was pointed out when the Charter was being drafted.[942] The difficulty is in knowing what "permitted to establish" means. It would seem, at the least, to exclude seasonal workers. It appears that it goes further than this and incorporates the idea of permanent settlement or residence that is found in the immigration laws of a number of the signatory states. Thus, in

[938]CM (61) 95 rev., 3. Art. 10, EEC Regulation 1612/68, note 893 *supra*, Art. 13 of the ILO Migrant Workers (Supplementary Provisions) Convention 1975, note 835 *supra*, and Art. 12 of the European Convention on the Legal Status of Migrant Workers 1977, note 840 *supra*, apply to a "spouse" of either sex. The EEC and ILO texts (but not the European Convention on the Legal Status of Migrant Workers) also contain more generous definitions of "dependents."

[939]C IV 124.

[940]*CF*. note 841 *supra*.

[941]*See*, however, the reference to "permanent residents" at C IV 127 (U.K.).

[942]It was pointed out by Italy in the CMSC at its Ninth Session in April 1960. An attempt then made by Italy to have the wording "permitted to establish himself in" changed to include, in effect, all migrant workers lawfully within a state's territory was unsuccessful.

the U.K., which was responsible for the introduction of the phrase into Article 19(6),[943] a person who is admitted for employment to the U.K. with a work permit is eligible for "permanent settlement" after four years' residence. He then ceases to need a work permit and to be subject to other controls.[944] If this is correct, the scope of Article 19(6) *ratione personae* is considerably narrower than the Committee of Independent Experts would seem to assume.

The Committee of Independent Experts has interpreted the obligation to "facilitate" the reunion of a migrant's family as meaning that a contracting party must eliminate "any legal obstacle preventing the members of a migrant worker's" family from joining him.[945] Despite the use of the word "any" in this passage, the fact that parties are required only to facilitate "as far as possible," and not to ensure, the reunion of a migrant worker with his family, must mean that limitations upon the entry or continued presence of migrant worker's family are not wholly prohibited. This has been recognized by the Committee of Independent Experts, which has accepted that a state does not have to allow the families of all migrant workers to join them as soon as they take up residence. In the F.R.G., for example, the family of nationals of non-EEC members[946] may by law be prevented from joining them for three years, although "as a rule" they are allowed to do so after one year. The Committee of Independent Experts would appear to be prepared to accept the one-year waiting period as conforming with Article 19(6) provided that it is converted into a rule of law.[947] A requirement that a migrant worker be able financially to support his family is also permissible.[948] So

[943]In the CMSC at its Ninth Session in April 1960.

[944]*See* I. MACDONALD, *supra* note 795, at 55.

[945]C II 197 (Cyprus).

[946]The family of EEC nationals have an immediate right of entry under Art. 10, EEC Regulation 1612/68, note 893 *supra*.

[947]C VI 125 (F.R.G.). The CIE had earlier wanted to know why it was not "possible" (in the terminology of Art. 19[6]) to have a more generous rule than the three-year one. C III 96 (F.R.G.). It has asked no such question about a one-year waiting period. Nor has it questioned a 1976 French law, Decree 76/383, which provides for a waiting period of one year if the worker does not have adequate resources to support his family: *see* Kojanec, *supra* note 934, at 7.

[948]C III 96 (Norway), C IV 126 (Norway). The question put to Norway in *Conclusions III* on the meaning of its requirement that a migrant worker lead an "orderly life" was satisfactorily answered in the sense indicated in the text in the Fourth Norwegian Report. *Kojanec, supra* note 934, at n.9, has suggested that one-year wait-

is the exclusion of members of a migrant worker's family suffering from a contagious disease in "particularly serious cases."[949] In the first cycle, the U.K. was found to be in breach of Article 19(6) because its immigration authorities were empowered to exclude a worker's child if it was suffering from a disability which called for special care and treatment where, having regard to the financial situation of the parents, the disability was such as to be likely to involve reliance upon free public health services.[950] In response to further information from the U.K., the Committee of Independent Experts ruled that it would not be contrary to Article 19(6) to refuse admission to a worker's dependent on the ground that the sole reason for the worker's taking employment in the immigrant state was to obtain the benefits of its free public health service.[951] But the U.K. position was not such as to permit the finding against it to be changed on the basis of this ruling.[952]

The U.K. has also been held to be in violation of Article 19(6) because of its policy of not admitting the families of migrant workers in domestic service.[953] The U.K. explained in its Third Report that "the rule is . . . that a work permit is not issued to a domestic worker who has a spouse and/or dependent children, except where a married couple without children are taking a joint domestic post."[954] Consequently, the U.K. argued, no question of a violation of Article 19(6) could

ing period and financial resources requirements are permissible only as alternatives, the justification of the former being the likelihood that the migrant worker will need that period of time to establish himself financially. This reasonable suggestion is not yet reflected in the CIE's *Conclusions.*

[949]C III 95 (Austria). The CIE is here relying impliedly upon the "public health" exception allowed in Art. 31. *See* note 11 of Chapter IV. It is submitted that it would not be permissible to exclude a family member in other cases of physical illness or in cases of mental illness. *See also* C VI 133 (Austria), C V 134 (Cyprus), C VI 124 (France).

[950]C I 85 (U.K.).

[951]C II 69 (U.K.), C III 87 (U.K.).

[952] In the fourth cycle, the U.K. reported that wives and children under 18 of workers who had been accepted as permanent residents would not be refused admission on medical grounds as of 1973. Fourth U.K. Report, at 147. *See* Statement of Immigration Rules for Control of Entry of EEC and Other Non-Commonwealth Nationals 1973, paras. 33, 53–54, and 60–62, H.C. 81, Parl. Papers, Sess. 1972–73, Vol. XXXI, 487. Although this brought the position "very largely into line" with Art. 19(6), it did not do so entirely because that provision applies to children up to the age of 21. C IV 127 (U.K.). *See* in defense of the U.K., Lord Selsdon, EUR. CONSULT. ASS. DEB. 27TH SESS. 82–83. The point is not pursued in later *Conclusions.*

[953]See, most recently, C VII 106 (U.K.).

[954]Third U.K. Report, at 166.

arise except where a worker has obtained a work permit by the false pretense that he is not married or has no dependent children. The Committee of Independent Experts accepted that Article 19(6) would not apply in a case of fraud.[955] It considered, however, that although the work permit rule took care of most other cases, it did not "cover all eventualities, such as the case of an unmarried foreign domestic servant who, while employed in the U.K., becomes a father or gets married abroad."[956]

Article 19(6) is concerned with the expulsion, as well as the admission, of members of a migrant worker's family. It seems that family members may be expelled only for the reasons listed in Article 19(8) in respect to the expulsion of migrant workers themselves, that is, they endanger national security or offend against public interest or morality. They should not be expelled, for example, simply because they become physically or mentally ill; however serious the illness, they should be provided treatment instead.[957]

Compliance with the obligation to "facilitate" the reunion of a migrant's family requires not only the absence of legal constraints but also the introduction of "appropriate practical administrative and social measures" to assist reunion, "particularly in regard to housing."[958] These include steps to place migrant workers and their families in suitable public housing and to help them find private accommodation. Action need not be taken if migrant workers are not experiencing difficulty in finding suitable accommodation for themselves and their families[959] or where, for some good reason, effective intervention would not be possible.[960] In the last case, the wording "as far as possible" in Article 19(6) would apply. Affirmative action may also not be required if the number of migrant workers who need assistance is very small.[961] Applying these rules to housing, the Committee of Independent

---

[955]C III 95 (U.K.).

[956]*Id.*

[957]*Cf.* C III 95 (Austria, Cyprus).

[958]C I 85 (Norway), C II 70, 197 (U.K., Cyprus), C III 94, 95 (Cyprus), C V 133 (Austria), C V 134 (France). On the need for the host state to have a housing policy for migrant workers, and on the level of accommmodation required, see Kojanec, *supra* note 934, at 11–12.

[959]C III 94.

[960]C II 69 (Norway).

[961]C II 69 (Ireland).

Experts found Norway to be in violation of Article 19(6).[962] Norway had taken no steps to assist migrant workers to find accommodation for their families. Nor had it shown that none were necessary (there was, in fact, evidence to the contrary) or that it was impossible for Norway to have taken appropriate action. Migrant workers in Norway had experienced more difficulty than Norwegians in finding accommodation for their families.[963] Presumably the Committee of Independent Experts would have reached the conclusion even if the experience of migrant workers and Norwegians had not been different. Article 19(6) does not contain an equality of treatment clause;[964] it imposes an obligation in respect to the treatment of migrant workers that does not exist in respect to others.[965] Article 19(6) thus adds to the equality of treatment provision of Article 19(4) in respect to housing.

Article 19(7): Equal Treatment in Respect to Legal Proceedings[966] By Article 19(7), the contracting parties undertake in respect to migrant workers "to secure for such workers lawfully within their territories treatment not less favourable than that of their own nationals in respect of legal proceedings relating to matters referred to in this Article." Migrant workers must accordingly be allowed access to courts and tribunals, to lawyers, and to legal aid on the same conditions as nationals of the contracting party in whose territory they are working.[967] They must also be treated equally in matters of security for costs or deposits.[968] The undertaking extends to legal proceedings relating to all "matters referred to" in Article 19, including proceedings in respect to deportation, membership of trade unions, and housing arrangements. It is "therefore insuffi-

[962]C III 96 (Norway), C IV 126 (Norway), C V 136 (Norway), C VI 124 (Norway); C VII 105 (Norway). The U.K. also has been found to be in violation of Art. 19(6) in this respect. *See,* most recently, C VI 126 (U.K.). *But see* C VII 106 (U.K.).

[963]C II 69 (Norway).

[964]C III 94.

[965]*Cf.* C IV 125 (Austria), where the CIE rejected a government argument that the question of accommodation was governed solely by Art. 19(4) and not Art. 19(6). The GC takes the same view as Austria. GC V 15. *But see* GC VII 14.

[966]Art. 19(7) is based upon Art. 6(1)(d) of the ILO Migration for Employment Convention (Revised) 1949, note 808 *supra. See also* ILO Migration for Employment Recommendation (Revised) 1949 and European Convention on Establishment 1955, Arts. 7–9, note 767 *supra.*

[967]*Cf.* European Convention on Establishment 1955, Arts. 7 & 8, note 767 *supra.*

[968]*Cf. id.* Art. 9.

cient for a state to guarantee it only in some fields, for example in criminal law and the law concerning contracts of employment."[969] It does not extend to legal proceedings beyond the limits of Article 19, however, to include legal proceedings in such matters as marriage or divorce or most aspects of the law of real or personal property. Although the text refers only to "workers," it can probably be taken to require that equal rights be accorded also to the members of their families insofar as any legal proceedings in which they might be involved (e.g., in respect of their admission to the country) come within Article 19. The wording "lawfully within their territories" does not exclude from the protection of Article 19(7) someone whose work permit is revoked and who is still in the territory of the contracting party to which he has gone as a migrant worker; it means only that the worker should have arrived lawfully in the territory of the party concerned.[970] Article 19(7) has caused no difficulty in practice.

Article 19(8): Freedom from Expulsion
By Article 19(8), the contracting parties undertake in respect to migrant workers "to secure that such workers lawfully residing within their territories are not expelled unless they endanger national security or offend against public interest or morality."[971] This provision is based upon Article 3(1) of the European Convention on Establishment 1955. It is identical to it in substance, the only difference being that the Establishment Convention is concerned with the expulsion of the nationals of other contracting parties generally and not just with the expulsion of migrant workers. There is also a similar provision relating to the admission as well as the expulsion of migrant workers in the "freedom of movement" provision in European Communities law.[972]

Of the three grounds for deportation, "national security" presents little difficulty. "Public interest" can be taken to have the meaning of its equivalent—*ordre public*—in the French text. This interpretation is supported, first, by the fact that whereas "public interest" could have a variety of meanings, *ordre public*

---

[969]C I 217.

[970]This point was made by a U.K. delegate at the TC. REC PROC TC 225.

[971]In the French text, migrant workers may not be expelled unless "ils menacent la securité de l'Etat ou contreviennent à l'ordre public ou aux bonnes moeurs."

[972]Treaty of Rome, Art. 56(1), 298 U.N.T.S. 11.

is a term of art in French law, the meaning of which is reasonably clear. There is also the fact that Article 3 of the European Convention on Establishment, upon which Article 19(8) is based, used *ordre public* in the French and the English texts. It is reasonable to suppose that "public interest" in the Charter is an attempt to find an English translation of *ordre public* in the Establishment Convention.[973] If this is correct, some indication of the meaning of "public interest" in Article 19(8) of the Charter is to be found in the Protocol to the Establishment Convention, Section III of which reads: "The concept of *'ordre public'* is to be understood in the wide sense generally accepted in continental countries. A Contracting Party may, for instance, exclude a national of another Party for political reasons, or if there are grounds for believing that he is unable to pay the expenses of his stay or that he intends to engage in a gainful occupation without the necessary permits." The three examples of the meaning of *ordre public* given in this extract are particularly relevant to the admission and expulsion of aliens but do not exhaust its possibilities in that context. It permits the expulsion of a migrant worker for any reason that can be explained in terms of the protection of the existing state institutions and social order. The bribery of public officials, the evasion of tax liabilities, the commission of other criminal offenses,[974] and political agitation are other examples of what this protean concept might include in cases of expulsion. The implied acceptance by the Committee of Independent Experts of the consistency with Article 19(8) of Sweden's 1973 law permitting the expulsion of political terrorists was based either upon this ground or that of "national security."[975]

---

[973]*See also* the use of "public interest"/*ordre public* and its interpretation in Art. 31 of the Charter, note 11 of Chapter IV. *Ordre public* has often presented difficulties of translation in treaty texts. In Art. 6(1) of the ECHR, note 1 *supra*, it is rendered as "public order" but *ordre public* is kept in the English text of Art. 2(3) of the Fourth Protocol to the ECHR, note 768 *supra*. The composite phrase "public order (*ordre public*)" is used in the English text of Art. 14 of the International Covenant on Civil and Political Rights. International Covenant on Civil and Political Rights, Dec. 16, 1966, G.A. Res. 2000A, 21 U.N. GAOR, Supp. (No. 16) at 52, U.N. Doc. A/6316 (1966). For the meaning of *ordre public* in the European Communities rules on freedom of movement, see Case 36/75 Rutili v. Minister of the Interior, 1975 E.C.R. 1219 (Eur. Court of Justice).

[974]The CIE has taken the view that a one-year prison sentence could be considered an adequate reason for expulsion.

[975]C IV 129 (Sweden). Whereas the CIE expressed doubts about the procedural side of the law, it did not question the law's consistency with the Charter in terms of its substance.

Finally, expulsion is permissible on the ground of "morals", or, in the French text, *bonnes moeurs*. Here too, the French text is the more helpful in that *bonnes moeurs* is a legal term of art whereas "morals" is not. It includes, but extends beyond, sexual morality; gambling, for example, would be against *bonnes moeurs*.

If the grounds for expulsion that are listed are somewhat wide, it is important to note that they are exceptions. Deportation is not permitted on any ground other than the three listed. For example, Cyprus was found to be in breach of Article 19(8) until the sixth cycle because a migrant worker could be deported under its law (later changed), inter alia, if he was destitute, if he was for any other reason unable to take care of himself, or if he was considered to be "an undesirable person."[976] It is contrary to Article 19(8) to deport a migrant worker because another member of his family is being deported unless it can be shown that this is justifiable in the interests of family unity.[977] Nor may a migrant worker be deported because of high unemployment.[978] Deportation is not permitted because of mental or other illness, except in the case of refusal of treatment or where it can be shown to be in the patient's own interest for medical reasons.[979] The Committee of Independent Experts has found the F.R.G. to be in breach of Article 19(8) on this last ground because "migrant workers in the Federal Republic of Germany who were found to have—or were suspected of having—certain diseases (epidemic diseases subject to notification or contagious veneral diseases) could be expelled if special protective measures did not

[976]C IV 128 (Cyprus), C V 137 (Cyprus), C VI 126 (Cyprus).

[977]The U.K. was able to satisfy the CIE that Immigration Act 1971, sec. 3(5)(c) (which permits the deportation of an alien migrant worker because another member of his family has been lawfully deported), is used only to preserve family unity and to prevent dependents being left destitute in the U.K. C V 139 (U.K.).

[978]*See* Laroque, *supra* note 591, at 12.

[979]C IV 130 (U.K.), C V 139 (U.K.). *Quaere* what is the ground in Art. 19(8) permitting these two exceptions. In the U.K., a migrant worker may be deported if he is receiving treatment for mental illness as an in-patient in a hospital or mental hospital or institution provided that it appears to the Home Secretary that (1) proper arrangements have been made for his removal to another country and for his treatment there and (2) it is in the interests of the patient to remove him. Mental Health Act 1959, sec. 90, and Mental Health Act (Scotland) Act 1960, sec. 82, as both provisions are amended by Immigration Act 1971, sec. 30. *See further* I. MacDonald, *supra* note 795, at 108. The U.K. was able to satisfy the CIE that removal was effected only very rarely and then only on the recommendation of the competent medical authorities that it was in the patient's own best interests.

suffice, in such cases, to prevent the health of third parties from being endangered."[980] The F.R.G. argued that its action could be justified as being in the interest of "public health" and hence in the "public interest" in the sense of Article 19(8). The Committee of Independent Experts rejected this argument because "public interest" in Article 19(8) means only *ordre public,* as indicated above, and *ordre public* does not extend to considerations of "public health". While the Committee of Independent Experts is correct in its interpretation of the Charter, it is interesting to consider the effect of Article 31, which permits restrictions upon the obligations that a contracting party accepts in Part II of the Charter so far as they are necessary for the protection of the "public interest" or "public health."[981] The Committee of Independent Experts has acknowledged, as is clearly the case, that Article 31 applies to the obligations in Article 19.[982] The problem is that in the case of Article 19(8) the drafters of the Charter borrowed a text from the European Convention on Establishment which has its own restrictive wording (contrast the other paragraphs of Article 19) and would seem to have done so without taking into account the relationship between Article 19(8) and Article 31. Faced with this drafting weakness, the better interpretation is not that Article 31 adds to the restrictions permitted by the text of Article 19(8), but that the intention was to limit the permissible kinds of restrictions to those actually inserted in Article 19(8) when that clause was being drafted. Article 19(8) contains its own *lex specialis* on the question of restrictions. Finally, in the sixth cycle, the Committee of Independent Experts raised the question whether U.K. law is consistent with the Charter insofar as it permits the deportation of an alien where this is for the "public good" in the interests of the "relations between the United Kingdom and any other country or for other reasons of a political nature."[983] The Committee has asked for further information as to the interpretation and application of these grounds for deportation in practice.

The Committee of Independent Experts has interpreted Article 19(8) as meaning not only that a state must provide by law that a person may not be expelled other than on the

[980]C V 138 (F.R.G.). *Cf.* C VI 127 (F.R.G.).
[981]*See* note 11 *supra.*
[982]C V 134 (Cyprus).
[983]Immigration Act 1971, sec. 3(5). C VI 129 (U.K.).

grounds which it lists, but also that it must "provide suitable guarantees against the possibility of arbitrary decisions" concerning expulsion.[984] In particular, a party must allow migrant workers a right of recourse to a court "or other independent body" to challenge a decision to expel him. Although the Committee of Independent Experts refers to a "right of appeal," it would seem a right to challenge the decision by way of judicial review (*recours en annulation*) is sufficient; a right of appeal on the merits of the decision is not required.[985] The Committee of Independent Experts has ruled against Sweden because of this second obligation in Article 19(8) in respect to the Swedish 1973 law on political terrorism.[986] The Committee has also ruled against the U.K. in respect to the remedy available in cases in which an alien is deported for the "public good" in the interests of "national security" or "of the relations between the United Kingdom and any other country or for other reasons of a political nature."[987] In such cases, the only remedy is an appeal to three advisers who are independent, but whose recommendations are not binding upon the government. This remedy is not provided by statute; it has been made available at the discretion of the Government.[988] Although a hearing occurs before the three advisers, the procedure followed is not such that an appellant is given a fair hearing in any accepted sense. The courts exercise a power of judicial review over the procedure, but, at least in cases of national security, it is a very modest one. There is a duty to act fairly, which the courts will ensure is observed, but they will not insist that the rules of natural justice are followed. In

---

[984]C I 86.

[985]Thus the F.R.G., Italy, and Cyprus have been held to comply with Art. 19(8) (*see* C I 218 [F.R.G.], C II 70 [Italy], C III 97 [Cyprus]), although what their law provides in all or some cases is only a right to judicial review. *Cf.* C V 138 (France), C VI 127 (France). In Cyprus, the remedy provided is the general right of recourse to the Supreme Court provided by Art. 146 of the Cyprus Constitution. There is a possibility of appealing to the Council of Ministers, but this is composed of Ministers and is not an independent body. In the F.R.G., a decision taken by the Aliens police may be the subject of review under Art. 19(4) of the Basic Law (Grundgesetz) and Art. 42(2) of the Code of Administrative Procedure, Law of Jan. 21, 1960 Bundesgesetzblatt, Tiel 1 at 17. In Italy, where a person is expelled as a police measure the ordinary administrative law remedies apply; there is no right of appeal on the merits.

[986]C VI 128 (Sweden). Under the 1973 law, the decision to expel an alien in the interest of national security lies with the Government; no recourse to an independent body is provided.

[987]Immigration Act 1971, sec. 15(3). C VI 128 (U.K.).

[988]*See* J. Evans, Immigration Law 126 (1976).

particular, the courts have accepted that the appellant does not have to be told of the case against him.[989] In the sixth and seventh cycles, the Committee of Independent Experts found that this remedy did not provide the "suitable guarantees" against abuse required by Article 19(8).

The Committee did not indicate whether this was because the three advisers' recommendations were not binding,[990] because the possibilities for judicial review were so limited,[991] or for some other reason or reasons. It is interesting to note that a challenge to the three-advisers procedure was unsuccessful under the European Convention on Human Rights.[992]

Clearly, it is desirable that a migrant worker should not be expelled without having the opportunity to challenge the executive's decision before an independent body. Nonetheless, the Committee of Independent Experts' interpretation of Article 19(8) by which it contains a procedural requirement of this sort as well as a substantive requirement concerning the grounds for expulsion is, although agreed to by the Governmental Committee,[993] open to question. The text of Article 19(8) expressly contains only a substantive obligation. An obstacle to implying a second, procedural obligation is the text of Article 3 of the European Convention on Establishment. Article 19(8) of the Charter repeats, mutatis mutandis, the undertaking and wording of Article 3(1) of the Convention. This is followed in Article 3(2) by a procedural guarantee which compliments the, consequently, exclusively substantive guarantee

---

[989]*See* R v. Secretary of State for Home Affairs, ex parte Hosenball [1977] 1 W.L.R. 766. The courts can quash an order because it is made in bad faith, but this is very difficult to prove. R. v. Briston Prison Governor, ex parte Soblen [1963] 2 Q.B. 243.

[990]It seems unlikely that this was crucial since the U.K. was found to comply with Art. 19(8) in the second cycle (C II 70 [U.K.]) in cases of deportation on the ground of "public good" even though the remedy provided—appeal to the Chief Metropolitan Magistrate—led only to an opinion that was not binding in law upon the Home Secretary. The opinion of the Chief Magistrate had, however, always been followed. It is interesting that although the CIE chose to emphasize the above remedy, it was only available during the second cycle in cases of deportation for the "public good" when the migrant worker had been in the U.K. for two years and where the particular ground of "public good" was not "national security." *Quaere* where the very limited possibilities for judicial review (*see* R. v. Brixton Prison Governor, ex parte Soblen, [1963] 2 Q.B. 243), were sufficient in other cases.

[991]*But see* note 990 *supra.*

[992]*See* Agee v. U.K., 7 DECISIONS AND REPORTS OF THE EUROPEAN COMMISSION OF HUMAN RIGHTS 164 (1977).

[993]GC V 15.

in paragraph (1). Since Article 19(8) of the Charter is clearly modeled on Article 3(1) of the Convention and was not expressly supplemented by a procedural guarantee, it is reasonable to suppose that none was intended.

Article 19(8) only applies to migrant workers who are "lawfully residing within" the territory of a contracting party other than that of their national state. By "lawfully residing" is meant that a worker "must be in possession of all papers legally required by the country of residence for regular residence, including if need be, a residing permit and a work permit."[994] Consequently, a person who loses his work permit because he loses his job loses also the protection of Article 19(8) if, as a result, he is no longer entitled to reside in the territory of the party concerned.[995] As the Committee of Independent Experts has stated, this is a situation which, although consistent with the Charter, allows an employer to bring "intolerable pressure" to bear upon the migrant worker.[996]

Article 19(9): Transfer of Earnings and Savings[997]

By Article 19(9), the contracting parties undertake in respect to migrant workers "to permit, within legal limits, the transfer of such parts of the earnings and savings of such workers as they may desire." This is a very important provision for migrant workers. It has caused no difficulty in practice. By "transfer" is meant the transfer of funds while the worker continues to work in the territory of the contracting party, when he leaves it,[998] or afterwards. Transfers may be subjected to "legal limits." As the Committee of Independent Experts has indicated, this qualification must be interpreted so as not to rob the undertaking of any meaning. In its opinion, the wording "within legal limits," "while authorising some limit on what might be transferred for currency reasons, could not be considered as permitting a state which had accepted paragraph 9 to place any obstacles in the way of transferring a reasonable amount of earnings and savings, having regard to

---

[994]C II 197.

[995]C II 198 (Cyprus).

[996]*Id.*

[997]*Cf.* ILO Migration for Employment Convention (Revised) 1949, Art. 9, note 808 *supra*, upon which Art. 19(9) is based. *See also* ILO Migration for Employment Recommendation (Revised) 1949.

[998]C I 87 (Norway).

the situation of the migrant and his family."[999] Applying this approach, the Committee of Independent Experts held that an Italian restriction during the first cycle by which a foreign worker might transfer up to 500,000 lire each month to his country of origin complied with Article 19(8).[1000] It also found the limitations imposed by the U.K. to be permissible. By these, a migrant worker who is temporarily resident in the U.K. may "transfer to his country of origin through a bank any amount of money up to the total of his net earnings, provided he has paid his income tax and deducted 'reasonable' current expenses"; if he becomes a permanent resident, he is subject in principle to the same restrictions as any resident of the U.K., except that any transfer he may wish to make to his home country to continue payment of certain family obligations, such as the education of his children, will be given consideration.[1001] A limit of 50% of annual earnings is permissible.[1002] Equality of treatment with nationals does not meet the requirements of Article 19(9); a migrant worker must not be subject to restrictions that are more severe than those that meet the Committee of Independent Experts' concept of a reasonable limitation, whatever the treatment afforded to nationals.[1003]

Article 19(10): Extension to Self-Employed Workers

By Article 19(10), the contracting parties undertake "to extend the protection and assistance provided for in this Article to self-employed migrants insofar as such measures apply." By Article 19(10), the Charter improves upon the International Labor Organization Migration of Employment Convention (Revised) 1949,[1004] which applies only to employed persons. It follows, instead, the European Convention on Establishment, which applies "whether the person concerned is self-employed or is in the service of an employer."[1005] The undertaking ap-

---

[999]C I 86.

[1000]C I 87 (Italy).

[1001]C I 87 (U.K.). *See also* C I 218 (Ireland) for a third example of permissible restrictions. In the case of Ireland also, the worker is only free to transfer funds to his home country.

[1002]Laroque, *supra* note 591, at 13.

[1003]C IV 131 (Italy), C V 123, C V 140 (France).

[1004]ILO Migration for Employment Convention (Revised) 1949, Art. 11(1), note 808 *supra*.

[1005]*Id.* Art. 10.

plies "insofar as such measures [i.e., those in Article 19(1)–(9)] apply." The only one that would not seem to apply is that in Article 19(4) (a) concerning "remuneration and other employment and working conditions." The obligation in Article 19(10) is met by treating the self-employed equally with employed persons in respect to matters within the paragraphs that the contracting party has accepted *whether the standards set in those paragraphs are met or not.* A contracting party may thus comply with Article 19(10) even though it is in breach of another paragraph of the Article.[1006]

MAINTENANCE OF A SYSTEM OF LABOR INSPECTION

Article 20(5) reads: "Each Contracting Party shall maintain a system of labour inspection appropriate to national conditions." This provision, which is the only part of the legal guarantee in the Charter that parties must accept,[1007] started life as a proposal for a much more substantial undertaking in Part II by which contracting parties would undertake to have a system of labor inspection to ensure that the guarantees in Part II concerning conditions of work and the protection of the worker were complied with.[1008] As such, it could have served an important role.[1009] Unfortunately, the substance of Article 20(5) was watered down considerably to its present anemic form and moved from Part II to Part III where it is not the subject of scrutiny by the Committee of Independent Experts. As a result, it has so far proved to be of no importance.

THE RECORD OF COMPLIANCE[1010]

Having examined the substance of the guarantee in Part II provision by provision, it is proposed in the final two sections of this chapter to review the record of compliance with it and to consider generally the standards set by the Charter. Table 1 indicates the overall record of compliance as determined by

---

[1006]*See, e.g.,* C III 145, 149 (F.R.G.). But positive measures must be taken to ensure equal treatment for the self-employed. C III 99 (Italy).

[1007]*Cf.* note 13 *supra.*

[1008]It was proposed in this form by Belgium at the TC. REC PROC TC 225. *Cf.* ILO Labour Inspection Convention 1947, note 174 *supra.*

[1009]*Cf.* the similar but much more restricted guarantee in Art. 3(2) concerning the enforcement of health and safety regulations.

[1010]For details of compliance by each state, see Appendix II.

Table 1. Overall record of compliance

Cycle	I	II	III	IV	V	VI	VII
Undertakings fulfilled	232	287	317	326	328	336	343 (81%)
Undertakings not fulfilled	57	62	61	60	64	69	73 (17%)
No decision for lack of information	131	71	42	34	28	15	8 (2%)

the Committee of Independent Experts of the seven states[1011] that reported during all of the first seven cycles of supervision.[1012] The figures for undertakings fulfilled has risen substantially from 55% in the first cycle to 81% in the seventh. This has been achieved partly by changes in law and practice and partly by the presentation of further information permitting a decision for the first time. The figure of undertakings that have not been fulfilled has increased slightly from 13 ½% to 17% for the reason that some cases in which further information has allowed a decision to be made, the information has revealed a situation of noncompliance. A striking change in the figures is the sharp fall in the number of cases in which a decision has not been possible.

Table 2, for the sixth and seventh cycles, contains figures for all of the ten states[1013] reporting during those two most recent cycles. It shows a similar pattern of compliance, etc.[1014]

Table 3 indicates the record of compliance of each of the contracting parties at the end of the seventh cycle as determined by the Committee of Independent Experts. The level of compliance varied considerably from state to state. No state complied with all of its obligations. Cyprus (which has considerable internal problems) had complied with the least number, less than that required for ratification. The worst records of compliance with accepted provisions were those of Ireland and the U.K., although in the case of the U.K. six of the findings against it concerned just the Isle of Man and/or Northern Ire-

[1011]Denmark, the F.R.G., Ireland, Italy, Norway, Sweden, and the U.K.

[1012]The table contains no figures for Art. 1(4) because of the CIE's practice in the first six cycles of not making a ruling on it for those states which have accepted all parts of Arts. 9, 10, and 15.

[1013]The seven referred to, note 1011 *supra*, plus Austria, Cyprus, and France. No figures are included for Iceland.

[1014]The table again ignores Art. 1(4). *See* note 1012 *supra*.

Table 2. Compliance during sixth and seventh cycles

Cycle	VI	VII
Undertakings fulfilled	470	478 (81½%)
Undertakings not fulfilled	87	94 (16%)
No decision for lack of information	26	15 (2½%)

Table 3. Record of compliance of contracting parties

	Paragraphs accepted[1]	Complied	Information lacking	Not Complied
Austria	62	53	1	7[2]
Cyprus	34	28	0	5
Denmark	45	38	1	5
FRG	67	59	1	6[2]
France	70	54	6	9
Ireland	63	43	0	19
Italy	72	54	3	14
Norway	60	55	0	4
Sweden	62	51	3	7
UK	62	43	0	18[2]

1. This figure indicates the total number accepted. The figures in the other columns in this table add up to one short of this in each case. No figure is given for compliance with Art. 1(4). *See* note 1012 *supra*.

2. The rulings against the F.R.G., Austria, and the U.K. on Art. 1(4) are not included. *Cf.* note 1012 *supra*.

land. The F.R.G. had complied with the largest number of provisions. The case of Italy is that of a state which accepted all of Part II when it was not really in a position to do so. Even so, its high number of provisions not complied with is matched by the high number of obligations that it has honored.

The guarantees that have caused the most difficulty for the contracting parties as a whole concern the protection (mainly in employment) of children and young persons and women. Article 7(1) (minimum age of employment) is the only provision that has not yet been complied with by any state. Other provisions that have caused particular difficulties of compliance are:

Article 4(1), (4) (right to adequate remuneration and reasonable notice of dismissal, respectively)
Article 6(4) (collective action in industrial disputes)

Article 7(3),(6) (employment of schoolchildren and day release of young workers, respectively)

Article 8(2) (dismissal during maternity leave)

Article 18(2),(3) (simplification and liberalization of rules concerning migrant workers)

At the other extreme, the following provisions have been satisfied with little or no difficulty:

Article 9(vocational guidance)

      10 (vocational training)

      11 (protection of health)

      12 (social and welfare services)

      15 (rights of the disabled)

      16 (protection of the family)

As will be apparent from these lists, most problems have arisen in respect to economic rather than social rights.

Many of the infringements that have been found by the Committee of Independent Experts are on matters of real importance for the contracting parties and for the individuals concerned. Certainly there are some breaches which are quite peripheral to the protection of economic and social rights in any basic sense. For example, the provision in Irish law (since repealed) whereby a person recently in receipt of public assistance was disqualified from local authority office had not been a grievance in practice.[1015] There are others, however, which are central to the protection of economic and social rights. The denial of the right to strike to the civil service is an example.[1016] So are the breaches of the right to equal pay[1017] and of the rights of migrant workers.[1018] Overall, the number and importance of the undertakings not complied with, as determined by the Committee of Independent Experts, is disappointingly large.[1019] The record displays, in the context of Western Europe, some surprising gaps in the protection afforded. And this, of course, is quite apart from the undertakings in Part II that have not been accepted.

[1015]See note 665 *supra.*

[1016]See note 339 *supra.*

[1017]See note 260 *supra.*

[1018]See note 835 *supra.*

[1019]For details, see Appendix II.

THE STANDARDS SET BY THE CHARTER

The Charter protects most of the rights that are thought of as economic and social rights, but there are omissions. Of these, the right to education is the most important.[1020] Whereas the plan at first was to include it, the Committee of Ministers eventually decided not to do so, largely on the ground that it was not a matter of social policy as clearly as were the other rights being protected.[1021] Its absence contrasts sharply with the detailed guarantee of primary, secondary, and tertiary education in the International Covenant on Economic, Social and Cultural Rights[1022] and results in an omission in the European arrangements for the protection of human rights which the negative and limited guarantee in the European Convention on Human Rights does not remedy.[1023] The failure to include the right to education is particularly disappointing because of its ramifications for some of the other rights that are protected, education being a necessary prerequisite, for example, to the full realization of the right to work and to equality of opportunity in employment. Although it is arguable that the right to education is a cultural rather than an economic or social right,[1024] there are no hard and fast lines between these categories. The practice has been to protect them all in the same document. The right to education has always had a prominent part in any such combined list, and its protection in the Charter would have been in keeping with this tradition. The same is true of the absence of cultural rights generally from the Charter and hence from the Council of Europe

[1020]The guarantee in Art. 10(1) of "facilities for access to higher technical and university education . . ." is relevant but is by no means sufficient. *See* note 535 *supra*.

[1021]Decision taken at its meeting in February 1958. Other factors may have been the problem of drafting a text guaranteeing free education and of providing for federal states within which education is the province of local government. The presence of a partial guarantee in the ECHR may also have been relevant. *See* note 1023 *infra*.

[1022]ICESCR, Art. 13, note 29 *supra*.

[1023]First Protocol to the ECHR, Art. 2, *done* Mar. 20, 1952, 1954 Gr. Brit. T.S. No. 46 (Cmd. 7778), Europ. T.S. No. 9. By this states do not undertake to ensure that there is an adequate educational system within their jurisdiction; they undertake instead not to deny any person the right to be educated and, insofar as they assume any functions in relation to education and teaching, to "respect the right of parents to ensure such education and teaching in conformity with their own religious and philosophical convictions."

[1024]*See* Benvenuti, *supra* note 10, at 661.

scheme of human rights protection as a whole.[1025] Again, the contrast with the International Covenant on Economic, Social and Cultural Rights, which does protect cultural rights, is a clear one.[1026]

Another omission is the right to protection of the environment. In this case, the drafters of the Charter are scarcely to blame since the quality of the environment came to be seen as an issue largely after they completed their work. The Committee of Independent Experts has recently asked for information on environmental control under Article 11,[1027] but there is a limit to the action it can take under this heading since pollution is not just a matter of health and needs to be regulated systematically in a separate provision.[1028] There is here an interest which is "coming to be recognized by modern law"[1029] and which can justifiably be formulated in terms of a social right.[1030]

The Charter also contains no provision in Part II equivalent to Article 14 of the European Convention on Human Rights, by which the rights included are guaranteed without discrimination on grounds of sex, race, etc. This is achieved in varying degrees in respect to certain particular provisions of the Charter,[1031] but there is no provision applying to Part II as a whole. The Preamble to the Charter does, however, contain a

---

[1025]European Cultural Convention 1954, *adopted* Dec. 19, 1054, Europ. T.S. No. 8, 218 U.N.T.S. 139, and other particular steps which the CE has taken (*see* MANUAL OF THE COUNCIL OF EUROPE 228–42 [1970]) are of limited scope, are not framed in human rights terms, and are not subject to any system of supervision.

[1026]Contrast ICESCR, Art. 15, note 29 *supra*.

[1027]C IV 75.

[1028]*Cf.* the Programme of Action of the European Communities on the Environment, Annex to the Declaration of the Council of Ministers on the Programme of Action, etc. 16 O.J. EUR. COMM. (No. C 112) 1 (1973). The 1973 Programme was supplemented in 1977 and 1982. See 20 O.J. EUR. COMM. (No. C 139) 1 (1977) and 26 O.J. EUR. COMM. (No. C 56) 1 (1983). For a full account, see G. JOHNSON, THE POLLUTION CONTROL POLICY OF THE EUROPEAN COMMUNITIES (1979).

[1029]Pound, *A Theory of Social Interests*, 15 PAPERS AND PROCEEDINGS OF THE AMERICAN SOCIOLOGICAL SOCIETY 44 (1921), *reprinted in* J. HALL, READINGS IN JURISPRUDENCE 245 (1938).

[1030]The Declaration on the Management of the Natural Environment of Europe adopted by the European Conservation Conference in 1970 proposed that a Protocol to the ECHR (not to the Social Charter) be drafted guaranteeing "the right of every individual to enjoy a healthy and unspoiled environment." The CM of the CE rejected this decision but referred the question of protection against environmental health hazards to the CIE acting under Art. 11 of the Charter.

[1031]*See especially*, Arts. 1(2) & 4(3).

nondiscrimination clause[1032] which may be used to interpret Part II and to achieve the same result where the wording of the provision concerned is not clearly to the contrary. It could be used, for example, to ensure that the right to organize a trade union in Article 5 is one that is guaranteed without discrimination on any of the grounds listed in the Preamble.

Although the Charter pays (inevitably) considerable attention to the rights of the individual as a worker, there are certain gaps, most of which were apparent in 1961, in the provisions concerning employment. Freedom from arbitrary dismissal, entitlement to redundancy payments, and the right to retire at sixty-two (or earlier) are the three clearest cases.[1033] Other more controversial provisions that were argued for unsuccessfully concerned profit-sharing with workers in industry, worker participation in industry, and the protection of savings from inflation.[1034]

The absence of certain other rights is more apparent than real. In particular, the rights of everyone to leisure and to "an adequate standard of living for himself and his family, including adequate food, clothing and housing, and to the continuous improvement in living conditions," which are recognized by the International Covenant on Economic, Social and Cultural Rights (Art. 2[1]) but not included as such in the Charter, are indirectly protected by provisions such as those concerning "reasonable . . . working hours,"[1035] remuneration that will allow "a decent standard of living" for workers and their families,[1036] and family housing.[1037] Several of the above

---

[1032]The Preamble reads: "Considering that the enjoyment of social rights should be secured without discrimination on grounds of race, colour, sex, religion, political opinion, national extraction or social origin."

[1033]The first and the third of these were included in the first draft referred to the CM by the CA. Eur. Consult. Ass., 8th Sess., Doc. No. 536 (1956), Art. 1(a) & (h). Old-age pensions come within Art. 12 of the Charter and Part V of the European Code of Social Security 1968, note 583 *supra*, but the right to retire is not directly guaranteed. *See also* the CM Resolution on Social Security Measures to be Taken in Favour of Pensioners and Persons Remaining in Activity after Pensionable Age 1976, CM Resolution (76) 32.

[1034]*See* the draft of the CA Committee on Social Questions. Eur. Consult. Ass., 7th Sess., Doc. No. 403 (1955), Arts. 4 & 13.

[1035]Art. 2(1) of the Charter. This, of course, does not guarantee the right to retirement.

[1036]Art. 4(1).

[1037]Art. 16. *But see* Laroque, *Drawing up and Implementation of the European Social Charter*, Working Paper for the 1977 Strasbourg Symposium on the European Social Charter, CE Doc. AS/Coll/Charte 1-E, at 9, who is very critical of the absence of a full right to housing.

undertakings are framed, however, in terms of the worker and his family when a commitment to individuals generally would have been preferable. Some more explicit provisions protecting the elderly would also have been useful.

Turning from the rights themselves to the substantive undertakings given in relation to them, it is interesting to note that despite the argument put during the drafting of the Charter that it would be a statement of specifically European objectives, there is little that is noticeably European about the standards which the Charter sets. Those concerning economic rights are closely geared to International Labor Organization standards, which have universal application, and the guarantees concerning other rights are not essentially different from those in the equally universal International Covenant on Economic, Social and Cultural Rights. This does not mean that the Charter cannot serve a valuable role as the source of a common commitment for European states. It does mean that the social aspirations of the Council of Europe do not differ essentially from those of states generally. This is not a surprising conclusion in view of the wide economic and cultural cross section of states that form the Council's membership. There are signs that when deciding what to expect of states in a particular respect, the Committee of Independent Experts looks to the "current state of society and of ideas about society reflected in law and regulations in the Member states of the Council of Europe."[1038] This approach, which must be the correct one, is not inconsistent with what has been said above. For example, the above quotation is taken from a passage in which the Committee of Independent Experts was taking account of the change in attitudes that has occurred toward the status of children born out of wedlock, a change which is not specifically European.

As far as economic rights are concerned, there is, as stated above, in most cases a clear parallel with the standards set in the conventions and recommendations of the International Labor Organization in existence in 1961.[1039] In a few places, these standards (and even those in later ILO conventions) are

---

[1038]C IV 104.

[1039]COMPARISON BETWEEN THE PROVISIONS OF THE DRAFT EUROPEAN SOCIAL CHARTER AND THE CORRESPONDING ILO STANDARDS, published by the International Labour Office in 1958 for the Tripartite Conference, and *The European Social Charter and International Labour Standards*, 84 INT'L LAB. REV. 354 (1961).

improved upon. Thus, certain of the Charter guarantees on equal pay,[1040] on maternity leave,[1041] and on the rights of migrant workers[1042] surpass those of the International Labor Organization. The Charter guarantees on vocational guidance and training predated the International Labor Organization convention on this subject,[1043] and the specific guarantees of the rights of the handicapped to vocational training, etc., still have no full parallel in International Labor Organization conventions.[1044] But in other places the Charter falls short. The principle of the forty-hour working week, which is recognized in the International Labor Organization Forty-Hour Week Convention 1935[1045] provides the clearest case of this. Strenuous efforts were made to write it into the text, but, in the event, it was not included.[1046] The guarantee of two weeks' annual holiday with pay has now been bettered by the three-week guarantee in the International Labor Organization Holidays with Pay Convention (Revised) 1970.[1047] The overall impression of Part II in the field of economic rights is of a conservative text rather than one that sets many new standards. The reason for this is not in doubt. The emphasis was upon the need to draft a text imposing legal obligations that states could accept at once. Even though states did not have to accept all of Part II, there was thought to be a serious risk that a more ambitious text of a binding legal character would not be sufficiently widely accepted to make it worthwhile.

Undertakings with regard to social rights are less cautious and, in the main, a good deal more vague and general in their wording. This latter characteristic is not necessarily a disadvantage. Although the generality of many of the provisions of Part II—including those concerning workers—was initially criticized as a weakness,[1048] the presence of an independent supervisory organ capable of filling in the details has meant

[1040]Art. 4(3). See note 255 supra.

[1041]Art. 8(2). See note 504 supra.

[1042]Arts. 18 & 19 (3),(6). See notes 767, 894, & 934 supra.

[1043]Arts. 9 & 10. See notes 517 & 530 supra.

[1044]Art. 15. See note 701 supra. But see ILO Vocational Rehabilitation and Employment (Disabled Persons) Convention 1983 (ILO Convention No. 159), adopted June 1983.

[1045]See note 125 supra.

[1046]See note 132 supra. This may well have proved fortunate as expectations are now of a working week of less than 40 hours.

[1047]See note 125 supra.

[1048]See, e.g., Delpérée, Les Droits Sociaux et la Charte Sociale Européenne, 1 HUMAN RIGHTS J. 549, 576 (1968).

that this is not necessarily so, although some provisions, e.g., Article 11 (the right to protection of health) and Article 16 (the right to the family to be protected), offer such a broad canvas that it has yet to be fully filled in.[1049] Insofar as the Charter has dated, it has done so in respect to certain of the more precisely worded of its provisions. Thus, certain of the very specific provisions concerning the employment of children in Article 7 have been overtaken by the raising of the school-leaving age, and the paternalistic approach to women underlying part of Article 8 is fast losing conviction in some of the contracting parties. Similarly, the tendency to reduce the age of majority to eighteen in national law has made Article 19(6) (which specifies twenty-one) out of date.[1050]

If Part II could have been more demanding in the obligations which it imposes, it must be stressed that it is still far from being without meaning or substance. In the first place, it contains a commitment which cannot (without denunciation of the Charter or the relevant part of it and the loss of face that this entails) be gone back upon so far as it is accepted by a contracting party. This is particularly important in times of economic recession.[1051] Second, most economic and social rights are in fact included and are protected at a level which, as is apparent from the number of provisions accepted by states[1052] and their record of compliance, presents a sizable hurdle. And it is, perhaps worth stressing again that a guarantee which does not appear ambitious on paper may nonetheless stretch or grow with time if it has an independent and demanding supervisory body to mark its limits and to adjust them as conditions and

[1049]It is interesting to recall in this connection the differences that emerged in the drafting of the ECHR, with some states wanting as much detail as possible so that they would know where they stood before ratification and other states preferring a more general text. *See* Robertson, *The European Convention for the Protection of Human Rights* 27 BRIT. Y.B. INT'L L. 145, 147–52 (1950). In the case of the Convention, the supervisory organs have found such general provisions as those guaranteeing freedom from "inhuman or degrading treatment or punishment" (Art. 3) and the right to a "fair hearing" (Art. 6[1]) capable of extensive development.

[1050]Although out of date as far as the age of majority is concerned, Art. 19(6) still, of course, offers valuable protection to dependents over 18.

[1051]Thus a party that accepted the obligation to provide free employment services (Art. 1[3]) could not rely on changed economic circumstances as a defense. Allowance for economic conditions can be made for provisions that are progressive or "dynamic" in either of the two senses in which Part II provision may be said to be such. *See* note 24 *supra*. Such provisions are in the minority.

[1052]The 13 contracting parties have not accepted 17% of the provisions that they could have accepted.

aspirations change. The drafting fathers of the American Constitution would certainly not have recognized the American Bill of Rights as it now stands interpreted.

The Committee of Independent Experts are, however, bound by the clear limits of the Charter's text. The deficiencies of that text, whether those apparent in 1961 or others that have materialized since, caused the Parliamentary Assembly in 1978 to propose amendments to the Charter to strengthen it.[1053] The Assembly's proposals for the addition of new rights to the Charter and for the improvement of existing ones were later submitted for government consideration within the Council of Europe. The Assembly has proposed the addition of the following new rights: the right to worker participation in industry; the right of workers to be protected against the effects of rationalization and of new technology; the right of men and women to equality of opportunity and treatment in the economic, social, and cultural fields; the right to a basic education; the right to educational leave; the right to decent housing; the right of frontier workers to social and economic protection; the right of elderly people to such protection; and the right of the least favored sectors of the population to reinforced social and economic protection. The Assembly has also proposed the updating of some of the existing standards, including four weeks' annual holiday with pay (instead of two); further protection of health and safety at work; better protection of the right to strike; a guarantee of basic social security rights and old-age pensions; and the right of the disabled to a properly planned place of work. At the same time, the Assembly has recommended that a small number of economic and social rights be added to the European Convention on Human Rights (with its different enforcement system).[1054] It is a matter of conjecture

---

[1053]Recommendation 839, Texts Adopted, September 1978.

[1054]Recommendation 838, *id.* The rights to which it is proposed to add are: the right freely to choose or to accept a paid activity; the right of access to free employment services, vocational guidance, and vocational training; the right to an adequate standard of living in the event of involuntary unemployment; and the right to be affiliated to a social security scheme. *Cf.* Arts. 1(2) and (3), 9, 10, & 12 of the Charter, which cover much of the same ground. *See also* Eur. Parl. Ass., 39th Sess., Doc. No. 3214 (1978), and Jacobs, *The Extension of the European Convention on Human Rights to Include Economic, Social and Cultural Rights*, 3 Human Rights Rev. 166 (1978). Concern was expressed during the debate on the proposal that the Charter should not be prejudiced by this development. *See* Mr. Craig, Eur. Parl. Deb. 30th Sess., at 296.

whether, despite the Committee of Ministers' commitment to the extension of the protection of social and economic rights within the Council of Europe,[1055] member states are yet prepared to adopt many, or any, of these proposals in Protocols to either the Charter or the Convention.[1056]

[1055]Declaration of Human Rights adopted by the Committee of Ministers at its 62d Session on Apr. 27, 1978, para. 7, 1978 Y.B. EUR. CONV. ON HUMAN RIGHTS 82.

[1056]At present, the Committee of Ministers has under active consideration proposals to include the following rights in a Protocol to the Charter: freedom from sexual discrimination in employment; the right of consultation of workers; the right of workers to participate in the determination of their working conditions and environment; and the right of the elderly to social protection. In addition, it is considering proposals to add the following economic and social rights to the ECHR by Protocol: the right to equal pay for equal work; the right to social and medical assistance; the right to free compulsory education; the right to equal treatment in respect of one's vocation and employment; and the right to adequate compensation for expropriated property.

CHAPTER III

The System of Supervision

Supervision of the Charter's implementation is based upon national reports from the contracting parties. These reports are examined first by the Committee of Independent Experts, which, as its name indicates, is an independent body. The Experts prepare their *Conclusions* on the reports. These *Conclusions* then are submitted, together with the reports, to the Govermental Committee of the Social Charter. This Committee, which consists of civil servants representing the contracting parties, makes a *Report* to the Committee of Ministers in which it comments upon the national reports and the *Conclusions*. The *Conclusions* and the *Report* are transmitted to the Parliamentary Assembly, which adopts an *Opinion* based on them. The Committee of Ministers completes the process by considering whether, in the light of the three documents thus generated by the supervisory process, any recommendations should be made to one or more of the contracting parties concerning the implementation of the Charter. As recommendations, they are not binding in law. The system of supervision does not include a right of petition. Further, there is no provision for a reference to a court of law. The system is concerned only with Part II of the Charter; no direct provision is made for the supervision of the general policy commitment in Part I.

NATIONAL REPORTS

There are two kinds of reports. In accordance with Article 21 of the Charter, contracting parties submit biennial reports "concerning the application of such provisions of Part II of the Charter as they have accepted." By Article 22, they must also report "at appropriate intervals as requested by the Committee of Ministers" on the provisions of Part II that they have not accepted.

Reports on Accepted Provisions

The first set of biennial reports made by the contracting parties under Article 21 were for a part of 1965 and for the calendar years 1966 and 1967. So far, seven further sets of reports have been presented. These cover the second to eighth cycles, for the years 1968–69 to 1980–81. Seven contracting parties submitted reports for the first cycle.[1] Eight parties did so for the second cycle, [2] nine for the third and fourth cycles, [3] and ten for the fifth and sixth.[4] Eleven parties submitted reports for the most recently completed seventh cycle.[5] The reports for the first seven cycles have been through all of the stages of the supervisory process; those for the eighth cycle have so far been considered by the Committee of the Independent Experts only.

The reports are submitted in one of the two official languages of the Council of Europe, English and French.[6] They are prepared in response to a Report Form adopted by the Committee of Ministers.[7] Reports other than the first report

---

[1]The Charter came into force for the first five contracting parties (the U.K., Norway, Sweden, Ireland, and the F.R.G.) on Feb. 26, 1965. *See* Appendix I. For those parties, the First Report covered the period from that date to the end of 1967 (i.e., nearly three years). By the time the machinery of implementation was established, two more states (Denmark and Italy) had ratified the Charter. The First Report for these states also covered the period from the time the Charter entered into force for them (Apr. 2, 1965 and Nov. 21, 1965, respectively) to the end of 1967.

[2]The eighth ratifying state—Cyprus—submitted its First Report for this cycle. The Report covered the period from the date of the entry into force of the Charter for Cyprus (Apr. 7, 1968) to the end of 1969.

[3]The ninth ratifying state—Austria—submitted its First Report for the third cycle. The Report covered the period from the date of the entry into force of the Charter for Austria (Nov. 28, 1969) to the end of 1971.

[4]The tenth ratifying state—France—submitted its First Report for the fifth cycle. The Report covered the period from the date of the entry into force of the Charter for France (Apr. 8, 1983) to the end of 1975.

[5]The eleventh party—Iceland—should have submitted its First Report during the previous cycle (covering the period from Feb. 14, 1976—when the Charter entered into force for Iceland—to the end of 1977) but failed to do so. The report it made during the seventh cycle covered the period of the sixth. Spain and the Netherlands, which both ratified the Charter in 1980, submitted their First Reports in the eighth cycle.

[6]This is a matter of practice; there is no provision in the Charter to this effect. The CIE has asked that accompanying documents (legislation, reports, etc.) also be sent in an official language wherever possible. In the third cycle, it asked for translations of certain Austrian legislation. C III 40 (Austria). In the fourth cycle, it asked Denmark for a summary of amendments to its legislation in an official language. C IV 180 (Denmark). Austria submitted its report for the sixth cycle in German at first. An English translation was sent five months later. C VI 135.

[7]*See* Art. 21. The Form was adopted by the CM on Jan. 26, 1968. It was based upon a draft prepared by the CIE. Sur, *La Charte Sociale Européenne: Dix Années*

also take account of the questions put to each contracting party by the Committee of Independent Experts in its *Conclusions*. The Report Form, which is 83 pages long and has 171 questions, is a detailed and closely structured questionnaire asking for a considerable amount of information concerning the undertakings in Part II of the Charter.[8] It has been the subject of criticism. The Govermental Committee has recommended its revision on the grounds that "it is too detailed and sometimes implies a tendentious interpretation of the provision concerned."[9] The Committee of Independent Experts also has asked for the Form to be changed and has prepared drafts[10] for two new report forms—one for first reports and one for subsequent reports—to replace it. The Committee of Independent Experts has found that some questions are ambiguous or obscure, while others are misdirected or in need of supplementation and that the Form as a whole is inappropriate for the largely updating role of subsequent reports. The Govermental Committee has drafted its own revised Form, which, like the present one, would apply to both first and subsequent reports. The draft takes as its main concern the need to ensure that the supervisory process is not made "unduly arduous" and to "simplify the work of national governments departments."[11] It omits most of the new questions proposed by the Committee of Independent Experts as well as some of the questions asked now. The revised, single report form approved by the Committee of Ministers contains few changes from the original form.[12]

During the first five cycles of implementation, no state

d'Application, 1974 EUR. Y.B. 88, 91. In the covering letter which the Secretary-General of the CE sent with it to contracting parties for the first cycle, it was stated, on the instruction of the CM, that "the enclosed form is only intended to indicate the lines on which your Government's report is to be prepared and, therefore, has no mandatory character." Smyth, *The Implementaion of the European Social Charter,* in MELANGES MODINOS 290, 295 (1968). On the interpretative value of the Report Form, *See* Kojanec, *Droit au Travail, Droit de la Famille à une Protection Sociale, Juridique et Economique, Droit de la Mère et de l'Enfant à une Protection Sociale et Economique,* 4, paper presented to the Brussels Colloquium on the European Social Charter, Institut d'Etudes Européennes (1971).

[8]It is more detailed than the questionnaires for the equivalent ILO conventions.

[9]GC III 4. The proposal was made as part of a more general proposal by the GC to reduce the biennial reporting commitment of contracting parties. *See* GC III 3.

[10]SOC (71) 2 & 3.

[11]GC V 4.

[12]The CM took its decision after referring the two rival proposals to the PA for an opinion.

failed to submit its report. Iceland spoiled this record when it failed to present its report for the sixth cycle.[13] Even so, compared to the experience of the International Labor Organization,[14] this is a remarkably good response. It was nonetheless predictable because the contracting parties are members of a small and politically homogeneous group of states within which a large-scale failure to submit reports would be surprising. Most reports, however, are submitted late. The filing deadline is six months after the end of each cycle. In the most recent cycle (the sixth) for which records are complete, reports were submitted on average some six months after this. No report was on time; one was a year late. The small size of the Secretariat at present available to deal with reports has meant that this delay has not greatly affected the process of supervision because all of the reports cannot be handled at once. If the Secretariat were increased in size, as it is submitted it should be, the situation would be different. The Committee of Independent Experts has expressed regret at the delay in the submission of reports.[15] Delays have been due, in part, to the fact that information has to be culled from a large number of governmental departments[16] and, in some cases, from regional governments.[17] A report may be held up for lack of just one or two pieces of information.[18]

The reports presented during the first seven cycles show that states have, for the most part, been diligent in the execution of what is, as the Committee of Independent Experts has acknowleged,[19] a demanding reporting obligation. It is such mainly because of the scope of the Charter, which covers the ground of a large number of International Labor Organiza-

---

[13]C VI xii. *Contra* note 5 *supra*.

[14]*See* E. LANDY, THE EEFFECTIVENESS OF INTERNATIONAL SUPERVISION: THIRTY YEARS OF I.L.O. EXPERIENCE 151–53 (1966). In recent years, about 85% of the reports due have been submitted.

[15]C IV x. *See also* C V xi and C VI x. In the sixth cycle, it demonstrated its concern by indicating in Part II of its *Conclusions* the date on which each report reached Strasbourg.

[16]The U.K. report, for example, is assembled from contributions from approximately 20 Whitehall Departments.

[17]Even a unitary state such as the U.K. has to obtain information from Northern Ireland and the Isle of Man.

[18]Some contracting parties, on occasion, have overcome this problem by sending in their reports in two or more parts. In other cases, a contracting party has set its own deadline and sent in its report without the missing information.

[19]C I 6 and C II xvii.

tion conventions as well as a wide range of social rights.[20] Most reports have been long and detailed.[21] This is particularly true of first reports. Subsequent reports provide further information requested by the Committee of Independent Experts or indicate changes in law and practice during the two years concerned. Often, reports have only to record that the situation has not changed in respect to a particular provision.

Despite the work put into the reports, the Committee of Independent Experts sometimes has found itself unable to decide whether a particular provision has been complied with for lack of information. One reason for this has been the shortcomings of the Report Form. In addition to those shortcomings referred to above,[22] the Form allows states to submit summaries or copies of reports that have been prepared for the International Labor Organization in respect to obligations in International Labor Organization conventions that correspond with those in the Charter.[23] Although this practice reduces the work load of reporting states, it has been found to have certain weaknesses. States have sometimes only summarized or submitted their most recent (and usually updating) International Labor Organization report, and not their earlier reports which the Committee of Independent Experts has needed to complete the picture. The arrangement also has proved to be inherently unsatisfactory because the Charter undertakings are seldom precisely the same as those in the comparable International Labor Organization conventions. The questions put by the International Labor Organization supervising authorities consequently are by no means the same as those put in the Report Form and so do not always provide the information needed by the Committee of Independent Experts. The reporting periods for the International Labor Organization conventions also may not exactly coincide with those for the Charter so that, for example, the most recent report for the International Labor Organization may stop short of the end of the reporting period for the Charter.

---

[20]The exact size of the commitment will depend upon the number of provisions of Part II that have been accepted.

[21]First reports have varied from 100 pages to over 300. Later reports have been shorter, ranging from 20 to 200 pages. These figures do not include the sometimes substantial annexes (statutes, reports, etc.) commonly submitted with the reports.

[22]Note 8 *supra*.

[23]Approximately one-third of the questionnaire may be answered in this way.

Because of these difficulties, the Committee of Independent Experts has taken the view that "the submission of copies of International Labour Organization reports cannot always be regarded as constituting an adequate or satisfactory reply to the questions put in the form."[24]

Another problem is that of defining the extent of a state's reporting obligation. Although it is generally agreed that a state is required to provide such information as is necessary for the supervisory organs to determine whether it is complying with its obligations, there is disagreement over what this requirement means. The Governmental Committee has questioned whether the Committee of Independent Experts is entitled, as it claims to be, to ask for further information from a state about a provision in the Charter that it has already found to comply with. In the opinion of the Governmental Committee, "requests should be limited to those indispensable for enabling the Committee of Independent Experts to determine whether or not a Contracting Party had fulfilled its 'undertakings.' "[25] This criticism is mistaken. A finding in favor of a contracting party, particularly in the early years when the Committee of Independent Experts is familarizing itself with its legal system, must be conditional upon the absence of subsequent contradictory information. The Committee of Independent Experts would be failing in its duty if it were not to continue probing, cycle by cycle, the law and practice of the contracting parties.[26] But the problem has arisen most commonly and most acutely in connection with the Committee of Independent Experts' requests for statistical information. Such requests have been largely, but not entirely,[27] concerning undertakings that are subject to Article 33 and which, therefore, are met if "the great majority of the workers concerned," which the Committee of Independent Experts has taken to mean 80%, are protected.[28] Statistics are clearly important in the assessment of compliance with such undertakings. The main difficulty has been that the states have not always had the necessary statistics available, or available in the right form,

[24]C III xvii.
[25]GC III 6.
[26]The CIE has maintained its practice despite the GC's criticisms. *See, e.g..,* C IV 131 (Sweden).
[27]*See, e.g.,* C III 34 (F.R.G.) concerning Art. 6 (2).
[28]See note 21 to Chapter IV *infra.*

and, upon being requested to compile them for the purposes of the Charter, have been reluctant, or have refused, to do so. In the fourth cycle, for example, the U.K. flatly refused to compile statistics on the wages of young workers and apprentices in the form wanted by the Committee of Independent Experts (distinguishing between the wages of the two groups) on the ground that the cost would not be justified.[29] In the same cycle, while maintaining its opinion that a contracting party is obliged to provide such statistics as are necessary for the supervision of the Charter, the Committee of Independent Experts made the following compromise suggestions:

> when it proves impossible or too costly to assemble genuine statistics, the necessary data can be obtained through the use of modern aids which, these days, are usually available to public authorities (polls, surveys, etc.). Failing this sort of data the government concerned could always submit official estimates based on factors that could be checked, particularly if the required information relates to the second year of reference, for which statistical data are not always available.[30]

Although these suggestions were welcomed by the Governmental Committee,[31] the Committee of Independent Experts noted in the next cycle that they "apparently have not met with the approval of all of the states concerned" and sought further cooperation.[32] Cases still occur of states not providing all of the statistical and other information requested by the Committee,[33] which has noted with concern that questions have sometimes gone unanswered for more than one cycle of supervision. The Committee has suggested that "failure to submit the information requested . . . is ultimately the same as a failure to comply with" the reporting requirement.[34]

But in the great majority of cases, the problem is simply one

---

[29]Fourth U.K. Report, at 53.

[30]C IV xvi. The statement was made in respect to Art. 33 undertakings but can be taken to apply to all requests for statistical information.

[31]GC IV 3.

[32]C V xvii.

[33]See e.g., the refusal of the U.K. in the sixth cycle to conduct the survey requested by the CIE on Art. 2 (5) because of the cost. Sixth U.K. Report, at 48. See also the following GC comment (GC V 3): "Another problem . . . is the propensity of the Independent Experts to ask for statistics. The Committee wishes to emphasise once more that there may be cases where it is difficult to bring such data together, and often impossible to provide figures that are recent."

[34]C V xvi. See also C VII 25 (a breach if eighth Italian report lacks information).

of communication—of the reporting state not understanding what information is required.[35] This is apparent from the steadily declining number of cases in which the Committee of Independent Experts has been unable to take a decision. In the first cycle of implementation, the Committee of Independent Experts was unable to take a decision on approximately 30% of the undertakings reported upon by the seven states that participated in the cycle.[36] This figure has been reduced to 2% for the same states after the seventh cycle.[37] Altogether, including all of the ten states which reported in the seventh cycle, the figure for that cycle was 2 1/2%.[38] The Committee of Independent Experts has expressed its satisfaction at this continuing downward trend, although it did in the third cycle consider it necessary to reprimand two of the reporting states whose reports it felt were not so full or helpful as they might have been.[39]

The level of "undecided" cases has been reduced partly by the practice of seeking supplementary information from contracting parties during the examination of their reports. Such a practice has been established by the Committee of Independent Experts in accordance with the following rules:

i) if with regard to a certain paragraph of the Charter such report contains no reply to any of the questions asked in the form, the Secretariat shall be empowered, on the Committee's behalf, to request the government concerned to provide the missing information.

ii) if the information given in the report is apparently at variance with other data in the hands of the Secretariat, the Chairman of the Committee may authorize the Secretariat to ask the government concerned for explanations to clear up the discrepancy. The same rule covers the case of a member of the Committee himself discovering an inconsistency of this nature.

iii) In the event of difficulties as to interpretation, i.e. if it is evident from the report from a government that the latter construes a given provision of the Charter in a manner open to ques-

---

[35]*Cf.* C II xiv.

[36]*See* the table in C III xvi. The CIE was unable to take a decision in respect to 131 of the 421 undertakings reported upon in the first cycle. These figures (and those in the following notes) do not take into account Art. 1 (4) (which overlaps with other provisions).

[37]The actual number of undecided cases was 8.

[38]The actual number was 15.

[39]C III xvii. The two states were Italy and Denmark.

tion, it will be for the Committee itself to decide whether or not to instruct the Secretariat to request further information from the said government. The Committee recognized that a similar procedure ought to apply in cases where, on a given question, a government's report did not contain replies on all points in respect of which, in the Committee's opinion, information should have been furnished by the said government.

The Committee of Independent Experts also has empowered the Secretariat to ask governments to send copies of legislative and other texts referred to in national reports either on the Secretariat's own initiative or at the request of a Committee member whenever the document in question appears essential to an understanding of the relevant report. The Secretariat has obtained supplementary information in a number of cases in accordance with these rules and has taken the initiative in some other cases not covered by them to ask a state to clarify or amplify what has been said in a report. It seems likely that this sort of personal and flexible approach could usefully be developed further, especially for first reports when new contracting parties are unsure of the sort of information and level of detail that is required. It would be even more helpful if a member of the Secretariat could discuss the first report with the civil servant responsible for its collation during its preparation.[40] Such initiatives can be helpful not only in reducing the number of cycles it takes for the information to be provided but also in preventing the deadlock that has resulted in a few cases in which a state has simply refused to provide the information sought.[41] The Secretariat's role in this regard is all the more important in the absence of any provision for an oral hearing of the contracting parties before the supervisory organs which could reduce misunderstanding.[42] Another development which should help to reduce the number of undecided cases in future cycles is the practice which the Committee of Independent Experts has adopted of asking questions "ahead" where, either from earlier reports or

[40]This would be a natural extension of the present practice by which the Secretariat is available to discuss the Charter with a state that is considering ratifying it. For the CIE's proposal for "direct contacts" with contracting parties along ILO lines (as to which, see E. LANDY, *supra* note 14, at 33–34), *see* C III xiii.

[41]See, e.g., the positions taken up at one stage by the CIE (C III 91 [U.K.] and C IV 118 [U.K.]) and the U.K. (Third U.K. Report, at 163, and Fourth U.K. Report, at 144) on Art. 19(3).

[42]*See also* E. LANDY, *supra* note 14, at 44–46.

from some other source, it has information about an imminent change in the law.[43] In this way, a contracting party is informed in advance of what the Committee of Independent Experts considers relevant information for inclusion in its next report.

The Charter contains no provision for the publication of reports, which are treated within the Council of Europe as confidential.[44] Although this is a sensible precaution on the Council's part, there would seem to be nothing in the reports to merit such a classification. They contain little more than summaries of the law and practice of the member states relevant to the provisions of the Charter. Insofar as these reports contain explanations of or comments on policies or possible shortcomings, they are not controversial to the point where the "frankness and candor" argument that is normally used to justify secrecy for government documents could apply. Their publication would help to ensure that Governments continue to take their reporting obligations seriously. It also would make it easier to follow the comments upon a particular state's report in the Committee of Independent Experts' *Conclusions* and assist generally in facilitating an understanding of the substance and system of supervision of the guarantee. Moreover, although limited by the scope of the provisions of the Charter and the demands of the Report Form, the reports—particularly first reports—contain information on the law and practice of the growing number of contracting parties, thereby making the reports a useful source of comparative law.[45] For these reasons, the reports should be made public.[46] This

[43]*See, e.g.,* C IV 124 (F.R.G.), where the CIE asked the F.R.G. for information in the fifth cycle on draft federal legislation that it had been informed would be law by then and which would impose a special tax upon the employers of migrant workers.

[44]The CIE has decided to treat the reports and papers relating to them as confidential. The GC follows the same practice.

[45]This is particularly true if the annexes containing the texts of national laws, regulations, etc., are taken into account. To some extent these texts overlap with the ILO legislative series. To the extent that the Charter covers rights not within the terms of reference of the ILO or the state concerned has accepted a Charter undertaking but not a comparable ILO convention, the annexes are an additional source. A more ambitious and valuable exercise would be for the CE, using the texts submitted with the Charter as a starting point, to publish in the official languages of the Council a comparative collection of the legislation of the parties of the Charter.

[46]Copies of some of the British Reports have been placed in the House of Commons Library. There are copies of all of the British Reports in the Library of the Department of Employment in London.

would be consistent with United Nations practice by which comparable national reports under the two International Covenants on Human Rights and the Convention on the Elimination of All Forms of Racial Discrimination are made public as United Nations documents.

In 1974 the Governmental Committee proposed a major alteration to the reporting system under Article 21.[47] It suggested that contracting parties which had submitted their first report should thereafter report in detail in each cycle on only one-third of the articles in Part II.[48] A detailed report thus would be made on each provision of Part II only once every six years. Contracting parties would make a "brief report" on the provisions that they had accepted and that were not reported upon in detail in a given cycle. In this, they would, "if they so wished," report on "changes they consider important which have occurred since the previous biennial report."[49] This proposal was made because of the increased work load that would fall upon the supervisory organ and the contracting parties as more states ratified the Charter and if (as has now happened) the provision for reporting on unaccepted provisions in Article 22 was implemented, as the Governmental Committee agreed should happen elsewhere in its report.[50] The Committee also noted that a large number of issues concerning the interpretation of the Charter and the functions of the supervisory organizations had been resolved during the first three cycles with the result that the need for a biennial consideration of every provision had declined.[51]

The proposal, which was opposed by the Committee of Independent Experts,[52] was rejected by the Committee of Ministers as contrary to the terms of the Charter. Whether this was

---

[47]GC III 3.

[48]The GC divided Part II into three groups of interrelated Articles for this purpose: Arts. 1, 2, 3, 4, 9, 10, and 15; Arts. 5, 6, 7, 8, 18, and 19; and Arts. 11, 12, 13, 14, 16, and 17. Each group would be reported upon by a contracting party so far as it has accepted the provisions in them in the above sequence every third cycle.

[49]GC III 3.

[50]See GC III 4.

[51]The GC felt that although this had also reduced the work load of the supervisory organs, on balance that work load had increased or would increase because of the work resulting from the other previously listed developments.

[52]C IV xix. For the intermediate position of the Parliamentary Assembly, see Opinion No. 71, para. 10, n.1, TEXTS ADOPTED, Apr. 1975, and Opinion No. 75, paras. 5–7, TEXTS ADOPTED, September 1976.

a correct interpretation or not,[53] the Ministers' decision was in the interest of the effectiveness of the system of supervision. A large part of the role of the supervisory organs is to remind the contracting parties of their obligations so that they will bring their law and practice into line with the Charter. A conscience that speaks every two years is less easily ignored than one that will not come again for another six.[54] Although there would have been some reduction in the work load of the contracting parties, it would not have been sufficient to have outweighed the harmful effect of an essentially six-year cycle. The question raised by the Governmental Committee's proposal is really one of the importance attached to the Charter. It is difficult to see that the work load generated by the present biennial reporting system can be said to be unduly great if the Charter is treated with the seriousness that it merits as the "pendant" of the European Convention on Human Rights in the field of economic and social rights.

Reports on Unaccepted Provisions

Article 22 provides that contracting parties must make reports "at appropriate intervals as requested by the Committee of Ministers" on the provisions of Part II of the Charter that they

---

[53]*Quaere* whether Art. 21 requires a detailed report on every provision in each cycle. It is interesting to relate the GC's proposal to the experience of the ILO. Art. 22 of the ILO Constitution requires members to "make an *annual* report on the measures which it has taken to give effect to the provisions of Conventions to which it is a party." (Emphasis added.) In 1959, at the suggestion of the Committee of Experts, which was concerned with its ability to cope with the increasing number of reports (5,000 in 1959) it was having to deal with annually, the Governing Body agreed that detailed reports could be submitted biennially instead of annually subject to the conditions that in "off years" a general report indicating important changes should be made; that first reports should be made immediately after ratification; and that requests for information in an "on year" should be taken up the next year. This arrangement differs from that proposed by the GC in that the change was from annual to biennial, and not from biennial to six-yearly, reporting. In 1976 the ILO made a further change by which reports are now made in detail every four years instead of two, except for the more important conventions and subject to certain other qualifications; *see* Report of the CE, Int'l Lab. Conf., 61st Sess., Report III (Part 4A) (1976). This change was again made because of the pressure of work upon the Committee of Experts, which is greater than that upon the supervisory organizations of the Charter in view of the larger number of reports involved, even allowing for the wider scope of the Charter.

[54]The system proposed by the PA is less subject to this criticism than that proposed by the GC because "additional information" sought by the CIE would have been provided in the next cycle.

have not accepted. No reports were called for until 1978, when the Committee of Ministers required contracting parties to submit reports on four provisions in Part II. The provisions were Articles 4 (3), 7 (1), and 8 (1) and (2). In 1981, a second series of reports was called for on Articles 2(4), 7(4), 8(4), and 19(8).

The Committee of Independent Experts[55] and the Consultative Assembly[56] had pressed for the implementation of Article 22 from the end of the first cycle. The Governmental Committee opposed its implementation in the second cycle because of the work already involved for contracting parties in the preparation of Article 21 reports for that cycle.[57] It maintained its opposition to the implementation of Article 22 in the third cycle on the ground that such implementation would be premature because of the small number of states that had ratified the Charter. The argument would seem to have been partly that it would have been hard on the states that had ratified the Charter to ask them for information about provisions which they had not accepted when a large number of Council of Europe members had not accepted any provision at all, and partly that a lot of extra reporting would be required. In its report in the third cycle, the Governmental Committee changed its mind and proposed the implementation of Article 22 as a part of its plan for a revision of the reporting arrangements for Article 21.[58]

It is both surprising and disappointing that Article 22 remained unimplemented for more than ten years after the Chapter came into force. It is surprising because there was an unequivocal legal obligation placed upon the Committee of Ministers to set Article 22 in motion.[59] Although the Committee has considerable discretion as to the frequency, form, and content of reports, it is not free to allow Article 22 to lie entirely dormant. It is disappointing since the comparable provision of the International Labor Organization Constitu-

[55]C I 9, C II XV, C III, C IV xvii. The CIE called for its implementation as early as 1967.

[56]Opinion No. 57, para. 16, TEXTS ADOPTED, May 1971; Opinion No. 64, para. 24, TEXTS ADOPTED, September/October 1973; Opinion No. 71, para. 10, TEXTS ADOPTED, April 1975.

[57]GC I 14. Italy, the only party then to have accepted all of the provisions of Part II, dissented.

[58]GC III 4.

[59]Cf. Eur. Consult. Ass., 25th Sess., Doc. No. 3276L, at 13–14 (1973).

tion[60] requiring reports on International Labor Organization conventions that have not been accepted by members has proved important in practice. The reports submitted under the International Labor Organization system have reminded member states of the existence and need for ratification of the conventions concerned and pointed to difficulties standing in the way of acceptance that have been taken into account in the revision of convention texts and in the drafting of new conventions in the same area. It is already apparent that Article 22 reports can serve some of the same functions. They also, as the Committee of Independent Experts had predicted,[61] help the supervisory organs to understand the situation in the contracting parties concerning related undertakings in the Charter that they have accepted. The Committee of Independent Experts has given Article 7 (1), which provides that the minimum age of admission to employment shall be fifteen years, as an example. Most contracting parties have not accepted this undertaking but have accepted the great majority of the closely related undertakings in the other paragraphs of the same Article. The Committee of Independent Experts has found it difficult to decide whether these other undertakings are being complied with without knowing why Article 7 (1) has not been accepted.

The Report Form for unaccepted provisions sent to contracting parties in 1978 required them "to give a concise summary of current law and practice in the field covered [by the listed provisions] . . . and indicate the difficulties inherent in the international standard in question, or in legislation, etc., that prevent or delay its acceptance." The wording of the Report Form had been the subject, again, of disagreement between the Committee of Independent Experts and the Governmental Committee. The Report Form follows the recommendation of the Committee of Independent Experts.[62] The Governmental Committee had recommended that contracting

---

[60]Art. 19 (5) (e) requires a state that is not a party to an ILO convention to: report to the Director-General of the International Labour Office, at appropriate intervals as requested by the Governing Body, the position of its law and practice in regard to the matters dealt with in the Convention, showing the extent to which effect has been given, or is proposed to be given, to any of the Convention by legislation, administrative action, collective agreement, or otherwise and stating the difficulties which prevent or delay the ratification of such Convention.

[61]C I 10.

[62]*See* C I 10.

parties not be asked to explain the position concerning a particular undertaking in their law and practice; they should instead "simply be invited to state the reasons why they have not accepted the provision or provisions in question."[63] The comparable reporting obligation in the International Labor Organization Constitution[64] requires an account of a state's law and practice concerning a provision, as well as the reasons for nonacceptance. Since the *trauvaux préparatoires* of the Charter indicate, and the pattern of its text confirms, that Article 22 is based upon the practice of the International Labor Organization,[65] it is reasonable to suppose that the International Labor Organization Constitution spells out in more detail what is implied in Article 22. The same conclusion follows from the function that the reports are intended to serve[66] and is as consistent with the very concise text of Article 22 as any other.[67]

It will be necessary for the Committee of Ministers to decide how frequently and upon which articles reports should be made in the future. The provisions selected for the first two sets of reports under Article 22 are those which the Committee of Independent Experts had listed as being ones which had not been widely accepted or respected and upon which therefore Article 22 reports would be particularly valuable.[68]

Comments upon Reports by National Employers Organizations and Trade Unions

Employers organizations and trade unions have an obvious interest in the majority of the undertakings upon which the

[63]GC III 4.

[64]For the text of Art. 19(5) (e) of the ILO Constitution, see note 60 *supra*.

[65]This is stated in the Report of the Working Party of the CMSC, which drafted the final version of the relevant part of Art. 22 in October 1957. Note also that the Working Party had before it Belgian and German draft texts which called for "reports on the state of . . . legislation and practice relating to the provisions" of the Charter which have not been accepted and a Secretariat version based upon them. The words "on the state of . . . legislation and practice" were omitted from the text finally adopted for a reason that is not indicated. One possibility is that they were omitted to bring Art. 22 into line with the ILO position by allowing the reports to include the reasons for nonacceptance as well as an account of the position in law and practice. What is clear is that the GC's selection of the reasons for nonacceptance as the one thing to be reported upon gains no support from the *travaux préparatoires*.

[66]*See* note 61 *supra*.

[67]The difference in wording of Art. 22 ("reports relating to the provisions of Part II") and Art. 21 ("a report . . . concerning the application of such provisions of Part II as they have accepted") is not instructive.

[68]C III xviii. First CIE Report on Unaccepted Provisions, p. 26.

contracting parties report. This interest is reflected in the provision made in the Charter for their participation, albeit modest, at various stages in the supervisory process. The first form of such participation is found in the requirement that a contracting party must send copies of the report it makes under Articles 21 and 22 to "such of its national organizations as are member of the international organizations of employers and trade unions" that are currently entitled to be represented at the meetings of the Govermental Committee of the Social Charter.[69]

These organizations may comment upon the report, and the contracting party must transmit such comments as are made to the Secretary-General of the Council of Europe, if asked to do so by the organization concerned. The comments then must be placed before the Committee of Independent Experts for consideration when the reports are examined. In practice, this arrangement has not proved very satisfactory. During the first seven cycles, very few organizations made comments.[70] As the Committee of Independent Experts has stressed continually,[71] such organizations' apparent lack of interest deprives the supervisory system of a potentially valuable source of information. The views of these organizations on the application of the Charter in their national state could, especially in the absence of a system of petitions, throw the reports submitted by governments into valuable relief. In the sixth cycle, the Governmental Committee interpreted the absence of comments by employers and employees organizations on all but one (the French) national report as "tacit approval" of the

[69]Art. 23.

[70]The Federation of German Trade Unions and the Confederation of British Industry made comments on their national reports in the third cycle: C III xviii. The *Conseil du Patronat Français* and the *Confédération Genérale du Travail/Force Ouvrière* made comments in the fifth cycle. C V xix. The Irish Congress of Trade Unions did so in the sixth cycle. C VI xvi. Until recently the ILO had experienced a similar, though not so complete, lack of interest in recent to a comparable practice in the ILO system. E. LANDY, *supra* note 14, at 184. Beginning with 1974, the number of comments made has increased markedly to the point where 51 were recorded in 1976. Report of the CE, Int'l Lab. Conf., 61st Sess., 1976, Report III (Part 4A), at 15. In one case at least, the CIE has made use of information provided by a trade union to the ILO which the ILO has forwarded. Some organizations have commented on Art. 22 reports.

[71]C I 7, C II xvii, C III xvii, C IV xvii. In the sixth cycle, the CIE suggested that it might increase the interest of national trade unions and employers organizations if they were informed of the results of the previous cycle for their state and of the matters that had caused difficulty. C VI xix.

other reports as "providing a faithful picture of reality."[72] A more accurate opinion is that it reflects their (mistaken) view of the potential importance of the Charter for them. If any weakness in the arrangement had been foreseen, it had not been the absence of cooperation of trade unions and employers organizations, but the fact that contracting parties are not required to send their reports for comments to other kinds of national organizations that are concerned with the rights in Part II that do not focus upon the individual as a worker.[73] Such organizations could play an equally valuable role and would, one feels, probably be more cooperative.

THE COMMITTEE OF INDEPENDENT EXPERTS[74]

The national reports of the contracting parties under Articles 21 and 22 are first examined by the Committee of Independent Experts. The Committee adopts *Conclusions* based on these reports, which are submitted with the national reports to the Governmental Committee.

Membership

The rules in the Charter concerning membership of the Committee of Independent Experts are found in Article 25. They are supplemented by other rules adopted by the Committee of Ministers, the organ seized with the task of appointing members, or developed in the practice of the Committee of Independent Experts itself. The principle underlying the rules added by the Committee of Ministers is the achievement of as wide a geographic representation of member states of the Council of Europe on the Committee as possible. This accords with the role of the Charter in setting social standards for the membership of the Council of Europe as a whole.

Article 25 (1) provides that the Committee "shall consist of not more than seven members." In fact, the Committee of Ministers has established that, in accordance with the principle of wide geographic representation, it will always have seven members. In contrast with the European Commission of Hu-

[72]GC V 2.
[73]*See* Arts. 11–17.
[74]The Charter refers to "The Committee of Experts" (Art. 25). The Committee altered its name to emphasize its independence.

man Rights,[75] the size of the Committee of Independent Experts is not the same as the number of contracting parties, thus necessarily departing from the principle of state equality. Although this departure has the merit of emphasizing the independence of the Committee, it also has the following disadvantage. Coupled with the decision that members should be recruited from the membership of the Council of Europe as a whole and not just from the contracting parties, it means that the Committee is unlikely to have expert knowledge of the law and practice of all of the contracting parties. In view of the limited and, at present, ineffective tripartite element in the supervisory system and the absence of any right of petition, this is a weakness, and one that will grow with the number of contracting parties. Reading the national reports that have been submitted during the first seven cycles, one feels that the presence within the Committee of Independent Experts of someone knowledgeable in the area of law and practice of the contracting party concerned can do much to clarify an ambiguity in a report or to point out something which the contracting party has forgotten, or was not called upon, to report. His presence may be to the advantage or disadvantage of the contracting party concerned, but, in either case, it assists in the operation of the system of supervision by reducing the element of chance that exists in any report system and by helping to avoid misunderstanding. It may also lessen the signs of lack of familiarity with national legal systems that have occasionally crept into the Committee's *Conclusions*[76] and induce a general sense of confidence in the Committee on the part of existing or potential contracting parties. If the work load of the Committee were to require an increase in its membership, it is submitted that the Charter should be amended to introduce a rule similar to that governing the composition of the European Commission of Human Rights.

Each member of the Committee of Independent Experts is appointed for six years.[77] The term of office of two of the first

[75]*See* European Convention on Human Rights and Fundamental Freedoms, Art. 20, *signed* Nov. 4, 1950, 1950 Gr. Brit. T.S. No. 70 (Cmd. 8969), 213 U.N.T.S. 221.

[76]*See* note 228 *infra.*

[77]Art. 25 (2). The term of office of the first seven members ran from the date of the first election by the Committee of Ministers during its 153d meeting, Sept. 19–26, 1966.

members was restricted to four years to ensure continuity of membership.[78] A member may be reappointed.[79] A member "appointed to replace a member whose term of office has not expired shall hold office for the remainder of his predecessor's term."[80] The Committee is at present composed as follows:[81]

Mr. B. Bull (Honorary Chairman)	Norwegian	1966–
Mr. A. Loizou (Chairman)	Cypriot	1972–
Mr. B. Zanetti (Vice-Chairman)	Swiss	1972–
Mr. G. Kojanec (General Rapporteur)	Italian	1972–
Mr. F. Fabricius	W. German	1976–
Mr. W. de Gaay Fortman	Dutch	1978–
Mr. P. Laurent	French	1982–

There have been eleven other members of the Committee:

Mr. P. Laroque (Chairman)	French	1966–76
Sir O. Kahn-Freund (General Rapporteur)	British	1966-72
Mr. H. Armbruster	W. German	1966–76
Mr. S. Busuttil	Maltese	1966–72
Mr. R. Geary	Irish	1966–72
Mr. C. Arena	Italian	1966–67[82]
Mr. F. Parrillo	Italian	1967–70[83]
Mr. R. Strasser	Austrian	1970–73[84]
Mr. L. Troclet (Chairman)[85]	Belgian	1972–78
Mr. A. Morgan	British	1976–80[86]
Mr. W. James	British	1980–82

Article 25 (1) requires that members be "independent experts of the highest integrity and of recognised competence in international social questions."[87] The fact that its members are independent of governments and other sources of influence is crucial to the conception of the Committee and is well recognized. A working knowledge of at least one of the official

[78]*Id.* The two members were Mr. Laroque and Mr. Arena.

[79]*Id.*

[80]Art. 25(4).

[81]The nationality of the members does not comply with the nationality group rules discussed at p. 220, *infra;* these were adopted in their present form after the most recent round of appointments.

[82]Died; replaced by Mr. Parrillo for the remainder of his term of office (until Sept. 18, 1970).

[83]*See* note 82 *supra.*

[84]Resigned; replaced by Mr. Armbruster for the remainder of his term of office (until Sept. 18, 1976).

[85]Chairman from 1976 to 1978.

[86]Resigned; replaced by Mr. James for the remainder of his term of office.

[87]Art. 25 (1).

languages of the Council of Europe (English and French) is clearly essential. Although there is no mention of legal qualifications, the background of those who have served on the Committee so far indicates an awareness of the legal competence required by the Committee.[88] Six of the present members are law professors[89] or persons who hold[90] or have held[91] judicial office.[92] Although it is important for the Committee to have an adequate representation of labor and other lawyers,[93] the varied and specialized nature of the fields covered by the Charter raises the question whether more room should be found for persons from other disciplines. It is surprising that there have been few trained economists on the Committee (none at present). The importance of Articles 18 and 19 of the Charter is such that the presence of a person versed in the problems of migrant workers also would be helpful. Despite the presence of an International Labor Organization observer at the Committee's meetings,[94] the Committee could also benefit from having more members who have had firsthand experience of the work of the International Labor Organization than it has had so far.[95] It is noticeable that the Committee as yet has no woman member. At least two members have held political office in a national government.[96] Current membership of the Government of a contracting party would be contrary to the requirement of independence.[97]

The Charter is silent on the question of the nationality of

[88]*Cf.* the practice of the ILO Committee of Experts (hereinafter ILO CE), E. LANDY, *supra* note 14, at 22.

[89]Messrs. Kojanec, Zanetti, and Fabricius. Mr. de Gaay Fortman is a former professor of law and Vice President of the European Commission of Human Rights.

[90]Mr. Loizou is a judge of the Supreme Court of Cyprus.

[91]Mr. Bull is a former chairman of the Norwegian Labour Court.

[92]The seventh—Mr. Laurent—is the President of the Social Section of the French Conseil d'Etat. The two most recent British members have been retired U.K. civil servants (from the Overseas Division, Department of Employment).

[93]For the view that members are "en principe des jurists" because of their role in applying a legal text, see Troclet, note 10 of Chapter II *supra*.

[94]*See* Art. 26.

[95]Mr. Troclet (former President of the ILO), Mr. James (former Chairman of the ILO Conference Committee), and Mr. Morgan (former U.K. Govt. Representative on the ILO Governing Body) would appear to be the only members who have served in the ILO system.

[96]Mr. Troclet was formerly a Belgian Government Minister; Mr. de Gaay Fortman was formerly a Dutch Government Minister. Mr. Bull was formerly a Mayor of Oslo.

[97]For further details of the background of CIE members, see Sur, *supra* note 7, at 91.

members of the Committee of Independent Experts. Although there are now too many parties to the Charter for each contracting party to have a national on the Committee of Independent Experts,[98] it would be possible for the Committee to be composed only of nationals of the contracting parties. This would have the advantage of ensuring that the Committee would have among its members specialists with knowledge of the law, practice, and conditions of at least seven of the contracting parties.[99] In fact, the Committee of Ministers has adopted a different approach in accordance with the principle of wide geographic representation. It has ruled that no state may have more than one national on the Committee of Independent Experts; that nationals of all of the member states of the Council of Europe, whether parties to the Charter or not, are eligible for membership;[100] and that members are appointed according to the following nationality group rules:

> The Committee of Experts shall consist of seven members elected in respect of the following groups of States as follows:
> 1. Three experts in respect of the following member States: Federal Republic of Germany, France, Italy, United Kingdom, Austria, Liechtenstein, and Switzerland, but not more than one national of any one country;
> 2. One expert a national from the Benelux countries, Portugal, and Ireland;
> 3. One expert a national from the Scandinavian countries: Denmark, Norway, Sweden and Iceland;
> 4. Two experts nationals from the Mediterranean member states: Cyprus, Greece, Malta, Spain, and Turkey.

Members are appointed by the Committee of Ministers of the Council of Europe.[101] In contrast with the rules on the membership of the European Commission of Human Rights and the European Court of Human Rights, the Parliamentary Assembly plays no part in the election process.[102] The matter

[98] It would have been possible at the time of the first election when there were only seven contracting parties to the Charter.

[99] *Cf.* note 228 *infra* (increased difficulty in finding expertise to manage law of increasing number of contracting parties).

[100] A national of a nonmember state is thus not eligible. Several nationals of member states not parties to the Charter are or have been members of the Committee, including the first Chairman.

[101] Art. 25(1).

[102] The PA has proposed that the procedure be changed so that the Assembly would play a part. Eur. Parl. Ass., 30th Sess., Doc. No. 4198, at 6 (1978). Such a change would ensure that an independent person was seen to be appointed.

is left entirely in the hands of the Governments of the member states. Article 25 (1) provides that members are to be appointed "from a list of independent experts . . . nominated by the Contracting Parties." The Committee of Ministers has added another stage to the procedure prior to the nomination of candidates by the contracting parties which, again, is intended to assist in achieving wide geographic representation. By this, each member state of the Council of Europe, whether a party to the Charter or not, is invited to transmit to the Secretary-General of the Council of Europe the names of candidates no more in number than the number of vacancies to be filled and in accordance with the rules concerning nationality groups.[103] A list of names thus compiled is sent to the contracting parties, who must choose from it when nominating candidates in accordance with Article 25 (1). Each contracting party nominates a number of candidates from the list no larger than the number of vacancies to be filled and in accordance with the rules concerning nationality groups. A retiring member may be renominated if he is on the list sent to the contracting parties. The election is held by the Committee of Ministers by secret ballot. To be appointed, a nominee must receive an absolute majority vote of those members of the Committee of Ministers present and voting. If more nominees meet this requirement than the number of vacancies to be filled in a particular nationality group, the nominee or nominees in the group with the highest number of votes are elected. If the number of nominees in a nationality group meeting the requirement is less than the number of vacancies to be filled, a second election is held among the nominees in the group concerned who have not been elected. In this second election, the nominee or nominees who receive the highest number of votes elected so far as there are places to be filled in the nationality group concerned whether they have obtained an absolute majority vote or not. The procedure is complicated and time-consuming. It is possible that it will be simplified in the future by eliminating the first stage involving all member states. Its value in achieving a wide geographic representation has declined as more states have become parties to the Charter.

Membership of the Committee is part-time. The Charter is

---

[103]*See* note 100 *supra*.

silent on this point; it would be possible to make member-ship[104] full-time if the work justified it without amending the Charter. Members are paid per diem. There is no provision for the dismissal or resignation of members. In practice, resignations have occurred.[105] There also is no provision equivalent to that concerning the European Commission of Human Rights by which members, after being replaced, "shall continue to deal with such cases as they already have under consideration."[106] Fortunately, the periodic elections to the Committee of Independent Experts occur in even years when its work load is light. Members of the Committee have no international privileges or immunities comparable to those of the members of the European Commission of Human Rights.

The International Labor Organization is invited to send a representative "to participate in a consultative capacity in the deliberations" of the Committee.[107] Such a representative (sometimes more than one) has come from Geneva regularly and contributed a great deal from his experience of the problems encountered in the implementation of International Labor Organization conventions. He also has helped to secure uniformity in the interpretation and application of such conventions and the Charter.

Organization of Work[108]

The Committee of Independent Experts meets at the headquarters of the Council of Europe in Strasbourg, France. Its meetings are held in private, and documents relating to them are treated as confidential. The meetings are conducted in English and French. A definite pattern has evolved as a result of the biennial nature of the reporting system under Article 21. In each of the odd years, when most of the work of examining Article 21 national reports occurs, the Committee of

[104]Or perhaps just the chairmanship.
[105]See notes 84, 86 supra.
[106]ECHR, Art. 22 (4), note 75 supra.
[107]Art. 26.
[108]See Laroque, Drawing Up and Implementation of the European Social Charter, Working Paper for the 1977 Strasbourg Symposium on the European Social Charter, CE Doc. AS/Coll/Charte I-E, at 21–23. The CIE has yet to adopt any rules of procedure. Although the Charter gives it no express power to do so, it can be taken to have one. The GC, which is in the same position, has adopted rules of procedure. The CIE considered the question at its First Meeting but decided not to adopt any for the time being. It has taken a number of uncollated decisions as to procedure, and other rules of practice have developed.

Independent Experts has held six or seven meetings a year lasting twenty-five to thirty days altogether. In even years, when there is less work to be done under Article 21, there have been three meetings a year lasting a total of twelve days.[109] There is no provision for a quorum. Most decisions are taken by consensus.[110] If a vote is needed, it is taken by a simple majority of members present and voting.[111]

The Committee of Independent Experts has established in its practice the offices of Chairman, Vice-Chairman, and General Rapporteur. Officeholders are elected by a simple majority vote of the members of the Committee of Independent Experts present and voting. They are elected for two years[112] and may be reelected.

The method of work the Committee has adopted in examining Article 21 reports is set out in *Conclusion I*.[113] Each member of the Committee of Independent Experts is made responsible for two or three of the nineteen articles in Part II and examines all of the reports so far as they concern these articles. He has available for this purpose analyses of the reports made by the Secretariat on the same article-by-article basis.[114] In the first five cycles, each member was also made responsible for the overall examination of the reports of one or two states, but this practice has been discontinued. The member's assessment of the position concerning "his" articles is made in a written report or orally. This provides the basis for discussion by the Committee of Independent Experts when it adopts its *Conclusions*. The Committee of Independent Experts also will have before it any comments on the reports made by the employers organizations or trade unions in accordance with Article 23 of the Charter.[115] The Committee of Independent Experts has stated that it can only consider any

---

[109]The implementation of Art. 22 has increased the work load in even years.

[110]*Cf.* the practice of the ILO CE, E. LANDY, *supra* note 14, at 31.

[111]This rule was agreed upon in 1968 for voting on the adoption of the CIE's *Conclusions*. It has come to have general application.

[112]The Chairman and General Rapporteur were first elected for one year. Their term of office was extended to two years in keeping with the biennial nature of the CIE's work under Art. 21. The Vice-Chairman (first appointed in 1972) has always been elected for two years.

[113]C I 7. The CIE's method of work for Art. 22 reports is described in 1st CIE Report on Unaccepted Provisions, p. 7.

[114]*CF.* The analyses made by the International Labour Office for the ILO CE, E. LANDY, *supra* note 14, at 29.

[115]Art. 23.

such comments if they are received at least one month before the date it takes up the report.

The competence of the Committee of Independent Experts to adopt its *Conclusions* is only obliquely given by the Charter. Article 24 simply states that the Committee of Independent Experts shall "examine" the national reports submitted to it. It does not refer to any report or other document which the Committee of Independent Experts might draft on the basis of its examination. Articles 27 and 28, which define the functions of the Governmental Committee and the Consultative Assembly respectively, refer to the "conclusions" of the Committee of Independent Experts. It is from these provisions that the constitutionality and title of the Committee of Independent Experts' report derive.

The *Conclusions,* which have in each of the first six cycles of supervision run to between two hundred and three hundred pages in length, are divided into three parts. The first part is a General Introduction which is the responsibility of the General Rapporteur. This Introduction includes comments upon the Committee of Independent Experts' role and work of a general character, whether arising out of the reports examined in the *Conclusions* or not. The Committee also makes general comments on the social and economic situation in the contracting parties and on developments during the cycle in their law and practice. It may also identify particular social problems that have arisen in Europe within the framework of the Charter. It is followed by Parts I and II. Part I of the *Conclusions* contains a commentary upon each of the undertakings of Part II of the Charter in turn and consists partly of the Committee of Independent Experts' interpretation of the undertakings and comments upon their application in the contracting parties generally. But it consists mainly of the determinations made by the Committee of Independent Experts on the question of compliance by each party with the undertakings that the party has accepted and requests by the Committee for further information. The Committee of Independent Experts may determine that a contracting party has fully complied with an undertaking during the two-year period to which the *Conclusions* relate or that the party has complied with it provisionally. In the latter case, the Committee of Independent Experts may have sufficient evidence to conclude provisionally that a state has fulfilled the requirements of the undertaking, but it seeks confirmation in one or more respects. Otherwise, it will decide that a contracting party has not fulfilled its obligation, or that it lacks sufficient information to take any decision on the question of compliance. Part II of the *Conclusions* consists of a summary of the position of each contracting party in turn.

There is no provision in the Charter on the public or private nature of the *Conclusions*. In practice, they become public when they are sent for consideration to the Parliamentary Assembly under Article 28, i.e., as of 1981, as soon as they are adopted by the Experts.

The Committee of Independent Experts does not regard itself as bound by its interpretation of the Charter. It may change its mind, if persuaded that a different meaning is to be preferred.[116] A determination that a state complies with the Charter in a particular cycle is res judicata. A state, however, may be found to be in breach of an undertaking in a subsequent cycle not only because the position as it previously existed has deteriorated but also because the Committee of Independent Experts has discovered a feature of the law or practice of a contracting party that had existed in a previous cycle but had been unknown to it.[117] In the third cycle, for example, the Committee of Independent Experts found that Italy was in breach of Article 12 (4) because its "social pension" was not available to nationals of other contracting parties.[118] This had been the case during the second cycle, when the Committee of Independent Experts had not been aware of the pension. Its earlier favorable decision, which was

---

[116]The approach taken by the CIE was explained in a letter from the CE Secretariat as follows:

The experts do not consider themselves *as formally* bound by the Committee's previous interpretations of the Charter, although they prefer not to change these unless there are very serious reasons for doing so. The Committee has, however, taken the habit of summarising or reformulating more clearly its opinion on the contents of certain provisions of the Charter, in each of its Conclusions (cf. Conclusions V, articles 7, paragraph 1, 7, paragraph 3, 19, etc.). This practice makes room for a certain development in its interpretation of the Charter. An example may be provided by Article 1, paragraph 2, with respect to certain forms of "forced labour" in legislation regarding seamen. In Conclusions III (page 5) the Committee admitted for the first time that ". . . penal measures could, in appropriate circumstances, be justified when they are applied in cases where the act giving rise to the change endangered, or was capable of endangering, the safety of the ships or the life or health of those on board."

[117]C I 8, C II XVI, C III xviii.

[118]C III 65 (Italy).

thus based upon inadequate evidence, remained undisturbed, but Italy was found to violate the Charter in the third cycle. As noted above,[119] it is possible for a decision by the Committee of Independent Experts regarding compliance or the need for further information to be taken by a simple majority of those present and voting, although it is normally taken by consensus. If a majority decision is taken after a vote, a member in the minority may ask that his dissent be recorded in the *Conclusions* or may write a dissenting "judgment" to be appended to it.[120]

In deciding whether a contracting party has complied with its undertakings, the Committee of Independent Experts does not limit itself to the information that contracting parties provide in their national reports[121] but uses any information that it has at hand. Most of this information comes from the International Labor Organization, which provides the Committee of Independent Experts with copies of national reports submitted to it by contracting parties to the Charter respecting International Labor Organization conventions and in response to "direct requests" for supplementary information sent by the International Labor Office to such states in the same connection.[122] The Committee has also relied upon information obtained from the implementation of other Council of Europe conventions (particularly the European Code of Social Security and the European Convention on Establishment)[123] and from Organization for Economic Cooperation and Development[124] and United Nations[125] documents. The collective knowledge of the members of the Committee of Independent Experts and the Secretariat is similarly valuable. The comments of representative trade union and employers organizations should be of help too, but, as noted,[126] very few have been made.

---

[119]Note 111 *supra.*

[120]For the only examples of an expression of dissent in accordance with this rule, see notes 314 and 399 of Chapter II.

[121]The CIE has become adept at finding information submitted under one provision of Part II and applying it to another. *See, e.g.,* C 12 (Norway).

[122]The ILO representative sitting with it also provides information.

[123]*See* note 54 of Chapter I and C I 79 respectively.

[124]*See* C IV 4 (Ireland).

[125]The ruling concerning Sweden in respect to Art. 4 (3) in the second cycle, C II 20 (Sweden), was based in part upon a document submitted by Sweden to the U.N. on the status of women in Sweden.

[126]*See* note 70 *supra.*

It is arguable from the text of Article 24 of the Charter that the Committee of Independent Experts is intended to rule on the question of compliance with Part II on the basis solely of the national reports and any comments upon them made by trade union or employers organizations. This has not been the approach of the International Labor Office Committee of Experts, which, like the Committee of Independent Experts, has used information that it has obtained from any source.[127] Nor have the contracting parties to the Charter objected to a practice which is not expressly prohibited by Article 24, which is consistent with the object and purpose of the exercise, and which may as well lead to a determination in favor of a contracting party.[128] What is curious, however, is the cloak of secrecy with which the Committee of Independent Experts sometimes hides the identity of its source. In the third cycle, for example, it asked the U.K. a question concerning Article 19 (4) on the basis of "certain information in the Committee's possession," the source of which (an International Labor Organization "direct request" for supplementary information) it did not identify.[129] In its Fourth Report, the U.K. stated that it understood the information had come from "an article in an unidentified newspaper" and said that "in the absence of more precise information" than that given in *Conclusions III* based upon this source it was "not possible to respond on this point."[130] In *Conclusions IV,* the Committee of Independent Experts denied that its information had been based upon a newspaper report, indicating that it had come "from a reliable source," which the Committee of Independent Experts still did not identify.[131] This reluctance to disclose a source of information[132] would be best abandoned in the interest of gaining the confidence of contracting parties and of eliciting information from them.

---

[127]*See* E. Haas, Beyond the Nation State 255 (1964).

[128]E.g., in the first cycle, the F.R.G. was found by the CIE to comply with Art. 13(4) "on the basis of information at its disposal" when the F.R.G. has given no information relevant to that provision in its report. C I 204 (F.R.G.). *Cf.* C IV 4 (Ireland).

[129]C III 93 (U.K.).

[130]Fourth U.K. Report, at 145.

[131]C. IV 122 (U.K.).

[132]For other cases, see, e.g., C IV 114 (Italy) (where the Committee stated that it had learned "from other sources of clandestine immigration into Sicily") and C III 39 (Italy) ("certain information which the Committee had received").

Function

The Committee of Independent Experts' function is stated to be the examination of national reports made by the contracting parties and to draw conclusions from them.[133] No more is said. The *travaux préparatoires* and the experience of the first seven cycles do much to fill in the details. The Committee of Independent Experts' role varies according to whether it is examining Article 21 reports on accepted provisions or Article 22 reports on those that have not been accepted.

Article 21 Reports

The *travaux préparatoires* make it clear that the Committee of Independent Experts is intended to exercise in respect to Article 21 reports a role similar in kind to that which the International Labor Office Committee of Experts has come to exercise at the same, initial stage in the International Labor Organizaton implementation system.[134] It is an independent and impartial body whose task is to discover what the law and practice of the contracting parties are, to consider whether they comply with the undertakings in Part II that the parties have accepted, and to do so solely in accordance with the meaning of those undertakings in law.[135] The fact that its work is such as to require technical expertise in such subjects as industrial relations, social administration, and economics is indicative of the specialized areas in which this function is exercised without taking

---

[133]Arts. 24 & 27.

[134]The idea of a committee of independent experts to conduct the first stage of the supervisory process was suggested by Belgium in a note dated May 15, 1957, for the Fifth Session of the Social Committee. Although the eventual composition of the Committee differed from that proposed in the note, the conception of it as a body that would exercise a role similar to that of the ILO Committee was never subsequently challenged. For an account of the role of the ILO CE, see E. LANDY, *supra* note 14, at 19–34.

[135]*See* Laroque, *supra* note 108, at 24. *Cf.* the following interpretation by the ILO CE of the nature of its functions:

...the Committee, which is composed of members appointed in their personal capacity by the Governing Body, has always believed that its functions consist in pointing out in a spirit of complete independence and entire objectivity the extent to which it appears to the Committee that the position in each State is in conformity with the terms of the Convention and the obligations which that State has undertaken in virtue of the Constitution of the International Labour Organization. The members of the Committee have always attached the greatest importance to avoiding all political considerations in the technical and juridical examination of the matters entrusted to it.

Report of the CE, Int'l Lab. Conf., 40th Sess., Report III (Part 4A), at 3 (1957).

away from its juridical nature. The Committee of Independent Experts has interpreted its role in the above sense when describing it as being "to determine whether the legislation and practice of the contracting states are in conformity with the undertakings accepted"[136] and its determinations as "legal findings."[137] It also has noted that "it was conceived as an 'impartial' body capable of interpreting objectively the provisions by which the states are bound and assessing their application, uninfluenced by the states themselves."[138] The Parliamentary Assembly has taken the same view of the Committee of Independent Experts' role.[139] The Governmental Committee also has done so, but with the qualification that in making its determinations the Committee of Independent Experts "should bear in mind the social, economic, historical and institutional context of each situation."[140] Clearly, such factors are relevant in the sense that national circumstances must be considered in the application of the "dynamic" provisions of Part II[141] and of undertakings such as that in Article 4 (1) concerning a wage or salary that will provide "a decent standard of living."[142] The circumstances of the contracting parties as a whole may be relevant in some cases when deciding at what level the requirements of an undertaking should be pitched for all of them. Insofar as the Governmental Committee goes further than this and suggests that the clear legal meaning of a provision should be suspended or modified in its application to a particular state for any of the reasons which the Governmental Committee mentions, its suggestion is inconsistent with the intention of the drafting states, who conceived of the Committee of Independent Experts interpreting and applying the terms of Part II as a legal text and in a uniform manner in accordance with the ordinary rules of treaty interpretation.[143]

The Committee of Independent Experts has claimed not only that it is competent to interpret the Charter and to rule upon legal compliance with Part II, but that the other supervis-

[136]C I 5.
[137]C III xii.
[138]C III xi.
[139]Opinion 57, para. 11, TEXTS ADOPTED, May 1971.
[140]GC I 3.
[141]Note 24 of Chapter II and accompanying text.
[142]See C III xiv.
[143]Cf. the view of the CA. Opinion 57, paras. 11 and 12, TEXTS ADOPTED, May 1971.

ory organs ought normally to accept its interpretations and its findings.[144] What it has suggested, in fact, is a division of labor between itself and the other supervisory organs by which the Committee of Independent Experts would take primary responsibility for the "legal" stage of the supervisory process and the other organs would take over at what might be called the "political" stage.[145] The Committee of Independent Experts, that is, should be given the responsibility of identifying cases of noncompliance, and the Govermental Committee, the Parliamentary Assembly, and the Committee of Ministers should concern themselves with the reasons for noncompliance, the steps to be urged upon a state to rectify the situation, and questions concerning the implementation of the Charter generally.[146] In making this suggestion, the Committee of Independent Experts is claiming, in effect, that the Charter incorporates the division of functions that has evolved over the years between the Committee of Experts and the Conference Committee in the International Labor Organization system of supervision.[147] The Committee of Independent Experts is not claiming that the other supervisory bodies are never entitled to challenge its interpretations or findings, but that a challenge should be "exceptional"; it should not happen "except when this is rendered imperative by, for example, new facts. . . ."[148] Should another supervisory organ make a challenge, the Committee of Independent Experts "should be informed of the grounds on which it is being challenged and asked to consider all the implications."[149]

This is a possible interpretation of the very brief terms of the

---

[144]C III xiii.

[145]*Cf.* Papadotos, *The European Social Charter,* 7 J. Int'l Comm'n Jurists 214, 236 (1966); Valticos, *La Charte Sociale Européenne: sa Structure, son Contenu, le Contrôle de son Application,* 26 Droit Social 466, 478 (1963); Valticos, *Mise en Parallèle des Actions et des Mechanismes de Contrôle au Niveau du Conseil et de l'Organisation Internationale du Travail,* 19, paper presented to the Brussels Colloquium on the European Social Charter, Institut d'Etudes Européennes, 1976; and Van Asbeck, *La Charte Sociale Européenne: sa Portée Juridique, sa Mise en Oeuvre, in* Mèlanges Offerts à Henri Rolin: Problèmes de Droit des Gens 424, 444 (1964), who also use the term "political" to describe the second stage of the supervisory process, i.e., that which follows the technical examination of the national reports by the CIE. *See also* Golsong, *Implementation of International Protection of Human Rights,* 110 Recueil des Cours (Hague Academy of International Law) 1, 36 (1963–III).

[146]C III xii.

[147]For a description of that system, see E. Landy, *supra* note 14, at Chapter I.

[148]C III xii–xiii.

[149]C III xiii.

Charter. In practice, the Parliamentary Assembly has accepted it, [150] but the Governmental Committee has not.[151] In the opinion of the Governmental Committee, each supervisory organ has an equal competence to interpret and rule upon the application of the Charter for its own purposes, and the Committee of Independent Experts is no different from any of the other organs in this regard.[152] Given the Governmental Committee's composition and the somewhat controversial way in which the Committee of Independent Experts has approached its role, it is not surprising that the Governmental Committee has taken this stand. Even the tripartite Conference Committee of the International Labor Organization was suspicious of the International Labor Office Committee of Experts in its early years and for a time had its own "sub-reporters" whose advice supplemented that of the Committee of Experts.[153] It soon became apparent, however, that this was impracticable, and the idea was dropped. With this precedent in mind, it is interesting to note that the Governmental Committee has already conceded that it is unable to review the application of the whole of the Charter in each cycle and limits itself instead to a consideration of just some of the questions that have arisen from the Committee of Independent Experts' *Conclusions.*[154]

Whether, in view of the difference in composition between the Governmental Committee and the tripartite Conference Committee of the International Labor Organization, the former will ever come to rely upon the determinations of the Committee of Independent Experts as fully as the latter does, after fifty years of experience, upon those of the International Labor Office Committee of Experts is impossible to say.[155] It is to be hoped that it will because it would be sensible for only one supervisory organ to have this "legal" role and because the Committee of Independent Experts is, as it claims, the best-qualified body to make the sort of objective, juridical judgment that is required.

In the first two cycles, the Committee of Independent Ex-

[150]Opinion 71, para. 5, TEXTS ADOPTED, Apr. 1975.

[151]GC III 6. *See also* GC III 6. For the CM's implied support of the CIE's position, see note 102 *supra*.

[152]*See* note 198 *infra.*

[153]*See* E. LANDY, *supra* note 14, at 40.

[154]*See* note 198 *infra.*

[155]For an optimistic view, see Wiebringhaus, *L'Etat d'Application de la Charte Social Européenne, 19* ANNUAIRE FRANÇAIS DE DROIT INTERNATIONAL 928, 932 (1973).

perts not only drew conclusions as to compliance with Part II but, in cases of noncompliance, proposed that the Committee of Ministers make recommendations to the defaulting states under Article 29 calling upon those states to bring their law and practice into line with the Charter. In the first cycle, the Committee of Independent Experts proposed that recommendations be made in all of the fifty-seven cases in which it found a breach by a contracting party of its obligations under the Charter. In the second cycle, the Committee proposed fifty-two recommendations concerning most, but not all, of the breaches found. However, none of the recommendations proposed by the Committee of Independent Experts—nor any recommendations at all—were made by the Committee of Ministers.[156] In later cycles, the Committee of Independent Experts has not proposed any recommendations, although in the third cycle[157] it did maintain its competence to do so. Whereas the Parlimentary Assembly supported the Committee of Independent Experts in its action in the first two cycles,[158] the Governmental Committee took the view that it—the Governmental Committee—is competent to make proposals but, by implication, that the Committee of Independent Experts is not.[159] Although the very general wording of Article 24 does not contradict the Committee of Independent Experts' interpretation, the Governmental Committee's interpretation is to be preferred. The latter is consistent with the distinction between the "legal" and "political" stages in the supervisory process that the Committee of Independent Experts itself has drawn,[160] and also with the practice of the International Labor Office Committee of Experts, which has served to insulate the Committee from politics. Insofar as it might be argued that the Governmental Committee's failure to propose any recommendations at all so far strengthens the argument for the Committee of Independent Experts' ability to propose them, it should be remembered that the Parliamentary Assembly is in a position to bring moral and political pressure on the Committee of Ministers to make re-

---

[156]See GC II 8–9.

[157]C III xii.

[158]Opinion No. 57, para. 6, TEXTS ADOPTED, May 1971, and Opinion No. 64, para. 7, TEXTS ADOPTED, September/October 1973.

[159]GC II 7. See also GC III 5.

[160]See note 145 supra.

commendations and in fact has made its own proposals for recommendations in the third and later cycles. The Committee of Independent Experts' decision not to make proposals since the second cycle may indicate an acceptance of this point of view.

The Committee of Independent Experts also has claimed the competence to supplement its conclusions on the question of compliance by "general suggestions with reference to the development of the social legislation and institutions in the Contracting states."[161] Accordingly, it makes such suggestions in the General Introduction to its *Conclusions*. In the first four cycles, it also did so in passages introducing its consideration of each Article in Part I and of each national report in Part II. Thus, in the fourth cycle, the Committee of Independent Experts made a number of suggestions in its *Conclusions* on the impact of the economic crisis that had developed during the cycle upon the protection of the rights guaranteed. None of the other supervisory organs have seriously questioned in their reports the Committee of Independent Experts' competence in this regard. Although the Governmental Committee expressed doubts in the first cycle about the appropriateness of such suggestions at the "formative stage" in the implementation of the Charter,[162] it has not since done so.

Article 22 Reports

The first two series of reports under Article 22 have been considered by the Committee of Independent Experts. The Committee has defined its role in the case of Article 22 reports as being to consider a state's reasons for nonacceptance and to draw conclusions therefrom.[163] As in the case of Article 21 reports, it claims the competence to make "general suggestions with reference to the development of the social legislation and institutions in the contracting states."[164] To this end, contracting parties should report upon the reasons for nonacceptance and explain "the exact position of their respective countries" with regard to unaccepted provisions.[165]

[161]C I 6.
[162]GC I 3.
[163]C I 5. *See also* the First CIE Report on Unaccepted Provisions, Part I.
[164]C I 6.
[165]C I 9.

This information also may help the Committee of Independent Experts exercise its role in respect to Article 21 reports.[166]

The Governmental Committee's initial reaction to the Committee of Independent Experts' analysis of the latter's role in respect to Article 22 reports was to accept that "the Independent Experts will have to examine the position of each state with respect to the non-accepted provisions" but to reject the view that the Committee of Independent Experts was entitled to consider the reasons for nonacceptance.[167] The reason for the Governmental Committee's reaction was that a state is not obliged to accept more than the number of undertakings necessary for ratification; it therefore would be an intrusion upon its sovereignty for a body such as the Committee of Independent Experts to examine and comment upon those reasons. Since, however, contracting parties accept in Part I of the Charter the realization of all of the rights guaranteed in it as the "aim of their policy," and since the primary purpose of Article 22 reports is to foster the achievement of this objective by the further acceptance by contracting parties of undertakings in Part II, it would seem to follow that an important part of the Committee of Independent Experts' examination of "the position of each state with respect to the non-accepted provisions" would be to consider the reasons for nonacceptance. It would seem correct to suppose that the Committee of Independent Experts' role is to consider these reasons in the context of the law and practice of the contracting party concerned and to make suggestions as to what alterations, if any, in that law and practice would be necessary to permit acceptance and to encourage it to make them. This in fact was the view taken by the Committee in its first two reports; however, it agreed with the Governmental Committee that in the context of the Article 22 procedure "it would be improper to exert any pressure whatsoever on contracting parties to accept additional provisions."[168] In the event, the Experts and the Governmental Committee are agreed that the Article 22 exercise is of value.

---

[166]See note 134 supra.

[167]GC I 4. The Danish representative dissented.

[168]Second Report, p. 3. See also First Report, p. 5.

THE GOVERNMENTAL COMMITTEE OF THE EUROPEAN SOCIAL CHARTER

Article 27 (1) states that the "reports of the Contracting Parties and the conclusions of the Committee of Experts shall be submitted for examination to a Sub-committee of the Governmental Social Committee of the Council of Europe."

Membership

The "Governmental Social Committee of the Council of Europe" (now referred to as the Steering Committee for Social Affairs) is a committee of the Committee of Ministers. It is composed of civil servants who represent their respective governments and has the function of considering social questions within the ambit of the Council's work. One of its first tasks was the drafting of the Social Charter.[169] Article 27 of the Charter establishes a Sub-Committee of the Committee whose sole function is to assist in the supervision of the implementation of the Charter. There is in fact no real link betweeen the Social Committee and the Sub-Committee, as the latter has sought to stress by changing its title to "Governmental Committee of the European Social Charter."[170] The Governmental Committee of the Charter reports directly to the Committee of Ministers and is not otherwise responsible to the Social Committee. It is composed of one representative of each of the contracting parties.[171] At the moment there are thirteen members who are civil servants drawn from the government departments concerned. Members are appointed by their governments and may be changed at any time. They need not be members of the Social Committee of the Council of Europe. They are paid per diem. The Chairman and Vice-Chairman, two offices created by the Governmental Committee, are elected at the beginning of each session by a majority of the votes cast and are eligible for reelection.[172]

---

[169]*See* note 18 of Chapter I.

[170]*Cf.* Smyth, *supra* note 7, at 10.

[171]Art. 27 (2). For a list of members in 1974, see Sur, *supra* note 7, at 93. A representative may be accompanied by one or more advisers. Rules of Procedure of the GC, Art. 2(2).

[172]Rules of Procedure of the GC, Art. 4.

Organization of Work

The Governmental Committee meets at the headquarters of the Council of Europe in Strasbourg, France. Its meetings are held in private[173] and are conducted in English and French, although a member may speak in another language if he arranges for translation into English and French.[174] As in the case of the Committee of Independent Experts, the biennial nature of the reporting system under Article 21 has shaped the distribution of meetings of the Governmental Committee so that, in its case, most of its work is done in even years. The Committee has held three to five meetings lasting from ten to twenty-one days altogether in each even year and met no more than once or twice in the intervening odd years. The implementation of Article 22 will increase the Committee's work load in odd years. A quorum for meeting purposes is two-thirds of the membership.[175] Voting on questions other than procedural ones is by a two-thirds majority of members present and voting; decisions on procedural questions are taken by a simple majority of the members present and voting.[176] The *Report* of the Committee, however, "shall not be adopted by means of a vote but shall indicate the number of representatives who approve it and any differing opinions."[177]

Unlike the Committee of Independent Experts, the Governmental Committee is not assisted by an International Labor Organization official. This is unfortunate because such a person could assist the Governmental Committee, drawing on the experience of the somewhat comparable International Labor Organization Conference Committee. Some members of the Governmental Committee have, however, had ILO experience themselves.

There is provision for participation by international trade unions and employers organizations in the Governmental Committee's work. The Committee "shall invite no more than two international organizations of employers and no more than two international trade union organisations as it may designate to be represented as observers in a consultative ca-

[173] *Id*. Art. 8.

[174] *Id*. Art. 7.

[175] *Id*. Art. 9.

[176] *Id*. Art. 10. The decision whether a question is procedural or not is taken by a two-thirds majority of the members present and voting.

[177] *Id*. Art. 11. It was thought better to act by consensus if possible rather than to take a vote.

pacity at its meetings."[178] At the moment, the Union of the Industries of the European Community (UNICE) and the European Trade Union Confederation (ETUC) participate as observers in accordance with this provision.[179] As such, they receive the documentation for the Committee's meetings[180] and are allowed to circulate their own papers on any topic under discussion.[181] They may also participate in the discussions leading up to the adoption of the Committee's *Report*[182] and are entitled to have their observations included as an appendix to it.[183] As observers, they have no vote.

The arrangement for a tripartite element in the Governmental Committee has not worked well in practice. Although both employers and trade union organizatons have made useful written and oral contributions to the work of the Governmental Committee, the trade union organizations at least have found that their status as observers and not members of the Committee has limited substantially the value of their participation.[184] One of the (then) two designated trade union organizations—the World Confederation of Labor—withdrew from the Committee in 1972 on the ground that the Governmental Committee had failed to take account of its views in the Committee's *Reports*. On several occasions there has been no trade union organizations represented at the Committee's meetings.[185] In a letter to the Secretary-General of the Council

[178]Art. 27(2). Invitations are valid for two years. Rules of Procedure of the GC Art. 13 (1), note 171 *supra*.

[179]UNICE replaced the International Organization of Employers. Two workers organizations—the International Confederation of Free Trade Unions (ICFTU) and the World Confederation of Labor (WCL)—were initially designated. These were replaced in 1974 by the European Trade Union Confederation (ETUC), which now incorporates the European national trade unions organizations that belong to ICFTU and WCL.

[180]Rules of Procedure of the GC Art. 13(2), note 171 *supra*. The expenses of one representative from each of the organizations represented are refunded.

[181]GC III 12.

[182]*Id.*

[183]*Id.*

[184]Observers have also been hampered by the absence of comments by national employers and trade unions organizations on national reports. *See* note 70 *supra*. In the second cycle, the ICFTU representative was able to rely upon the comments that its "national centres" had made upon the CIE's *Conclusions* as they affected the contracting parties concerned. Forrest, *Towards the European Welfare State*, FREE LABOUR WORLD, April 1973, at 15, 16. As that representative stated, "it is easier to take a position on six pages of conclusions on a national report than on the national report itself." *Id.*

[185]This was true of three of the first thirteen meetings of the GC. Although the GC stated in its Second Report that the participation of the employers and trade union

of Europe the World Confederation of Labor stated that a renewal of its participation in the work of the Governmental Committee "could only be guaranteed if a new procedure was adopted permitting a fair and honest dialogue within the Committee."[186] Although the Governmental Committee made it clear in its third *Report* that "it was itself in favour of such a dialogue taking place within the framework of Article 27,"[187] it seems likely that the difficulties experienced so far are symptoms of a basic problem—the absence of a tripartite element in the composition of the Committee comparable to that in the International Labor Organization Conference Committee—which cannot be overcome without an amendment to the Charter involving a radical change in its conception of the Government Committee. The Parliamentary Assembly proposed such a change in 1978, recommending that the Committee should become a fully tripartite body along International Labor Organization lines.[188] The proposal, which was welcomed by the Committee of Independent Experts,[189] would, if the experience of the International Labor Organization is a guide, greatly strengthen the Charter's system of implementation.

Unlike International Labor Organization conventions, the Charter protects social rights that do not concern the individual as a worker so that organizations other than employers organizations and trade unions have an interest in its effective implementation. This fact is recognized by Article 27 (2) of the Charter, which provides that the Governmental Committee "may consult no more than two representatives of international non-governmental organizations having consultative status with the Council of Europe in respect of questions with which the organizations are particularly qualified to deal, such as social welfare, and the economic and social protection of the family." There is a long list of nongovernmental organiza-

organizations in the second cycle had "contributed to a balanced report," GC II 6, the representative of the ICFTU who attended the meetings during its preparation has stated that he "could find little or no trace of the various interventions" which he had made in the report and for that reason had asked—and been allowed—to append his views to it. Forrest, *supra* note 184, at 16.

[186]GC III 2.

[187]*Id.*

[188]Recommendation 839, TEXTS ADOPTED, April 1978.

[189]In the same year, the CIE wrote to the CM proposing, more modestly, that the international organizations of employers and employees participating in the work of the GC under Art. 27 should be joined by "three or four national delegations, whose expenses would be covered by the Council of Europe." C VI xvi.

tions with consultative status with the Council of Europe.[190] Their status under Article 27 (2) differs from that of such employers and trade union organizations as are designated under Article 27 (1) in that whereas the latter may participate as observers in the Governmental Committee's meetings, the former are merely entitled to be consulted by the Governmental Committee on the initiative of the Committee.[191] Presumably, consultation could be by a special meeting between the organization and the Governmental Committee, as well as by written consultation. To date this provision has remained a dead letter; the Governmental Committee has not consulted any organization under Article 27 (2).[192] This is unfortunate since the employers and trade unions organizations that participate in the work of the Governmental Committee have no direct interest in the undertakings in Articles 11–17 of Part II. There is a real need for observer status (at least) for organizations that have an interest in the rights dealt with in these articles; short of that, it is to be hoped that the Governmental Committee will give further consideration to the possibilities of consultation offered by Article 27,[193]

Function

As with the Committee of Independent Experts, the Governmental Committee's function is only cryptically described in the Charter. Article 27 simply states that the Committee must examine the reports of the contracting parties under Articles 21 and 22 and the *Conclusions* of the Committee of Independent Experts and report to the Committee of Ministers in the light of them.[194] No indication is given of what the Governmental Committee should be looking for when conducting its examination or of the kind of report it should prepare. In practice, the Governmental Committee has evolved for itself the role of advising the Committee of Ministers on all matters

---

[190]*See* MANUAL OF THE COUNCIL OF EUROPE 97–99 (1970). Certain of the organizations designated under Art. 27 (1) as observers have consultative status.

[191]This is apparent from the text of Art. 27 (2). *See also* Rules of Procedure of the GC, Art. 14 (2), note 170 *supra*.

[192]The International Union of Family Organizations wrote indicating its interest in the work of the GC in the first cycle, but the GC decided that since the CIE had not proposed any recommendation be sent to a contracting party in connection with Art. 16, to which the Union had referred, there was no need to consult with it.

[193]The proposals made by the PA and the CIE for strengthening the tripartite character of the GC are limited to the representation of employers and employees.

[194]Art. 27 (1), (3). On the role of the GC, see Laroque, *supra* note 108, at 27–29.

concerning the Charter; it is competent to consider and advise on the question of compliance with it in law, on the action to be taken in cases of noncompliance, and on any other matter about the Charter. The Committee's examination of the first two series of Article 22 reports has raised no difficulties.

Regarding compliance with the Charter, the Committee considers itself as having the same general power as the Committee of Independent Experts has to interpret the undertakings in Part II and to judge whether they have been met. It rejects entirely the opinion of the Committee of Independent Experts[195] that the Governmental Committee has "only a limited right to challenge the interpretations and findings of the Committee of Independent Experts."[196] In the Governmental Committee's opinion, these provide "useful guidelines"[197] but are "made to assist that Committee in the formulation of its conclusions and do not bind the other supervisory organs."[198] In its opinion, the Committee of Independent Experts and the Governmental Committee have an equal competence; the latter may express its views on questions of compliance as freely as the former, and the views of the two organs have equal weight.

In practice, the Governmental Committee has not undertaken the same detailed examination and appraisal of national reports as precede the Committee of Independent Expert's *Conclusions*. Instead, it has, largely without examining the national reports available to it, confined itself to reviewing the Committee of Independent Expert's *Conclusions* in each cycle and to commenting upon a limited number of points of interpretation and application arising out of them.

The Governmental Committee has adopted this policy partly because of the amount of time it has been able to give to its work and partly because of its conception of its relationship with the Committee of Independent Experts. The latter is seen by the Governmental Committee as a technical body which conducts an exhaustive examination of the national reports and draws up a comprehensive set of conclusions on the question of compliance. It is then for the Governmental Com-

---

[195]*See* C III xii–xiii.

[196]GC III 6.

[197]GC III 2.

[198]GC II 4. This statement was made about the interpretation of the Charter; it can be taken to concern its application to the facts of particular cases too.

mittee, reviewing the Committee of Independent Experts' *Conclusions,* to take up and comment upon such points in them as call for comment and ought to be drawn to the attention of the Committee of Ministers, the organ which the Governmental Committee advises. In restraining itself in this way, the Governmental Committee is, however, not to be taken as accepting the Committee of Independent Experts' findings on matters upon which it does not comment.

In accordance with this policy, the Governmental Committee by the end of the third cycle had examined "closely the fifteen provisions of Part II of the Charter which seem to have given rise to divergencies of opinion and/or interpretations."[199] In the fourth cycle, it adopted a different approach, choosing to comment in response to points raised by the Committee of Independent Experts' *Conclusions* upon just the seven articles that together would have been considered in that cycle if the Committee's plan for an essentially six-year cycle had been adopted.[200] The Committee's examination of these articles was of a general nature and did not deal with the details of cases specific to individual contracting parties because it felt that through the medium of the biennial reports "any misunderstandings could be cleared up and any additional information could be brought to the notice of the Committee of Independent Experts."[201] Accordingly, its examination consisted to a greater extent than formerly of abstract interpretations of the Charter and omitted entirely any consideration of its application in particular cases. The Committee followed essentially the same approach in the later cycles, examining the Committee of Independent Experts' comments on other groups of Articles, and did so, again, largely in an abstract way. The Committee did, however, to some extent revert to its previous practice of considering particular cases in the light of the Committee of Independent Experts' findings. After seven cycles, the Governmental Committee remained in disagreement with the Committee of Independent Experts in

[199]GC III 2. These were Art. 1 (2), Art. 3 (2), Art. 4 (3), Art. 5, Art. 6 (4), Art. 7 (3), Art. 8 (1), Art. 13 (1), Art. 17, Art. 18 (1), (2), (3), and Art. 19 (3), (6). Art. 7 (4) is also mentioned in the Third Report, GC III 2, as a provision that has been examined in the third cycle, but there is no discussion of it in the Report. Some undertakings were examined in more than one cycle.

[200]*See* GC III 3. These were Arts. 1, 2, 3, 4, 9, 10, and 15.

[201]GC IV 2.

its interpretation of over twenty of the seventy-two provisions of Part II of the Charter.[202]

The Governmental Committee's stand and its disagreement with the Committee of Independent Experts on the interpretation of a large number of the undertakings in Part II draw attention to the fact that there is no body (apart from the Committee of Ministers) that is competent to resolve such differences concerning Part II[203] or to rule authoritatively on the meaning of any other provision of the Charter.[204] The Constitution of the International Labor Organization gives the International Court of Justice jurisdiction to rule definitively upon any question or dispute concerning the interpretation of the Constitution or of International Labor Organization conventions.[205] There is no comparable provision in the Charter. An amendment to the Charter would be necessary to give such competence to an appropriate body, such as the European Court of Human Rights.[206] The International Labor Organization has made a reference to the World Court on only one occasion, and that as long ago as 1932.[207] This is because the interpretation of International Labor Organization conventions adopted by its supervisory organs during the examination of reports, particularly by the International Labor Office Committee of Experts, has come to be recognized over time as being "of high authority."[208] The same is true of the opinions given by the International Labor Office in response to re-

---

[202]These provisions were Art. 1 (3)(4), Art. 3 (2), Art. 4 (1), (3), Art. 5, Art. 6 (3), (4), Art. 7 (1), (3), (6), (9), Art. 10 (1)(2), Art. 12 (3)(4), Art. 13 (1), Art. 17, and Art. 19 (4)(6)(8). The only case in which the GC gave a provision a wider meaning than the CIE is that of Art. 6 (3). The GC has indicated (GC I 1 and GC II 2) that the absence of comment on other provisions does not mean that the GC necessarily shares the views of the CIE on their meaning.

[203]The CIE's claim to a primary interpretative role applies to "conclusions reached by the Committee within its sphere of competence." C III xii. This would appear to limit its role to the interpretation and application of the undertakings reported upon by contracting parties in accordance with Art. 24.

[204]Apart from the question of the respective competences of the CIE and the GC to rule upon the question of compliance with Part II, another question of interpretation that has arisen concerns the meaning of "consultation with the Consultative Assembly" in Art. 29. See note 239 infra.

[205]Art. 37, ILO Constitution.

[206]The Appendix to the Charter reads: "It is understood that the Charter contains legal obligations of an international character, the application of which is submitted solely to the supervision provided for in Part IV thereof."

[207]Interpretation of the 1919 Convention concerning the Employment of Women during the Night Case, 1932 P.C.I.J. ser. A/B, No. 50. The possibility that a case may be referred to the ICJ may itself have a beneficial effect.

[208]C. JENKS, LAW FREEDOM AND WELFARE 124 (1963).

quests for advice by member states.[209] The interpretations rendered in this way have not given rise to clashes or inconsistencies so as to make recourse to the International Court of Justice for an outside opinion necessary. It remains to be seen whether the same will be true within the Charter system of supervision once it has settled down.[210]

Just as the Governmental Committee, in principle at least, has not been prepared to concede primary responsibility for the interpretation and application of the Charter to the Committee of Independent Experts, it similarly has not taken up its "political" role in quite the way that the Committee of Independent Experts has imagined. It is true that the Governmental Committee has agreed with the Committee of Independent Experts in asking states to supply the information needed to allow that Committee to reach a decision,[211] although the two Committees have not always agreed upon the information needed. There have also been dissenting voices within the Governmental Committee on matters concerning future arrangements for the implementation of the Charter.[212] To this extent, the Governmental Committee is not quite the monolithic apologist for states that might have been feared. Nonetheless, the Committee has yet to break ranks to the extent of expressly agreeing in its *Report* with the Committee of Independent Experts that a contracting party has infringed the Charter[213] It is also rare for it to interpret the Charter in a way contrary to that suggested by a party at odds with the Experts.[214] The contrast between the Committee and the

---

[209]*Id* at 122.

[210]*See* notes 145 & 167 *supra.*

[211]GC II 3.

[212]*See* note 57 *supra.*

[213]The closest the GC has come to this was in the fifth cycle when it "took note of the position in Austria and Italy" concerning Art. 8 (2) when the CIE had found these states did not comply with it. GC V 14. Earlier, in the second cycle, the GC had recognized, without being more specific, that a prima facie examination of the national reports might lead to the opinion that certain obligations are not wholly satisfied. GC II 3.

[214] The GC did agree by a majority in the seventh cycle to the CIE's reading of Art. 13 (4) that was challenged by France. GC VII 12. When the CIE found Austria in breach of Art. 19 (6) in the third cycle, Austria questioned the CIE's interpretation of that provision. C IV 124 (Austria). The CIE's interpretation was tolerated by the GC in the third cycle. GC III 9. When it next considered the matter, in the fifth cycle, the GC adopted the Austrian interpretation. GC V 15. The decision of the GC to support the F.R.G. in its dispute with the CIE on the meaning of Art. 6 (4) so far as it affects civil servants was taken by a majority decision only. GC V 9.

Conference Committee of the International Labor Organization is quite striking in this respect. Whereas the Conference
Committee probes hard into the reasons for noncompliance
and publishes each year a list of serious offenders, the Governmental Committee holds meetings that, together with its
Reports, serve as a vehicle for the presentation of a largely
unchallenged governmental view of the Committee of Independent Expert's *Conclusions* and has yet to propose to the
Committee of Ministers that any recommendation be made to
a contracting party under Article 29.[215]

None of this is very surprising. Even if it was expected—and
it is not at all clear that the states which insisted upon its
present composition had this in mind—that the Governmental
Committee should have the same role in respect to the
Charter as the Conference Committee has in the International
Labor Organization system, it was quite in keeping with its
governmental and essentially nontripartite character for the
Governmental Committee to develop in this way in the absence of an instruction to the contrary. Ulterior political motives apart, states do not go out of their way to criticize each
other in respect to their social and economic policies and
achievements. This is particularly so when they are represented by civil servants, who must be "constantly looking over
their shoulders to their Ministers,"[216] and when the forum is a
politically homogeneous and friendly institution such as the
Council of Europe. The decision of the nominated international employers and workers organizations not to participate
fully in the consultative role permitted them has increased the
relevance of this fact; the inquisitorial atmosphere of the
International Labor Organization Conference Committee is
generated less by the government members than by the employers' and, particularly, the workers' members of the Committee. As mentioned earlier, the Parliamentary Assembly has
proposed an amendment to the Charter to make the Governmental Committee a properly tripartite body. The experience
of the Committee to date suggests that this would be desirable.
The approach adopted by the Committee of Independent Experts, particularly in the first two cycles, has also been a factor.
If the natural tendency of civil servants is to protect their

---

[215]*See further* the comparison made by Valticos, *supra* note 145, at 35.
[216]Mr. Voogd, Eur. Consult. Ass. Deb. 25th Sess. 294 (Sept. 26, 1973).

ministers or governments, the Committee of Independent Experts' uncompromising stance inevitably triggered reactions of collective self-defense.

In addition to its role as adviser to the Committee of Ministers on the substance of the reports presented under Articles 21 and 22, the Governmental Committee also regards itself as competent to advise the Committee of Ministers on any other matter that may arise concerning the operation of the Charter. For example, it has given its opinion on the revision of the reporting system under Article 21 and on the timing and form of the implementation of Article 22.[217] It would be consistent with the object and purpose of the Charter for the Committee to give advice to the Committee of Ministers on matters unconnected with the reporting system, such as the Charter's amendment, the implementation of Part I, or the relationship between the Charter and the International Covenant on Economic, Social and Cultural Rights.

RELATIONS BETWEEN THE COMMITTEE OF INDEPENDENT EXPERTS AND THE GOVERNMENTAL COMMITTEE

As indicated in the earlier sections of this chapter, there are a number of points of disagreement between the Committee of Independent Experts and the Governmental Committee on the interpretation and application of Part II of the Charter and on the operation of the system of implementation. This was always likely in view of the composition of the two Committees. What has been unfortunate is that the perhaps inevitable differences of opinion have been accompanied by a lack of rapport which has made cooperation between the two Committees difficult. This was particularly true of the first two cycles. If, as is undoubtedly the case,[218] there has been a mellowing of attitudes, so that agreement or understanding has been achieved regarding some matters since then, the relationship between the two Committees is still not a harmonious one.

The difficulties between the two Committees began with *Conclusions I*. There the Committee of Independent Experts

[217]*See* GC III 3 and GC I 14.
[218]*Cf.* Sur, *supra* note 7, at 99. The decision of the CM that the GC Report should henceforth be referred officially to the CIE is also a step in the right direction. C V xix. So was the holding of the first joint meetings of the two Committees in 1981 and 1983.

found that 57 (14%) of the undertakings accepted by the contracting parties were not being complied with and that it was
unable to take a decision on another 130 (30%) undertakings.
It ruled, accordingly, that the contracting parties had complied with little more than half of the undertakings that they
had accepted collectively. The reaction of the members of the
Governmental Committee was predictable. They or their col-
leagues had recommended that their national governments
ratify the Charter on the assumption that their law and practice were consistent with all of the undertakings which they
chose to accept. The Governmental Committee members were
shocked to learn that, in the opinion of the Committee of
Independent Experts, the record of compliance was so poor;
that the Commitee of Independent Experts proposed the
making of formal recommendations against all of the contracting parties and in respect to every single breach; that the
national reports, which had taken a lot of work to compile,
were thought to be inadequate and in need of considerable
supplementation; and that the work load of the contracting
parties might be added to further by the immediate implementation of Article 22. This situation was all the more dis-
turbing since the majority of members of the Council of Europe had not accepted the Charter at all. Not unexpectedly,
the contracting parties defended themselves through the *Report* of the Governmental Committee. A similar pattern was
repeated in the second cycle, and an adversary relationship
was established for which both Committees, one feels, were
partly to blame.

A large part of the burden of the Governmental Committee's complaint against the Committee of Independent Experts has been the "surprisingly strict" attitude that, it is
claimed, the latter has taken in the interpretation and application of the Charter.[219] This is an opinion that is difficult to
accept. If the Committee of Independent Experts has been
concerned with interpreting the human rights guarantee in its
care in accordance with its object and purpose, this has not
been done at the expense of the clear wording of the Charter

---

[219]GC I 3. Although the words quoted were used to describe the CIE's treatment
of the reports presented in the first cycle in particular, they would seem apt to
describe the reaction of the GC to the CIE's approach to the interpretation and
application of the undertakings in Part II since then as well.

and is in accordance with the rules of treaty interpretation.[220] Inevitably, states tend to see their treaty obligations primarily from a national point of view, bearing in mind national difficulties, achievements, and standards; it is the function of an independent body, such as the Committee of Independent Experts, to apply an international corrective. Moreover, so far as the complaint is addressed to *Conclusions I,* the Committee of Independent Experts probably was correct to begin as it meant to continue. There is an interesting contrast here with the experience of the European Commission of Human Rights in the implementation of the European Convention on Human Rights. In its earlier years, the European Commission of Human Rights was very cautious and only later began to assert itself.[221] But such an approach is not a good precedent for implementing the Charter. Whereas the European Commission of Human Rights and the Committee of Independent Experts both needed to gain the confidence of states, the former also needed to feel its way slowly because it was the first international institution seized with the task of enforcing a comprehensive guarantee of civil and political rights. In contrast, the Committee of Independent Experts was able to draw on the long experience of the International Labor Organization, with whose practice the contracting parties were familiar, in the interpretation of most of the undertakings in Part II. Moreover, the Committee of Independent Experts at once was called upon to rule on the meaning of every provision in Part II of the Charter and to say whether the law and practice of the contracting parties were consistent with them. Whereas it has not proved difficult for the European Commission of Human Rights to reinterpret as new cases have arisen the few provisions of the Convention which in its early years it had pitched at the wrong level, it would not have been so easy for the Committee of Independent Experts to have undertaken what would have been a much more comprehensive task.[222]

At the same time, it would have been wise for the Committee of Independent Experts during the first two cycles (while indicating clearly its interpretation of the Charter and the

---

[220]*See* note 56 of Chapter I.
[221]*See* C. MORRISON, THE DEVELOPING EUROPEAN LAW OF HUMAN RIGHTS 203 (1967).
[222]*Cf.* Evans, *The European Social Charter* in FUNDAMENTAL RIGHTS 278, 287 (J. Bridge ed. 1973).

likely effect for each contracting party) to have deferred until
the third cycle some of its findings against a contracting
party, thus giving the party a full opportunity to change its
law and practice or to present further information. Although
the Committee did this in some cases, it is clear with hind-
sight that it would have been better for the Committee to
have adopted this approach on a larger scale.[223] The lack of
familiarity with the Charter and the system of implementation on the part of states during the first two cycles particularly and the length of time that each cycle took (so that the
subsequent reports were submitted before the previous cycle
was completed)[224] suggest this.[225] It would also have been
preferable for the Committee of Independent Experts not to
have made any proposals for recommendations under Article
29 in the first and second cycles. Apart from the question of
its competence to make them, a more cautious approach
would have been sensible in this early period. This would
have been so at a national level; it was even more advisable at
the international level, at which the success of a system of
implementation, even in as homogeneous an institution as
the Council of Europe, depends almost entirely upon the
cooperation and goodwill of states.

There are other aspects of the Committee of Independent
Experts' approach which continue to merit criticism. In particular, the Committee should be more explicit and accurate in
its *Conclusions*. Some of its pronouncements have been delphic
in quality and have left states wondering what is expected of
them. There have also been simple mistakes in the reading of

---

[223]*Cf.* the approach of the ILO CE as described in E. Haas, *supra* note 127, at 257.
It is a standing feature of the Committee's skillful persistence that ordinarily no
evidence regarding a non-implementation of a ratified Convention is published for
two years after discovery, thus giving the Office and the Committee time to persuade the delinquent government to make appropriate changes in law or practice
before word of the situation reaches the Organization and the public. The information is made public only when the Committee is convinced that the infraction will
continue, or when a serious infraction comes to light.

[224]*See* Valticos, *supra* note 145, at 44.

[225]For an indication that the CIE is more inclined to delay an adverse finding than
used to be the case, see the ruling in the third cycle by which the CIE held that it
could not decide whether Austria, which was presenting its first report, was complying with Art. 19 (3). C III 90 (Austria). In the first cycle, four states had been found
to violate Art. 19 (3) in circumstances comparable to those of Austria in the third
cycle.

a national report[226] or in the citation of a law.[227] Although these may seem small matters, it is important to a contracting party that a body which is criticizing its law should be able to handle that law properly.[228] What also has upset the Governmental Committee has been the forthright manner in which the Committee of Independent Experts has expressed some of its views. If the General Introduction and much of Parts I and II of the *Conclusions* are in courteous, indeed complimentary, language, there are places, mainly in the early cycles, where the Experts' language has been less diplomatic.[229] Whereas the International Labor Office Committee of Experts now uses equally robust language in its criticisms of states, it did not do so in its early years and still uses the neutral term "observation" when indicating a breach of a convention.[230]

But whatever the reasons, the fact remains that the two central organs in the system of supervision remain in disagreement on the interpretation of quite a number of provisions of the Charter and that this situation has been in part engendered or exacerbated by a lack of sympathy between them. This is a situation which cannot but be harmful to the Charter's prospects of success.

THE PARLIAMENTARY ASSEMBLY

The Parliamentary Assembly of the Council of Europe is composed of "representatives of each member state" who, in prac-

[226]See, e.g., the assessment by the CIE in the third cycle, C III 67 (U.K.), of the U.K. position concerning unemployment benefits reported in the Second U.K. Report, at 123–25, and commented upon by the Fourth U.K. Report, at 107. In the same cycle the CIE asked for information concerning the application of Act. 6 (1) to the Channel Islands, C III 34 (U.K.), when, as the U.K. pointed out in the Fourth U.K Report, at 34, no part of the Charter extended to them.

[227]See, e.g., the wrong date given for the Irish Local Election Act 1972 in the third cycle (C III 68 [Ireland]); the wrong name given to the Aliens Order 1953 (C III 94 [U.K.]); and the reference to "articles," not "sections," of the Merchant Shipping Act 1970 (C III 7 [U.K.]).

[228]A difficulty here is that it may, especially with the small size of the CIE and of the Secretariat available to help it, become increasingly difficult to find the expertise to handle competently the law of the increasing number of contracting parties.

[229]To take a recent example, see the CIE's comments concerning Art. 19 (4) in which it "learnt with astonishment" that the U.K. had not taken certain steps. C IV 122 (U.K.).

[230]E. HAAS, *supra* note 127, at 257; and Van Asbeck, *Une Commission d'Experts*, in SYMBOLAE VERZIJL 9, 18 (1958).

tice, are almost entirely members of the national parliaments of the member states.[231] During the drafting of the Charter, in which it played a large part,[232] the Assembly pressed successfully for a role in the system of supervision. Article 28 of the Charter reads: "The Secretary-General of the Council of Europe shall transmit to the Consultative Assembly the conclusions of the Committee of Experts. The Consultative Assembly shall communicate its views on these Conclusions to the Committee of Ministers." As a result of Article 28, the Charter was the first— and remains the only—Council of Europe Convention in whose implementation the Parliamentary Assembly plays a direct part. Article 28, which applies to both Article 21 and Article 22 reports, provides that the Committee of Independent Experts' *Conclusions* shall be transmitted to the Assembly for its views; no mention is made of the Governmental Committee's *Report*. During the first cycle of supervision, the Committee of Ministers agreed to the Assembly's request that these *Reports* also be referred to it so that it could consider the Committee of Independent Experts' *Conclusions* in the light of them.[233]

In the case of Article 21 reports,[234] the *Conclusions* and the *Report* first are considered by the Assembly's Committee on Social and Health Questions. At this point a tripartite element enters into the system of supervision for a third and final time in that representatives of international employers and trade union organizations are entitled to be present as observers at the meetings of this Committee.[235] The Committee has established the practice of appointing for each cycle an independent expert who is not a member of the Assembly to act as a consultant and to assist in the preparation of the Committee's Explanatory Memorandum commenting on the *Conclusions* and the *Report*.[236] This Memorandum has proved to be a valuable document which has concentrated upon the main points

---

[231]On the composition and powers of the Assembly, see generally the MANUAL OF THE COUNCIL OF EUROPE, Ch. 4 (1970).

[232]*See* Chapter I, *supra*.

[233]*See* CA I 6 and Mr. Grütter, EUR. CONSULT. ASS. DEB. 23D SESS. 237–38 (May 14, 1971).

[234]A similar procedure for Art. 22 reports has been adopted.

[235]*Cf.* Sur, *supra* note 7, at 123–24. They do not attend regularly.

[236]The consultants so far have been Mr. Troclet, later Chairman of the CIE, in the first cycle, and Mr. Berenstein in subsequent cycles. For the qualifications of Mr. Troclet, see notes 95 & 96 *supra*. Mr. Berenstein is a Swiss Federal Judge and a Professor of Labor Law.

at issue between the Committee of Independent Experts and the Governmental Committee and the working of the system of implementation generally. Although comments are made in the Memorandum on the interpretation and application of some undertakings in each cycle, no attempt is made to assess comprehensively whether each state has complied with all its undertakings. As in the case of the Governmental Committee's *Report,* the Memorandum leaves this to the Committee of Independent Experts. It is largely on the basis of the Memorandum that the Assembly, possibly after a debate in plenary session,[237] adopts its "views" for submission to the Committee of Ministers, in the form of an *Opinion.*[238]

Under Article 29 of the Charter, the Committee of Ministers only may make a recommendation to a contracting party or the contracting parties "after consultation with the Consultative Assembly." It is not clear from the text of the Charter whether the process leading to the adoption of an *Opinion* by the Assembly on the *Conclusions* of the Committee of Independent Experts in accordance with Article 28 constitutes "consultation" for the purposes of Article 29 or whether, after receiving the Parliamentary Assembly's *Opinion,* the *Conclusions* of the Committee of Independent Expert, and the *Report* of the Governmental Committee, the Committee of Ministers must, or may, go back to the Assembly for further consultation on the specific questions whether it should make a recommendation. Either interpretation is consistent with the underlying conception of the relationship between the Committee of Ministers and the Assembly, reflected in the original name—Consultative Assembly—of the latter, which is that the Committee of Ministers normally should consult the parliamentary organ of the Council of Europe before acting. In 1970 the Committee of Ministers declined the Assembly's request to indicate which interpretation was the correct one on the ground that the matter con-

---

[237]For the debates on the first three cycles, see EUR. CONSULT. ASS. DEB. 23D SESS. 236–44 (May 14, 1971); *id.,* 25th Sess. 292–303 (Sept. 26, 1973); *id.,* 27th Sess. 77–93 (Apr. 22, 1975). The draft opinions for the fourth, fifth, and sixth cycles were not debated in the plenary Assembly. That for the seventh cycle was, but only after argument and then before a poorly attended Assembly.

[238]*See,* concerning the first seven cycles, Opinion 57, TEXTS ADOPTED, May 1971; Opinion 64, TEXTS ADOPTED, September/October 1973; and Opinion 71, TEXTS ADOPTED, April 1975; Opinion 83, TEXTS ADOPTED, April 1977; Opinion 95, TEXTS ADOPTED, June 1979; Opinion 106, TEXTS ADOPTED, September/October 1981; Opinion 113, TEXTS ADOPTED January 1983.

cerned the Assembly's powers under the Charter and was therefore a matter for the Assembly. Without expressly ruling upon the point, the Parliamentary Assembly has adopted the first interpretation in its practice.[239] Its *Opinions* refer to its competence under Articles 28 and 29 and offer the Assembly's view on the question whether recommendations should or should not be made. This is undoubtedly the more sensible interpretation. A procedure by which the Committee of Ministers would come back to the Assembly for guidance just on the question of recommendations would be cumbersome.

The question arises whether the contribution of the Assembly under Article 28 is such as to justify the length of time (six months or so) that the Assembly's participation adds to the process of implementation.[240] Were relations between the Committee of Independent Experts and the Governmental Committee better than they are, the answer probably would be in the negative. As matters stand, the Assembly provides a public, political forum for the regular consideration of the problems of the system of supervision which, on balance, is of value.[241] Although some members of the Assembly have tended to see their function as defenders of their national states' Charter records,[242] a sufficient number of them do not so as to make the Assembly an essentially independent element in the system of supervision.[243] The Assembly's *Opinions*,

[239]In contrast the GC had assumed in the second cycle that there would be two separate stages of consultation. GC II 6.

[240]On the value of Art. 28 from the CE point of view in developing consensus within the Assembly, see E. HAAS, CONSENSUS FORMATION IN THE COUNCIL OF EUROPE 40, 61 (1960).

[241]The Assembly can play a role in fostering the Charter in other ways than its participation in the system of implementation. It has asked its members to question their governments in their national parliaments on the acceptance of and compliance with the Charter and has itself called upon member states to ratify it (Recommendation 710, TEXTS ADOPTED, September/October 1973). Note also the Assembly's support for the revsion of the Charter. *See* note 1054 of Chapter II. The Assembly also initiated the 1977 Strasbourg Symposium on the Charter. *See* Resolution 649, TEXTS ADOPTED, January 1977.

[242]*See* the speeches by Dame Joan Vickers (U.K.), Miss Bergegren (Sweden), and Mr. Desmond (Ireland) in the debate on the second cycle of implementation, EUR. CONSULT. ASS. DEB. 25TH SESS., 292 (Sept. 26, 1973), and those by Lord Selsdon (U.K.) and Mrs. Cattaneo Petrini (Italy) in the debate on the third cycle, EUR. CONSULT. ASS. DEB. 27TH SESS. 77 (Apr. 22, 1975).

[243]For the view that the parliamentary background and constituency work of the great majority of the members of the Assembly make it particularly competent to represent the views of the individuals whose rights are being protected, see Dame Joan Vickers (U.K.). EUR. CONSULT. ASS. DEB. 23D SESS. 240 (May 14, 1971). In

which usually, though not always,[244] have supported the Committee of Independent Experts, therefore have provided the Committee of Ministers with an independent commentary upon the *Conclusions* and *Reports*. Although the Assembly's record over the years suggests that its influence upon the Committee of Ministers is generally not very great, there are some signs that its work under Article 28 of the Charter has been taken into account. In particular the Assembly's proposals on the making of recommendations would appear to have been of assistance to the Committee of Ministers.[245]

THE COMMITTEE OF MINISTERS

The Committee of Ministers is responsible for the final stage of the supervisory process. Article 29 of the Charter reads: "By a majority of two-thirds of the members entitled to sit on the Committee, the Committee of Ministers may, on the basis of the report of the Sub-Committee, and after consultation with the Consultative Assembly, make to each Contracting Party any necessary recommendations." Article 29 allows the Committee to make recommendations to the contracting parties as a whole or to one or more particular contracting parties.[246] Such recommendations are not binding in law.[247] They are made "on the basis of" the Governmental Committee's *Report,* which for this purpose includes the Committee of Independent Experts' *Conclusions* since these are appended to the *Report.*[248] The Committee therefore may address itself to any matter concerning the Charter generally or concerning national reports made under Articles 21 or 22 which arises out of the Governmental Committee's *Report* or the Committee of Independent Experts' *Conclusions*. The Committee of Minis-

practice, such plenary debates of the Assembly on the supervisory process as have been held do not support this thesis.

[244]In particular, the Assembly has taken a middle road betwen the CIE and the GC on the questions of recommendations under Art. 29, *see* note 252 *infra,* and the revision of the biennial reporting system, *see* note 52 *supra.*

[245]*See* CM Resolution (74) 16.

[246]Contrast the more limited power of "general recommendation" under the ICESCR, Art. 19, note 75 *supra. Cf.* Wiebringhaus, *Première Mise en Oeuvre du Système de Contrôle Instauré par la Charte Sociale Européenne,* 14 ANNUAIRE FRANÇAIS DE DOIT INTERNATIONAL 784, 786 (1968).

[247]Contrast the powers of decision given to the CM (Art. 32 [1]) and the European Court of Human Rights (Art. 53) under the ECHR.

[248]Art. 27 (3).

ters also has before it the *Opinion* of the Parlimentary Assembly, in which the Assembly expresses its "views" on the Committee of Independent Experts' *Conclusions* and on the questions whether and to whom any recommendations should be made. In practice, any recommendations that are made are likely to concern the question of compliance with the undertakings in Part II of the Charter accepted by the contracting parties. The decision to make a recommendation is taken by "a majority of two-thirds of the members entitled to sit on the Committee."[249] A contracting party may vote or participate in the discussion on a possible recommendation against it. States that have not ratified the Charter are qualified to vote as well as those that have done so. Presumably, a state which had not accepted the Charter would be unlikely to take the initiative in supporting a recommendation that would criticize a state or states that had done so.

During the seven cycles or reports under Article 21 that have been completed, the Committee of Ministers has made no recommendations under Article 29. In the first cycle it was asked to make fifty-seven recommendations by the Committee of Independent Experts.[250] The Governmental Committee considered this to be premature at this stage because the contracting parties had not had an opportunity to comment on the Committee of Independent Experts' *Conclusions* and proposed that no recommendations be made at all.[251] The Parliamentary Assembly proposed that no recommendations should be sent "in the special circumstances governing this initial stage of the supervision of the application of the Charter," but suggested instead that the Committee of Ministers should forward the Committee of Independent Experts' *Conclusions* to the contracting parties, commending the comments contained therein and drawing their attention to the Committee of Independent Experts' proposals for recommendations so that they might be able to take these into account in the preparation of their next reports.[252] In the

[249]*Id.* Art. 29. *Cf.* ECHR, Art. 32 (1), note 75 *supra.*

[250]*See* GC II 8–9.

[251]GC I 2. It also gave other reasons applicable to particular proposals: the fact that the proposal was based on incomplete information or had been overtaken by events; GC disagreement with the CIE interpretation of the provision of the Charter upon which it was based; and the presence of the subject concerned in the Work Programme of the CMSC. *Id.*

[252]Opinion 57, para. 14, TEXTS ADOPTED, May 1971.

event, the Committee of Ministers accepted the Governmental Committee's advice not to make any recommendations because it was the first cycle of supervision but agreed with the Assembly in deciding to transmit the Committee of Independent Experts' *Conclusions* to the contracting parties since these offered "useful guidance which may assist in achieving the full application of the principles enshrined in European Social Charter."[253] It also decided to transmit to the contracting parties the *Report* of the Governmental Committee and the *Opinion* of the Assembly.

The same pattern was followed in the second cycle, except that the Parliamentary Assembly joined with the Committee of Independent Experts to the extent that it proposed[254] that recommendations should be sent in some of the cases in which the Committee of Independent Experts proposed them;[255] in other cases, it proposed that a procedure not expressly provided for in the Charter should be followed, viz., that the Committee of Ministers transmit the recommendations proposed by the Committee of Independent Experts in the form of "suggestions." These would not carry the weight of full recommendations made under Article 29 but would provide the contracting party concerned with guidelines for its law and practice. While taking the view that a recommendation should be made "in principle" whenever a state has failed to comply with an undertaking in Part II which it has accepted, the Assembly considered that "suggestions," rather than formal recommendations, should be sent "when the states in question are clearly endeavouring to make good any gaps in their laws or imperfections in their practice, or when these gaps are of minor importance."[256] The Committee of Ministers did not accept this idea. It agreed instead with the Governmental

[253]CM Resolution (71) 30.

[254]Opinion 64, para. 22, TEXTS ADOPTED, September/October 1973.

[255]*See* GC II 8–9.

[256]Opinion No. 64, paras. 14 and 15, TEXTS ADOPTED, September/October 1973. Applying this criterion to eight "particularly important provisions of the Charter" (Art. 1 [2], Art. 2 [1], [3], [4], [5], Art. 3 [2], Art. 5, and Art. 6 [4]), the Assembly proposed that 12 of the 26 recommendations suggested by the CIE concerning these articles be sent to the contracting party concerned. The Assembly's Committee on Social and Health Questions was not unanimous in the adoption of the criterion indicated in the text above. Miss Bergegren (Sweden) (Chairman), in particular, argued that recommendations should only be made where there is no dispute between the CIE and the GC on the interpretation of the Charter provision concerned. *See* EUR. CONSULT. ASS. DEB. 25TH SESS., 297 (Sept. 26, 1973).

Committee[257] and declined to send any recommendations at all. Again, however, it sent the Committee of Independent Experts' *Conclusions*, together with the Governmental Committee's *Report* and the Assembly's *Opinion*, to all of the contracting parties and drew "the attention of the governments of these states to the observations formulated in the documents . . . [sent to them], especially as regards the action required to make their national legislation and practice comply with the obligations deriving from the Charter."[258] These remarks, with their reference to what was "required" of contracting states, were clearly a step further along the road toward the making of recommendations under Article 29, but still fell short of actually making any. They are interesting also, as Sur[259] has pointed out, because they imply recognition of the special authority of the Committee of Independent Experts, as opposed to the Governmental Committee, in indicating what is required to comply with the Charter. This follows from the fact that the reference to "action required" must be to the Committee of Independent Experts' *Conclusions* because this is the only one of the documents mentioned in which "action" is proposed.

The third cycle produced another variation on the same pattern. On this (and subsequent) occasions, the Committee of Independent Experts did not propose any recommendations, although maintaining its competence to do so. The Committee of Independent Experts did, however, indicate the policy that it thought the Committee of Ministers should follow. In particular, the Experts recognized that there might be some circumstances in which a recommendation would not be appropriate, viz., where the situation in the contracting party concerned has changed between the conclusion of the cycle and the making of its report or where the contracting party concerned has indicated its intention to amend its law or practice to comply with its obligations.[260] The Governmental Committee did not propose any recommendations.[261] In contrast, the Parliamentary Assembly expressed "its acute disappointment that the Committee of Ministers should have taken virtu-

[257]*See* GC II 8–9.
[258]CM Resolution (74) 16.
[259]*Supra* note 102, at 101.
[260]C III xii.
[261]GC III *passim*.

ally no action ... [to make] recommendations to contracting parties under Article 29, nor even any precise suggestion regarding the failure of certain national laws or practices to comply with the provisions of the Social Charter accepted by those Contracting Parties."[262] It urged the Committee of Ministers "most strongly" to make recommendations to seven of the nine contracting parties that had reported concerning their obligations under certain specified provisions of Part II. The Assembly proposed that the Committee of Ministers should invite the states concerned to bring their law and practice into line with their obligations under these provisions and to indicate a date on which they would be required to report on the measures taken to that end.[263] It further proposed that the Committee of Ministers should communicate to each of the reporting states concerned "by way of suggestions" the other observations of the Committee of Independent Experts, indicating three cases in which it thought that it would be particularly important for the Committee of Ministers to take this step.[264] Nonetheless, without giving any reasons, the Committee of Ministers again declined to make any recommendations.[265] However, it did transmit to the nine contracting parties that had reported the documents that it had sent to them in the first two cycles and drew their attention to the comments in them, particularly to those indicated above made by the Parliamentary Assembly "concerning the steps necessary to bring national legislation and practice more closely into line with the obligations ensuing from the Charter." Here too there is a veiled acceptance of the determinations by the Committee of Independent Experts that the Charter had been infringed.

In *Conclusions IV*, the Committee of Independent Experts expressed the view that it was "to be deplored" that no recommendations had yet been made, "particularly in cases of obvious and persistent failure to comply with the Charter."[266] The fourth *Report* of the Governmental Committee did not mention the question of recommendations. Following its approach in the second and third cycles, the Parliamentary Assembly

[262]Opinion 71, para. 4, TEXTS ADOPTED, April 1975.

[263]*Id.* paras. 6 & 7.

[264]*Id.* para. 8.

[265]CM Resolution (75) 26.

[266]C IV xvii.

regretted that the Committee of Ministers had made no recommendations and proposed that recommendations be made
in the fourth cycle to six of the nine reporting contracting
parties in respect to certain adverse findings of the Committee
of Independent Experts listed by the Assembly; it also urged
that the Experts' observations in the other cases be sent to the
contracting parties as "suggestions."[267] The Committee of
Ministers again refused to make any recommendations and
repeated what it had done in the previous cycle.[268] In the fifth,
sixth, and seventh cycles, neither the Committee óf Independent Experts nor the Governmental Committee made any
mention of recommendations. In the fifth cycle, the Assembly
noted "with regret" that the Committee of Ministers had
"never made use of Article 29" and suggested once more that
recommendations be made.[269] The Committee of Ministers
did not make any. It communicated to the reporting states the
documents that it had sent to them previously. It also drew

> the attention of the Governments of [the reporting] states to the
> observations made in [the GC *Report,* the CIE *Conclusions,* and the
> PA *Opinion*] . . . , in particular those referring to the considera-
> tions in paragraph 6 of the aforementioned Assembly Opinion
> relating to equal pay for men and women workers (Article 4,
> paragraph 3 of the Charter), the right to organise (Article 5) and
> the right of children and young persons tó protection (Article 7),
> concerning which steps may have to be taken in order to bring
> domestic legislation and practice more fully into line with the
> obligations ensuing from the Charter.[270]

The same pattern was followed in the sixth and seventh cycles.
    It is surprising that the Committee of Ministers has not
found any occasion so far to make a recommendation under
Article 29. The decision not to do so in the first two explora-
tory cycles was a sound one, as has been any policy that the
Committee of Ministers may have been following in not making recommendations in respect to the first and second re-

[267]Opinion 83, paras. 8 & 9, TEXTS ADOPTED, April 1977.
[268]CM Resolution (78) 9.
[269]Opinion 95, paras. 4 & 5, TEXTS ADOPTED, June 1979. In particular, it recommended that "the Committee of Ministers . . . address recommendations to those
countries, namely Austria, Cyprus, Denmark, the F.R.G., Ireland, Italy, Norway,
Sweden and the U.K., who to some extent do not respect their obligations under the
Charter." The list includes all of the reporting states except for France, which was
reporting for the first time.
[270]CM (80) 1.

ports presented since the first cycle. It is submitted, however, that recommendations should be made in cases of clear breaches of the Charter that have persisted over more than two cycles and that the contracting party concerned is not taking active steps to rectify. It is difficult to accept that there have not been any cases in which recommendations would not have been called for on the basis of these criteria.[271]

The Committee of Ministers' reluctance to act under Article 29 is particularly disappointing when it is compared with its contribution to the supervision of the European Code of Social Security 1964.[272] In the case of the latter, the reports submitted by the contracting parties are examined by the International Labor Office Committee of Experts, the Council of Europe Steering Committee for Social Security,[273] and the Committee of Ministers in turn.[274] The first two Committees present their conclusions on the reports to the Committee of Ministers, which then decides whether a breach of the Code has occurred; if it decides that it has, it is obliged to "invite" the contracting party concerned to take steps to rectify the situation.[275] The parallel between the Committee of Ministers' role under the Code and under the Charter is not an exact one since the Committee of Ministers is obliged to act under the Code if it—and the decision rests with the Committee of Ministers, not with either of the two committees of experts that participate in the system—finds that a breach has occurred, and because the question of compliance is, to some extent, a mathematical one and not one of judgment. Even so, the comparison is instructive. The Code is more recent than the Charter, covers to some extent the same ground, and has

---

[271]This is so even if a "clear" breach is not regarded as existing where it is based upon an interpretation of the Charter by the CIE which the GC does not accept.

[272]European Code of Social Security and Protocol, *opened for signature* Apr. 16, 1968, 1968 Gr. Brit. T.S. No. 10 (Cmd. 3871), 648 U.N.T.S. 235.

[273]Formerly the CE Committee of Experts on Social Security. The Steering Committee is composed of government representatives. The Steering Committee has the conclusions of the ILO CE on the reports before it, and when "certain points appear to it to be ambiguous, it asks the ILO's Committee of Experts for an opinion in order to clarify the legal position and to avoid disputes with the contracting parties." Villars, *Social Security Standards in the Council of Europe: the ILO Influence,* 118 INT'L LAB. REV. 343, 350 (1979).

[274]European Code of Social Security, Art. 74, note 272 *supra.*

[275]*Id.* Art. 75. The Committee of Ministers "has always accepted the interpretations of the ILO Committee of Experts, though it sometimes suggests that there may be more than one way of looking at a given problem." Villars, *supra* note 274, at 350.

many of the same contracting parties. An element of discretion is left to the Committee of Ministers in deciding whether a breach has occurred, with the consequent need for an "invitation." Given these similarities and the lack of difficulty that the Committee of Ministers has found in establishing breaches of the Code and making recommendations, it is reasonable to conclude that at least one element in the Committee of Ministers' continuing reluctance to act under the Charter is the relationship that has developed between the Committee of Independent Experts and the Governmental Committee and the problem that this has presented for the Committee of Ministers when faced with conclusions from the Committee of Independent Experts which differ markedly from the advice given to it by its own Sub-Committee.[276] The contrast with the International Labor Organization system of supervision is equally striking. There, the tripartite Conference accepts each year the list of serious offenders sent to it by the Conference Committee, and this is not thought to present difficulties in terms of an unacceptable affront to the dignity of states. If the International Labor Organization system has been established for a much longer period than that in the Charter, it is also true that members of the Council of Europe are parties to large numbers of International Labor Organization conventions and have accepted the "observations" of the International Labor Office Committee of Experts and the Conference Committee for many years.

In many cases, the mere publication of the findings and comments of the Committee of Independent Experts may precipitate remedial action by a party found in default of its obligations. The reduction of the number of cases in the first seven cycles in which a state has been found to be in breach of the Charter or to have failed to provide the information requested suggests that this is so.[277] Nonetheless, it would be unfortunate if Article 29 were to become a dead letter. There are several cases of clear and persistent infringement of the

---

[276]Compare (also in a human rights context) the disappointing record of the CM under the ECHR. See, e.g., the failure of the CM to find that the defendant state had violated the ECHR in The Inhabitant of Les Fourons against Belgium 1974 Y.B. EUR. CONV. ON HUMAN RIGHTS 542 (Comm. of Ministers), when it was required to do so by the terms of the Convention. See F. JACOBS, THE EUROPEAN CONVENTION ON HUMAN RIGHTS 268 (1975). For the view expressed in 1960 that the CM is generally not greatly interested in the work of the CE, see E. HAAS, supra note 240, at 12.

[277]See note 1012 of Chapter II.

Charter in which it is evident that the contracting party does not propose to take action as matters stand and in which a recommendation from the Committee of Ministers might be less easily ignored.[278] The complete absence of recommendations suggests a lack of confidence in the Committee of Independent Experts which must, in time, affect its authority. It must also cast doubt on the Council of Europe's intention to protect economic and social rights.

THE SYSTEM OF SUPERVISION AS A WHOLE: SOME COMMENTS

It is an important commonplace that a human rights guarantee is as good as its system of supervision.[279] *Ubi remedium, ibi jus.* The system that has been established to implement the Social Charter is something of a curate's egg. It is good in that it requires states to report on a regular and sufficiently frequent basis on its undertakings in Part II of the Charter. Moreover, the reports are examined and measured against the Charter by an independent body, and one that has demonstrated considerable vigor and enthusiasm for its role. To this extent it is more satisfactory than the report system in the International Convenant on Economic, Social and Cultural Rights[280] is likely

[278]The fact that a recommendation is not legally binding does not contradict this conclusion. Although the moral force that attaches to a legally binding ruling is not to be denied, the fact that a state has been formally adjudged by its peers to be in breach of its legal obligations is not without weight. The question has been raised whether the CM's failure to make recommendations under Art. 29 should be referred to the Joint Committee of the CE. Opinion 83, TEXTS ADOPTED, April 1977.

[279]*Cf.*, the statement by the British representative to the General Assembly in the debate in 1968 on the International Covenants that "the effectiveness of the Covenants would lie in the strength of their implementation clauses." 21 U.N. GAOR C.3 (1415th mtg.) at 219, 222 U.N. Doc. A/2929 (1966). *Cf. also* the ineffectiveness of the report provision in Art. 57 of the ECHR, note 75 *supra,* in the absence of any mechanism for examining and ruling upon the reports presented and of Art. 20(5) of the Charter, which is not subject to CIE scrutiny.

[280]International Covenant on Economic, Social and Cultural Rights, Arts. 16–22, *adopted,* Dec. 19, 1966, G.A. Res. 2200, 21 U.N. GAOR, Supp. (No. 16) at 49, U.N. Doc. A/6316 (1966), 1977 Gr. Brit. T.S. No. 6 (Cmd. 6702), Arts. 16–22. National reports on one-third of the provisions only are made biennially. The reports are examined by an ECOSOC Working Group, composed of 15 government representatives (*cf.* the GC of the Charter). Although the Group conducts an oral examination of each report, questioning a government spokesman, there is no provision for any nongovernmental element in the procedure. While, in the context of the U.N., government representatives may not all speak with the same voice, nongovernmental, expert supervision would be much preferable. *See further* on the ICESCR system of supervision, Schwelb, *Some Aspects of the Measures of Implementation of the International Covenant on Economic, Social and Cultural Rights,* 1 HUMAN RIGHTS J. 363 (1968).

to prove. There are, however, certain structural weaknesses, as well as weaknesses in the way that the Charter system has evolved, that make it less than wholly satisfactory.

In the first place, the second committee that examines the reports—the Governmental Committee—compares unfavorably with its equivalent in the International Labor Organization system—the Conference Committee. The latter serves a most valuable function by insulating the International Labor Office Committee of Experts from the actual enforcement process and by providing a forum in which states can be made to answer, orally as well as in writing, the criticisms of the Committee of Experts and in which moral persuasion can be brought to bear. The Conference Committee's satisfactory performance of this function is attributable to its tripartite character and, particularly, to the presence of trade union representatives among its members.

The contrast with the Governmental Committee is at once apparent. When the idea of a second committee was introduced during the drafting of the Charter, it was as a tripartite body along the lines of the International Labor Organization Conference Committee.[281] The idea of a committee was kept, but its composition was changed on the ground that the Council of Europe was an intergovernmental body in which a tripartite body would be out of place. This was a barren, dogmatic argument that did not merit the overriding importance attached to it. If wholly independent bodies such as the Committee of Independent Experts can participate in the functioning of the Charter, there seems to be no good reason why a tripartite body could not do so, particularly when the final decision is left in any case with the exclusively governmental Committee of Ministers and when the member states have for years participated with employers and trade unions representatives in the tripartite organs of the International Labor Organization. Although the result of giving the Governmental Committee an exclusively governmental composition was to make the contracting parties judges in their own cause, the drafting states maintained their position.[282] The consequence is a body whose natural instinct is to defend its ministers

[281]The idea was put forward by Belgium in a note dated May 15, 1957, for the Fifth Session of the CMSC.
[282]See REC PROC TC 234–36.

rather than to call them to account.[283] It is this, coupled with the fact that the final stage is in the hands of the Committee of Ministers, that, in the words of some of the participants in the 1977 Strasbourg Symposium on the Charter, makes the system of supervision one of "self supervision"[284] to an important extent.

Quite apart from this institutional weakness, the Charter system has suffered in the manner of its implementation. The existing arrangements would work better if the employers and workers organizations were to take more advantage of the (admittedly modest) tripartite elements that they contain and if the arrangements were to be brought fully into force through the implementation of Article 29. As important, however, is the clash between the Governmental Committee and the Committee of Independent Experts that has been described earlier.[285] The experience of the International Labor Organization has shown that the essence of a successful reporting system is persuasion.[286] Since this depends largely upon the goodwill and confidence of states, the Charter system of implementation cannot be said to have had a good start. It should be stressed, however, that the International Labor Organization system of supervision had similar teething troubles in its early days[287] and that there are some signs of a better understanding between the Committee of Independent Experts and the Governmental Committee.[288] Nonetheless, it may require more diplomacy on the part of the former and a considerable effort on the part of the latter to look beyond national interests for the Charter to realize its full potential as an instrument for social progress in Europe. It may be that the Parliamentary Assembly's proposal for making the Governmental Committee a tripartite body would need to be implemented for this to occur.[289]

---

[283]*Cf.* Lannung, *Human Rights and the Multiplicity of European Systems for International Protection,* 5 HUMAN RIGHTS J. 651, 654 (1972).

[284]Eur. Parl. Ass., 30th Sess., Doc. No. 4198, at 9 (1978) *Cf. Villars, supra* note 273, at 353, who criticizes the "self-judging" character of much of the system of supervision of the European Code of Social Security.

[285]Note 218 *supra.*

[286]On the need for publicity also (inter alia to help persuade), see note 4 of Chapter V.

[287]*See* E. HAAS, *supra* note 127, at 252–53.

[288]Note 218 *supra.*

[289]Note 193 *supra.*

Another serious weakness in the system is the length of time that the supervisory process takes. In each of the first six cycles of Article 21 reports, the decision of the Committee of Ministers under Article 29 bringing the cycle to a close had been taken approximately four years after the reporting period had ended. The seventh cycle was completed more expeditiously, taking only three years and three months.[290] Even so, following such a long lapse of time, the law of the contracting parties may have changed considerably, and any recommendations that are made may have only historic value.[291] The same is true, to a lesser extent, of the Committee of Independent Experts' *Conclusions* even at the moment when they are adopted, since, in the first seven cycles, this has been from eighteen months to two years after the reporting period concerned had ended. This time scale also makes it difficult for the contracting parties when completing their reports.[292] In most cycles so far the parties have not known the outcome of the Committee of Ministers' consideration of their previous reports, or even of that the Parliamentary Assembly or (in a final form) the Governmental Committee, when their next reports have been due. It also has presented problems for the Committee of Independent Experts, which has not always had before it the Resolution of the Committee of Ministers from the previous cycles when preparing its *Conclusions* for the next.

The length of time that the process takes results partly from the inherently cumbersome nature of the system of implementation, which involves a consideration, in varying degrees of detail, of the national reports and/or other documents by four supervisory organs.[293] It also is attributable to the manner in which the system is implemented. If the Council of Europe were to increase the size of the Secretariat assigned to the Charter,[294] if national governments were to feel a greater

[290]The 1981 CM decision that the CIE *Conclusions* should henceforth be referred to the PA on adoption and not later with the GC *Report* (*see* C VII xi) is to be welcomed. For the much shorter ILO time scale, see Valticos, *supra* note 145, at 44.

[291]This was apparent, for example, in the treatment of the U.K.'s industrial relations law during the third and fourth cycles of implementation as the star of the Industrial Relations Act 1971 waxed and waned. *See also* EUR. CONSULT. ASS. DEB. 25TH SESS. 299 (Sept. 26, 1973).

[292]*CF.* Valticos, *supra* note 145, at 44.

[293]On the question of whether the participation of the PA is desirable in view of the time it adds to the supervisory process, see E. HAAS, note 240 *supra*.

[294]This has been recommended by the PA. Eur. Parl. Ass., 30th Sess., Doc. No. 4198, at 6 (1978).

sense of urgency in presenting their reports on time, and if the supervisory organs were to speed up their part of the work, the length of the whole process could be cut by at least a year. It is particularly difficult to understand why it should take so long after the Committee of Independent Experts has adopted its *Conclusions,* for the rest of the review process to be completed. If, as has been suggested earlier, the Charter is to be treated seriously as the "pendant" to the European Convention on Human Rights that it was designed to be, it would seem necessary to assign more resources to its implementation and to take other steps to accelerate the process by which reports are examined.

Another way of improving the system would be to provide the contracting parties with an oral hearing before the Committee of Independent Experts, during which questions arising out of the reports submitted in a particular cycle could be discussed before the Committee's *Conclusions* were adopted. A somewhat similar procedure applies within the International Labor Organization system in the form of the hearing that occurs before the Conference Committee after the Committee of Experts has made its observations and requested such further information as it considers to be necessary.[295] In the absence of a tripartite body, an oral stage to the proceedings could only usefully occur in the Charter system before the Committee of Independent Experts. Such a stage undoubtedly would help in eliciting information. It might also avoid the kind of misunderstanding that can easily occur in a reporting system that operates solely on the basis of question and response without any personal contact.[296] It is interesting to note that a practice already has developed within the United Nations system whereby contracting parties voluntarily appear before the Committee on the Elimination of Racial Discrimination, the Human Rights Committee, and the ECOSOC Working Group to answer questions about their national reports made under the Convention on the Elimination of All Forms of Racial Discrimination, the International Covenant

[295]See E. LANDY, *supra* note 14, at 44.

[296]*Cf.* C I 14 on the role of the Secretariat in obtaining information. *See also* Mr. Desmond, EUR. CONSULT. ASS. DEB. 25TH SESS. 299–300 (Sept. 26, 1973). For an example of a case in which an oral hearing would probably have helped in both of the respects mentioned in the text see the exchange between CIE and the U.K. concerning Art. 19(6), note 952 of Chapter II.

on Civil and Political Rights, and the International Convenant on the Economic, Social and Cultural Rights respectively. There seems no good reason why a similar practice, which would not require an amendment to the Charter, should not be introduced at Strasbourg if states take their obligations under the Charter seriously. The difficulty of finding a representative who could cover the wide range of rights protected by the Charter applies equally to the International Covenants and could be overcome, for example, by giving notice of the areas in which questions would be put.

Finally, reference must be made to the proposal of the Parliamentary Assembly in 1978 that the system of supervision in the Charter should be revised to allow a right of petition and to establish a European Court of Social Rights.[297] Individuals and groups protected by the Charter would be allowed to petition the Committee of Independent Experts claiming that the protection which should be theirs was not being provided. The Committee would be competent to refer appropriate cases to the Court. The new system of petitions would supplement the present reporting arrangements. Somewhat inconsistently, at the same time the Assembly proposed that a small number of economic and social rights should be added by protocol to the European Convention of Human Rights, and hence made subject to its system of petitions.[298] Both proposals are currently under government consideration.

These proposals raise the long-standing question of the best way of enforcing an international guarantee of economic and social rights. No suggestion of a right of state or individual petition, whether leading to adjudication by a court or not, was made during the drafting of the Charter.[299] It was assumed without argument that the correct manner of implementation of an international guarantee of economic and social rights was a report system in accordance with the International Labor Organization precedent.[300] The same approach

---

[297]Recommendation 839, TEXTS ADOPTED, September 1978. *See also* Eur. Parl. Ass., 30th Sess., Doc. No. 3198 (1978). Villars, *supra* note 273, at 353, has suggested a European Social Court for the European Code of Social Security.

[298]*See* note 1054 of Chapter II.

[299]For the proposal that came the closest to being one of this sort, see Eur. Consult. Ass., 7th Sess., Doc. No. 403 (1955), Arts. 35–37.

[300]The ILO Constitution, Arts. 24 and 26, provide for complaints by trade unions and employers and by states, although not by individuals. This possibility had not proved important in practice at the time of the drafting of the Charter. States had

was adopted in the International Covenant on Economic, Social and Cultural Rights. There are advantages to such a system,[301] to which the experience of the Charter bears witness. There is no need to wait upon the chance of a petition being brought by a person with the *locus standi,* knowledge, time, inclination, and, possibly, funds to do so; the initiative lies with the supervisory organs. It took a long time, for example, for the spotlight to fall upon trade union matters under the European Convention on Human Rights,[302] and the question of "forced labor" by merchant seamen has yet to arise. In contrast, every part of the law and practice of the contracting parties (including the law on the above two subjects) is examined automatically every two years under Article 21 of the Charter. But there are disadvantages too. The Committee of Independent Experts may not discover how a law or practice actually operates without the sort of information that appears from the facts of particular cases and that emerges from the sharpness of conflict in adversary proceedings.[303] This is particularly so in the absence of an effective tripartite element in the Charter system of supervision.[304] The need to resort to local remedies, which normally will be present in a system of petitions, will mean that a national court usually will

been reluctant to bring complaints against other states, and trade unions and employers organizations had preferred to raise matters at a national level rather than antagonize their governments by embarrassing them before the ILO. State complaints under Art. 26 have become more numerous since 1961 with the increasing diversity of membership of the ILO, but it is unlikely that many would be brought within the context of the CE. Complaints to the special Committee on Freedom of Association by employers and workers organizations have also increased in number since 1961. There has been one case of a complaint being submitted to the Strasbourg authorities in connection with the Charter from a trade union. The union was informed that there was no procedure for handling the complaint. The only effective system of petitions that might have been provided for in the Charter would have been one allowing petitions by individuals *à la* ECHR.

[301]*See* Valticos, *Un Système de Contrôle International: la Mise en Oeuvre des Conventions Internationales du Travail,* 123 RECUEIL DES COURS (Hague Academy of International Law) 311, 321 (1968–I).

[302]*See* note 317 *infra.*

[303]In a report system, a lot turns upon the way in which an answer to a questionnaire is put and whether the expertise of the supervisory organ is such to allow it to know when and how to probe further. The national reports that have been presented so far under the Charter system contain, for example, many short, comprehensive statements which, in some cases, have been questioned further as a result of the presence on the CIE of a member with specialist knowledge.

[304]This does not mean that a tripartite element is the complete answer. In the field of employment, at least, there is often a discrepancy between the interests of organized labor and of particular individuals.

have the opportunity to provide a remedy locally or at least to clarify the meaning of a national law before a claim is brought at an international level.[305] There is also the fact that a finding against a state in favor of a particular individual that is binding in law is likely to make a much greater impact upon public opinion than an abstract ruling upon the question of compliance.[306] Above all, from the standpoint of the individual whose rights are directly or indirectly in issue, there is no substitute for a remedy directly available to him.

If a choice is to be made, it is likely that a system of petitions is the more effective. Although it operates just in areas in which claims arise, it not only provides a remedy for the particular individual who brings the petition, but in most cases it will, like a report system, cause the law or practice in question to be changed to the advantage of all. Moreover, it is likely to have this general effect more speedily and more certainly than a report system. At least this is so when the report system is one which, like the Charter's, provides only for recommendations and has the other weaknesses described earlier in this chapter. It is true that progress in the protection of economic and social rights may be achieved better by persuasion than by confrontation. But a petition system usually has a conciliation stage, and the existence of a case against a state may help to concentrate its mind. The Assembly's proposal for the revision of the Charter is, of course, for petitions *and* reports.[307] Such a combination would offer the best of both worlds.

But the question remains whether a petition system for economic and social rights is feasible. Most commentators take the view that it is not.[308] The argument to this effect starts from the

---

[305]See, e.g., the position concerning the Irish Trade Union Act 1941 in respect to negotiating licenses. The CIE has found the requirements as to the size of a union and deposits to be in breach of the Charter, *see* note 324 of Chapter II, when these requirements could be challenged in the Irish High Court and possibly be found illegal on the ground of public interest as a matter of Irish law. The CIE ruling has been made without any ruling by the Irish High Court on the question.

[306]The difficulty in some petition cases is to achieve the necessary publicity without rendering the dispute so political that the state's goodwill is forfeited. *See* Valticos, *supra* note 301, at 321.

[307]Insofar as the rights which it is proposed to add to the ECHR overlap with the Charter, see note 1054 of Chapter II. The Assembly's proposal for revising the ECHR is to the same effect.

[308]*See, e.g.,* LAUTERPACHT, *supra* note 13 of Chapter I, at 284–85, 354–55; Bossuyt, *supra* note 13 of Chapter I, at 793–94; and Cohen-Jonathan, *supra* note 39 of Chapter I, at 641. On the question whether economic and social rights are "justiciable" and

proposition that economic and social rights are essentially different from civil and political rights in that whereas the latter are always within the capacity of all governments to protect fully (by abstaining from interfering with them), the former depend upon economic conditions and can only be realized progressively and variably by positive action by states as the economic circumstances of each permits. It is thought to follow from this proposition, which is essentially correct,[309] that economic and social rights are not justiciable, or not generally so. It is not possible, it is argued, to call a state to task in respect to its realization of economic and social rights at any particular moment in the way that this would occur within a system of petitions; moreover, the nature of economic and social rights is such that individuals cannot be given rights which would be theirs to enforce by means of a petition. It is claimed that in both of these respects the position of civil and political rights is different.

The first part of this argument is not supported by the experience of the European Social Charter. A finding of a breach of the Charter under its report system, which is juridically no different from any such finding as might result from the operation of a system of petitions, has presented no inherent difficulties. In particular, it has proved possible to set appropriate levels of achievement for states and to take sufficient account where necessary of the economic circumstances of individual states or of states generally at a given time when doing so.[310] The fact that many of the obligations in a guarantee of economic and social rights may be limited to the "pro-

hence properly the subject of a system of petitions, see Jacobs, *supra* note 1054 of Chapter II, at 172.

[309]But the protection of some civil and political rights may be dependent upon the provision of funds. Free legal aid, adequate court systems, and satisfactory prison conditions are obvious examples. *See* Airey Case, 32 Eur. Ct. of Human Rights, para. 26 (Council of Europe 1979). On the obligation to take positive action to protect the right to "respect for family life" in Article 8, ECHR, see Marckx Case, *supra* note 727 of Chapter II, para. 31.

[310]See, e.g., the jurisprudence of the CIE on Article 4 (1), note 213 of Chapter II *supra*, and Article 1 (1), note 52 of Chapter II *supra*. But there are limits to the adjustments that can be made in the case of nondynamic obligations in the Charter. For example, obligations to provide free services or facilities of various kinds (*see, e.g.,* Art. 1 [3] [employment services] and Art. 19 [1] [services to assist migrant workers]) cannot be adjusted in this way. So far, no contracting party has suggested that it has reached the point where compliance with such obligations has presented financial difficulties. If that point were reached, the party could denounce the particular provision (*see* Art. 37 [2] of the Charter), provided that sufficient Charter obligations were still accepted.

motion" or "encouragement" of certain objectives[311] or by such provisions as Article 33 of the Charter[312] has more to do with the likelihood of a successful outcome of a petition than with the feasibility of a petition system. The conclusion that a system of petitions would generally be viable is supported by the experience of national courts and tribunals.[313] These deal daily with matters covered by a wide range of undertakings present in the Charter. In states in which treaties may be applied by the national courts as part of the local law, self-executing provisions of International Labor Organization conventions, which cover much of the ground of the Charter, have also been applied.[314] Another factor which might be thought to militate against a system of petitions could be the politically contentious or damaging nature of some of the findings that might result from a system of petitions for economic and social rights. But allegations of torture, which would appear to be as problematical in this respect as allegations, for example, that a state is not pursuing a policy of full employment or is not providing wages affording a decent standard of living, have been dealt with successfully by the European Court of Human Rights.

The second part of the argument has no application to a system of state petitions. As far as petitions by individuals are concerned, although, for the most part, economic and social rights may have to be expressed, as they are in the Charter, in terms of interstate obligations rather than in terms of the rights of individuals, there is still no overriding reason why individuals should not be given the *locus standi* to call attention to the possible breach of these obligations in circumstances in which they are directly and specifically affected.[315] Rules as to

---

[311]*See, e.g.,* Arts. 1 (4) & 10 (4).

[312]*See* note 21 of Chapter IV.

[313]In the case of national law, of course, it is legally possible for a government to lower the level of protection afforded by law to economic and social rights to reflect economic circumstances—subject, that is, to any national bill of rights or treaty obligation to the contrary.

[314]*See* Valticos, *supra* note 145, at 46. Although most of the undertakings in Part II of the Charter are not self-executing, it does not follow that states cannot be held to them in a complaint system any more than it follows that they cannot be the subject of a report system.

[315]This is in fact the scheme of the ECHR as that document was eventually drafted. An individual application under Art. 25 of the ECHR, note 75 *supra*, is not the initiation of proceedings for the enforcement of a legal right of the individual applicant; it is instead a way of bringing to the attention of the Strasbourg authorities

admissibility and arrangements for a conciliation stage similar to those in the European Convention on Human Rights would be necessary and attainable safeguards. The need for a workable *locus standi* rule might, however, effectively rule out a challenge to certain undertakings by individuals. Few people or groups, for example, would be directly and specially affected by an obligation to provide satisfactory and educational facilities for the promotion of health.[316] Even so, such considerations would still leave the great majority of rights—at least as they are formulated in the Charter—as ones in respect to which a petition system would be perfectly viable. Support for this view in respect to some of the rights in the Charter can also be found in the fact that the Charter coincides with the European Convention on Human Rights in certain respects and that, in cases that have originated from individual petitions brought under the European Convention on Human Rights in this area of overlap, the European Court of Rights has had no difficulty in ruling upon the legal guarantee in the European Convention on Human Rights.[317]

It seems likely that the argument that obligations concerning economic and social rights cannot by their nature be properly made the subject of a system of petitions stems more from tradition than from a thorough assessment of the practical situation. It so happens that civil and political rights have been the subject of legal protection and of courtlike remedies longer than economic and social rights have and that the states most likely to agree to a system of petitions are the ones that

---

a possible breach of an obligation which each contracting party owes to its fellow contracting parties, and not to the individual. This is why the applicant has no *locus standi* before the European Court of Human Rights. It is true, however, that the ECHR has been recognized as creating enforceable rights for individuals in the national courts of some contracting parties and that the practice of the Strasbourg authorities has moved a lot in the direction of treating "victims" as enforcing their own rights.

[316]*See* Art. 11 (2).

[317]*See* National Union of Belgian Police Case, 1975 Y.B. EUR. CONV. ON HUMAN RIGHTS 294 (Eur. Court of Human Rights); Swedish Engine Drivers' Union Case, 1976 Y.B. EUR. CONV. ON HUMAN RIGHTS 478 (Eur. Court of Human Rights); and Schmidt and Dahlström Case, at 484 (Eur. Court of Human Rights). All of these cases concerned the rights of trade unions under Art. 11 of the ECHR, note 75 *supra*, which overlaps to some extent with Arts. 5 and 6 of the Charter. The Court in fact interpreted Art. 6 of the Charter in all three cases. *See* notes 346 & 355 & 379 of Chapter II. *See also* Marckx Case, 1979 Y.B. EUR. CONV. ON HUMAN RIGHTS 410 (Eur. Court of Human Rights), on illegitimate children, a matter which is controlled by Art. 16 of the Charter, note 54 of Chapter I.

emphasize economic and social rights the least. A quite separate question is whether there is the political will within the membership of the Council of Europe at present to translate either of the Assembly's two proposals into law.

CHAPTER IV

Restrictions on the Application of the Charter

This chapter discusses a number of Charter provisions that limit the application of the Charter.

DEROGATION FROM CHARTER OBLIGATIONS IN TIME OF WAR OR PUBLIC EMERGENCY

Article 30 allows contracting parties to derogate from their obligations under the Charter in certain circumstances and in accordance with a specified procedure. No contracting party to date has found it necessary to invoke Article 30; consequently, no practice elaborating its meaning has emerged.[1] There have been several cases interpreting Article 15 of the European Convention on Human Rights, on which Article 30 is based.[2] Although the Charter and the Convention are separate documents and although most of the jurisprudence concerning Article 15 postdates the drafting of the Charter, nonetheless it may be helpful to examine Article 30 in the light of that jurisprudence.

Article 30 (1) reads: "In time of war or other public emergency threatening the life of the nation any Contracting Party may take measures derogating from its obligations under this Charter to the extent strictly required by the exigencies of the

---

[1]The Turkish invasion of Cyprus in 1974 has led to a situation in which Art. 30 could be invoked in respect to that state. So far, however, no derogation has been made. *Cf.* C V xvi. The CE continues to recognize the Greek Cypriot Government of Cyprus. It is that Government, therefore, that continues to submit reports under the Charter and could act under Art. 30. Whereas the U.K. derogated from its obligations under the ECHR in respect to Northern Ireland in view of the current public emergency there, it has not made such a derogation in respect to its obligations under the Charter. In some cases it may be sufficient for a state to rely upon the general restriction clause in Art. 31 of the Charter, *see* note 11 *infra*, which has the advantage that it does not require any notification of derogation.

[2]*See also* European Convention on Establishment 1955, Art. 28, *done* Dec. 13, 1955, 1971 Gr. Brit. T.S. No. 1 (Cmnd. 4573), 529 U.N.T.S. 141.

situation, provided that such measures are not inconsistent with its other obligations under international law." "War" can be taken to have the meaning that it has in customary international law.[3] The Appendix to the Charter states that the wording "in time of war or other public emergency" shall be understood as including the "*threat* of war" also. Insofar as this follows from the presence of the wording "public emergency threatening the life of the nation," it is submitted that it is not indicative of the whole of the meaning of that wording, which was defined more fully in the applicaton of Article 15 (1) of the European Convention on Human Rights in the *Lawless* case as being "an exceptional situation of crisis or emergency which affects the whole population and constitutes a threat to the organized life of the community of which the State is composed."[4] In the same case, in considering whether the measures taken were "strictly required by the exigencies of the situation," the Court inquired whether any lesser measures would have met the situation. Measures can be taken by a contracting party under Article 30 (1) only if they "are not inconsistent with its other obligations under international law." Such "obligations" include treaty and customary international law obligations. Where the Charter overlaps with the European Convention on Human Rights, the obligations under the latter qualify.[5] In contrast with the European Convention on Human Rights,[6] any Charter obligation may be derogated from.

The question whether any of the conditions in Article 30 (1) upon which the exercise of the power to derogate depends is

[3]*See L.* Oppenheim, 2 International Law, para. 54 (7th ed. 1948).

[4]The "Lawless" Case, 1961 Y.B. Eur. Conv. on Human Rights 480. The Court found that a "public emergency" did exist on the facts of that case. For two other ECHR cases in which the Strasbourg authorities have ruled on the presence or absence of a "public emergency," *see* The Greek Case, 1969 Y.B. Eur. Conv. on Human Rights 76 (Eur. Comm'n on Human Rights) (no public emergency) and Ireland v. U.K. 1978 Y.B. Eur. Conv. on Human Rights 25 (Eur. Court of Human Rights) (public emergency found).

[5]*E.g.,* Charter, Art. 1 (2), and European Convention on Human Rights and Fundamental Freedoms, Art. 4 (2), *signed* Nov. 4, 1950, 1950 Gr. Brit. T.S. No. 70 (Cmd. 8969), 213 U.N.T.S. 221. Both concern "forced labour." *See* note 60 of Chapter II. If the provision in the Convention is one that can be derogated from under Art. 15, ECHR, and such a derogation is in fact made, a derogation may also be made under Art. 30 of the Charter without a contracting party's "obligations under international law" thereby being violated.

[6]ECHR, Art. 15 (2), note 5 *supra.*

met must be one for determination by the supervisory organs at Strasbourg. This has been the interpretation of Article 15 of the European Convention on Human Rights, and it would seem to be a necessary interpretation of Article 30 also to ensure its effectiveness. The European Court of Human Rights has lessened the rigor of this approach by developing a "margin of appreciation" doctrine by which a contracting party is allowed a measure of discretion in deciding whether a condition in Article 15 is met. There is, as it were, a presumption in favor of the government's assessment of the facts.[7] Such a doctrine reasonably could be read into Article 30 in order to allow for special knowledge and responsibilities of the government.

By Article 30 (2), a "Contracting Party which has availed itself of this right of derogation shall, within a reasonable lapse of time, keep the Secretary-General of the Council of Europe fully informed of the measures taken and of the reasons therefor." Although there is thus an obligation to keep the Council of Europe informed, there is no need to do so before or at the time that the measures are taken. It is sufficient if the required information is given "within a reasonable lapse of time" of their being taken.[8] By Article 30 (2) a contracting party also must inform the Secretary-General of the Council of Europe when the measures in derogation of its obligations have ceased to operate, which must be when the reasons for them cease to apply.[9] It is not clear whether the failure to provide the required information under Article 30 (2) should be taken as invalidating a derogation, or whether it is just an independent breach of the particular obligation in Article 30 (2). Although the former interpretation would make the reporting obligation more effective, the latter is likely to be preferred. Like the European Convention on Human Rights, the Charter is defective in not requiring that the fact and extent of any derogation be made public in the territory of the contracting party concerned.

Finally, Article 30 (3) requires the Secretary-General of the

---

[7]See Ireland v. U.K. 1978 Y.B. EUR. CONV. ON HUMAN RIGHTS 602 (Eur. Court of Human Rights).

[8]Cf. the interpretation of the less fully worded Art. 15 (3) of the ECHR, note 5 supra, in the "Lawless Case," 1961 Y.B. EUR CONV. ON HUMAN RIGHTS 430, 484 (Eur. Court of Human Rights) (delay of twelve days permissible).

[9]Cf. in respect to Art. 15 of the ECHR, note 5 supra, and the "Lawless Case," id.

Council of Europe to inform the other contracting parties and the Director-General of the International Labor Organization of "all communications" received under Article 30 (2).[10]

RESTRICTIONS IN THE PUBLIC INTEREST, ETC.

Article 31 (1) provides that the undertakings in Parts I and II "shall not be subject to any restrictions or limitations not specified in those Parts, except such as are prescribed by law and are necessary in a democratic society for the protection of the rights and freedoms of others or for the protection of public interest, national security, public health, or morals."[11]

The reference to restrictions or limitations "specified" in Parts I and II is to such restrictions or qualifications as those in Paragraph 18 of Part I ("subject to restrictions based upon cogent economic or social reasons") and in Article 5 of Part II ("The extent to which the guarantees provided for in this Article shall apply to the police shall be determined by national laws or regulations. . . .") which are designed to suit the needs of particular undertakings. Article 31 (1) supplements these by a general restrictions clause applying to all of the undertakings in the Charter, including those which are subject to their own restrictions where these are narrower than those in Article 31 (1). Restrictions are permitted on one of five grounds. The "rights and freedoms of others" is a concept that has no precise, foreseeable limits. It will presumably be used to protect such "rights or freedoms" recognized by the

---

[10]There is no comparable obligation in Art. 15 of the ECHR, but the CM has decided that the Secretary-General should in practice inform the other contracting parties and the European Commission of Human Rights of any notification sent to him under Art. 15. CM Res. (56) 16.

[11]*Cf.* International Covenant on Economic, Social and Cultural Rights, Art. 4, *adopted* Dec. 19, 1966, G.A. Res. 2200, 21 U.N. GAOR Supp. (No. 16) at 49, U.N. Doc. A/6316 (1966), 1977 Gr. Brit. T.S. No. 6 (Cmd. 6702) ('. . . the State may subject such rights only to such limitations as are determined by law only insofar as this may be compatible with the nature of these rights and solely for the purpose of promoting the general welfare in a democratic society") and ('. . . such limitations as are determined by law solely for the purpose of securing due recognition and respect for the rights and freedoms of others and of meeting the just requirement of morality, public order and the general welfare in a democratic society"). The ECHR has no such general clause; tailor-made restriction clauses are inserted in particular articles where appropriate. For a comment on the different roles that a restriction clause plays in respect to economic and social rights on the one hand and civil and political rights on the other, see Mr. Whitlam (Australia) in the U.N. Commission on Human Rights. U.N. Doc. E/CN.4/SR.235, at 7.

laws of a contracting party as appear acceptable limitations upon the Charter right in question.[12] The "public interest" ground reads "pour protéger l'ordre public" in the French text, which incorporates the concept of "ordre public" in civil law systems.[13] "National security" was impliedly relied upon by the Committee of Independent Experts when it referred to Article 31 as the basis for its ruling that U.K. law on the status of the armed forces did not infringe the "forced labor" prohibition in Article 1 (2).[14] The grounds of "public health" and "morals" might be relevant, for example, to the undertaking in Article 19 (6) concerning the admission of the families of migrant workers. The exclusion of persons with contagious diseases or who live off immoral earnings might be justified in this way.[15]

A restriction only may be imposed where it is "prescribed by law" and is "necessary in a democratic society." The first of these conditions must be understood to refer to a restriction that emanates from any source of law in the legal system concerned, including case law.[16] The second condition narrows the scope of Article 31 considerably. A "democratic society" can be taken to be a political society of the sort required for the membership of the Council of Europe.[17] If a contracting

[12]For examples of situations in which the "rights and freedoms of others" might permit a restriction, see the discussion during drafting by the U.N. Commission of Human Rights of the comparable Art. 4 of ICESCR. U.N. Doc. E/CN.4/SR.235, at 4, and E/CN.4/SR.236, at 6. The scope of the same words of limitation in several articles of the ECHR has yet to be clearly defined. See Connelly, *The Protection of the Rights of Others*, 5 HUMAN RIGHTS REV. 119 (1980).

[13]The CM adopted an interpretation of Art. 31 (1) which reads: "The concept of 'ordre public' is to be understood in a wide sense." CM (61) 95 rev., 3. As orginally proposed, the interpretation had read: "The concept of 'ordre public' is to be understood in the wide sense generally accepted in continental countries." The wording finaly adopted was not intended to change the sense of the original text. On the meaning of "ordre public, *see* note 973 of Chapter II.

[14]C IV 10 (U.K.). The CM adopted an interpretation of Art. 31 by which a contracting party "may reserve for its own nationals the exercise of public functions or of occupations connected with national security or defense, or make the exercise of these occupations by aliens subject to special conditions." CM (61) 95 rev., 3. It added that this "interpretation would not preclude a contracting party from reserving other occupations to its own nationals in accordance with the terms of Art. 31." *Id.*

[15]See note 949 of Chapter II. The wording "as far as possible" in Art. 19 (6) might make recourse to Art. 31 unnecessary.

[16]Report of the CMSC to the CM, December 1960. CM (60) 156, 14. For the fuller meaning given to this wording in the ECHR, *see* the Sunday Times Case, 58 I.L.R. 491, 524–25 (Eur. Court of Human Rights 1979) ("adequately accessible" and "formulated with sufficient precision").

[17]See also Bleckmann, *Interprétation et Application en Droit Interne de la Charte Sociale Européenne, Notamment du Droit de Grève*, 1967 CAHIERS DE DROIT EUROPÉEN 388, 395.

party has a restriction that other contracting parties—who are necessarily members of the Council of Europe—lack, this is strong evidence that the restriction is not "necessary" in a democratic society. It may be an accepted and long-established restriction in the community concerned, but still will not be "necessary" in a democratic society. This point was made by the Committee of Independent Experts when considering the West German law preventing civil servants (the *beamte*) from striking; since many of the parties to the Charter had no such restriction, it was not possible to accept the positon that the ban was "necessary in a democratic society."[18]

Article 31 (1) only rarely has been referred to expressly by the Committee of Indepdent Experts.[19]

ABUSE OF POWER

Article 31 (2) reads: "The restrictions permitted under this Charter to the rights and obligations set forth herein shall not be applied for any purpose other than that for which they have been prescribed." "Restrictions" mean restrictions allowed by Article 31 (1) and those allowed by particular paragraphs of Part I or provisions of Part II. The purpose of Article 31 (2) is to ensure that restrictions are only introduced or used for their proper purpose. It incorporates, in other words, the doctrine of "abuse of power," or *détournement de pouvoir,* that is commonly found in the law of the contracting parties. Thus a migrant worker must not be expelled on a ground permitted by Article 19 (8), even though his expulsion could be justified thereunder, if the real reason for expelling him is not allowed by Article 19 (8). Article 31 (2) is based upon Article 18 of the European Convention on Human Rights, and its wording is virtually identical to it. Like Article 18 of the European Convention, it makes explicit what would probably be implied.[20]

---

[18]C IV 49 (F.R.G). Note that this question concerned the application of Art. 6 (4), in respect to which there is a special provision in the Appendix to the Charter. On the different approach (more favorable to states) to the meaning of the phrase "necessary in a democratic society" in the ECHR, *see* Handyside Case, 58 I.L.R. 150, 174 (Eur. Court of Human Rights 1976), and the Sunday Times Case, 58 I.L.R. 491, 529–31 (Eur. Court of Human Rights 1979). The ECHR approach, which rewrites the limitation to require the existence of a "pressing social need," seems more realistic.

[19]*See, e.g.,* C IV 8 (Italy).

[20]*CF.* F. JACOBS, THE EUROPEAN CONVENTION ON HUMAN RIGHTS 203–04 (1975).

ARTICLE 33: IMPLEMENTATION BY COLLECTIVE AGREEMENTS

The general rule is that a contracting party must comply with a particular provision in Part II with respect to all of the persons to whom it extends. An exception is allowed by Article 33 (1) pertaining to certain provisions concerning workers' rights when the guarantees they contain are "matters normally left to agreements beween employers or employers' organizations and workers' organizations, or are normally carried out otherwise than by law." Where this is so, the contracting party concerned will be understood to comply with the provision if it is "applied through such agreements or other means[21] to the great majority of the workers concerned." The exception applies to the following twelve provisions:

Article 2 (1), (2), (3), (4), (5)
Article 7 (4), (6), (7)
Article 10 (1), (2), (3), (4).[22]

The Committee of Independent Experts and the Governmental Committee have interpreted "a great majority" to mean 80%.[23] Although a precise figure of this sort is useful as a general guide, common sense suggests that it should not be rigidly followed.[24] Statistics, the need for which the Committee of Independent Experts has stressed in relation to Article 33 provisions,[25] as Mark Twain noted, can be misleading. When considering whether a provision is being applied to the "great majority" of workers, it does not matter that the provision is not being applied to the "great majority" of a particular group of workers, such as agricultural workers, or workers in a particu-

---

[21]E.g., by custom or administrative measures.

[22]Exceptions similar to those in Art. 33 are allowed by the Appendix to the Charter in respect of Arts. 4 (5) and 7 (8).

[23]See C V 13 (Italy), C VI 14 (U.K.), GC V 11. Thus, in the third cycle, Denmark was found to comply with Art. 2 (5) when the workers not protected by it amounted to 17.5%. C III 16 (Denmark, Ireland). In the fourth cycle, the Committee would appear to have applied a 20% rule to Ireland with respect to Art. 2 (1) and (5). C IV 23 and 29 (Ireland).

[24]The *travaux préparatoires* suggest the same. A proposal by the workers' delegates to the TC to replace "a great majority" by "90 per cent" was rejected as introducing too rigid a rule. REC PROC TC 237. A system of exact percentage figures is used in ILO Social Security (Minimum Standards) Convention (ILO Convention No. 102), *adopted* June 28, 1952, 210 U.N.T.S. 131, and European Code of Social Security 1964, *opened for signature* Apr. 16, 1968, 1968 Gr. Brit. T.S. No. 10 (Cmnd. 3871), 648 U.N.T.S. 235. *Cf.* GC VII 15.

[25]C I 9.

lar region (e.g., Northern Ireland), if it is being applied to the great majority of the "workers concerned."[26]

One question which arises is whether a state is obliged to take action if the "great majority" of the workers concerned are not protected. The drafting history of Article 33 suggests that it is not; a contracting party must legislate, take administrative action, or persuade the interested parties as far as its system of industrial relations allow, but it is not required by the Charter to go beyond this.[27]

To avoid discrimination against contracting parties who regulate a matter covered by Article 33 (1) by law, Article 33 (2) provides that for states in which the matters dealt with in the provisions covered by Article 33 (1) are "normally the subject of legislation," the undertakings concerned will be held to have been complied with if "the provisions are applied by law to the great majority of the workers concerned." In some cases, a contracting party may deal with a matter by legislation for some workers and by collective agreements for others. The test, then, is whether the "great majority" of workers concerned are protected, either by legislation or by collective agreements or by other means.[28]

Article 33 provides a more general rule for contracting parties than that which applies to International Labor Organization conventions. Under the International Labor Organization Constitution,[29] states must "take such action as may be necessary to make effective" the provisions of any convention which it accepts. This has been interpreted as allowing a state to satisfy an International Labor Organization convention by means of collective agreement.[30] The provisions of the convention, however, must be applied to all the persons protected by it, and a contracting party has a residual obligation to take the necessary steps by law to ensure compliance if this does

[26]As to particular groups of workers, see, e.g., C II 7 (F.R.G.) and C III 14 (Sweden).

[27]See the Opinion of the Legal Adviser to the TC, REC PROC TC 238, and the rejection by the CMSC at its Sixth Session, Dec. 20, 1957, of a proposal to require contracting parties to "attempt to exercise some influence on the labour market partners in order to have the provisions of the Charter complied with."

[28]Report of the CMSC to the CM, December 1960. CM (60) 156, 14.

[29]Art. 19 (5) (d).

[30]See E. LANDY, THE EFFECTIVENESS OF INTERNATIONAL SUPERVISION: THIRTY YEARS OF ILO EXPERIENCE 114–18 (1966). Some ILO conventions specifically provide for implementation by collective agreements. See INT'L LAB. CODE, Arts. 701, n. 24 & 876.

not happen. The argument that prevailed in the case of the Charter was that "if the obligation were to be stricter, the government would have either to supervise the operation of collective agreements in order to make sure that no small part of the field was left uncovered or they would have to legislate in order to achieve the same effect."[31] This, it was argued, would be a situation which no one would want.

APPLICATION RATIONE PERSONAE[32]

Nationally Limitations
The Appendix to the Charter reads:

> Without prejudice to Article 12, paragraph 4 and Article 13, paragraph 4, the persons covered by Articles 1 to 17 include foreigners only insofar as they are nationals of other Contracting Parties lawfully resident or working regularly within the territory of the Contracting Party concerned, subject to the understanding that these Articles are to be interpreted in the light of the provisions of Articles 18 and 19.
>
> This interpretation would not prejudice the extension of similar facilities to other persons by any of the Contracting Parties.

A contracting party thus undertakes to apply the provisions of Articles 1 to 17 to its own nationals and to such of the nationals of other contracting parties as are "lawfully resident or working regularly within . . . [its] territory." A particular provision applies to a national of another contracting party even though his national state has not accepted it. The requirement that a national of another contracting party be "lawfully resident" within the territory of a contracting party excludes visitors, such as persons on holiday or on a family or business visit. However, a person does not have to be allowed to settle in the territory of a contracting party, i.e., to establish himself, for the Charter to apply to him. The alternative requirement of "working regularly" would be met by a person who commutes to work across a border from one contracting party to another, or by a seasonal

---

[31]Mr. Veysey, U.K. Government delegate to the TC. REC PROC TC 67. For the view that Art. 33 is an undesirable limitation upon the application of the Charter, see Laroque, *Drawing Up and Implementation of the European Social Charter*, Working Paper for the 1977 Strasbourg Symposium on the European Social Charter, CE Doc. AS/Coll/Charte 1-E.

[32]*See* Wiebringhaus, *Le Champ d'Application "Ratione Personae" de la Charte Sociale Européenne*, in LIBRO-HOMENAJE AL PROFESSOR LUIS SELA SAMPIL OVIEDO 525 (1970).

agricultural or other worker. Whether a person who makes regular business trips would qualify is not clear. A person who goes to work in the territory of another contracting party for a limited period in connection with a single job (e.g., a one-year construction project) would be covered as being "lawfully resident" there.

The above rule is "without prejudice to Article 12, paragraph 4 and Article 13, paragraph 4," which contain rules requiring equality of treatment betweeen all nationals of contracting parties, regardless of questions of residence, etc. It is also "subject to the understanding that these Articles [Articles 1 to 17] are to be interpreted in the light of the provisions of Articles 18 and 19." The reference to Article 18 is presumably intended to confirm that nationals of other contracting parties are protected by the provisions in Articles 1 to 17 concerning employment only if they have permission to work in a contracting party in accordance with Article 18 (which leaves contracting parties considerable discretion in the granting of such permission). What follows from looking at Articles 1 to 17 "in the light of" Article 19 is less clear. Possibly the intention is just to draw attention to Article 19 (4), by which, quite independently of Articles 1 to 17, migrant workers from other contracting parties are entitled to equal treatment with respect to certain matters covered in.certain of the provisions in Articles 1 to 17 (in which case it is unnecessary).

Article 18 (1), (2), and (3) apply to all nationals of other contracting parties regardless of residence.[33] The paragraphs of Article 19 apply to such nationals more or less restrictively according to the terms of each particular paragraph of it.[34]

Part II does not protect the nationals of noncontracting parties at all. This is so whether they are nationals of member states of the Council of Europe or not. The question of the scope of the Charter *ratione personae* did not arise until after the Tripartite Conference and the Consultative Assembly had given their views. At that late stage, despite pangs of conscience

---

[33]C I 79. The Appendix to the Charter contains no wording that would narrow the Charter's scope beyond this as far as Art. 18 is concerned, and the text of Art. 18 (unlike that of Art. 19) does not impose its own limits. For confirmation that Art. 18 (and Art. 19) does not apply to persons who are not nationals of the contracting parties, see C I 79. Although the Appendix is not clear on this point, the *travaux préparatoires* leave no doubt. *See* note 35 *infra.*

[34]C I 81. *See* Laroque, note 591 of Chapter II. *supra.*

by the representatives of some states, the Committee of Ministers Social Committee[35] adopted a rule that smacks more of the reciprocal arrangements found in bilateral treaties of friendship than a human rights guarantee and that compares most unfavorably with similar instruments. The International Covenant on Economic, Social and Cultural Rights applies without discrimination "as to . . . national . . . origin . . . or other status"[36] and most International Labor Organization conventions apply in a similar, unlimited fashion.[37] Likewise, the European Convention on Human Rights applies to "everyone" within the contracting party's "jurisdiction," regardless of nationality.[38] The more restrictive rule in the Charter is particularly open to criticism because the Charter does not limit a state's power to control entry into its territory. If a contracting party allows an alien to take up residence or work within its territory, it is difficult to justify excluding that person from the rights guaranteed in the Charter solely on the basis of his nationality.[39] Nonetheless, despite these criticisms, the Charter does protect the great majority of persons likely to be subject to a state's action, viz., the state's own nationals. The Charter's Appendix contains a special provision applicable to refugees.[40]

The Self-Employed

With one exception, the Charter does not state whether the employment provisions of Part II apply to the self-employed. The exception is Article 19 (10), which contains an express undertaking, which states may or may not accept, extending the provisions in the remainder of the article to the self-

---

[35]*See* the Report to the CM by the CMSC, December 1960. CM (60) 156, 21–27.

[36]ICESCR Art. 2 (2), note 11 *supra*. An exception is made for "developing countries," which need not guarantee fully the economic rights protected to nonnationals. Art. 2 (3).

[37]*See The European Social Charter and International Labour Standards*, 84 INT'L LAB. REV. 354, 375 (1961).

[38]ECHR, Art. 1, note 5 *supra*.

[39]Green, *Droits Sociaux et Normes Régionales*, 96 JOURNAL DU DROIT INTERNATIONAL 58, 69 (1969).

[40]The Appendix to the Charter reads:

Each Contracting Party will grant to refugees as defined in the Convention relating to the Status of Refugees, signed at Geneva on 28th July 1951, and lawfully staying in its territory, treatment as favourable as possible, and in any case not less favourable than under the obligations accepted by the Contracting Party under the said Convention and under any other existing international instruments applicable to those refugees.

employed. Although it is arguable from this that the absence of a similar arrangement with respect to the other provisions of Part II means that they do not apply to the self-employed, the Committee of Independent Experts has taken the view, which is supported by the *travaux préparatoires,* that in principle the provisions of Part II apply to the self-employed except where the context requires that they be limited to employed persons.[41] The Governmental Committee would appear to agree.[42]

Workers in Agriculture

The Preamble ("urban and rural populations") makes it clear that agricultural workers are covered by the Charter, as does the practice of the supervisory organs.[43] The protection afforded to such workers in the Charter has been supplemented by the European Convention on the Social Protection of Farmers.[44]

Territorial Application

By Article 34 (1), the Charter applies to the "metropolitan territory" of the contracting parties. A state, upon signature, ratification, or approval, may specify by declaration the territory that it regards as its metropolitan territory for this purpose. So far, four states have made such declarations.[45] Presumably, the Strasbourg authorities are free to make their own decision on this point should a contracting party not make a declaration at one of the times indicated, although they would no doubt be strongly influenced by what the contracting party

[41]C I 8.

[42]GC II 10.

[43]See, e.g., their application of Art. 3, as to which see note 186 of Chapter II. The same view was taken by the CMSC at its Ninth Session, April 1960.

[44]European Convention on the Social Protection of Farmers, *done* May 6, 1974, 1982 Gr. Brit. T.S. No. 3 (Cmd. 8447), Europ. T.S. No. 83. The Convention applies only to the nationals of contracting parties and is subject to many limitations.

[45]Denmark has declared that its metropolitan territory consists of "the territory of the Kingdom of Denmark with the exception of the Faroe Islands and Greenland." 1 European Conventions and Agreements 361 (1971). Norway has declared its to be "the territory of the Kingdom of Norway with the exception of 'Svarlbard (Spitzbergen) and Jan Mayen'; the Charter does not apply to the Norwegian dependencies." *Id.* at 364. The Netherlands has declared that it understandings its metropolitan territory to be its "European" territory. *Id.* at 363. The F.R.G. has declared that the Charter applies to *Land* Berlin, presumably under Art. 34 (1) rather than Art. 34 (2). *Id.* at 362.

concerned suggested. The Charter applies to a contracting party's ships, aircraft, and oil rigs. These can all be assimilated to territory for jurisdictional purposes.[46]

By Article 34 (2), a contracting party, upon ratification or approval, or thereafter, may make a declaration extending the application of the Charter to a "non-metropolitan territory or territories specified in the said declaration for whose international relations it is responsible or for which it assumes international responsibility." The second alternative in this wording was added to allow for French overseas departments and territories.[47] The Charter may be extended to a territory "in whole or in part." Such a declaration, which may be added to later,[48] must specify the articles or paragraphs of Part II which are accepted as binding for the territory named. The declaration or any addition to it takes effect thirty days after the Secretary-General of the Council of Europe has received notification of it.[49] To date two declarations have been made under Article 34 (2).[50]

The Secretary-General of the Council of Europe must communicate to the other signatory Governments and to the Director-General of the International Labor Organization any notification transmitted to him in accordance with Article 34 (1) to (2).[51]

The rules in Article 34 concerning the territorial application of the Charter have to be read in conjunction with the rule concerning the scope of the Charter *ratione personae*.[52] By the latter, the Charter only applies to foreigners if they are nationals of another contracting party who are "lawfully resident or working regularly within the territory of the contracting party concerned." No such limitations applies in the case of a contracting party's own nationals. It is submitted that with

[46]*See* notes 782 & 846 of Chapter II.

[47]The comparable Art. 63 of the ECHR, note 5 *supra*, refers only to "territories for whose international relations it is responsible."

[48]Art. 34 (4).

[49]Art. 34 (3).

[50]The U.K. has extended the Charter to the Isle of Man. 1 EUROPEAN CONVENTIONS AND AGREEMENTS 364 (1971). The same Part II provisions as apply to the U.K. apply to the Isle of Man. The Charter has not been extended to the Channel Islands. The Netherlands has accepted "Articles 1 and 5, Article 6 (except for civil servants) and Article 16" for the Netherlands Antilles. 7 INFORMATION BULLETIN ON LEGAL ACTIVITIES WITHIN THE CE AND MEMBER STATES 3 (1980).

[51]Art. 34 (5).

[52]*See* note 32 *supra*.

respect to the few undertakings for which this would be relevant,[53] the Charter applies to the nationals of a contracting party not within its territory; for such persons the rule *ratione personae* supplements Article 34.

Should any part of a signatory state's "metropolitan territory" cease to be its territory, it is submitted that the Charter ceases to apply to the territory, and that this is so whether or not the signatory state has made a declaration under Article 34 (1). Where a contracting party makes a declaration under Article 34 (2) for a territory within its control and the territory ceases to be a territory "for whose international relations . . . [the contracting party] is responsible or for which it assumes international responsibility," the declaration as a matter of international law should be treated as being terminated. When a territory to which the Charter has applied by virtue of Article 34 (1) or (2) becomes a state, it is submitted that the new state does not succeed to the treaty by operation of law,[54] nor has it any right to do so unless it is eligible to become, and does become, a member of the Council of Europe, in which case the ordinary rule by which the Charter is open to members of the Council of Europe applies.[55]

RESERVATIONS

Unlike the European Convention on Human Rights,[56] the Charter contains no reservations clause. The Committee of Independent Experts has taken the view that reservations to Part II provisions are not permitted.[57] It has done so on the ground that "the Charter's very structure compelling as it does every Contracting Party ratifying the Charter to accept the obligations laid down in a certain number of paragraphs, necessarily implies that acceptance of a particular paragraph extends to all the obligations embodied therein so that none of them may be evaded by means of a reservation or otherwise." This is not a convincing argument. Provided that a contracting

[53]E.g., those in Art. 12.
[54]*See* Vienna Convention on Succession of States in Respect of Treaties, *done* Aug. 23, 1978, Arts. 15 & 16, 17 I.L.M. 1488, 1496 (1978).
[55]*See* Art. 35. *Cf.* the practice in respect to Art. 63 of the ECHR, note 5 *supra*, discussed in F. JACOBS, *supra note 20, at 14–15*.
[56]ECHR, Art. 64, note 5 *supra*.
[57]C IV 49 (F.R.G.).

party accepts the minimum number of provisions in their entirety, there is no reason in the scheme of Article 20 why that party should not be allowed to make reservations to such provisions as it accepts in excess of that minimum, if this is what was intended. There is some evidence in the *travaux préparatoires* to suggest that the intention of the drafting states was not to permit reservations to Part II and that this was so far a reason similar (but not identical) to that expressed by the Committee of Independent Experts above, i.e., that sufficient discretion was already given to the contracting parties under Article 20 to choose the obligations that they would accept; they could not expect the further freedom to attach limitations to the obligations that they choose to accept.[58] The subsequent practice of the contracting parties suggests otherwise. Both Norway and the Netherlands have made reservations without attracting any comment from the other contracting parties.[59] The better view would appear to be that reservations to Part II are permitted provided that the minimum number of provisions are fully accepted and provided that the object and purpose of the Charter is otherwise not infringed.[60] Reservations to any Part of the Charter other than Part II are clearly permitted provided that they are not incompatible with the object and purpose of the Charter.

A question has arisen concerning the significance of a

[58]This was stated, seemingly without contradiction, to have been the opinion of the Social Committee by the Netherlands at the 98th Meeting of the Minister's Deputies, Apr. 20–22, 1961. CM/Del./Concl. (61) 98, 13. It was also the understanding of the U.K. Government; see a letter in the U.K. Government files on the drafting of the Charter dated May 18, 1961, from S. W. Spain to D. Anderson. On the limited value, however, of the unilateral and uncommunicated statements of individual drafting states, see note 76 of Chapter II.

[59]Norway made a "reservation" to Art. 12 (4). For text, *see* 1 EUROPEAN CONVENTIONS AND AGREEMENTS 364 (1971). More recently, in its 1980 instrument of ratification, the Netherlands accepted Art. 6 (4) except insofar as it applies to civil servants. This was clearly a reservation (although that word is not used). In both cases, the details of the instrument of ratification were communicated to contracting parties, with no response. The French instrument of ratification in 1980 was accompanied by two "reservations" and a "declaration of interpretation." The former are not reservations in a legal sense; they are explanations for the nonacceptance of certain provisions in Part II in toto. The "declaration of interpretation" is an acknowledgement that French law is not in conformity with Art. 12 (4) (a), which France has accepted, and indicates that France is taking steps to bring its law into line.

[60]*See* Reservations to the Convention on the Prevention and Punishment of the Crime of Genocide, 1951 I.C.J. 15, 24; Vienna Convention on the Law of Treaties, Art. 19 (c), *adopted* May 22, 1969, 1969 Gr. Brit. Misc. No. 31 (Cmnd. 4140).

declaration[61] made by the F.R.G. shortly before the Charter was opened for signature on October 18, 1961, concerning the scope of Article 6 (4) and its application to the *Beamte* (the West German established civil service). In the declaration, which was sent to the Deputy Secretary-General of the Council of Europe by a letter of September 28, 1961, and registered with the Secretariat-General on October 4, 1961, the F.R.G. indicated that in its view Article 6 (4) did not apply to the *Beamte.* The Deputy Secretary-General communicated the declaration to the member states of the Council of Europe, these being the states that were qualified to sign the Charter. In his letter making this communication, the Deputy Secretary-General stated that the "declaration, for which there is no provision in the European Social Charter, is solely concerned with defining the position of the Federal Republic of Germany on a specific in that Charter." No state to which the declaration was sent commented upon it. When the Committee of Independent Experts later found that the F.R.G. had violated Article 6 (4) because the *Beamte* were not allowed to strike,[62] the F.R.G. relied upon its declaration to challenge this finding. In *Conclusions IV* the Committee of Independent Experts concluded that the declaration was not a reservation.[63] This would appear to be correct. If it is the case that reservations to Part II are permitted, the declaration was made before the F.R.G. signed the Charter and does not qualify as a reservation on that ground alone.[64] It would seem instead to be an "instrument" in the sense of Article 31 (2) (b) of the Vienna Convention on the Law of Treaties.[65] An "instrument" may be unilat-

---

[61]1 EUROPEAN CONVENTIONS AND AGREEMENTS 361. The Declaration also applies to Art. 6 (2) but has not given rise to any difficulty in this regard.

[62]*See* note 405 of Chapter II.

[63]C IV 49 (F.R.G.). While maintaining this view, the CIE (influenced by the fact that the Netherlands had successfully avoided the effect of Art. 6(4) in respect of its civil service by a declaration in proper form and by its understanding that the F.R.G. "intended its declaration to have a similar effect to a reservation") in the seventh cycle decided not to raise the question of the F.R.G.'s compliance with Art. 6(4) on this matter again. C VII 39 (F.R.G.).

[64]A reservation is "a unilateral statement, made by a State, when signing, ratifying, accepting, approving, or accepting to a treaty . . .," Art. 2 (1) (d) of the Vienna Convention on the Law of Treaties 1969, note 60 *supra.*

[65]Note 60 *supra*. The CE Director of Legal Affairs has interpreted the F.R.G. declaration as an "agreement" in the sense of Art. 31 (2) (a). *See* GC V Appendix III. The GC has accepted this interpretation. GC V 9. The declaration is not, it is submit-

eral, as was the West German declaration. It has "to be accepted by the other parties as an instument related to the treaty." The declaration was communicated to the other member states of the Council of Europe, and their lack of response can be taken to be acceptance.[66] The declaration is therefore a part of the "context" of the Charter for the purposes of interpretation. As such, it contains admissible, though not by itself conclusive, evidence of the meaning of Article 6 (4).[67]

ted such an "agreement." It is a unilateral document which was sent by the F.R.G. to the Deputy Secretary-General of the Council of Europe. So far as is known, copies were not sent directly to the other member states of the Council by the F.R.G. There is no suggestion in the covering letter sent with the declaration by the F.R.G. to the Secretary-General that the declaration should be communicated to the other member states. The decision by the Secretary-General to send the declaration to them implies that it was being transmitted for purposes of information only. The other member states would find nothing in it suggesting that the F.R.G. wished to negotiate an agreement with them interpretative of the Charter. Both the declaration and the covering letter indicate that the F.R.G. was instead giving notice of its own, unilateral point of view. In these circumstances, it is impossible to conclude that the elements of agreement in accordance with general principles of law were present. There is, in particular, no evidence of an intention to create consensual legal relations.

[66]That acquiescence is sufficient for this purpose was the view of the Special Rapporteur of the ILC, Sir Humphrey Waldock, Sixth Report on the Law of Treaties, 1966 Y.B. INT'L L. COMM'N 98. It is also consistent with the analogous rule concerning consent to reservations in Art. 20 (5) of the Vienna Convention on the Law of Treaties 1969, note 60 *supra*.

[67]It is not the interpretation which an instrument contains that the other states accept but the fact that it is "related to the treaty" and so forms a part of its "context." It is then one of several kinds of evidence to be taken into account for interpretational purposes. *See* Vienna Convention on the Law of Treaties 1969, Art. 31 (1), note 60 *supra*. The question of the importance to be attached to presignature declarations or "understandings" which are circulated among the drafting states was discussed in connection with the many declarations of "undertakings" made prior to the signature of the Briand-Kellogg Pact of 1928. *See* G. Hackworth, 5 DIGEST OF INTERNATIONAL LAW 144–46 (1927) for a list of them. For differing views then expressed, see Wright, *The Interpretation of Multilateral Treaties*, 23 AM. J. INT'L L. 94, 105 (1929), and D. MILLER, THE PEACE PACT OF PARIS 119 (1928), cited in Wright, *id.* Wright states:

> In the case of bilateral treaties, such notes, if accepted or not protested by either party, have been regarded as authoritative. They indicate the meaning, intended by the parties. In the case of multilateral treaties, however, there is a strong presumption that the terms of the text have the established meaning recognised throughout the family of nations. Such notes may furnish evidence of that meaning, but they are not conclusive of it.

In contrast, writing of the Pact of Paris in particular, Miller states that "the interpretations and declarations made in the diplomatic correspondence before the signature of the treaty, and either agreed or not dissented from, are just as binding and just as much within the meaning of the treaty as if they were written into the treaty text." It is submitted that Wright's view is preferable as a general rule. *See further*, Bowett, *Reservations to Non-Restricted Multilateral Treaties*, 48 BRIT. Y.B. INT'L L. 67, 68–69. (1976–77).

RELATIONS BETWEEN THE CHARTER AND MUNICIPAL LAW[68]

The Appendix to the Charter reads: "It is understood that the Charter contains legal obligations of an international character, the application of which is submitted solely to the supervision provided for in Part IV[69] thereof." This language was added to establish that no part of the Charter is self-executing.[70] It does not, therefore, create rights and duties enforceable in the courts of those contracting parties whose constitutions make self-executing treaties a part of their law. Even in the absence of this express provision, the great majority of the undertakings are so worded that it seems likely that they would not be regarded as self-executing.[71]

In this respect, the Charter falls short of the European Convention of Human Rights, which contains no such express limitations and which, in varying degrees, has been held to be self-executing in those states whose constitutions provide for this possibility.[72] The Convention system of supervision thus

---

[68]See W. WENGLER, DIE UNANWENDBARKEIT DER EUROPÄISCHEN SOZIALCHARTA IM STAAT (1969), and Schambeck, *Bild und Recht des Menschen in der Europäischen Sozialcharta*, in 2 FESTSCHRIFT FÜR H. SCHMITZ 216 (1967).

[69]I.e., the report system described in Chapter III.

[70]The CM approved the above paragraph with this in mind at the suggestion of the F.R.G. 99th Meeting, Ministers' Delegates, May 1961. *But see* Purpura, *L'Elaborazione Della Carta Sociale Europea, 1961* RASSEGNA DEL LAVORO 25, 42 1961. *See also* Bleckmann, *supra* note 17, at 407, who, relying upon Purpura's account, argues that the Appendix is intended to indicate that Part IV provides the only international remedy available. It seems unlikely that the F.R.G. would have accepted a text with such a meaning.

[71]This is true of the obligation (which, in any event, is political only) in Part I in which the contracting parties simply accept the attainment of certain conditions as "the aim of their policy." All but two of the undertakings in Part II are also cast in terms of action which the contracting parties agree to take ("the contracting parties undertake to provide . . . to promote . . . to ensure . . . etc.") and not in terms of an immediate commitment to the presence upon ratification of certain rights of individuals in their law. The two exceptions are Arts. 6 (4) and 18 (4) in which the contracting parties "recognise" (as opposed to "undertake to recognise") the two rights concerned. *Cf.* Papadatos, *The European Social Charter*, 7 J. INT'L COMM'N JURISTS 214, 239 (1966).

[72]See Buergenthal, *The Effect of the European Convention on Human Rights on the Internal Law of Member States*, in BRITISH INSTITUTE OF INTERNATIONAL AND COMPARATIVE LAW, THE EUROPEAN CONVENTION ON HUMAN RIGHTS 79 (1965). ILO conventions may also be self-executing: *see* Valticos, *supra* note 145 of Chapter III (Brussels Colloquium Paper). Valticos suggests that national courts, applying their own constitutional law, may decide to treat the Charter as a part of their law despite the provision in the Appendix. It is submitted that it is unlikely that they will do so; the intention of the contracting states is usually followed by municipal courts: *cf.* Blackmann, *supra* note 17, at 405–6. *See.*however, Laroque *supra* note 31, at 14, who states

has an extra, national dimension which has proved important in practice and which the Charter lacks.

that some national counts have "thought nevertheless that they could apply the Charter." The Charter may, of course, be invoked by a national court in interpreting national law. For a case in which the Charter was referred to by a court in its reasoning, see the judgment of January 25, 1972, of the Milan Corte d'Appelo: COLLECTION OF DECISIONS OF NATIONAL COURTS REFERRING TO THE ECHR, 3d Supplement, 1973, No. 30.

CHAPTER V

The Charter: Achievements And Prospects

The progress of the Charter during the first fifteen or so
years of its existence has been mapped out in the preceding
chapters, and such conclusions as seem appropriate have been
fully drawn there. In this final chapter, it is intended to sum-
marize these conclusions and to comment upon the prospects
of the Charter for the future.

The Charter was intended partly as a statement of principles common to the membership of the Council of Europe in
the field of social policy and as a guide to the harmonization
of future social progress in Europe. It also was to provide an
immediate legal guarantee of economic and social rights comparable to that in the European Convention on Human Rights
for civil and political rights. It has played only a modest role in
the first of these two respects. It contains in Part I a fairly full
statement of the economic and social rights to which West
European (and probably most other) states would subscribe.
As such, it has provided a convenient place of reference in the
evolution of the Council of Europe's social policy. Even so, it
would be difficult to say that the Charter in practice has become the inevitable starting point of current developments
within the Council. Although some Council of Europe conventions and other documents refer back to it, the overall impression is that contemporary pressures and interests are more
important in shaping the Council's social policy than a con-
scious intention to build upon the groundwork set by the
Charter. It also is difficult to find evidence that the Charter
has fashioned the social policies of governments at a national
level other than in the sense that action may sometimes be
taken to bring a state's law and practice into line with its commitments under Part II.

It is the Charter's role as the counterpart of the European
Convention on Human Rights, through the obligations which
the contracting parties accept in Part II, that is the main
source of its present significance. Despite the mood of disap-

pointment that accompanied the adoption of the Charter, Part II has proved to have sufficient substance to qualify as a worthwhile guarantee of economic and social rights. Its provisions, like those of Part I, contain an impressive list of such rights, although there are a few omissions. The most obvious of these are the right to education, cultural rights generally, the right to protection of the environment, and certain economic rights, such as freedom from arbitrary dismissal, entitlement to redundancy payments, and retirement at a reasonable age. The weakness in the Charter resulting from the fact that a state does not have to accept much more than half of the undertakings in Part II in order to become a party has not, in practice, proved as serious as might have been supposed. Most contracting parties have accepted far more than this, and the thirteen contracting parties as a whole have accepted 83% of the provisions open to them. Another measure of the quality of the guarantee in the Charter is the fact that states have not found it easy to comply with their obligations. As the record of the first seven cycles shows, there is no reporting state that has been found by the Committee of Independent Experts to have complied with all of the provisions which it has accepted, and there are several with poor records. Two states—Ireland and the U.K.—were in breach of more than 25% of the obligations that they had undertaken at the end of the seventh cycle. Overall, the ten contracting parties that had reported remained in breach of approximately 16% of the provisions which they had accepted. The provisions that have caused the most difficulty have concerned the rights of children, young persons, women, and migrant workers. The provisions concerning economic rights generally have been more difficult to comply with than those concerning social rights. It is noticeable that the vague wording of some of the provisions has not proved the handicap that had been supposed when the Chapter was first drafted. On the contrary, the availability of supervisory organs capable of interpreting these provisions has meant that they are gradually being given a more detailed meaning, and the generality of their wording allows them to keep pace with change. It has been some of the more precisely worded provisions that have become dated instead. But even the most generally worded provision cannot protect a right that is not included at all. In the case of the Charter, such omissions have been deliberate (as in the case of the right to education) or the result of subsequent developments (as with the right to protection of the environment). Only a protocol could remedy such omissions.[1] Whether the proposals for one now under consideration in the Committee of Ministers will succeed is uncertain. The Charter has been supplemented further by Council of Europe conventions on particular topics. Unfortunately, most of these instruments do not provide for any system of supervision. Should a protocol to the Charter ever be adopted, an amendment to the rule concerning its application *ratione personae* would be desirable. The present rule limiting the Charter's applicability to nationals of contracting parties is inconsistent with the Charter's human rights character.

It is axiomatic that an international guarantee of human rights can only succeed if it is accompanied by a vigorous and independent system of supervision.[2] No one could say that the Committee of Independent Experts has failed in its role in this regard. It already has developed an extensive jurisprudence elaborating the meaning of the Charter and has set standards that are generally in tune with International Labor Organization precedents where these apply and are pitched at a level which puts the achievement of the contracting parties to a serious test. Most significantly, the Committee has stressed the dynamic character of the Charter and shown awareness of what continuing improvement can be expected of the contracting parties. This is not to say that the system of supervision was perfectly conceived or works as well as it might. The failure to follow the International Labor Organization pattern in the composition of the Governmental Committee is a serious flaw, and the conflict between the Governmental Committee and the Committee of Independent Experts that appeared during the first two cycles has proved a real handicap. But there are signs in the more recent cycles of an accommodation between the two committees which it is hoped may develop further. The International Labor Organization system of supervision experienced somewhat similar difficulties in its early

---

[1]*Cf.* the Protocols to the European Convention on Human Rights and Fundamental Freedoms: Protocol No. 1, *done* Mar. 26, 1952, 1954 Gr. Brit. T.S. No. 46 (Cmd. 9221), 213 U.N.T.S. 262; Protocol No. 2, *done* May 6, 1963, Europ. T.S. No. 44; Protocol No. 3, *done* May 6, 1963, Europ. T.S No 45; Protocol No. 4, *done* Sept. 16, 1963, Europ. T.S. No. 46; Protocol No. 5, *done* Jan. 20, 1966, Europ. T.S. No. 55.

[2]Witness the fate of Art. 20 (5) of the Charter, which is not subject to a report system and which has become a dead letter.

years when states were extremely wary of its Committee of Experts. It remains to be seen whether the Committee of Independent Experts can generate greater confidence in its role in the minds of the contracting parties and whether the Governmental Committee can look beyond national considerations and develop further its concern for overall European progress in the social field. It is already true that the *Conclusions* of the Experts have become the main source for the interpretation of Part II, a development which could not confidently have been predicted from the text of the Charter and which provides a good example of the importance of subsequent practice in the exegesis of a treaty.[3] If the Governmental Committee has not agreed in theory to the primary role of the Experts in the interpretation of Part II, it has in practice left this task mostly to them and only taken up particular points itself. Should the International Labor Organization precedent be followed further, so that the Governmental Committee would not normally challenge the Experts' interpretation, the absence from the Charter of a body competent to give a final ruling on the meaning of the Charter, such as the European Court of Human Rights, would not be such a weakness as it is at present.

The system of supervision would also work better if trade unions were to show more interest in it. This is particularly so in view of the lack of a system of petitions and the Charter's non-self-executing character. The opinion bluntly expressed to the present author by one trade union official was that there was "nothing in it" for trade unions. The results of the first seven cycles do not support his view. There is a lot in the jurisprudence that has evolved during that period which could support an argument for further national improvement. The introduction of a genuinely tripartite element in the functioning of the Governmental Committee would help to overcome the present trade union lack of interest and would strengthen the system of supervision.

There are other developments that should occur if the Charter is to realize its full potential. More states need to ratify it,[4] and the existing contracting parties need to be per-

---

[3]*Cf.* Kahn-Freund, *The European Social Charter,* in EUROPEAN LAW AND THE INDIVIDUAL 181, 205 (F. Jacobs ed. 1976).

[4]There is no immediate prospect of additional ratifications. Belgium and Switzerland have had the matter under consideration for some time. Portugal has taken the matter up more recently.

suaded to accept more provisions. Pressure by the Committee of Ministers upon states to translate good intentions into action in both regards would be welcome. Another serious weakness in the Charter is that, as it has operated to date, a cycle of supervision takes as many as four years to complete, so that national reports for one cycle are due for submission before a final ruling is given on those submitted for the previous one. Sometimes the law or practice of a state has changed long before a ruling is given so that the ruling is only of historical interest. The effectiveness of the system of supervision generally would be greatly assisted if the size of the Secretariat and other resources made available to the Charter were increased. The making of recommendations by the Committee of Ministers under Article 29 is also long overdue. It is difficult to accept that there have not been cases of clear and serious breaches of the Charter which have persisted over a sufficient length of time to justify such action under Article 29. The absence of recommendations is particularly striking when compared to the practice of the International Labor Organization and the willingness of the Committee of Ministers to make them under the European Code of Social Security. Implementation of Article 29 would do a great deal to show a commitment to the Charter on the part of the Committee of Ministers that has so far been lacking. Another welcome development would be the introduction of an oral hearing in which contracting parties would respond to questions about their reports before the Committee of Independent Experts. Such a procedure has evolved without express textual authorization in the examination of United Nations human rights treaties and could do so to advantage in the case of the Charter. The Charter's usefulness could be further improved if its human rights charter were stressed. At the moment, the European Convention on Human Rights is treated in Council of Europe publications and affairs under the heading of "human rights," while the Charter is not. The latter instead is characterized as being concerned with economic and social affairs. This ignores the original conception of the Charter as a "pendant" of the European Convention of Human Rights and robs it of the moral force that attaches to the concept of human rights.

In addition, the Charter would have a greater impact if it were given more publicity. Publicity must be the mainspring of any effective system for the international protection of human rights.[5] States value their reputations and in an area not affecting vital national interests may bow to public and moral suasion. Publicity is easier to achieve in a petition system of supervision where the issues are narrowly and personally defined than it is in a report system such as that of the Charter. The non-self-executing character of the Charter similarly detracts from national awareness of it. The answer must be for the Council of Europe,[6] national parliaments,[7] and others to stimulate interest and awareness. An instructive contrast can be found in the treatment of the European Convention on Human Rights and the Charter by English courts. While these courts have used the Convention as a criterion in a number of cases in the course of defining and applying civil and political liberties in British law, there has been no case as yet in which the British courts have referred to the Charter.

A valuable development within the Council of Europe would be the collection of the *Conclusions, Reports, Opinions,* and *Resolutions* of the supervisory organs and their publication in a more convenient form. Other documents and practice concerning the Charter such as the *travaux préparatoires,* bibliographies, and extracts from debates of the Parliamentary Assembly and national parliaments could be treated similarly to advantage. The same is true of the national reports of the contracting parties. There appears to be no good reason why these should not be published. The equivalent reports to the United Nations under the International Covenants on Human Rights and the Convention on the Elimination of All Forms of Racial Discrimination are made public as U.N. documents. The reports made under the Social Charter are no more confidential in content

---

[5]*Cf.* Van Asbeck, *La Charter Sociale Européenne: sa Portée Juridique, sa Mise en Oeuvre,* in MÉLANGES OFFERTS À HENRI ROLIN: PROBLÈMES DE DROIT DES GENS 446 (1964); Golsong, *Implementation of International Protection of Human Rights,* 110 RECUEIL DES COURS (Hague Academy of International Law) 1, 38 (1963); Cohen-Jonathan, *Droits de l'Homme et Pluralité des Systèmes Européens de Protection International,* 5 HUMAN RIGHTS J. 613, 640 (1972).

[6]The CE Strasbourg Symposium on the Charter in 1977 was a step in the right direction. *Cf.* the Brussels Colliquium on the Charter organized by the Institut d'Etudes Européennes in 1976.

[7]For questions put to the U.K. government calling (so far unsuccessfully) for the acceptance of further provisions of Part II, see 360 PARL. DEB., H.L. (5th ser.) 1007 (1975); 365 PARL. DEB., H.L. (5th ser.) 1966 (1975); 373 PARL. DEB., H.L. (5th ser.) 1011 (1976).

than these. The contrast between the publication program for material concerning the European Convention on Human Rights and the Charter is striking.

Another question that a study of the Charter raises is whether the case for a report system of supervision of economic and social rights along International Labor Organization lines, rather than a system of petitions, is as overwhelming as has been commonly thought. The experience of the Charter tends to suggest that it is not, and that a system of petitions leading to adjudication by a court would be feasible for most of the obligations concerning economic and social rights in the Charter.

It is difficult to assess the impact that the Charter has had upon the law and practice of the contracting parties. There is evidence that some states have changed their law in order to become contracting parties.[8] Periodically, the Council of Europe publishes lists of changes made by contracting parties in their national law and practice that are attributed to the influence of the Charter.[9] It is not clear whether the changes listed really result from the operation of the Charter or merely coincide with it. Although coincidence is probably the answer in some cases, the Charter would seem to have had an effect in others.[10] Governments are slow to admit that the Charter has been responsible for a change in their law or practice.

A question which will become increasingly important during the Charter's second decade is its relationship with the European Communities.[11] More than half of the present contract-

---

[8]See Sur, *La Charte Sociale Européenne: Dix Années d'Application*, 1974 EUR. Y.B. 88, 103. This applies in particular to states ratifying the Charter following its entry into force when its meaning became clearer. France, for example, changed its practice on the deportation of migrant workers when it ratified the Charter and indicated its intention to take steps to bring its law into line with Art. 12 (4) (d).

[9]For the most recent list, see Appendix III. See also the list in GC III Appendix V. And see Wiebringhaus, *L'Etat d'Application de la Charte Social Européenne*, 19 ANNUAIRE FRANÇAIS DE DROIT INTERNATIONAL 21–31 (1973).

[10]The change in Irish law to permit a person formerly in receipt of public assistance to be a member of a local authority is probably an example. *See* note 665 of Chapter II *supra*. The F.R.G. is known to have consulted the CE Secretariat on the residence requirement for migrant workers and to have changed its practice to bring it into line with Art. 19 (6). *See* note 947 of Chapter II *supra*. The CIE will, as a matter of policy, not suggest in its *Conclusions* what alterations should be made to comply with the Charter.

[11]*See* Kahn-Freund, *supra* note 3, at 192–98.

ing parties are members of the Communities,[12] and their governments tend to look to Brussels rather than Strasbourg in areas in which the two documents overlap. This happens because Communities law applies directly within member states and because the European Communities has funds that can be distributed among member states for improvement in such matters as vocational training. The difference is essentially that between the international and federal, or quasi-federal, approaches, and the latter is quite clearly the more effective. Even in the case of Communities directives, which are normally not self-executing, the incentive to comply is much greater within the quasi-federal context of the Communities than it is in the international context of the Council of Europe. Nonetheless, the Communities social policy and other law does not cover the wide range of subjects of the Charter, and the states subject to each are not identical. To this large extent, the Charter can continue to serve a useful function in a European context. The Charter also may be of use as the European Court of Justice develops its concept of "fundamental rights" in Communities law.[13]

A somewhat similar question has arisen with the entering into force of the International Covenant on Economic, Social and Cultural Rights.[14] The substantive and reporting obligations of the Covenant and the Charter overlap so that a situation comparable to that already existing in the relationship between the Charter and International Labor Organization conventions will develop for those parties to the Charter that are also parties to the Covenant. Taken as a whole, there is not a great deal to choose between the substantive obligations in the two treaties. Although the Covenant contains some rights[15]

---

[12]Denmark, France, the F.R.G., Ireland, Italy, the Netherlands, and the U.K. are members.

[13]*Cf.* Kahn-Freund, *supra* note 3, at 198. For an account of the "fundamental rights" debate within the Communities, see WYATT AND DASHWOOD, THE SUBSTANTIVE LAW OF THE EEC 48–51 (1980).

[14]On the relationship between the Charter and the ICESCR, see the statement by Mr. Modinos, of the Council of Europe, before the U.N. Commission on Human Rights at its 23d Session in 1967, U.N. Doc. E/CN.4/SR.897, at 5. See also the Council of Europe Division of Social Affairs' Revised Draft Report on the Coexistence of the European Social Charter and the United Nations International Covenant on Economic, Social and Cultural Rights, CE/Soc (73) 11 rev.

[15]E.g., the right to education and cultural rights.

that the Charter omits, the reverse is also true.[16] For the most part, the Charter—generally worded as it is in certain places— is more specific in its definition of the obligations undertaken than is the Covenant. The Covenant has advantages over the Charter in that contracting parties are not free to pick and choose the obligations which they accept in the way that they may under the Charter (Article 20)[17] and the guarantee is not generally limited to nationals of contracting parties.[18] But the basic undertaking that each party gives in respect of each right recognized in the Covenant is less demanding than most of the specific obligations in the Charter.[19] At this stage one would say that the Charter is likely to prove the more effective document in view of the (admittedly limited) independent element in its system of supervision and the politically homogeneous nature of its clientele.

[16]E.g., the Covenant contains no provision on migrant workers or on social and medical assistance.

[17]Reservations to the Covenant are permitted, and some have been made.

[18]Developing countries may limit the application of the economic rights as far as nonnationals are concerned. International Covenant on Economic, Social and Cultural Rights, Art. 2 (3), *adopted* Dec. 19, 1966, G.A. Res. 2200, 21 U.N. GAOR Supp. (No. 16) at 49, U.N. Doc. A/6316 (1966).

[19] Art. 2 (1) of the ICESCR, note 18 *supra,* reads:

Each state party to the present Covenant undertakes to take steps, individually and through international assistance, and co-operation, especially economic and technical, to the maximum of its available resources, with a view to achieving progressively the full realisation of the rights recognized in the present Covenant by all appropriate means, including particularly the adoption of legislative measures.

Appendixes

Text of the European Social Charter

Bibliography

Table of Charter References

Index

Table of Signatories and Contracting Parties to the Charter

	Date of Signature	Date of Ratification	In force
Austria	7/22/63	10/29/69	11/28/69
Belgium	10/18/61		
Cyprus	5/22/67	3/7/68	4/6/68
Denmark	10/18/61	3/3/65	4/2/65
France	10/18/61	3/9/76	4/8/73
F.R.G.	10/18/61	1/27/65	2/26/65
Greece	10/18/61		
Iceland	1/15/76	1/15/76	2/14/76
Ireland	10/18/61	10/7/64	2/26/65
Italy	10/18/61	10/22/65	11/21/65
Luxembourg	10/18/61		
Netherlands	10/18/61	4/22/80	5/21/80
Norway	10/18/61	10/26/62	2/26/65
Portugal	5/28/82		
Spain	4/27/78	5/6/80	6/5/80
Sweden	10/18/61	12/17/62	2/26/65
Switzerland	5/6/66		
Turkey	10/18/61		
U.K.	10/18/61	7/11/62	2/26/65

Note: Malta and Liechtenstein are the two members of the Council of Europe that have not signed the Charter.

Appendix II

Table of Compliance with the Charter as Determined by the
CIE During the First Six Cycles

Key:*c:* compliance (a provisional ruling in favor of a contracting party is counted as a ruling of compliance)
n: noncompliance
i: decision not possible for lack of information
An empty space indicates that the provision has not been
accepted by the contracting party concerned.
Cyprus, Austria, and France did not begin reporting until
the second, third, and fifth cycles, respectively; Iceland
should have reported for the sixth cycle but did so too
late for the information to be included.

Article	Austria 34567	Cyprus 234567	Denmark 1234567	F.R.G. 1234567	France 567	Ireland 1234567	Italy 1234567	Norway 1234567	Sweden 1234567	U.K. 1234567
1(1)	ccccc	ccccc	iicccnc	ccccccc	icc	icccicc	cciccci	ccccccc	ccccccc	iiiicc
1(2)	iiccc	iiiic	cnncccc	inmccc	iin	nnnnnnn	iiinnnn	cnnccc	cnnccc	nnnnnn
1(3)	ccccc	iccccc	ccccccc	ccccccc	ccc	nnnnccc	ciiiccc	ccccccc	ccccccc	cccnnn
1(4)	(1)n	ccccc	(1)	icccccnn	(1)	(1)	(1)	(1)	(1)	(1)n
2(1)				ccccccc	ccc	inccccc	iiiiccc	ccccccc		
2(2)	ccccc		ccccccc	ccccccc	ccc	ccccccc	ccccccc	ccccccc	ccccccc	ccccccc
2(3)	cnccc		ccccccc	ccccccc	ccc	inncccc	iiiiccc	iccccc		iiccccc
2(4)	iinnn			iccccc		nnnnnnn	iiinnn	ccccccc		iccccc
2(5)	ccc			iccccc		innnccc	ccccccc	iccccc	ccccccc	cicccc
3(1)	cnccc	nnnnnn	iccccc	iiccccc	ccc	innnnnn	innnnnn	ccccccc	inccccc	ccccccc
3(2)	cncic	nnnnnn	ccccccc	iiccccc	ccc	innnnnn	innnnnn	ccccccc	iniicc	ccccccc
3(3)	ccccc	iccccc	ccccccc	iccccc	ccc	iiccccc	iccccc	iccccc	ccccccc	iccccc
4(1)	iiiin		iccccc	iccccc	iin	iiiinn	iiiiii	iccccc	iiccccc	icccinn
4(2)	ccccc		iiiiccn	iccccc	ccc	ccccccc	iiiccc	nnnnnnc	nnnnnnn	iccccc
4(3)	innmc		ccccccc	nnccccc	ccc	nnnnnnn	nnnnccc	ccccccc	(2)c	innninn
4(4)	ccccc		(2)i		ccc	nnnnnnn	nnnnnnn	ccccccc		innnicc
4(5)	ccccc			ccccccc	ccc	ccccccc	ccccccc	ccccccc	ccccccc	cnnnnnn
5	ccccc	nnnnnn	ccccccc	ccccccc	cnn	innnnnn	nnnnnnn	ccccccc	ccccccc	cnnnnnn
6(1)	ccccc	iccccc	ccccccc	ccccccc	ccc	innnnnn	iiccccc	ccccccc	ccccccc	iccccc
6(2)	ccccc	iccccc	ccccccc	ccccccc	ccc	innnnin	iiiccc	ccccccc	ccccccc	iccccc
6(3)	ccccc	ccccc	ccccccc	nnnnnnn	ccc	iccccc	ciiicc	ccccccc	ccccccc	ccccccc
6(4)		ccccc	iccinnn	nnnnnnn	inn	nnnnnnn	innnnnn / nnnnnnn	iccccc	ccccic	innmmnn
7(1)									(2)n	
7(2)	ccccc			iccccc	ccc	iccccc	ccccccc	ccccccc	ccccccc	ccccccc
7(3)	iniin			nnnnicc	ccc	inmmmm	ccccccc	iiiicc	iiccnn	iiccinn
7(4)	ccccc			ccccccc	ccc	nnnnnin	innmmmm		nccccccc	
7(5)	ciccc			iiccin	iii		iiiiii	iiccccc		iiiniicc
7(6)				ccccccc	iii	nniiicc	iinnnnn	iiiiin		iiiiic

Article	Austria 34567	Cyprus 234567	Denmark 1234567	F.R.G. 1234567	France 567	Ireland 1234567	Italy 1234567	Norway 1234567	Sweden 1234567	U.K. 1234567
7(7)	ccccc			cccccc	ccc		iiiccc	cccccc	cccccc	
7(8)	ccccc			cccccc	ccc	icccccc	cccccc	iiiiicc	cccccc	icccccc
7(9)	ccccc			nnncccc	ccc		cccccc		cccccc	ccciicc
7(10)	ccccc		iinnnnn	cccccc	iii	cccccc	nncccccc	cccccc	innmmic	cccccc
8(1)	ccncc			cccccc	ccc	nnnnnnn	nnccccc		innmmic	innmmm
8(2)	nnnnn				ccc		nnnnnnn			
8(3)	ccccc			cccccc	ccc		ccinnn		icccnn	
8(4)	ccccc				ccc		cccccc			
9	ccccc	iicccc	cccccc	cccccc	ccc	cccccc	iiinccc	cccccc	cccccc	cccccc
10(1)	iccc		iiccc	ccccinn	icc	iccccc	iiinccc	icccccc	cccccc	cccccc
10(2)	cccn		cccccc	ccccinn	ccc	iicccc	iciccc	icccccc	cccccc	icccccn
10(3)	ccci		cccccc	cccccc	ccc	iicccc	iiiccc	cccccc	cccccc	cccccc
10(4)	ccccc		cccccc	cccccc	ccc	iccccc	nncccccc	icccccc	cccccc	nnccccc
11(1)	ccccc	iccccc	cccccc	cccccc	ccc	iicicc	iiiccc	cccccc	cccccc	cccccc
11(2)	ccccc	ncccccc	cccccc	cccccc	ccc		iiiccc	cccccc	cccccc	cccccc
11(3)	iccc	iiccc	cccccc	cccccc	ccc	ncccccc	iiiccc	cccccc	cccccc	cccccc
12(1)	ccccc	iiccc	cccccc	cccccc	ccc	cccccc	cccccc	cccccc	cccccc	cccccc
12(2)	inccc	nnnnnn	cccccc	cccccc	icc	cccccc	cccccc	cccccc	cccccc	cccccc
12(3)	inccc	nnnnnn	cccccc	cccccc	icc	cccccc	ccnnnn	ccnnnnc	cccccc	
12(4)	ccnnc	cccccc	cccnnnc	cccccc	cm	cccccc	ccnnnnn	ccnnnnc	cccccc	cnnnnnn
13(1)	ccccc		cccccc	cccccc	ccc	cccccc	nnnnnnn	icccccc	cccccc	cccccc
13(2)	ccccc		cccccc	icccccc		nnccccc	cccccc	cccccc	cccccc	cccccc
13(3)	iccc		cccccc	iccccc	ccc	cccccc	iiiiic	icccccc	cccccc	cccccc
13(4)	cicc		ccinic	cccccc	ini	cccccc	cccccc	icccccc	cccicc	ccnnnn
14(1)	ccccc	ccccc	cccccc	cccccc	ccc	iccccc	iiiiic	iiiccc	cccccc	cccccc
14(2)	iccc	ccccc	cccccc	cccccc	ccc	iccccc	iiiiic	ncccccc	iccccc	cccccc
15(1)	iicc	ccccc	cccccc	cccccc	ccc	nnccccc	cccccc	ncccccc	cccccc	ccccccn
15(2)	ccccc	ccccc	cccccc	icccccc	ccc	nnccccc	cccccc	cccccc	cccccc	cccccc

Article	Austria 34567	Cyprus 234567	Denmark 1234567	F.R.G. 1234567	France 567	Ireland 1234567	Italy 1234567	Norway 1234567	Sweden 1234567	U.K. 1234567
16	ccccc		iiiccc	cccccc	ccc	icccccc	cccccc	cccccc	cccccc	cccccc
17	cmmn		cccccc	cccccc	ccc	innnnn	cccccc	cccccc	cccccc	nnnnnn
18(1)	iccc		niciccc	niccinc	icc	nicincc	niiccc		nccccc	niiccc
18(2)	iccc		nicinnn	nicinn	ccn	ninnnn	niiccc		nccccin	ninnnn
18(3)			nicinnn	niccinc	cmn	ninnnn	niiccc		nccccin	ninnnn
18(4)	cccc	innccc	cccccc	cccccc	ccc	cccccc	cccccc		cccccc	cccccc
19(1)	cccc	iiccc		cccccc	ccc	iicccc	iccccc	icccccc	iccccc	icccccc
19(2)	ciic	iiccc		iccccc	icc	icccccc	iiiccc	iiciic	cccccc	icccccc
19(3)	ciic	iiiccc		cccccc	icc	innnnn	ncccccc	nnnnnn	ncccccc	nnnnccc
19(4)		ciccc		ncccccc	inn	icccccc	cccccc	ciiiin	ccccii	cnnnnn
19(5)	iccc	cccccc		cccccc	ccc	icccccc	cccccc	cccccc	cccccci	cccccc
19(6)	niinn	iiiccc		inncii	iii	icccccc	cccccc	iinnnnn	cccccci	nnnnnnn
19(7)				icccccc	ccc	icccccc	cccccc	cccccc	(2)c	cccccc
19(8)		imnncc		cccccmn	icc	iiinnn	cccccc		cccccmn	icccmn
19(9)	ccc	cccccc		cccccc	iic	cccccc	iiiiic	nnnnccc	cccccc	cccccc
19(10)	ccc	ccc		ccc	iii	ccc	ccc	ncc	ccc	cc

Note: The three other ratifying states have accepted the following provisions:

Iceland has accepted Article 1, Article 2 (1) (3) (5), Articles 3–6, and Articles 11–18 (41 paragraphs).

The Netherlands has accepted all 72 paragraphs except Article 19 (8) (10). The Netherlands has accepted Article 6 (4) except insofar as it applies to civil servants.

Spain has accepted all 72 paragraphs.

1. The CIE has not made rulings for Article 1 (4) in respect to contracting parties which accept all of the provisions of Articles 9, 10, and 15 in the first six cycles.

2. Accepted after the sixth cycle.

Changes in National Law and Practice in Accordance with the Charter

The following extract in which the Council of Europe lists changes in national law and practice during the fourth to sixth cycles is taken from CE Doc. H (81)1:

Austria

Section 305 of the Penal Code, which provided for a certain form of "compulsory labour", has been rescinded in accordance with Article 1, paragraph 2, of the Charter.

The 1885 Vagrancy Act has been revised to delete those clauses which provided for certain forms of "compulsory labour" and thus bring the situation into conformity with Article 1, paragraph 2, of the Charter.

Act No. 782 of 1974 abrogated the 1935 Act on children employed in agriculture and forestry, thus bringing the situation into conformity with Article 7, paragraph 3, of the Charter.

The official commentaries of the assistance acts of the Länder give the Social Charter the same status as international treaties in this field; on this basis, equality of treatment in this matter is assured for the nationals of other Contracting States in accordance with Article 13, paragraph 4, of the Charter.

Cyprus

The law on employment of seamen, which provided for certain forms of "compulsory labour", has been amended in this respect to bring the situation into conformity with Article 1, paragraph 2, of the Charter.

The legislation on social security has been amended to raise the level of protection as required by Article 12, paragraph 1, of the Charter.

The law governing aliens has been revised in order to bring the guarantee secured to foreign workers in the event of expulsion into conformity with Article 19, paragraph 8, of the Charter.

Denmark

An act of 1973 repealed earlier legislation on the merchant navy which provided for certain forms of "compulsory labour" contrary to Article 1, paragraph 2, of the Charter.

Federal Republic of Germany

The law on the merchant navy, which provided for certain forms of "compulsory labour" contrary to Article 1, paragraph 2, of the Charter, has been amended in accordance with this provision.

The Federal Government reports that, in accordance with Article 2, paragraph 4, of the Charter, miners working underground have been granted additional paid leave.

Under a revision of the legislation applicable to young workers, medical check-ups have been made periodical in accordance with Article 7, paragraph 9, of the Charter.

The Federal Government states that the order relating to recruitment of foreign workers issued following the oil crisis will not apply to the nationals of other Contracting States bound by the Charter (Article 10).

By virtue of a decision taken by the Conference of Ministers of the Interior of the Länder, the time limit for authorisation of family reunion is reduced from three years to one year in the case of migrant workers who are national of other Contracting States bound by the Charter (Article 19, paragraph 6).

The Young Persons (Protection of Employment) Act, which came into force on 1 May 1976 contains provisions whereby the employment of young persons still subject to compulsory education, when authorised, is subject to firm restrictions and other conditions which are in compliance with the requirements of the Charter.

France

The French Government has declared its official intention of amending the provision in the Code of Social Security which permits discrimination against foreign women in respect of maternity allowance, in order to bring this provision into conformity with Article 12, paragraph 4, of the Charter.

The French Government has stated that Austrian nationals in France will be treated equally in the manner of assistance, both France and Austria being bound in this matter by Article 13, paragraph 4, of the Charter.

Under a decree of 1976, French regulations conform to Article 19, paragraph 6, of the Charter by stipulating that migrant workers who are nationals of another Contracting State bound by this instrument must enjoy conditions of family reunion in keeping with the requirements of this provision.

Ireland

The legislation barring married women from entering the civil service and requiring unmarried female civil servants to resign on marriage has been amended in this respect to bring it into conformity with Article 1, paragraph 2, of the Charter.

For the first time in the history of Irish labour law, there is an act which specifies minimum periods of notice of dismissal, thus meeting the requirements of Article 4, paragraph 4, of the Charter.

A law has been enacted abolishing an old provision of legislation permitting discrimination against persons receiving assistance benefits, in order to bring the situation into conformity with Article 13, paragraph 2, of the Charter.

Legislative changes have also taken place in the field of protection of children and young persons. Thus, the Protection of Young Persons (Employment) Act 1977 provides that the time spent on vocational training should count as hours worked, wages being unaffected. This change has brought Irish legislation in line with Article 7, paragraph 6, of the Charter.

Italy

Maternity benefits, which had stood at an extremely low level in the case of certain categories of employed women, have been substantially increased in order to bring the situation into conformity with Article 8, paragraph 1, of the Charter.

Norway

The legislation applicable to seamen, which contained provisions permitting certain forms of "compulsory labour" contrary to Article 1, paragraph 2, of the Charter, has been amended and now conforms with this provision.

Sweden

Swedish legislation on seamen, which contained provisions permitting certain forms of "compulsory labour" contrary to Article 1, paragraph 2, of the Charter, has been amended and now conforms with this provision.

The legislation on protection of workers has been amended to bring its provisions on the employment of children and adolescents in agriculture into line with the requirements of Article 7, paragraph 3, of the Charter.

United Kingdom

The legislation applicable to seamen has been revised in order to abolish or amend certain provisions which permitted a kind of "compulsory labour", and thus bring the situation in this respect more into conformity with Article 1, paragraph 2, of the Charter.

Periods of notice of termination of employment have been extended substantially in order to meet the requirements of Article 4, of the Charter.

Measures have been taken to ensure that the seriously ill or disabled children of migrant workers are no longer excluded from family reunion, in accordance with Article 19, paragraph 6, of the Charter.

European Social Charter

The Governments signatory hereto, being Members of the Council of Europe,

Considering that the aim of the Council of Europe is the achievement of greater unity between its Members for the purpose of safeguarding and realising the ideals and principles which are their common heritage and of facilitating their economic and social progress, in particular by the maintenance and further realisation of human rights and fundamental freedoms;

Considering that in the European Convention for the Protection of Human Rights and Fundamental Freedoms signed at Rome on 4th November 1950, and the Protocol thereto signed at Paris on 20th March 1952, the member States of the Council of Europe agreed to secure to their populations the civil and political rights and freedoms therein specified;

Considering that the enjoyment of social rights should be secured without discrimination on grounds of race, colour, sex, religion, political opinion, national extraction or social origin;

Being resolved to make every effort in common to improve the standard of living and to promote the social well-being of both their urban and rural populations by means of appropriate institutions and action,

Have agreed as follows:

Part I

The Contracting Parties accept as the aim of their policy, to be pursued by all appropriate means, both national and international in character, the attainment of conditions in which the following rights and principles may be effectively realised:

1) Everyone shall have the opportunity to earn his living in an occupation freely entered upon.
2) All workers have the right to just conditions of work.
3) All workers have the right to safe and healthy working conditions.

4) All workers have the right to a fair remuneration sufficient for a decent standard of living for themselves and their families.

5) All workers and employers have the right to freedom of association in national or international organisations for the protection of their economic and social interests.

6) All workers and employers have the right to bargain collectively.

7) Children and young persons have the right to a special protection against the physical and moral hazards to which they are exposed.

8) Employed women, in case of maternity, and other employed women as appropriate, have the right to a special protection in their work.

9) Everyone has the right to appropriate facilities for vocational guidance with a view to helping him choose an occupation suited to his personal aptitude and interests.

10) Everyone has the right to appropriate facilities for vocational training.

11) Everyone has the right to benefit from any measures enabling him to enjoy the highest possible standard of health attainable.

12) All workers and their dependents have the right to social security.

13) Anyone without adequate resources has the right to social and medical assistance.

14) Everyone has the right to benefit from social welfare services.

15) Disabled persons have the right to vocational training, rehabilitation and resettlement, whatever the origin and nature of their disability.

16) The family as a fundamental unit of society has the right to appropriate social, legal and economic protection to ensure its full development.

17) Mothers and children, irrespective of marital status and family relations, have the right to appropriate social and economic protection.

18) The nationals of any one of the Contracting Parties have the right to engage in any gainful occupation in the territory of any one of the others on a footing of equality with the nationals of the latter, subject to restrictions based on cogent economic or social reasons.

19) Migrant workers who are nationals of a Contracting Party and their families have the right to protection and assistance in the territory of any other Contracting Party.

Part II

The Contracting Parties undertake, as provided for in Part III, to consider themselves bound by the obligations laid down in the following Articles and paragraphs.

Article 1
The Right to Work

With a view to ensuring the effective exercise of the right to work, the Contracting Parties undertake:

1) to accept as one of their primary aims and responsibilities the achievement and maintenance of as high and stable a level of employment as possible, with a view to the attainment of full employment;

2) to protect effectively the right of the worker to earn his living in an occupation freely entered upon;

3) to establish or maintain free employment services for all workers;

4) to provide or promote appropriate vocational guidance, training and rehabilitation.

Article 2
The Right to Just Conditions of Work

With a view to ensuring the effective exercise of the right to just conditions of work, the Contracting Parties undertake:

1) to provide for reasonable daily and weekly working hours, the working week to be progressively reduced to the extent that the increase of productivity and other relevant factors permit;

2) to provide for public holidays with pay;

3) to provide for a minimum of two weeks annual holiday with pay;

4) to provide for additional paid holidays or reduced working hours for workers engaged in dangerous or unhealthy occupations as prescribed;

5) to ensure a weekly rest period which shall, as far as possible, coincide with the day recognised by tradition or custom in the country or region concerned as a day of rest.

Article 3
The Right to Safe and Healthy Working Conditions

With a view to ensuring the effective exercise of the right to safe and healthy working conditions, the Contracting Parties undertake:

1) to issue safety and health regulations;

2) to provide for the enforcement of such regulations by measures of supervision;

3) to consult, as appropriate, employers' and workers' organisations on measures intended to improve industrial safety and health.

Article 4
The Right to a Fair Remuneration

With a view to ensuring the effective exercise of the right to a fair remuneration, the Contracting Parties undertake:

1) to recognise the right of workers to a remuneration such as will give them and their families a decent standard of living;

2) to recognise the right of workers to an increased rate of remuneration for overtime work, subject to exceptions in particular cases;

3) to recognise the right of men and women workers to equal pay for work of equal value;

4) to recognise the right of all workers to a reasonable period of notice for termination of employment;

5) to permit deductions from wages only under conditions and to the extent prescribed by national laws or regulations or fixed by collective agreements or arbitration awards.

The exercise of these rights shall be achieved by freely concluded collective agreements, by statutory wage-fixing machinery, or by other means appropriate to national conditions.

Article 5
The Right to Organise

With a view to ensuring or promoting the freedom of workers and employers to form local, national or international organisations for the protection of their economic and social interests and to join those organisations, the Contracting Parties undertake that national law shall not be such as to impair, nor shall it be so applied as to impair, this freedom. The extent to which the guarantees provided for in this Article shall apply to the police shall be determined by national laws or regulations. The principle governing the application to the members of the armed forces of these guarantees and the extent to which they shall apply to persons in this category shall equally be determined by national laws or regulations.

Article 6
The Right to Bargain Collectively

With a view to ensuring the effective exercise of the right to bargain collectively, the Contracting Parties undertake:

1) to promote joint consultation between workers and employers;

2) to promote, where necessary and appropriate, machinery for

voluntary negotiations between employers or employer's organisations and workers' organisations, with a view to the regulation of terms and conditions of employment by means of collective agreements;

3) to promote the establishment and use of appropriate machinery for conciliation and voluntary arbitration for the settlement of labour disputes;

and recognise:

4) the right of workers and employers to collective action in cases of conflicts of interest, including the right to strike, subject to obligations that might arise out of collective agreements previously entered into.

Article 7
The Right of Children and Young Persons to Protection

With a view to ensuring the effective exercise of the right of children and young persons to protection, the Contracting Parties undertake:

1) to provide that the minimum age of admission to employment shall be 15 years, subject to exceptions for children employed in prescribed light work without harm to their health, morals or education;

2) to provide that a higher minimum age of admission to employment shall be fixed with respect to prescribed occupations regarded as dangerous or unhealthy;

3) to provide that persons who are still subject to compulsory education shall not be employed in such work as would deprive them of the full benefit of their education;

4) to provide that the working hours of persons under 16 years of age shall be limited in accordance with the needs of their development, and particularly with their need for vocational training;

5) to recognise the right of young workers and apprentices to a fair wage or other appropriate allowances;

6) to provide that the time spent by young persons in vocational training during the normal working hours with the consent of the employer shall be treated as forming part of the working day;

7) to provide that employed persons of under 18 years of age shall be entitled to not less than three weeks' annual holiday with pay;

8) to provide that persons under 18 years of age shall not be employed in night work with the exception of certain occupations provided for by national laws or regulations;

9) to provide that persons under 18 years of age employed in occupations prescribed by national laws or regulations shall be subject to regular medical control;

10) to ensure special protection against physical and moral

dangers to which children and young persons are exposed, and particularly against those resulting directly or indirectly from their work.

Article 8
The Right of Employed Women to Protection
With a view to ensuring the effective exercise of the right of employed women to protection, the Contracting Parties undertake:

1) to provide either by paid leave, by adequate social security benefits or by benefits from public funds for women to take leave before and after childbirth up to a total of at least 12 weeks;

2) to consider it as unlawful for an employer to give a woman notice of dismissal during her absence on maternity leave or to give her notice of dismissal at such a time that the notice would expire during such absence;

3) to provide that mothers who are nursing their infants shall be entitled to sufficient time off for this purpose;

4) (a) to regulate the employment of women workers on night work in industrial employment;

(b) to prohibit the employment of women workers in underground mining, and, as appropriate, on all other work which is unsuitable for them by reason of its dangerous, unhealthy, or arduous nature.

Article 9
The Right to Vocational Guidance
With a view to ensuring the effective exercise of the right to vocational guidance, the Contracting Parties undertake to provide or promote, as necessary, a service which will assist all persons, including the handicapped, to solve problems related to occupational choice and progress, with due regard to the individual's characteristics and their relation to occupational opportunity: this assistance should be available free of charge, both to young persons, including school children, and to adults.

Article 10
The Right to Vocational Training
With a view to ensuring the effective exercise of the right to vocational training, the Contracting Parties undertake:

1) to provide or promote, as necessary, the technical and vocational training of all persons, including the handicapped, in consultation with employers' and workers' organisations, and to grant facilities for access to higher technical and university education, based solely on individual aptitude;

2) to provide or promote a system of apprenticeship and other systematic arrangements for training young boys and girls in their various employments;

3) to provide or promote, as necessary:
   (a) adequate and readily available training facilities for adult workers;
   (b) special facilities for the re-training of adult workers needed as a result of technological development or new trends in employment;

4) to encourage the full utilisation of the facilities provided by appropriate measures such as:
   (a) reducing or abolishing any fees or charges;
   (b) granting financial assistance in appropriate cases;
   (c) including in the normal working hours time spent on supplementary training taken by the worker, at the request of his employer, during employment;
   (d) ensuring, through adequate supervision, in consultation with the employers' and workers' organisations, the efficiency of apprenticeship and other training arrangements for young workers, and the adequate protection of young workers generally.

Article 11
The Right to Protection of Health

With a view to ensuring the effective exercise of the right to protection of health, the Contracting Parties undertake, either directly or in co-operation with public or private organisations, to take appropriate measures designed *inter alia:*

1) to remove as far as possible the causes of ill-health;

2) to provide advisory and educational facilities for the promotion of health and the encouragement of individual responsibility in matters of health;

3) to prevent as far as possible epidemic, endemic and other diseases.

Article 12
The Right to Social Security

With a view to ensuring the effective exercise of the right to social security, the Contracting Parties undertake:

1) to establish or maintain a system of social security;

2) to maintain the social security system at a satisfactory level at least equal to that required for ratification of International Labour Convention (No. 102) Concerning Minimum Standards of Social Security;

3) to endeavour to raise progressively the system of social security to a higher level;

4) to take steps, by the conclusion of appropriate bilateral and multilateral agreements, or by other means, and subject to the conditions laid down in such agreements, in order to ensure:

(a) equal treatment with their own nationals of the nationals of other Contracting Parties in respect of social security rights, including the retention of benefits arising out of social security legislation, whatever movements the persons protected may undertake between the territories of the Contracting Parties;

(b) the granting, maintenance and resumption of social security rights by such means as the accumulation of insurance or employment periods completed under the legislation of each of the Contracting Parties.

Article 13
The Right to Social and Medical Assistance

With a view to ensuring the effective exercise of the right to social and medical assistance, the Contracting Parties undertake:

1) to ensure that any person who is without adequate resources and who is unable to secure such resources either by his own efforts or from other sources, in particular by benefits under a social security scheme, be granted adequate assistance, and, in case of sickness, the care necessitated by his condition;

2) to ensure that persons receiving such assistance shall not, for that reason, suffer from a diminution of their political or social rights;

3) to provide that everyone may receive by appropriate public or private services such advice and personal help as may be required to prevent, to remove, or to alleviate personal or family want;

4) to apply the provisions referred to in paragraphs 1, 2 and 3 of this Article on an equal footing with their nationals to nationals of other Contracting Parties lawfully within their territories, in accordance with their obligations under the European Convention on Social and Medical Assistance, signed at Paris on 11th December 1953.

Article 14
The Right to Benefit from Social Welfare Services

With a view to ensuring the effective exercise of the right to benefit from social welfare services, the Contracting Parties undertake:

1) to promote or provide services which, by using methods of social work, would contribute to the welfare and development of both individuals and groups in the community, and to their adjustment to the social environment;

2) to encourage the participation of individuals and voluntary or other organisations in the establishment and maintenance of such services.

Article 15

The Right of Physically or Mentally Disabled Persons to
Vocational Training, Rehabilitation and Social Resettlement

With a view to ensuring the effective exercise of the right of the
physically or mentally disabled to vocational training, rehabilitation and resettlement, the Contracting Parties undertake:

1) to take adequate measures for the provision of training facilities, including, where necessary, specialised institutions, public or
private;

2) to take adequate measures for the placing of disabled persons
in employment, such as specialised placing services, facilities for
sheltered employment and measures to encourage employers to
admit disabled persons to employment.

Article 16

The Right of the Family to Social, Legal and Economic
Protection

With a view to ensuring the necessary conditions for the full development of the family, which is a fundamental unit of society,
the Contracting Parties undertake to promote the economic, legal
and social protection of family life by such means as social and
family benefits, fiscal arrangements, provision of family housing,
benefits for the newly married, and other appropriate means.

Article 17

The Right of Mothers and Children to Social and Economic
Protection

With a view to ensuring the effective exercise of the right of
mothers and children to social and economic protection, the Contracting Parties will take all appropriate and necessary measures
to that end, including the establishment or maintenance of appropriate institutions or services.

Article 18

The Right to Engage in a Gainful Occupation in the Territory of
Other Contracting Parties

With a view to ensuring the effective exercise of the right to
engage in a gainful occupation in the territory of any other Contracting Party, the Contracting Parties undertake:

1) to apply existing regulations in a spirit of liberality;

2) to simplify existing formalities and to reduce or abolish chancery dues and other charges payable by foreign workers or their
employers;

3) to liberalise, individually or collectively, regulations governing
the employment of foreign workers;

and recognise:

4) the right of their nationals to leave the country to engage in a gainful occupation in the territories of the other Contracting Parties.

Article 19
The Right of Migrant Workers and Their Families to Protection and Assistance

With a view to ensuring the effective exercise of the right of migrant workers and their families to protection and assistance in the territory of any other Contracting Party, the Contracting Parties undertake:

1) to maintain or to satisfy themselves that there are maintained adequate and free services to assist such workers, particularly in obtaining accurate information, and to take all appropriate steps, so far as national laws and regulations permit, against misleading propaganda relating to emigration and immigration;

2) to adopt appropriate measures within their own jurisdiction to facilitate the departure, journey and reception of such workers and their families, and to provide, within their own jurisdiction, appropriate services for health, medical attention and good hygienic conditions during the journey;

3) to promote co-operation, as appropriate, between social services, public and private, in emigration and immigration countries;

4) to secure for such workers lawfully within their territories, insofar as such matters are regulated by law or regulations or are subject to the control of administrative authorities, treatment not less favourable than that of their own nationals in respects of the following matters:

  (a) renumeration and other employment and working conditions;
  (b) membership of trade unions and enjoyment of the benefits of collective bargaining;
  (c) accommodation;

5) to secure for such workers lawfully within their territories treatment not less favourable than that of their own nationals with regard to employment taxes, dues or contributions payable in respect of employed persons;

6) to facilitate as far as possible the reunion of the family of a foreign worker permitted to establish himself in the territory;

7) to secure for such workers lawfully within their territories treatment not less favourable than that of their own nationals in respect of legal proceedings relating to matters referred to in this Article;

8) to secure that such workers lawfully residing within their ter-

ritories are not expelled unless they endanger national security or offend against public interest or morality;

9) to permit, within legal limits, the transfer of such parts of the earnings and savings of such workers as they may desire;

10) to extend the protection and assistance provided for in this Article to self-employed migrants insofar as such measures apply.

Part III

Article 20
Undertakings

1) Each of the Contracting Parties undertakes:

(a) to consider Part I of this Charter as a declaration of the aims which it will pursue by all appropriate means, as stated in the introductory paragraph of that Part;

(b) to consider itself bound by at least five of the following Articles of Part II of this Charter: Articles 1, 5, 6, 12, 13, 16 and 19;

(c) in addition to the Articles selected by it in accordance with the preceding sub-paragraph, to consider itself bound by such a number of Articles or numbered paragraphs of Part II of the Charter as it may select, provided that the total number of Articles or numbered paragraphs by which it is bound is not less than 10 Articles or 45 numbered paragraphs.

2) The Articles or paragraphs selected in accordance with sub-paragraphs (b) and (c) of paragraph 1 of this Article shall be notified to the Secretary-General of the Council of Europe at the time when the instrument of ratification or approval of the Contracting Party concerned is deposited.

3) Any contracting Party may, at a later date, declare by notification to the Secretary-General that it considers itself bound by any Articles or any numbered paragraphs of Part II of the Charter which it has not already accepted under the terms of paragraph 1 of this Article. Such undertakings subsequently given shall be deemed to be an integral part of the ratification or approval, and shall have the same effect as from the thirtieth day after the date of notification.

4) The Secretary-General shall communicate to all the signatory Governments and to the Director-General of the International Labour Office any notification which he shall have received pursuant to this Part of the Charter.

5) Each Contracting Party shall maintain a system of labour inspection appropriate to national conditions.

Part IV

Article 21
Reports Concerning Accepted Provisions

The Contracting Parties shall send to the Secretary-General of the Council of Europe a report at two-yearly intervals, in a form to be determined by the Committee of Ministers, concerning the application of such provisions of Part II of the Charter as they have accepted.

Article 22
Reports Concerning Provisions Which Are Not Accepted

The Contracting Parties shall send to the Secretary-General, at appropriate intervals as requested by the Committee of Ministers, reports relating to the provisions of Part II of the Charter which they did not accept at the time of their ratification or approval or in a subsequent notification. The Committee of Ministers shall determine from time to time in respect of which provisions such reports shall be requested and the form of the reports to be provided.

Article 23
Communication of Copies

1) Each contracting Party shall communicate copies of its reports referred to in Articles 21 and 22 to such of its national organisations as are members of the international organisations of employers and trade unions to be invited under Article 27, paragraph 2, to be represented at meetings of the Sub-committee of the Govermental Social Committee.

2) The Contracting Parties shall forward to the Secretary-General any comments on the said reports received from these national organisations, if so requested by them.

Article 24
Examination of the Reports

The reports sent to the Secretary-General in accordance with Articles 21 and 22 shall be examined by a Committee of Experts, who shall have also before them any comments forwarded to the Secretary-General in accordance with paragraph 2 of Article 23.

Article 25
Committee of Experts

1) The Committee of Experts shall consist of not more than seven members appointed by the Committee of Ministers from a list of independent experts of the highest integrity and of recognised competence in international social questions, nominated by the Contracting Parties.

2) The members of the Committee shall be appointed for a period of six years. They may be reappointed. However, of the members first appointed, the terms of office of two members shall expire at the end of four years.

3) The members whose terms of office are to expire at the end of the initial period of four years shall be chosen by lot by the Committee of Ministers immediately after the first appointment has been made.

4) A member of the Committee of Experts appointed to replace a member whose term of office has not expired shall hold office for the remainder of his predecessor's term.

Article 26
Participation of the International Labour Organisation

The International Labour Organisation shall be invited to nominate a representative to participate in a consultative capacity in the deliberations of the Committee of Experts.

Article 27
Sub-Committee of the Governmental Social Committee

1) The reports of the Contracting Parties and the conclusions of the Committee of Experts shall be submitted for examination to a Sub-committee of the Governmental Social Committee of the Council of Europe.

2) The Sub-committee shall be composed of one representative of each of the Contracting Parties. It shall invite no more than two international organisations of employers and no more than two international trade union organisations as it may designate to be represented as observers in a consultative capacity at its meetings. Moreover, it may consult no more than two representatives of international non-governmental organisations having consultative status with the Council of Europe, in respect of questions with which the organisations are particularly qualified to deal, such as social welfare, and the economic and social protection of the family.

3) The Sub-committee shall present to the Committee of Ministers a report containing its conclusions and append the report of the Committee of Experts.

Article 28
Consultative Assembly

The Secretary-General of the Council of Europe shall transmit to the Consultative Assembly the conclusions of the Committee of Experts. The Consultative Assembly shall communicate its views on these Conclusions to the Committee of Ministers.

Article 29
Committee of Ministers

By a majority of two-thirds of the members entitled to sit on the Committee, the Committee of Ministers may, on the basis of the report of the Sub-Committee, and after consultation with the Consultative Assembly, make to each Contracting Party any necessary recommendations.

Part V

Article 30
Derogations in Time of War or Public Emergency

1) In time of war or other public emergency threatening the life of the nation any Contracting Party may take measures derogating from its obligations under this Charter to the extent strictly required by the exigencies of the situation, provided that such measures are not inconsistent with its other obligations under international law.

2) Any Contracting Party which has availed itself of this right of derogation shall, within a reasonable lapse of time, keep the Secretary-General of the Council of Europe fully informed of the measures taken and of the reasons therefor. It shall likewise inform the Secretary-General when such measures have ceased to operate and the provisions of the Charter which it has accepted are again being fully executed.

3) The Secretary-General shall in turn inform other Contracting Parties and the Director-General of the International Labour Office of all communications received in accordance with paragraph 2 of this Article.

Article 31
Restrictions

1) The rights and principles set forth in Part I when effectively realised, and their effective exercise as provided for in Part II, shall not be subject to any restrictions or limitations not specified in those Parts, except such as are prescribed by law and are necessary in a democratic society for the protection of the rights and freedoms of others or for the protection of public interest, national security, public health, or morals.

2) The restrictions permitted under this Charter to the rights and obligations set forth herein shall not be applied for any purpose other than that for which they have been prescribed.

Article 32
Relations Between the Charter and Domestic Law or International Agreements

The provision of this Charter shall not prejudice the provisions of domestic law or of any bilateral or multilateral treaties, conventions or agreements which are already in force, or may come into force, under which more favourable treatment would be accorded to the persons protected.

Article 33
Implementation by Collective Agreements

1) In member States where the provisions of paragraphs 1, 2, 3, 4 and 5 of Article 2, paragraphs 4, 6 and 7 of Article 7 and paragraphs 1, 2, 3 and 4 of Article 10 of Part II of this Charter are matters normally left to agreements between employers or employers' organisations and workers' organisations, or are normally carried out otherwise than by law, the undertakings of those paragraphs may be given and compliance with them shall be treated as effective if their provisions are applied through such agreements or other means to the great majority of the workers concerned.

2) In member States where these provisions are normally the subject of legislation, the undertakings concerned may likewise be given, and compliance with them shall be regarded as effective if the provisions are applied by law to the great majority of the workers concerned.

Article 34
Territorial Application

1) This Charter shall apply to the metropolitan territory of each Contracting Party. Each signatory Government may, at the time of signature or of the deposit of its instruments of ratification or approval, specify, by declaration addressed to the Secretary-General of the Council of Europe, the territory which shall be considered to be its metropolitan territory for this purpose.

2) Any Contracting Party may, at the time of ratification or approval of this Charter or at any time thereafter, declare by notification addressed to the Secretary-General of the Council of Europe, that the Charter shall extend in whole or in part to a non-metropolitan territory or territories specified in the said declaration for whose international relations it is responsible or for which it assumes international responsibility. It shall specify in the declaration the Articles or paragraphs of Part II of the Charter which it accepts as binding in respect of the territories named in the declaration.

3) The Charter shall extend to the territory or territories named in the aforesaid declaration as from the thirtieth day after the date on which the Secretary-General shall have received notification of such declaration.

4) Any Contracting Party may declare at a later date by notification addressed to the Secretary-General of the Council of Europe, that, in respect of one or more of the territories to which the Charter has been extended in accordance with paragraph 2 of this Article, it accepts as binding any Articles or any numbered paragraphs which it has not already accepted in respect of that territory or territories. Such undertakings subsequently given shall be deemed to be an integral part of the original declaration in respect of the territory concerned, and shall have the same effect as from the thirtieth day after the date of notification.

5) The Secretary-General shall communicate to the other signatory Governments and to the Director-General of the International Labour Office any notification transmitted to him in accordance with this Article.

Article 35
Signature, Ratification and Entry Into Force

1) This Charter shall be open for signature by the Members of the Council of Europe. It shal be ratified or approved. Instruments of ratification or approval shall be deposited with the Secretary-General of the Council of Europe.

2) This Charter shall come into force as from the thirtieth day after the date of deposit of the fifth instrument of ratification or approval.

3) In respect of any signatory Government ratifying subsequently, the Charter shall come into force as from the thirtieth day after the date of deposit of its instruments of ratification or approval.

4) The Secretary-General shall notify all the Members of the Council of Europe and the Director-General of the International Labour Office, of the entry into force of the Charter, the names of the Contracting Parties which have ratified or approved it and the subsequent deposit of any instruments of ratification or approval.

Article 36
Amendments

Any member of the Council of Europe may propose amendments to this Charter in a communication addressed to the Secretary-General of the Council of Europe. The Secretary-General shall transmit to the other Members of the Council of Europe any amendments so proposed which shall then be considered by the Committee of Ministers and submitted to the Consultative Assembly for opinion. Any amendments approved by the Committee of

Ministers shall enter into force as from the thirtieth day after all the Contracting Parties have informed the Secretary-General of their acceptance. The Secretary-General shall notify all the Members of the Council of Europe and the Director-General of the International Labour Office of the entry into force of such amendments.

Article 37
Denunciation

1) Any Contracting Party may denounce this Charter only at the end of a period of five years from the date on which the Charter entered into force for it, or at the end of any successive period of two years, and, in each case, after giving six months notice to the Secretary-General of the Council of Europe, who shall inform the other Parties and the Director-General of the International Labour Office accordingly. Such denunciation shall not affect validity of the Charter in respect of the other Contracting Parties provided that at all times there are not less than five such Contracting Parties.

2) Any Contracting Party may, in accordance with the provisions set out in the preceding paragraph, denounce any Article or paragraph of Part II of the Charter accepted by it provided that the number of Articles or paragraphs by which this Contracting Party is bound shall never be less than 10 in the former case and 45 in the latter and that this number of Articles or paragraphs shall continue to include the Articles selected by the Contracting Party among those to which special reference is made in Article 20, paragraph 1, sub-paragraph (b).

3) Any Contracting Party may denounce the present Charter or any of the Articles or paragraphs of Part II of the Charter, under the conditions specified in paragraph 1 of this Article in respect of any territory to which the said Charter is applicable by virtue of a declaration made in accordance with paragraph 2 of Article 34.

Article 38
Appendix
The Appendix to this Charter shall form an integral part of it.

Appendix to the Social Charter
Scope of the Social Charter in terms of persons protected:
1) Without prejudice to Article 12, paragraph 4 and Article 13, paragraph 4, the persons covered by Articles 1 to 17 include foreigners only insofar as they are nationals of other Contracting Parties lawfully resident or working regularly within the territory of the Contracting Party concerned, subject to the understanding

that these Articles are to be interpreted in the light of the provisions of Articles 18 and 19.

This interpretation would not prejudice the extension of similar facilities to other persons by any of the Contracting Parties.

2) Each Contracting Party will grant to refugees as defined in the Convention relating to the Status of Refugees, signed at Geneva on 28th July 1951, and lawfully staying in its territory, treatment as favourable as possible, and in any case not less favourable than under the obligations accepted by the Contracting Party under the said Convention and under any other existing international instruments applicable to those refugees.

Part I   Part II

Paragraph 18   and   Article 18, paragraph 1

It is understood that these provisions are not concerned with the question of entry into the territories of the Contracting Parties and do not prejudice the provisions of the European Convention on Establishment, signed at Paris on 13th December 1955.

Part II

Article 1, paragraph 2

This provision shall not be interpreted as prohibiting or authorising any union security clause or practice.

Article 4, paragraph 4

This provision shall be so understood as not to prohibit immediate dismissal for any serious offence.

Article 4, paragraph 5

It is understood that a Contracting Party may give the undertaking required in this paragraph if the great majority of workers are not permitted to suffer deductions from wages either by law or through collective agreements or arbitration awards, the exceptions being those persons not so covered.

Article 6, paragraph 4

It is understood that each Contracting Party may, insofar as it is concerned, regulate the exercise of the right to strike by law, provided that any further restriction that this might place on the right can be justified under the terms of Article 31.

Article 7, paragraph 8

It is understood that a Contracting Party may give the undertaking required in this paragraph if it fulfils the spirit of the undertaking by providing by law that the great majority of persons under 18 years of age shall not be employed in night work.

Article 12, paragraph 4

The words "and subject to the conditions laid down in such agreements" in the introduction to this paragraph are taken to imply *inter alia* that with regard to benefits which are available independently of any insurance contribution a Contracting Party may require the completion of a prescribed period of residence before granting such benefits to nationals of other Contracting Parties.

Article 13, paragraph 4

Governments not Parties to the European Convention on Social and Medical Assistance may ratify the Social Charter in respect of this paragraph provided that they grant to nationals of other Contracting Parties a treatment which is in conformity with the provisions of the said Convention.

Article 19, paragraph 6

For the purpose of this provision, the term "family of a foreign worker" is understood to mean at least his wife and dependent children under the age of 21 years.

Part III

It is understood that the Charter contains legal obligations of an international character, the application of which is submitted solely to the supervision provided for in Part IV thereof.

Article 20, paragraph 1

It is understood that the "numbered paragraphs" may include Articles consisting of only one paragraph.

Part V
Article 30

The term "in time of war or other public emergency" shall be so understood as to cover also the *threat* of war.

BIBLIOGRAPHY

For a more extensive bibliography, see the Council of Europe publication, BIBLIOGRAPHICAL INDEX OF ARTICLES RELATING TO THE EUROPEAN SOCIAL CHARTER, SOC (74) 6, published in 1974 EUROPEAN YEARBOOK 774.

Books

LYON-CAEN, G.	DROIT SOCIAL INTERNATIONAL ET EUROPÉEN, Dalloz, Paris, 83–93 (4th ed. 1976).
MEERSCH, VAN DER G.	ORGANISATIONS EUROPÉENNES, Vol. I, Establissements Emile Bruylant, Brussels, 377–81 (1966).
PURPURA, R.	LA CARTA SOCIALE EUROPA, Rome Instituto italiano di medicina sociale (1962).
ROBERTSON, A. H.	HUMAN RIGHTS IN EUROPE, Manchester U.P., Manchester, Ch. VIII (1st ed. 1963).
SCHAMBECK, H.	GRUNDRECHTE UND SOZIALORDNUNG: GEDANKEN ZUR EUROPÄISCHEN SOZIALCHARTA, Duncker and Humblot, Berlin (1969).
TROCLET, L.-E.	ELÉMENTS DE DROIT SOCIAL EUROPÉEN, Institut de Sociologie, Free University of Belgium, Brussels, 95–122 (1963).
WASESCHA, L.	LE SYSTÈME DE CONTRÔLE DE L'APPLICATION DE LA CHARTE SOCIALE EUROPÉENNE, Libraire Droz, Geneva (1980).
WENGLER, W.	DIE UNANWENDBARKEIT DER EUROPÄISCHEN SOZIALCHARTA IM STAAT, Verlag Gehlen, Bad Homburg (1969).

Articles, etc.

Asbeck, F. M. Van	*La Charte Sociale Européenne: sa Portée Juridique, sa Mise en Oeuvre,* in MÉLANGES OFFERTS À HENRI ROLIN: PROBLÈMES DE DROIT DES GENS 427–48 (1964).

Balzarini, R.　　　　　*La Carta Sociale Europa e la Costituzione Italiana*, 3 IL DIRITTO DELL'ECONOMIA 286–98 (1963).

Barile, G.　　　　　　*La Carta Sociale Europea e il Diritto Internazionale*, 1961 RIVISTA DI DIRITTO INTERNAZIONALE 624–44.

Benvenuti, L.　　　　*Les Buts Sociaux et Politiques de la Charte Sociale Européenne*, 4 REVUE BELGE DE SÉCURITÉ SOCIALE 657–66 (1962).

Benvenuti, L.　　　　*Le Finalità Sociali e Politiche della Carta Sociale Europea*, 1961 RASSEGNA DEL LAVORO 1493–1504.

Bleckmann, A.　　　　*Interprétation et Application en Droit Interne de la Charte Sociale Européenne, Notamment du Droit de Grève*, 1967 CAHIERS DE DROIT EUROPÉEN 388–412.

Bois, P.　　　　　　　*La Charte Sociale Européenne: Son Influence sur le Droit Suisse*, 33 ANNUAIRE SUISSE DE DROIT INTERNATIONAL 9–36 (1977).

Bourlard, M.　　　　*Droit à L'Assistance Sociale et Médicale, Droit au Bénéfice des Services Sociaux, Droit des Personnes Physiquement ou Mentalement Diminuées à la Formation Professionelle et à la Réadaption Professionelle et Sociale*, paper presented to the Brussels Colloquium on the European Social Charter, Institut d'Etudes Européennes (1976).

Brown, E.D.　　　　　*International Social Law in Europe*, 19 Y.B.W.A. 160–82 (1965).

Brugel, J. W.　　　　*Die Europäische Sozialcharta*, 17 EUROPA-ARCHIV 399–404 (1962).

Cannella, G.　　　　*Le Droit à la Sécurité Sociale et les Droits Connexes de la Charte Sociale Européenne*, 5 REVUE BELGE DE SÉCURITÉ SOCIALE 1–45 (1963).

Cohen-Jonathan, E.　*Droits de l'Homme et Pluralité des Systèmes Européens de Protection Internationale*, 5 HUMAN RIGHTS J. 613–49 (1972).

De Broeck, G.　　　　*Droit à la Sécurité et à l'Hygiene dans le Travail, Droit à la Protection de la Santé*, paper presented to the Brussels Colloquium on the European Social Charter, Institut d'Etudes Européennes (1976).

Deirmenzoglou-　　　*La Charte Sociale Européenne et l'Influence de la*
Panayotopoulou, S.　*Déclaration Universelle des Droits de l'Homme*, 18 REVUE HELLÉNIQUE DE DROIT INTERNATIONAL 137–47 (1965).

Delarbre, H. *Le Rôle du Sous-Comité Gouvernemental et la Charte Sociale Européenne*, paper presented to the Brussels Colloquium on the European Social Charter, Institut d'Etudes Européennes (1976).

Delpérée, A. *Les Droits Sociaux et la Charte Sociale Européenne*, 1 HUMAN RIGHTS J. 549–81 (1968)

Delpérée, A., and Gilon, C. *La Charte Sociale Européenne*, 1958 REVUE DU TRAVAIL (Brussels) 1216–23.

Deprez, U. *Droit à des Conditions de Travail Equitable, Droit à l'Orientation Professionnelle, Droit à la Formation Professionnelle*, paper presented to the Brussels Colloquium on the European Social Charter, Institut d'Etudes Européennes (1976).

Evans, M. *The European Social Charter*, in FUNDAMENTAL RIGHTS, Sweet & Maxwell, London, 278–90 (J. Bridge ed. 1973).

Fuks, F. *Les Dispositions de la Charte Européenne à la Lumière des Revendications des Syndicats Belges*, 1966 REVUE DE L'INSTITUT DE SOCIOLOGIE (Brussels) 29–63.

Golsong, H. *Implementation of International Protection of Human Rights*, 110 RECUEIL DES COURS (Hague Academy of International Law) 1, 36–38 (1963–III)

Green, N. Maryan *Droits Sociaux et Normes Régionales*, 96 JOURNAL DU DROIT INTERNATIONAL 58–71 (1969).

Harris, D.J. *The European Social Charter*, 13 INT'L COMP. L.Q. 1076–87 (1964).

Havie, H. *Den Europeiske Sosialpakt*, 1979 LOV OG RETT 351–62.

Heuskin, L. *Le Droit à la Protection de la Santé dans la Charte Sociale Européenne*, 1966 REVUE DE L'INSTITUT DE SOCIOLOGIE (Brussels) 65–81.

Hiou, T. *La Charte Sociale Européenne*, 25 REVUE HELLÉNIQUE DE DROIT INTERNATIONAL 311–33 (1972).

Jacobs, F. G. *The Extension of the European Convention on Human Rights to Include Economic, Social and Cultural Rights*, 3 HUMAN RIGHTS REV. 166–77 (1978).

Janssen-Pevtschin, G. *Les Engagements des Parties Contractantes et la Mise en Oeuvre de la Charte Sociale Européenne*, 1966 REVUE DE L'INSTITUT DE SOCIOLOGIE (Brussels) 9–28.

Kahn-Freund, O.   *Labour Relations and International Standards— Some Reflections on the European Social Charter,* in 1 MISCELLANEA W. J. GANSHOF VAN DER MEERSCH 131–55 (1972).

Kahn-Freund, O.   *The European Social Charter,* in EUROPEAN LAW AND THE INDIVIDUAL, North Holland, Amsterdam, Ch. 10 (F. G. Jacobs ed. 1976).

Karisch, A.   *Die Europäische Sozialcharta,* 1963 OESTERREICHISCHE JURISTENZEITUNG 172–76.

Khol, A.   *Die Europäische Sozialcharta und die Oesterreichische Rechtsordnung,* 87 JURISTISCHE BLÄTTER 75–82 (1965).

Kiss, A. C.   *Entrée en Vigeur de la Convention Européenne d'Establissement et de la Charte Sociale Européenne,* 11 ANNUAIRE FRANÇAIS DE DROIT INTERNATIONAL 686–91 (1965–6).

Kojanec, G.   *Droit au Travail, Droit de la Famille à une Protection Sociale, Juridique et Economique, Droit de la Mère et de l'Enfant à une Protection sociale et Economique,* paper presented to the Brussels Colloquium on the European Social Charter, Institut d'Etudes Européennes (1976).

Kojanec, G.   *Reunion of the Familes of Migrant Workers,* Working Paper for the 1977 Strasbourg Symposium on the European Social Charter, CE Doc. AS/Coll/Charte 5-E.

Lannung, H.   *Human Rights and the Multiplicity of the European Systems for International Protection,* 5 HUMAN RIGHTS J. 651–61 (1972).

Laroque, P.   *Drawing Up and Implementation of the European Social Charter,* Working Paper for the 1977 Strasbourg Symposium on the European Social Charter, CE Doc. AS/Coll/ Charter 1-E.

Laroque, P.   *Droit à la Sécurité Sociale, Droit à l'Exercise d'une Activité Lucrative sur le Territoire des Autres Parties Contractantes, Droit des Travailleurs Migrants et de Leurs Familles à la Protection et à l'Assistance,* paper presented to the Brussels Colloquium on the European Social Charter, Institut d'Etudes Européenes (1976).

Mazzoni, G.   *Carta Sociale Europea,* in 2 STUDI IN ONORE DI G. ZINGALI 410–21 (1965).

Papadatos, P. *The European Social Charter*, 7 J. INT'L COMM'N JURISTS 214–42 (1966).

Pugsley, D. *The European Social Charter*, 39 Y.B.A.A.A. 97–100 (1969).

Purpura, R. *L'Elaborazione della Carta Sociale Europea*, 1961 RASSEGNA DEL LAVORO 25–60.

Rehn, G. *Attainment and Maintenance of Full Employment*, Working Paper for the 1977 Strasbourg Symposium on the European Social Charter, CE Doc. AS/Coll/Charte 2-E.

Schambeck, H. *Bild und Recht des Menschen in der Europäischen Sozialcharta*, in 2 FESTSCHRIFT FÜR H. SCHMITZ 216–37 (1967).

Schoetter, P. *La Charte Sociale Européenne: Considérations Critiques*, 1966 REVUE DE L'INSTITUT DE SOCIOLOGIE (Brussels) 109–17.

Scotto, I. *La Carta Sociale Europea*, 18 DIRITTO COMUNITARIO E DEGLI SCAMBI INTERNAZIONALI 709–20 (1979).

Smyth, J. F. *The Implementation of the European Social Charter*, in MÉLANGES MODINOS 290–303 (1968).

Sur, F. D. *La Charte Sociale Européenne: Dix Années d'Application*, 1974 EUR. Y. B. 88–136.

Taquet, M., and Gosseries, P. *La Charte Social Européenne*, 77 JOURNAL DES TRIBUNAUX 181–88, 202–05 (1962).

Tennfjord, F. *The European Social Charter—an Instrument of Social Collaboration in Europe*, 1962 EUR. Y.B. 71–83.

Tessari, G. *Considerazioni sulla Carta Sociale Europea, l'Integrazione Sociale Europea e il Consiglio d'Europa*, 14 RIVISTA DI DIRITTO EUROPEO 235–59 (1974).

Troclet, L. E. *Dynamisme et Contrôle de l'Application de la Charte*, paper presented to the Brussels Colloquium on the European Social Charter, Institut d'Etudes Européennes (1976).

Valticos, N. *L'Influenze delle Convenzioni e delle Raccomandazioni Internazionali del Lavoro sulla Carta Sociale Europea*, 1961 RASSEGNA DEL LAVORO 1585–1611.

Valticos, N. *La Charte Sociale Européenne: Sa Structure, son Contenu, le Contrôle de son Application*, 26 DROIT SOCIAL 466–82 (1963).

Valticos, N.   *Les Systèmes de Contrôle non Judiciares des In-struments Internationaux Relatifs aux Droits de l'Homme,* in MÉLANGES MODINOS 331, 351–52 (1968).

Valitcos, N.   *Un Système de Contrôle International: la Mise en Oeuvre des Conventions Internationales du Travail,* 123 RECUEIL DES COURS (Hague Academy of International Law) 311, 396–98 (1968-I).

Valticos, N.   DROIT INTERNATIONAL DU TRAVAIL, Dalloz, Paris, 1970, and 1973 supplement (see indexes).

Valticos, N.   *Mise en Parallèle des Actions et des Mécanismes de Contrôle au Niveau du Conseil et de l'Organisation Internationale du Travail,* paper presented to the Brussels Colloquium on the European Social Charter, Institut d'Etudes Européennes (1976).

Vogel-Polsky, E.   *L'Article 6 de la Charte Sociale Européenne,* 1966 REVUE DE L'INSTITUT DE SOCIOLOGIE (Brussels) 83–107.

Vogel-Polsky, E.   *The Right of Employed Women to Equal Pay and to Protection,* Working Paper for the 1977 Strasbourg Symposium on the European Social Charter, CE Doc. AS/Coll/Charte 4-E.

Wiebringhaus, H.   *La Charte Sociale Européenne,* 9 ANNUAIRE FRANÇAIS DE DROIT INTERNATIONAL 709–21 (1963).

Wiebringhaus, H.   *Première Mise en Oeuvre du Système de Contrôle Instauré par la Charte Sociale Européenne,* 14 ANNUAIRE FRANÇAIS DE DROIT INTERNATIONAL 784–89 (1968).

Wiebringhaus, H.   *Le Champ d'Application "Ratione Personae" de la Charte Sociale Européenne,* in LIBRO-HOMENAJE AL PROFESOR LUIS SELA SAMPIL OVIEDO, 525–42 (1970).

Wiebringhaus, H.   *Jurisprudence du Droit Social Européenne,* 12 RIVISTA DI DIRITTO EUROPEO 169–201 (1972).

Wiebringhaus, H.   *L'Etat d'Application de la Charte Social Européenne,* 19 ANNUAIRE FRANÇAIS DE DROIT INTERNATIONAL 928–40 (1973).

Wiebringhaus, H.   The European Social Charter: its Application and Implementation, lecture delivered at Edinburgh University, 1974.

Wiebringhaus, H.   *La Charte Sociale Européenne—Dix Années d'Application,* paper presented to the Brussels Colloquium on the European Social Charter, Institut d'Etudes Européenes (1976).

Wiebringhaus, H.   *La Convention Européenne des Droits de l'Homme et la Charte Sociale Européenne,* 8 HUMAN RIGHTS J. 527–44 (1975).

Wiese, W.   *Die Europäische Sozialcharta,* 16 JAHRBUCH FÜR INTERNATIONALES RECHT 328–53 (1973).

Zacher, H. F.   *The Right to Organise and the Right to Take Collective Action under Article 5 and Article 6, Paragraph 4, of the European Social Charter,* Working Paper for the 1977 Strasbourg Symposium on the European Social Charter, CE Doc. AS/Coll/Charte 3-E.

Zanetti, B.   *Droit à une Rémunération Equitable, Droit Syndical, Droit de Négotiation Collective,* paper presented to the Brussels Colloquium on the European Social Charter, Institut d'Etudes Européennes (1976).

Anon.   *The European Social Charter,* BULLETIN OF THE INTERNATIONAL COMMISSION OF JURISTS No. 18, 1–9 (March 1964).

Anon.   *The European Social Charter and the International Labour Standards,* 84 INT. LAB. REV. 354–75, 462–77 (1961).

Table of Charter References

Index